# THE JUSTICES OF
# THE PEACE
# IN ENGLAND
## 1558 TO 1640

# THE JUSTICES OF
# THE PEACE
# IN ENGLAND
## 1558 TO 1640

A LATER *EIRENARCHA*

BY

J. H. GLEASON

OXFORD

AT THE CLARENDON PRESS

1969

*Oxford University Press, Ely House, London W.1*

GLASGOW NEW YORK TORONTO MELBOURNE WELLINGTON
CAPE TOWN SALISBURY IBADAN NAIROBI LUSAKA ADDIS ABABA
BOMBAY CALCUTTA MADRAS KARACHI LAHORE DACCA
KUALA LUMPUR SINGAPORE HONG KONG TOKYO

TO
M.E.G.
J.G.
R.H.G.

# PREFACE

THIS study of the justices of the peace in Elizabethan and early Stuart England divides rather sharply into five parts. Chapters I, II, and III are concerned with the method requisite to consider in some depth a large group of men—approximately thirteen hundred individuals. They suggest criteria by which to gauge the whole body of J.P.s of Kent, Norfolk, Northamptonshire, Somerset, Worcestershire, and the North Riding of Yorkshire in 1562, 1584, 1608, 1626, and 1636. So discrete are the data which must be assembled that they inhibit any flow of discussion; absolutely essential, the facts about the lives of those justices are thus best segregated into Appendices A–F, one for each of the counties. Two further appendices treat certain somewhat tangential evidence with regard to taxation and property. Chapters IV to VII are built on the facts of the appendices, but they also set forth data of a different sort. In Chapter VIII an assessment is made of the stature of the J.P.s during the eighty years which preceded the civil wars and of their significance in the history of England.

It is my hope that I may have provided a standard of comparison which will prove useful for cognate studies dealing with other counties or other aspects of the social history of the same six shires. The series of rosters of justices, with their information about membership in the two universities and the four inns of court, may be a particularly useful feature of the book. Explanation of the assumptions which were made in compiling the data in the rosters is made in note 1 on page 28 and in Chapter III. The method followed in the citation of sources is also explained in note 1. In order to minimize the listing of names various symbols have been used in the rosters of justices. They are included in the List of Abbreviations. In the rosters for 1608 there have been included the figures of the assessments for the subsidy in 1609, which are derived from an Ellesmere memorandum in the Huntington Library in San Marino, California, which is transcribed in Appendix G. In connection with Worcestershire and the North Riding extra symbols—W or N—indicate membership of the Council of Wales or the Council of the North. There are two indexes: General and Persons. A note at the head of the Index of Persons explains the emphasis given to certain entries. Only when there is other information about the principal residences of J. P.s—shown in the rosters—is there an entry in the General Index. To have included the J.P.s whose names constitute Appendix G would have been merely to alphabetize the same lists; such duplication is unwarranted.

Although I am grateful to them all, the friends who have helped me in some fashion are far too numerous for individual acknowledgement. I mention gladly, however, the particular assistance of a few. First must come my wife, my daughter, and my son; in gratitude for their patience and good cheer, this book is dedicated to them; they shared in it in many ways. The expert knowledge and skill of my sister-in-law, Madeleine Rowse Gleason, made it possible to put the manuscript in presentable form. Mrs. Thomas Pinney corrected proofs and compiled the Index of Persons with unflagging care. She shared typing with Mrs. Shelton Beatty and Mrs. John Campbell. Dr. Nelly J. Kerling transcribed many documents in London. My colleagues, J. H. Kemble, F. R. Mulhauser, W. T. Jones, and D. W. Davies made varied and valuable suggestions. Professor Margaret Gay Davies, also of Pomona College, read a large portion of the manuscript, gave it her great critical skill, and was ever helpful on difficult points. Very important revisions were suggested by the reader for the Clarendon Press. The members of its staff also played their important parts.

Outside Pomona College I have received great help from Professor W. K. Jordan of Harvard and from Professor V. H. Galbraith and Dr. A. L. Rowse of Oxford. Like other American historians I owe to Professor Sir John Neale the privilege of attending the Tudor seminar at the Institute of Historical Research. I wish profoundly that three other friends—the late R. B. Merriman and E. A. Whitney of Harvard and Godfrey Davies of the Huntington Library—could know of my gratitude to them for their inspiration and their fellowship.

In connection with this work I have been the fortunate recipient of a Fellowship at the Henry E. Huntington Library and for grants in aid by the American Philosophical Society, the Folger Shakespeare Library, the Haynes Foundation, Pomona College, and the Claremont Graduate School. I am grateful to all those responsible for this beneficence. My thanks go also to many members of the staffs of the libraries and archives where I have worked: the Honnold Library in Claremont, California, the Huntington Library—particularly Miss Mary Isabel Fry—the Folger Library, the Widener Library, the Bodleian Library, the British Museum, the Public Record Office, Somerset House, and the county archives and record offices in Kent, Northamptonshire—particularly P. C. King, esq.—Somerset, and Bristol. The Director of the Huntington Library kindly gave me permission to reproduce the Ellesmere MS. which forms Appendix G. The Director of the Folger Library approved my quoting considerable passages of its Lambarde MSS. which were published in *William Lambarde and Local Government*, and Dr. Mark H. Curtis gladly allowed me to quote passages from his *Oxford and Cambridge in Transition*.

J. H. G.

*Pomona College*
*Claremont, California*

# LIST OF CONTENTS

LIST OF ILLUSTRATIONS xiii

LIST OF ABBREVIATIONS xv

I. A Later *Eirenarcha* I

II. The Kent Commission of the Peace in 1584 8

III. Case Studies of J.P.s: Data and Categories 31

IV. The Complexion of the Commissions of the Peace 47

V. Religion and Politics 68

VI. The Education of the J.P.s 83

VII. The Burden of the Commission 96

VIII. The Historical Stature of the J.P.s 116

APPENDICES

A. Kent 123
B. Norfolk 145
c. Northamptonshire 164
D. Somerset 187
E. Worcestershire 207
F. North Riding 224
G. Assessments of J.P.s in 1609 246
H. A Note on the Wealth of the Gentry 263

GENERAL INDEX 265

INDEX OF NAMES OF PERSONS 269

LIST OF CONTENTS

# LIST OF ILLUSTRATIONS

Title-page of the original edition of *Eire-narcha* presented by Lambarde to Sir Thomas Egerton, later first Baron Elles-mere and Viscount Brackley      *facing page*   1

William Lambarde's *Ephemeris*, folios 2 and 3      ,,    ,,    10

Kent: the Lathes of Aylesford and Sutton-at-Hone      ,,    ,,    22

British Museum, Lansdowne MS. 1218 a *liber pacis* of *c.* 1 January 1559      ,,    ,,    62

# LIST OF ABBREVIATIONS

In addition to a few abbreviations whose significance is obvious the following have been used:

| | |
|---|---|
| *A.P.C.* | *Acts of the Privy Council* |
| *Alum. cantab.* | J. and J. A. Venn *Alumni cantabrigienses* (4 vols., Cambridge, 1922–7) |
| *Alum. oxon.* | Joseph Foster, *Alumni oxoniensis*, etc. (4 vols., Oxford, 1891–2) |
| *Arch. Cant.* | *Archaeologia Cantiana* |
| B.M. | British Museum |
| C | Cambridge University |
| *Cal. Pat. Rolls* | *Calendar of the Patent Rolls* |
| *Cal. S.P. Dom.* | *Calendar of State Papers Domestic* |
| *DNB* | *Dictionary of National Biography* |
| G | Gray's Inn |
| H.M.C. | Historical Manuscripts Commission |
| I | Inner Temple |
| I.P.M. | Inquisition Post Mortem |
| K | Mary F. Keeler, *The Long Parliament, 1640–1641; a Biographical Study of its Members* (Philadelphia, 1954) |
| L. | London; in the citation of published works |
| L | Lincoln's Inn; in the rosters of J.P.s |
| *L. & P.* | *Letters and Papers, Foreign and Domestic of the Reign of Henry VIII* |
| M | Middle Temple |
| N | Council of the North |
| N.R. | North Riding, Yorkshire |
| Norf. | Norfolk |
| Northants. | Northamptonshire |
| O | Oxford University |
| P | Parliament; as a member of the Commons |
| PCC | Prerogative Court of Canterbury |
| P.R.O. | Public Record Office |
| r | relative; a brother, grandson, or cousin |
| s | son |
| Som. | Somerset |
| *VCH* | *Victoria County History* |
| W | Council of Wales |

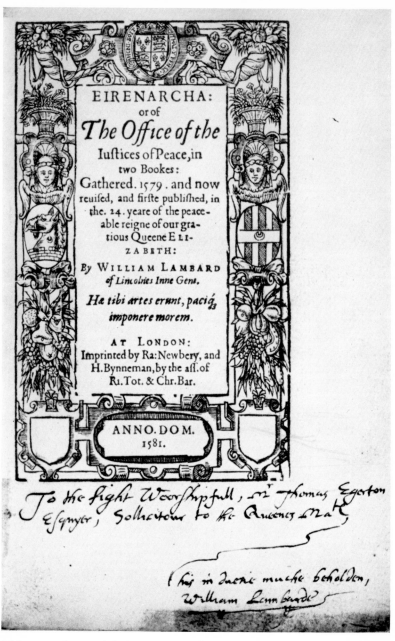

EIRENARCHA:
or of

*The Office of the*

Iustices of Peace, in
two Bookes:

Gathered. 1579. and now
reuised, and firste publifhed, in
the. 24. yeare of the peace-
able reigne of our gra-
tious Queene E li-
za beth:

*By* William Lambard
*of Lincolnes Inne Gent.*

*Hæ tibi artes erunt, paciq̃*
*imponere morem.*

At London:
Imprinted by Ra: Newbery, and
H. Bynneman, by the aff. of
Ri. Tot. & Chr. Bar.

ANNO. DOM.
1581.

Title-page of the original edition of *Eirenarcha* presented by Lambarde to Sir
Thomas Egerton, later first Baron Ellesmere and Viscount Brackley. Now in the
Huntington Library, San Marino, California

# I

## A LATER *EIRENARCHA*

THE justices of the peace symbolize the polity of England. Official but not professional, autonomous and powerful yet limited and directed, they have long served their land in unmatched fashion. Commissioned first in the fourteenth century to give a greater degree of order to a feudalistic society, after the Restoration they became the unchallenged rulers of their counties, and they remain important today in local criminal jurisdiction despite the development of the bureaucratic state.

By the time of Elizabeth I the J.P.s had achieved a stature which well deserved George Macaulay Trevelyan's incisive tribute that they were then 'the most influential class of men in England'. Much the same estimate was implicit in a remark by Sir William Holdsworth:

The old idea of local self-government subject to the law was retained in the system of local government, as newly organized under the justices of the peace. The fact that, in the sixteenth century, this idea was preserved, and these self-governing judicial officers of the later medieval period were adopted as the basis of the scheme of local government, is a unique phenomenon in Western Europe, of the utmost significance for the future of our constitution and our law.[1]

Nor have other students doubted their role in English affairs. Indeed, it is a formidable body of writing both for and about the justices which has accumulated since the publication in 1582 of William Lambarde's *Eirenarcha: or of the Office of the Justices of Peace*. Not quite the pioneer treatise, it remains pre-eminent, and an adaptation of the title in another, very different, book about the justices of the peace is not inappropriate.[2]

[1] G. M. Trevelyan, *English Social History* (L., 1941), p. 171; W. S. Holdsworth, *A History of English Law* (13 vols., L., 1922–52), iv. 136–7.

[2] 1581 is the date of *Eirenarcha* on its title page, in *DNB*, and in Wilbur Dunkel, *William Lambarde, Elizabethan Jurist, 1536–1601* (New Brunswick, New Jersey, 1965), pp. 66, 74, 190–3, but this is clearly old style since Lambarde's preface is: 'From Lincolnes Inne, this 27. day of Januarie: 1581.'

Lambarde was a professional lawyer, a barrister and
bencher of Lincoln's Inn, who became a master in chancery
in 1592. He was also a talented historian, having published
both his *Perambulation of Kent*, the first and still perhaps the
best of county histories, and his *Archainomia*, which initiated
the study of Anglo-Saxon law. He was first appointed a J.P.
in Kent in 1580, and *Eirenarcha* had a practical purpose. A
manual for the guidance of the author's fellow justices, its
frequent re-publication in the six decades before the outbreak
of the civil wars is evidence of its popularity among the men
to whom it was addressed, while the fact that it has served
subsequently as the basis of most of what has been written
about the office during the Tudor and Stuart periods indicates that historians too have understood its merits. Yet the
oddly inadequate paragraphs devoted to the J.P.s in several
recent books show that there is still much to be said about
the men who provided half the members of the Elizabethan
House of Commons and administered the Stuart countryside.

The twentieth-century literature dealing with the J.P.s
in some detail begins with Charles A. Beard's *The Office of
Justice of the Peace*, published in 1904, his first and probably
his least impressive book; that it should recently have been
deemed worthy of re-publication is itself eloquent evidence
of a gap in historical studies. Of much greater worth is the
extensive and varied work of Miss Bertha Putnam, almost
all of which, however, is devoted to the period before the
accession of Elizabeth. There are considerable chapters in
E. P. Cheyney's *History of England*, Wallace Notestein's
lively *The English People on the Eve of Colonization*, and
A. L. Rowse's sparkling *The England of Elizabeth*. Special-
ized treatment in a variety of fashions is found in such
important monographs as W. B. Willcox's *Gloucestershire,
a Study in Local Government, 1590–1640*, Margaret Gay
Davies's *The Enforcement of English Apprenticeship*, Alan
Simpson's *The Wealth of the Gentry*, and, though limited to
one county and a few years, T. G. Barnes's penetrating
*Somerset, 1625–1640*. In the fifth volume of the *Victoria
County History of Wiltshire* is a chapter on 'County Government, 1530–1660' by Joel Hurstfield.

Much valuable work has also appeared during the last thirty years under the imprint of county historical societies. The volumes of quarter sessions records and other official papers of local government have often included excellent introductions, each setting forth for its group of subscribing members the technicalities of the office in Elizabethan and Stuart times. Useful as these essays are, none attempts to compare the situations of the several counties nor to assess the role of the J.P.s in the life of the nation as a whole.

There are a few paragraphs about the J.P.s in several volumes of the *Oxford History of England* and in other standard histories of the Tudor and Stuart periods. Sections of such manuals as G. W. Prothero's *Select Statutes* and J. R. Tanner's *Tudor Constitutional Documents* have provided for students at many levels a synoptic view which has seemed often to constitute an adequate knowledge of a complex institution. The succinct survey in G. R. Elton's *The Tudor Constitution* stresses the comprehensive and multiform responsibilities performed by individual J.P.s, of which the commission of the peace was the core, but four pages are too few for such a protean topic.

The J.P.s have also received often unrecognized attention in another, less urbane, corpus of historical writing. Implicitly they were the subject of the controversy over the gentry, since few upper gentry were not in the commission whether that disputed social group was rising or not rising or merely affluent.[1] Even Lawrence Stone's *Crisis of the Aristocracy, 1558–1641* seems not to have resolved the enigma.

Too much of this literature shares a common flaw. Generalizations are based upon narrow data; doubtless, few statements are without foundation, but so often an illustrative example has been elevated into a uniformity. For instance, Tanner declared that the 'Lord Lieutenant was usually also Custos Rotulorum', a remark repeated by other scholars, including such a master as Conyers Read. Presumably Tanner had some—unstated—example in mind, but a comparison of the rosters of lords lieutenant and of J.P.s

---

[1] The extensive literature about the gentry is summarized in Appendix A of J. H. Hexter, *Reappraisals in History* (N.Y., 1963), pp. 149–52.

shows that seldom, if ever, in Elizabeth's reign did the same
man fill both offices. The Earl of Exeter, however, was Lord
Lieutenant and *Custos* in Northamptonshire in 1608, while
in Kent in 1636 the Earl of Pembroke held both charges. It
was only late in the Stuart period, whent he Lord Lieutenant
became in effect the viceroy of the county, that he began
as a matter of routine to have technical custody of the
county's rolls.[1]

Similarly even by experts the quorum has been described
as 'small', though in Kent it numbered fifty-five in 1584 and
ninety-two in 1608. Likewise it is commonly accepted that
the quarter sessions met four times a year, and such was the
case in some counties. Yet Kent, for quarter sessions as for
some other purposes, was in effect two counties, in each of
which in turn the justices met twice a year. In the North
Riding of Yorkshire, by the device of adjourning meetings
to another town, there were in some years eight or even more
essentially separate sessions. Other counties devised other
variations on the statutory practice.[2] Like the common law
the office of justice of the peace grew. How to generalize?

This is no small problem with regard to a group of men
who may have numbered fifteen thousand for all the English
counties during the eighty-odd years between the accession
of Elizabeth and the outbreak of the civil wars. Doubtless it
lies at the root of the faulty dicta which have been made even
by careful scholars. It was one element in the controversy
over the fortunes of the gentry, although that issue was complicated by fuzzy definition. There must, of course, be a
selection of individuals for study, but just as certainly every
effort should be made to avoid distortion. Justices Slender
and Shallow are not unknown.

A fortunate solution to the problems of choice and definition is at hand. Neutral—in the Elizabethan phrase 'indifferent'—groups were in fact distinguished by the
processes of the society itself. In the commissions of the

---

[1] J. R. Tanner, *Tudor Constitutional Documents* (Camb., 1940), p. 452; Conyers
Read, *The Government of England under Elizabeth* (Washington, 1960), pp. 18–19;
cf. Mary S. Gretten (ed.), *Oxfordshire Justices of the Peace* (Oxford, 1934), p. lviii;
Gladys Scott Thompson, *Lords Lieutenants in the Sixteenth Century* (L., 1923),
pp. 142–3.

[2] Cf. *infra*, p. 103, 109.

peace, shire by shire, and month by month, may be found a plethora of samples segregated by an innocent technique. There is no dearth of names of justices. Many of the local history publications contain lists which happen to have survived, sometimes by chance. The quarter sessions records —many now in print—indicate members of the county bench. Yet these are to some degree fortuitous examples, an insecure foundation for generalization.

More systematic lists are available. The *dorses* of the patent rolls contain a great many official copies of commissions which are hardly adventitious. Some county archives have the original documents as they passed the Great Seal. Another and more convenient series of rosters is the *libri pacis*, lists of the justices, county after county, which were prepared from time to time for use in government offices, much as internal directories are compiled in current military, civil, and commercial practice.[1] These will be the foundation of the present work.

Although not very many *libri* survive, the extant ones happen to be scattered in time well across the period, and they have the extra value that they contain significant *marginalia*. There is at least one *liber* for each decade, except for the years 1611–20, but seldom more than two or three. A distortion arising from a present-day bias is rendered less likely by the fact that choices must be made with little consideration of particular events. The very considerable identity between commissions dated as far apart as ten years—1626 and 1636, for instance—proves the general stability of personnel and indicates that intervals of approximately twenty years may be adopted with a loss of names which is not excessive. Other *libri* have in fact been consulted, and some reference to them will be made to demonstrate particular points. The most useful *libri* have been found to be the earliest (1559 and 1561, taken in conjunction with the patent-roll commissions of 1562 available in the published calendar), the latest (1636), and those of 1584, 1608, and 1626.

[1] Cf. Thomas G. Barnes and A. Hassell Smith, 'Justices of the Peace from 1558 to 1668—a Revised List of Sources', *Bulletin of the Institute of Historical Research*, xxxii (Nov. 1959), 221–42; M. G. Davies, *The Enforcement of English Apprenticeship* (Camb., 1956), pp. 286–9.

Selection in space is also necessary, and the available range is almost complete. Only the county of Lancaster, with a commission issued over the seal of the Duchy, was not included in the *libri pacis*, which on occasion even contained such special, non-county, jurisdictions as the Soke of Peterborough and the Isle of Ely. Thus a geographical bias may readily be minimized by an appropriate dispersal on the map. The selection of six counties appears to be adequate: Kent, Norfolk, Northamptonshire, Somerset, Worcestershire, and in Yorkshire the North Riding, which with regard to the commission of the peace constituted a separate county.

Each of these areas has its own character. Kent is one of the home counties, lying in part very much within the London metropolitan region even in 1558, yet also essentially rural; in Canterbury, the Cinque Ports, and the naval-dockyard communities of Deptford and Chatham it possessed towns of special significance. An East Anglian county, touching the Fens, Norfolk was notable for its woollen trades, and in Norwich had the city which was second in population, first in industry. Northamptonshire lies in the heart of the Midlands and borders on more counties than any other. A splendid grazing area, in Elizabethan times it was the home of many proud peers; today it is blessed by an exceptional record society and local archive. Somerset, on the edge of the extreme West Country, was important also for woollens and for mining; it was adjacent to Bristol, second city in the kingdom in commerce and third or fourth in population. Worcestershire was in the marches of Wales, in England but subject to Welsh influences, still somewhat backward, within the purview of the Council of Wales. The North Riding was a northern area, in Yorkshire, relatively close to the Scottish border, subject to the jurisdiction of the Council of the North; York was the second administrative city of the realm. Taken together the six counties exhibit most of the salient features of English society. The rosters of their commissions of the peace should include examples of all types of men who were J.P.s.

The justices of the peace of these six counties in these five years totalled not quite thirteen hundred different men. The gross sum is 1,792, if for the first group there are added to the patent-roll commissions of February 1562 the extra men whose names are found in the *libri pacis* of both January 1559 and December 1561. Then the elimination of duplications yields a net figure of 1,294. Even though these men constituted a series of groups ranging widely in time and space, thirty samples distinguished by processes of their own day, relatively far more generous than those which often suffice for the political polls of the twentieth century, there remains a serious problem of method. A book which endeavoured to include merely abbreviated sketches of the lives of so many men would be monstrous—heavy to hold, exhaustive to read, prohibitive to publish, impossible to write. Hence the present study begins with a survey of a representative commission —Kent in 1584—which happens to provide unusual insights. There follows a discussion of the classification of justices and of the problems inherent in the quantity of data available. These matters are illustrated by case studies of justices who, although they did not gain the immortality of the *Dictionary of National Biography*, show what could be done in similarly detailed accounts of most of the thirteen hundred men in the total group.[1] In appendices are surveys of the remaining twenty-nine commissions which furnish the basic data of the investigation. Chapters IV to VII develop the generalized statements which grow out of the materials in the appendices. The final chapter presents the conclusions to which the full study leads.

[1] When it is completed, the *History of Parliament* will include *vitae* of about two-fifths of the men who were J.P.s in the time of Elizabeth I and the early Stuarts.

## II

## THE KENT COMMISSION OF THE
## PEACE IN 1584

THE most revealing evidence with regard to Tudor justices of the peace is an *Ephemeris* which William Lambarde kept between 1580 and 1588. Since *Eirenarcha*
was first published in 1582, this diary cannot have been an
adjunct to its composition. Yet it is a most happy chance that
its author should have left such a record. As the title-page
declares, it is 'An Ephemeris of the Certifiable Causes of the
Commission of the Peace', and even a casual reading indicates that it was regularly used as an aid in the performance
of the duties of the office. A reader is taken directly into the
day-by-day operation of the Kent commission of the time.

In June 1580 Lambarde was 43 years old; he was a
remarkably talented addition to the bench. The son of a
prominent London draper and already a man of some distinction, both as a lawyer and as an author, he held an inherited estate in Greenwich. This property easily qualified
him for appointment to the commission, but his work as a
justice was carried forward in the neighbourhood of his
actual residence in Ightham, not quite ten miles from Maidstone; at that time he was living at St. Clere's with George
Moulton, a Kentish J.P. of many years' standing who was
the father of his deceased wife. In 1583 he married a second
wife, a daughter of Robert Deane and widow of William
Dalison, a Lincolnshire gentleman. As *Ephemeris* records, he
then moved to his new wife's inherited property in Halling,
where he continued to be the leading J.P. in western Kent.[1]

The opening portion serves to portray the character of
the author and to show in what manner and with whom he
served his queen. The full text for an adequate period—from
the beginning until the meeting of the quarter sessions in

---

[1] Conyers Read (ed.), *William Lambarde and Local Government* (Ithaca, 1962),
pp. 3–13 *et passim*; Dunkel, *William Lambarde*, Ch. V *et passim*.

October—is requisite for an understanding of the scope and method of Lambarde's work.[1]

## 1580

*April–May*   I was put in the commission of the peace 6 August 1579 et 21 Elizabethae Reginae, and I took the oath 3 June 1580 and 22 Elizabethae Reginae, and between these days I assisted Sir Christopher Alleyn, Sir Thomas Cotton, and Mr. Robert Byng in taking the musters at Shorne the 25 April and at Frindsbury the 26 April for the Lord Cobham's division. And likewise I assisted the justices of the other three divisions of the lathe of Aylesford in taking their musters at Malling, Tonbridge, and Borough Green, because the commission of the musters was a general commission by itself, etc.

*June–July*   The last of June 1580 and the first of July I joined with my father-in-law, George Moulton, in the examination of Baptiste Bristow, Edward Rootes, John Romyne, Thomas Brissenden, and Nicholas Miller concerning a robbery done upon the said Baptiste, etc. by virtue of letters from the lords of the Privy Council.

The 9 of July I assisted Mr. Willughby and Mr. Potter in the examination of Oliver Booby of Chipstead, by virtue of the said letters. All which examinations I have delivered to the Lord Chief Baron, upon his request of the same by his letters.

*August*   The 26 August, being at Tonbridge in the execution of the commission of sewers for Medway, Sir Thomas Fane, Sir Christopher Alleyn, and I sent Thomas Chambers, William Cosin, and Thomas Norham of Tonbridge to the gaol for keeping ale-houses obstinately and against the commandment of sundry justices which had put them down.

*September*   The 20 of September my father-in-law and I examined John Sone, by virtue of the said letters from the lords, and bound him to appear at the quarter sessions at Maidstone. The same day he and I sent Walter Pelsant of Borough Green to the gaol for keeping an alehouse there obstinately against the commandment of Mr. Byng and Mr. Richers.

The same day also he and I bound Sylvester Swan of Ightham to the peace against John Bound the younger of Ightham, tailor, the said Walter Pelsant and Edward Rootes of Ightham, shoemaker, being his sureties; but this was released.

---

[1] Read, *Lambarde*, pp. 15–17. Except for a few instances where Read appears to have misread the manuscript in the Folger Library, his text has been followed, including all his editorial emendations of spelling and punctuation. This text is far better than the earlier transcription in the *Huntington Library Quarterly*, xv (1952), 123–58.

The 26 of September Sir Thomas Fane and I took sureties of Thomas Chambers aforesaid, namely, Thomas Codd of Tonbridge, innholder, and William Lucas of the same, shoemaker; and likewise we took bond with the said William Cosin, William Atmer of Penshurst, yeoman, and John Cosin of Tonbridge, tailor, and with Thomas Norham, Isaac Fray of Hadlow, husbandman, and Nicholas Dynes of Tonbridge, laborer, the principals in 10 *li.* the piece and the sureties in 5 *li.* the piece, with condition that the principals shall no more keep alehouses, etc.

The 27 and 28 September the Lord Cobham and I licensed James Hawkes, Thomas Pigeon, and George Colt, all of Chalk, to keep alehouses in their then dwelling houses there, and we took the said Hawkes bound in 10 *li.*, Andrew Smith of Higham and Reignold Hawkes of [Shorne], his sureties, bound in 5 *li.* apiece, with the usual condition [which I] have devised for that purpose. Colt and Pigeon . . .

My father and I joined in certifying our knowledge to the bishop concerning the good behaviour of Margaret Tebold to be married, etc. Likewise bound, and with them, William Page of Shorne, gentleman, and Stephen Colt of the same, yeoman, as sureties in the like sums and under the like conditions.

The said Lord and I bound Richard Williams of Higham, yeoman, in 100 marks, to his good behavior, but that was released, etc.

*October*    The 3 of October my father-in-law and I bound Walter Pelsant aforesaid from keeping an alehouse any more; his sureties were Reignold Pelsant and Nicholas Miller of Wrotham, yeomen.

The 4 October I certified at the quarter sessions the said recognizances of Walter Pelsant, Thomas Chambers, William Cosin, and Thomas Norham for not keeping alehouses, and the said recognizances of James Hawkes, Thomas Pigeon, and George Colt for the keeping of good rule in their alehouses, and the said recognizance of John Sone for his appearance aforesaid, the said Walter Pelsant and John Usiner of Wrotham, butchers, being his sureties, which recognizance was then forfeit by his default of appearance.

This passage illustrates well both the variety of tasks which Lambarde performed and the fashion in which he used his *Ephemeris*. The statement that on October 4 he certified at quarter sessions the recognizances of certain men is followed in the manuscript by an 'X' in the margin and a line drawn across the page.[1] This was a procedure which Lambarde regularly followed when he had fulfilled his duties either at

---

[1] In the printed text, this and other significant annotations or marginalia were ignored.

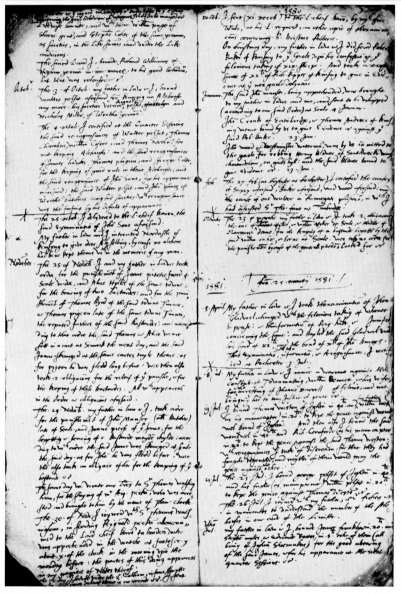

William Lambarde's *Ephemeris*, folios 2 and 3

Three examples of the X and of the line which are discussed on p. 10 are shown, as well as the last few entries of the passage which is quoted on that page.

the quarter sessions or at the assizes, using somewhat different symbols for the two sorts of sittings. Careful reading shows that the entry listed all the men whose recognizances he then held; since the bonds of Swan and Williams had been released before the meeting of the sessions, no certificates were required. The line must have been drawn to indicate that earlier entries were for Lambarde no longer of official concern. Unquestionably he used the *Ephemeris* as a practical tool in the effective performance of his duties; he was a methodical man.

It is also possible to follow in the diary the fortunes of several culprits. Chambers, Cosin, and Norham, who were committed to gaol on August 26, were released after they succeeded on September 20 in posting bonds, both their own and those of sureties. Walter Pelsant was that same day committed to gaol for the same offence. Yet his bond on behalf of Sylvester Swan was accepted simultaneously, and later he was bondsman for John Sone. By October 3 Pelsant had produced satisfactory bonds and he too was released. It was a close community. Lambarde must have known many of these men well.

In the manuscript the entry about Margaret Tebold appears at the head of a page, and it is clear that it was made at a later date than the passage which it interrupts. One other item—on 6 November 1582—also concerns a certificate in connection with a marriage. Perhaps these women had earlier been guilty of unchaste behaviour, for a certificate from a J.P. was hardly a standard preliminary to marriage. But these were only two of the considerable number of entries which concern acts beyond the scope described by the title-page of the *Ephemeris*: 'The Certifiable Causes of the Commission of the Peace.'

16 July [1582]   I wrote to my Lord of Dover in commendation of Simon Haxup, schoolmaster at Knole, to be admitted into the ministry of the church.

4 March [1583]   At the assizes at Rochester . . . we all of the commission of the peace agreed upon a draft for the house of correction which I had penned, and we also wrote in the behalf of a constable that was arrested by the Knight Marshal's men at the complaint of a purveyor.

20 July [1583]    At Cobham Hall my Lord, Sir Christopher Alleyn, and I wrote to all the constables of this division to notify the taxation of the money for the gaol and the house of correction.

23 June [1587]    We of this division sent out towards the Low Countries thirteen men for our part of fifty men allotted to this lathe of Aylesford; . . . the whole shire made out three hundred.[1]

Many other examples could be given of the very varied tasks which Lambarde and other justices undertook.

In one respect the opening portion of the diary was very unusual. Although it reflected two common forms of mis-behaviour—robbery and the disorders associated with ale-houses—there is no evidence of the consequences of human lust. An entry at Christmas-time, however, indicates in more characteristic fashion the misconduct which required so much of any J.P.'s attention.

24 December [1583]    Mr. Dr. William Lewyn and I took order that Margaret Dutton should be first whipped at Gravesend and then sent to the house of correction for a bastard woman child there born and begotten on her by Robert Cole, as it is thought, whom also we committed till he give sureties to appear at the Easter sessions, for to stand to the order of the bench there, because he refused to perform the order set down against him by my L. Cobham and Mr. Somer.

The same day also he and I took like order for the whipping of Abigail Sherwood for a bastard man child born by her at Chatham and for her like sending to the house of correction. But as touching the reputed father, we left the decision thereof to the ecclesiastical trial, for that she confessed herself to have been carnally known of many men. The child also was dead so that nothing was to be done in the behalf of the parish.[2]

Sometimes the J.P.s had cognizance of very serious crime.

23 Feb [1583]    Sir Christopher Alleyn and I examined sundry persons at Sevenoaks concerning the suspicion of willful poisoning of William Brightrede by Thomas Heyward and Parnel, his now wife, then wife of the said William.

28 February    Sir Christopher Alleyn, Mr. John Lennard, and I examined divers other persons concerning the said William Bright-rede's death and concerning the like suspicion of poisoning of Joan,

<hr />

[1] Read, *Lambarde*, pp. 25, 28, 29, 47.                   [2] Ibid., pp. 30–1.

late wife of the said Heyward. And we then committed the said Heyward and Parnel to the gaol.[1]

There were problems which today are not crimes.

23 August [1581]  Sir Christopher Alleyn, my father-in-law, and I joined in the examination of eight persons, that counterfeited their apparel and language as the rogues called Egyptians were wont to do, and we sent them to the gaol.[2]

It is tempting to quote even more extensively from the entries of a diary which combines a vivid reflection of the lives of the less fortunate of Elizabeth's Kentish subjects and most revealing evidence of the comprehensive activity of a justice of the peace. Both are indicated also in Lambarde's charge to the jury at the sessions held at Maidstone in September 1583.

It is evident then that you of the jury be the principal instruments of this business, put in trust by the law to solicit and procure the glory of God and service of the Queen, the quiet of the good and correction of the bad, the stay of the rich and relief of the poor, the advancement of public profit and the restraint of injurious and private gain.

And therefore, if God be dishonored by the imps of Satan and enemies of right religion, if the Majesty of our gracious Queen be contemned in breach of her laws by unbridled persons, if unlawful buyers and sellers do move dearth in the midst of this blessed store and plenty, if by countenance of retainers against the law many amongst us do not only escape common charge but do also vex and overcrow their neighbors, if by disorders in alehouse keepers your children and servants be corrupted in manners, bastards be multiplied in parishes, thieves and rogues do swarm in the highways, the lawful pastimes of the land be abandoned, and dicing, cards, and bowling be set up in place, finally, if neither public officers do content themselves with their due and allowable fees nor private persons of any sort do contain themselves within their lawful bounds . . . you that are called hither . . . cannot . . . but see and know and are also sworn to bewray the authors of these evils . . . and you above other are to answer unto God, the Queen's Majesty and your country for the same.[3]

Evidently Lambarde recognized that the J.P.s were expected to have concern for many matters unnoticed in his *Ephemeris*. Does the absence, then, from its text of all

---

[1] Ibid., pp. 27-8.    [2] Ibid., p. 21.    [3] Ibid., pp. 73-4.

mention of religion and of any reference to the defence of England against the Armada mean that it is a very incomplete account of the author's work as a magistrate?

To this question no sure answer can be given. A passage in Lambarde's charge to the jury in September 1588 reflects the point of view of a loyal Englishman.

Have not our most obstinate recusants and unnatural conspirators fetched their popish treason from beyond the seas? Have not Italy and France sent us swarms of Jesuits and seminaries, that privily minister poison to our souls and stir up Spaniards with open hostility to invade the realm?[1]

Lambarde was certainly exercised by the major issues of his time. Yet Kent was relatively free of recusancy, and there were several other justices in his division. It is not impossible that no cases of religious crime came to his personal attention. Furthermore there are so many entries of minor matters in the *Ephemeris*, so much detail with regard to the cases therein recorded, so many memoranda addressed to himself —e.g. 'Remember to send for Christopher Bowle, the borseholder . . . Remember to renew at the Easter sessions the Register of the Poor at Ightham'—that it is manifest that he leaned heavily on it in the performance of his duties.[2] Thus it seems probable that it does in fact record not all his public responsibility—the charges to the jury are not mentioned though there are several references to such extra tasks as the commission for sewers of Medway—but essentially all his acts performed as a justice of the peace outside quarter sessions.

During the eight years—1580 to 1588—covered by the *Ephemeris*, Lambarde made an average of some three entries a month. The only considerable gaps are the weeks from April to July 1581, January to March and September to December 1582. He was still an active lawyer—in 1588 the Privy Council instructed him in association with three other members of his inn to suggest reforms in the law which should be submitted to Parliament—and he may well have been in residence in his chambers during these intervals. Yet the *Ephemeris* records his presence at almost all the quarter

---

[1] Read, *Lambarde*, pp. 95–6.    [2] Ibid., pp. 23, 27.

sessions for west Kent, in Maidstone in April and September, and on at least seven occasions during these years he delivered the charge to the jury, which was a central feature of the proceedings. He was present also at many of the Kent assizes, whether held at Maidstone, at Rochester, or occasionally elsewhere.

The acts outside sessions which are recorded in his *Ephemeris* were performed at ten specified places in addition to his residence, all lying within the triangle formed by Maidstone, Rochester, and Sevenoaks. The houses of the J.P.s with whom he collaborated must have been the usual scene of these sittings. While he lived at Ightham, George Moulton, his father-in-law, was his partner on thirty-four occasions, and he acted with Sir Christopher Alleyn of the Mote in Ightham eleven times, with the nearby Wrotham J.P.s, Robert Binge and Robert Richers, six and five times respectively, and with Lord Cobham also five. He recorded twenty-five further formal acts in which he was associated with a dozen other justices, all men of some eminence.

After Lambarde moved to Halling, Moulton disappeared from the diary and John Leveson, who collaborated on twenty-four occasions, became the most frequent associate, while Lord Cobham and Edward Beecher, who was Cobham's son-in-law, each joined with Lambarde eleven times in a total of sixty-five recorded acts. Comparison with the records of other J.P.s shows that the 300-odd entries during eight years reflect much more than average devotion to duty.[1]

In the diary mention is made of twenty-two fellow J.P.s. They are a good sample, drawn from a commission of the peace in the middle years of Elizabeth I. A glance at the full roster shows that their names—marked below by an '*E*'—are scattered through the seventy-six men who constituted the Kent bench in 1584, a fact of some import, since in all commissions the justices were listed in order of legal and social precedence. Within each of the classes: the 'dignitaries' at the head of the roster—great officers of state, other peers, bishops, justices of assize—and the 'working group' —knights, doctors of the two universities, simple esquires— seniority of appointment was the usual order. A blank line

[1] Cf. *infra*, pp. 112–14.

indicates the division between the dignitaries and the working group.

### 1584[1]

| | No. | q | Name | Place | | | | Year | DNB |
|---|---|---|---|---|---|---|---|---|---|
| | 1 | q | Thomas Bromley, lord chancellor of England | | O | M | P | 1587 | DNB |
| | 2 | q | William [Cecil], lord Burghley, lord treasurer of England | | C | G | P | 1598 | DNB |
| | 3 | q | John [Young], bishop of Rochester | | C | | | 1605 | DNB |
| E | 4 | q | Henry [Neville], lord Burgavenny [Abergavenny] | | | | | 1587 | |
| E | 5 | q | William [Brooke], lord Cobham, lord warden [of the cinque ports] [lord lieutenant] | | C | | | 1597 | |
| | 6 | q | Thomas [Burgh], lord Burgh | | | | | 1602 | |
| | 7 | q | Henry [Carey], lord Hunsdon | | | | P | 1596 | DNB |
| | 8 | q | Thomas Sackville, knight, lord Buckhurst | | | I | P | 1608 | DNB |
| | 9 | q | Henry [Cheyney], lord Cheyney of Toddington | | | | P | 1587 | |
| | 10 | q | Henry Sidney, knight, lord president [of Wales] | | | | P | 1586 | DNB |
| | 11 | q | Christopher Hatton, knight | | O | I | P | 1591 | DNB |
| | 12 | q | Roger Manwood, knight [chief baron of the exchequer] | | | I | P | 1592 | DNB |
| | 13 | q | George Carey, knight | | C | | P | 1603 | DNB |
| | 14 | q | Thomas Gawdy, knight, justice [of the queen's bench] | | | I | P | 1589 | DNB |
| | 15 | q | Francis Gawdy, serjeant-at-law | | | I | | 1606 | DNB |
| | 16 | q | Henry Cobham, knight | Cobham | | G | P | 1619 | DNB |
| E | 17 | q | Thomas Randolph | Maidstone | O | | P | 1590 | DNB |
| E | 18 | | Thomas Cotton, knight | Oxenhoath | | | | 1585 | |
| E | 19 | | Christopher Alleyn, knight | Ightham | | | P | 1590 | |
| | 20 | | Warham St. Leger, knight | Leeds Castle | | | | 1597 | DNB |
| | 21 | | Thomas Scott, knight | Smeeth | | I | P | 1594 | DNB |
| | 22 | | Richard Baker, knight | Sissinghurst | | | P | 1594 | |
| | 23 | | James Hales, knight | Canterbury | C | G | | 1589 | |
| E | 24 | | Thomas Fane, knight | Badsell | | | | 1589 | DNB |
| | 25 | q | George Harte, knight | Lullingstone | | | | 1587 | |
| | 26 | q | Edward Hoby, knight | Queenborough | O | | P | 1617 | DNB |
| | 27 | q | Thomas Sondes, knight | Throwley | | L | | 1592 | |
| | 28 | q | Thomas Wotton [custos rotulorum] | Boughton Malherbe | | | | 1587 | DNB |
| | 29 | q | John Cobham | Newington | C | | P | 1594 | |
| | 30 | q | John Astley | Maidstone | | | P | 1595 | DNB |
| | 31 | q | William Cromer | Tunstall | | G | P | 1598 | |
| | 32 | q | Moyle Finch | Eastwell | | G | | 1614 | |
| | 33 | q | Thomas Smyth | Westenhanger | | | | 1591 | |
| E | 34 | q | John Lennard | Chevening | | L | | 1590 | |
| | 35 | q | Richard Payne | Horsmonden | | | | | |
| | 36 | q | Brian Annesley | Lee | | | | 1604 | |
| E | 37 | q | Thomas Willoughby | Chiddingstone | | | P | 1596 | |
| E | 38 | q | William Lewin, master | Otterden | C | | P | 1598 | DNB |
| | 39 | q | John Hawkins | Chatham | | | P | 1595 | DNB |
| E | 40 | q | George Moulton | Ightham | | | | 1588 | |
| E | 41 | q | Robert Rudston | Boughton Monchelsea | | | P | 1589 | |
| | 42 | | William Gresham | Lingfield, Surrey | O | G | P | 1624 | |
| E | 43 | q | John Somers | Rochester | | | | 1585 | |
| | 44 | q | John Parker | Bekesbourne | | | P | 1618 | |
| | 45 | q | Richard Cosin, doctor of laws | Doctors Commons | C | | P | 1597 | DNB |
| | 46 | q | John Scott | Nettlestead | O | | P | 1618 | DNB |

[1] See note on pp. 28–30.

| E | No. | q | Name | Place | C | O | | P | Date | |
|---|---|---|---|---|---|---|---|---|---|---|
| | 47 | q | Thomas Henley | Otham | | | | | 1591 | |
| | 48 | | John Fineux | Herne | | | | | 1592 | |
| E | 49 | q | Robert Binge | Wrotham | | | | P | 1595 | |
| E | 50 | q | Robert Richers | Wrotham | | | L | P | 1588 | |
| | 51 | q | George Clifford | Bobbing | | | G | P? | | |
| | 52 | | John Goldwell | Great Chart | C | | G | P | 1599 | |
| | 53 | q | Edward Boys | Nonington | | | G | | 1597 | |
| | 54 | q | Richard Hardres | Upper Hardres | | | G | | 1613 | |
| | 55 | q | Martin James | Eastling | | | | | 1592 | |
| | 56 | | George Mooreton | Chilham | | | | | 1594 | |
| | 57 | q | Thomas Palmer | Wingham | | | G | | 1626 | DNB |
| | 58 | q | William Partrige | Bredgar | | | | P | 1598 | |
| | 59 | q | George Finch | Norton | | | | | 1584 | |
| | 60 | q | Michael Sondes | Sheldwich | | | L | P | 1617 | |
| E | 61 | q | William Lambarde | Halling | | | L | P | 1601 | DNB |
| | 62 | q | Thomas Hales | Thannington | | | | | 1583 | |
| | 63 | | Martin Barnham | Hollingbourne | | | G | | 1610 | |
| | 64 | q | John Boys | Canterbury | | | M | P | 1612 | |
| | 65 | | Richard Argall | East Sutton | | | I | P | 1588 | |
| | 66 | | Nicholas St. Leger | Eastwell | | | | P | | |
| | 67 | q | Edward Monins | Waldershare | | | | | 1602 | |
| | 68 | | Justinian Champneys | Bexley | | | | P | 1596 | |
| | 69 | q | Robert Honiwood | Charing | | | G | | 1627 | |
| E | 70 | | Thomas Potter | Westerham | | | | | 1610 | |
| E | 71 | | Edward Beecher | Cobham | C | | M | | | |
| E | 72 | q | Thomas Fludd | Bearsted | | | | P | 1607 | |
| E | 73 | | Thomas Fane, junior | Hunton | | | | P | 1607 | |
| E | 74 | | Roger Twysden | East Peckham | | | G | | 1604 | |
| | 75 | | Ralph Heyman | Selling | | | | | | |
| | 76 | | John Ayscough | Lynsted | | | | | 1601 | |

The following, though mentioned in Lambarde's *Ephemeris*, were not members of the commission for Kent in 1584 as it is recorded in a *liber pacis*. Walsingham died early in that year, Leveson and Sedley were added in 1585.

| E | No. | q | Name | Place | O | | P | Date |
|---|---|---|---|---|---|---|---|---|
| E | 77 | q | Thomas Walsingham, knight | Chislehurst | | L | | 1584 |
| E | 78 | | John Leveson | Halling | O | G | P | 1615 |
| E | 79 | | William Sedley | Aylesford | O | L | | 1618 |

Lambarde's closest associates were a varied group of men. They included two dignitaries and one holder of national office. Lords Abergavenny and Cobham, the heirs of half a dozen generations of nobility, were the leading magnates of the county, the only distinctively Kentish peers at this time. Brothers-in-law, their principal estates at Birling and Cobham were each only a few miles from Lambarde's new home at Halling. Thomas Randolph, born of an undistinguished Kentish family, acquired at Oxford the knowledge of civil law which proved to be the entrance to a distinguished career in government. For Elizabeth he undertook several important diplomatic missions in France and Scotland and was appointed Master of the Posts in 1566. Like many of his associates he had a financial interest in overseas ventures. His wife was a sister of Sir Francis Walsingham; his office is the explanation of his place in the roster, ahead of all the knights who had no position at court.

Four such knights were mentioned in *Ephemeris*. Sir Thomas Cotton came, on his father's side, of prominent Cambridgeshire gentry, and through his mother was connected with the Colepepers, a comparable family in Sussex and Kent. Sir Christopher Alleyn was a relative parvenu who had acquired significant monastic property and then a knighthood at Mary's coronation. Sir Thomas Fane was descended from yeomen of the Tonbridge region, but his mother was a co-heiress of Sir Walter Henley, who had been Attorney of the Court of Augmentations and the grantee of much monastic land. Fane married a daughter of Lord Abergavenny; their son captured the heiress of the Mildmay fortune and became Earl of Westmorland in a new creation. Even in Tudor times this was a spectacular rise. Sir Thomas Walsingham was a cousin of the principal Secretary and head of a family of leading gentry.

Among the esquires were three who had connections with the court, four whose prominence derived from the law, two who inherited fortunes made in the commerce of London, and six who were the heirs of gentry of some antiquity. John Somers, a descendant of a Chancellor of the Exchequer, was Clerk of the Signet. Thomas Fludd, of a Shropshire family, held a number of official positions including the Keepership of Norwich Castle and the Surveyorship of Kent. Knighted in 1589, he was the Paymaster of the Forces sent to France in that year. Edward Beecher, though the son of a London mercer and alderman, married a daughter of Lord Cobham and thus became in time the brother-in-law of Robert Cecil. He lived at Cobham and moved in court circles.

John Lennard, Robert Richers, and William Sedley were Lincoln's Inn barristers—like Lambarde. Though never a serjeant or judge, Lennard held a number of legal offices and acquired such extensive lands in Kent that his son secured in marriage the heiress to a peerage and his grandson became Baron Dacre. A recognized legal scholar and

later treasurer of his inn, Sedley also prospered greatly and, 79
among other charitable legacies, founded at Oxford the
distinguished lectureship in natural philosophy. Richers was 50
less prominent, but he too was a professional lawyer. William
Lewin won his success in the civil law. In 1584 he was judge 38
of the Prerogative Court of Canterbury; he soon became
chancellor of the diocese of Rochester. Had he not later
become master in chancery, he might here be considered to
be a churchman rather than a lawyer.

Robert Rudston was the son of a Lord Mayor of London 41
of Yorkshire background. John Leveson, descendant of two 78
Lord Mayors and cousin of his colleague, William Gresham,
became Deputy Lieutenant and a leader of Kentish society.
He is considered in detail in the next chapter.

Roger Twysden was probably the most prominent of the 74
men who can be described simply as leading gentry. Thomas
Fane the younger was a brother of Sir Thomas; he too pros- 73
pered by marriage with a Henley heiress. The grandson of a
Chief Justice of the Common Pleas on whose success at the
law the family fortune rested, Thomas Willoughby was 37
another well-established member of the gentry. George
Moulton is best known as the father-in-law of William Lam- 40
barde. Robert Binge and Thomas Potter appear to have been 49, 70
gentry who barely qualified for the county bench, though
their descendants achieved greater prominence.

All these men owned sizeable estates in Kent. If the group
was heterogeneous—among its members were two peers
who held ancient titles and several parvenus—it was a closely
knit society. Lambarde knew them all well, and they must
have been in his mind when he wrote in his *Perambulation
of Kent*:

The Gentlemen be not heere (throughout) of so auncient stockes as
else where, especially in the partes nearer to London, from which citie
(as it were from a certaine riche and wealthy seed plot) Courtiers,
Lawyers, & Marchants be continually translated, & become new plants
amongst them. Yet be their revenues greater than any where else:
which thinge groweth not so muche by the quantitie of their possession,
or by the fertilitie of their soyle, as by the benefit of the situation
of the countrie itselfe, which hath al that good neighborhood, that
Marc Cato and other olde writers require to a well placed graunge,

that is to say, the Sea, the River, a populous citie, and a well traded highway, by the commodities wherof, the superfluous fruites of the grounde be dearly sold, and consequently the land yeeld a greater rent.[1]

The J.P.s were often friends as well as colleagues. Lambarde's diary demonstrates his ties with Moulton, Abergavenny, Cobham, Leveson, and Beecher. Something more than formal acquaintance is implied with Alleyn, the elder Fane, Binge, Richers, and Lewin. There were frequent marriages between members of these families, while evidence of intimacy and trust is in their wills. Lambarde served as executor or overseer under the wills of Lord Cobham, Somers, and Rudston. Leveson carried out these duties for Cobham, Lambarde, and Fludd. Randolph was Lambarde's colleague under Somers's will. Dr. Thomas Binge was overseer both for his brother and for Lewin.[2]

The wills show other facts about their makers. Specific holdings of land are frequently given; since the will commonly does not indicate whether the land was encumbered, real property is not very clear evidence of the wealth of the maker. More reliable testimony comes from money legacies, particularly those to unmarried daughters. Sir Thomas Fane left £1,000 to one daughter in addition to making generous bequests to three sons. Lennard provided legacies of £1,000 for two daughters. Randolph bequeathed to his wife and five daughters £500 each as well as providing for two sons. Leveson, who complained about his losses, left even larger legacies to two granddaughters. It was a wealthy group.[3] Lambarde knew that their lands yielded a great rent.

There is other evidence of their varied lives. Randolph devised to his second son 'all share or parts adventured beyond the sea in Persia, Media, Russia or elsewhere now amounting to £300'. Cotton gave to his grandson 'my seal of arms, my books, maps and cosmography and marine causes and all

---

1 William Lambarde, *A Perambulation of Kent* (L., 1576), p. 10.
2 Cobham: *Arch. Cant.* xx (1877), 206–15; Lambarde: ibid. v (1863), 253–6; Somers: PCC 1585, 49 Brudenell; Rudston: PCC 1589, 12 Drury; Fludd: PCC 1607, 54 Hudleston; Binge: PCC 1595, 76 Scott; Lewin: PCC 1598, 1 Lewyn; Fane: PCC 1590, 10 Sainberbe; Lennard: PCC 1591, 27 Sainberbe; Randolph: PCC 1590, 75 Drury; Cotton: PCC 1585, 35 Brudenell; Leveson: PCC 1615, 97 Rudd.
3 Cf. *infra*, Appendix H.

manner of armour . . . at Oxenhoth'. He also entreated his friends to defend the grandson against the boy's relatives, particularly against his uncle Robert, who had 'of late most unnaturally broken open doors and locks at Oxenhoth and taken out of Closets divers of my writings which my mind was he should never have had'. Lambarde provided that each of his three sons should have 'three pairs of sheets to be sent for use at school, the university, or an Inn of Court'. They were also to be allowed for their keep £20 each year while in grammar school, £30 at a university, and £35 at an inn. He left to Lord Keeper Egerton, to whom he had earlier presented inscribed copies of two editions of *Eirenarcha*,[1] 'the books and writings which belonged to Ralph Rokeby, Master of Requests'. To the benchers of Lincoln's Inn went £10 to be used for the purchase of plate. Bequests to the poor of the testator's parish were usual, and occasionally there was a gift to a community, such as the £10 which Somers left to Rochester. The Kent J.P.s had diverse interests.

Lambarde left another key to the commission of the peace in Kent. In the 1596 edition of the *Perambulation* he outlined the organization of the work of the J.P.s. Within the lathe of Aylesford, in which lay both Ightham and Halling, were three divisions: north, south, and east. For the north division Lord Cobham, his son Henry, Sir John Leveson, and Lambarde had responsibility. In the south division the tasks fell upon Sedley, Twysden, Thomas Fane the younger, who were mentioned in the *Ephemeris*, and upon several who were not: John Scott of Nettlestead, John Richers, who had succeeded his deceased father, and George Chowne of Wrotham, who had been put into the commission after 1588. In the east division Fludd and Lewin were Lambarde's collaborators. There were in that division seven men, including Sir Edward Wotton, who had been added to the commission since 1588 in his deceased father's place.[2]

Among the state papers is a manuscript summary of the organization of the Kent J.P.s as of June 1575. This shows that the justices then living in the lathe of Aylesford were: Lords Abergavenny and Cobham, Cotton, Alleyn, Thomas

---

[1] Now in the Henry E. Huntington Library, San Marino, California.
[2] William Lambarde, *A Perambulation of Kent* (L., 1596), pp. 31–5.

Fane the elder, Richers, Moulton, Binge, and Rudston, who have been shown to have worked actively with Lambarde after 1580; Thomas Watton, Thomas Coppinger, Nicholas Barham, who had all died before the *Ephemeris* began; and finally Sir Warham St. Leger, Nicholas St. Leger, Thomas Henley, Richard Argall, and Thomas Wotton, who were still alive but do not appear in its text. In conjunction these two outlines of the organization of the justices in the region where Lambarde lived demonstrate that almost all those men who lived in his close neighbourhood are mentioned in his account. They were active associates in fact.[1]

The day-to-day functioning of the commission is also shown by a survey of the sites where its members resided. Of the men whose seats were within ten miles of Ightham or Halling only John Astley (Master of the Jewel House) does not figure in the *Ephemeris*. Conversely William Lewin lived at Otterden, some sixteen miles from Halling. Neighbours often collaborated. The commission was accepted as a serious obligation; only for the dignitaries at the head of the roster was it a sinecure.[2]

Lambarde and his closer associates constituted one-third of the commission for Kent in 1584. Was the whole body significantly different? Altogether there were seventy-six men in the roster when the *liber pacis* was compiled, probably in July 1584. Several extra names were added while the book was in use, among them that of the new Archbishop of Canterbury, which then stood first. Twenty-two men were veterans from the commission of the early years of the reign.[3]

The dignitaries at the head of the roster need little comment. The Lord Chancellor (or the Lord Keeper of the Great Seal) and the Lord Treasurer were uniformly members of the commissions of all counties with an essentially honorary status in each. Equally *ex officio* but not merely formal members were the justices of assize assigned to the circuit in which the county lay, in this instance Sir Thomas Gawdy and

---

[1] P.R.O., S.P. 12/104.  [2] Cf. *infra*, Ch. VII.

[3] Lords Hunsdon, Burgavenny (Abergavenny), Cobham, Buckhurst, and Cheyney; Sir Henry Sidney, Sir Roger Manwood, Sir Thomas Cotton, Sir Christopher Alleyn, Sir Warham St. Leger, Sir Thomas Scott, Sir Richard Baker; Thomas Wotton, John Cobham, William Cromer, John Lennard, George Moulton, Robert Rudston, Thomas Henley, Robert Binge, Robert Richers, Thomas Hales.

Kent: the Lathes of Aylesford and Sutton-at-Hone
The residences of the J.P.s mentioned in Lambarde's *Ephemeris* are shown

Comptroller of the Navy he was much concerned with the functioning of the dockyards at Chatham and Deptford. 45,55 Cosin, Dean of the Arches, James, Registrar of the Court of 65 Chancery, and Argall, Registrar of the prerogative court of Canterbury, were lawyers who held significant official positions. 30 tions. Astley was the Master of the Jewel House as well as the owner of considerable properties in the county.

Basically county figures were seven men who were not 12 without connections and honour otherwise. Sir Roger Manwood, a native and for most of his life a leading citizen of Sandwich, was a very successful barrister who became Chief Baron of the Exchequer in 1578. Prominent by virtue of 29 their family were Lord Cobham's brother John and his son 16 Sir Henry, the eighth Baron, who was to be implicated in the plot of 1603 and to spend many years in the Tower. Sir 26 Edward Hoby, the son of a distinguished father, a diplomat and a man of letters, inherited estates in Berkshire and Worcestershire as well as in Kent. A nephew of Lord Burghley and a religious controversialist, he was knight of the shire in 1592 and was appointed *custos rotulorum* and 20 constable of Queenborough Castle. Sir Warham St. Leger of Leeds Castle was the noteworthy son of a still more eminent father, Sir Anthony, who had also been a J.P. Both father and son served in Ireland, and the son married a daughter of 28 Lord Abergavenny. Thomas Wotton, who had been *custos rotulorum* as early as 1562, was the son of a Treasurer of Calais who had been a Privy Councillor under both Henry VIII and Edward VI. His two sons, Sir Edward, who succeeded to his estates, and Sir Henry, the diplomatist and poet, 64 were even more distinguished than their father. John Boys— who is considered in detail in the next chapter—was a bencher and treasurer of the Middle Temple. He came from a well-known Kentish family and established a flourishing legal practice in Canterbury.

The City of London was the principal source of the wealth which qualified four Kentish justices for their appointments 33 to the commission. Thomas Smyth was the extremely successful haberdasher and merchant who secured the farm of the customs of London; 'Customer' Smyth had an estate at Westenhanger, and three of his sons were later J.P.s.

William Gresham was a grandson of Sir John Gresham, Lord 42
Mayor of London in 1547, and a nephew of the notable
financier, Sir Thomas. His estate at Lingfield near the Kent
border of Surrey explains his membership in the Kent commission. Martin Barnham was the very wealthy son of a 63
London merchant; sheriff for Kent in 1599, he was knighted
in 1603. Justinian Champneys, the son of a Lord Mayor, 68
was sheriff in 1583–4. A number of the men who have
already been considered in other categories also possessed
fortunes which derived from City sources.

There were twenty-eight men who are best described
simply as gentry. A few were connected with the nobility or
had some other distinction, and several were major figures in
Kent society; they merit brief notice. The others have left
such spare traces of their lives that even antiquaries and the
diligent local historian Hasted can indicate little except their
holdings in land and basic biographical facts. The data given
in the roster above, with the bibliographical references in the
notes, serve present purposes.

Knighthood itself gave distinction to three men. Sir
Thomas Scott (whose son John was his colleague in the com- 21, 46
mission) was the head of a family of gentry that had been
prominent in the county since the end of the fourteenth
century; Reginald Scott, whose putative place in the commission they may have pre-empted, was a more notable but
less wealthy cousin. Sir James Hales (whose cousin Thomas 23,
was also a J.P.) came from a family that had included three
judges in the past century. Sir Thomas Sondes, who held 27
lands in Surrey, Sussex, Nottinghamshire, and Lincolnshire
as well as in Kent, was another outstanding member of the
gentry. Moyle Finch, son of a distinguished soldier, was 32
knighted in 1584 and became a baronet in 1611; his brother,
Henry, and his sons, Heneage and John, all achieved fame
in law and in politics.

Among the esquires, John Parker merits mention. Son of 44
the late Archbishop of Canterbury, he lived for a time in
Kent but later moved to Cambridge, where in his later years
he subsisted on money grants from Corpus Christi, his
father's college. John Goldwell's forebears had held lands in 52
Great Chart since the twelfth century, but near the end of

the reign these holdings were dissipated; this is presumably
the explanation of the disappearance of the family from the
56 bench. George Mooreton was an interloper from Dorset, to
which he soon returned. Gentlemen of varying wealth and
prominence, the remaining justices do not require individual
attention.

Lambarde's closer associates were introduced as a sample
—not quite one-third—of the whole commission of 1584.
How do the two compare? Superficially the most striking
difference is the number of dignitaries: two in the *E* group—
Lords Abergavenny and Cobham, whose active participation
was in itself unusual—and fifteen in the whole body. If they
be disregarded, both certain similarities and one difference
become apparent. Among 61 active J.P.s (not including the
three extra names derived from *Ephemeris*) 10 had been
enrolled in one of the universities—4 from the *E* group—
while 22 had studied at one of the inns of court—5 in the *E*
group. Among Lambarde's immediate associates there were
one member each of Gray's Inn and the Middle Temple, and
three members of Lincoln's Inn, all barristers (Lambarde,
Lennard, and Richers). In the whole body Gray's Inn was
far in the lead: there was only one other barrister—John
Boys of the Middle Temple. In each case approximately one-
third had secured at least formal enrolment in one of the inns
of court. The figures for the universities were nearer a fifth;
there were only four men who had studied in both contexts.
The proportions of the barristers are notably different; three
of the four were in the *E* group. Chance may be the explanation, but probably geography played a part. The lathe of
Aylesford is close to London and it was convenient as a
residence for professional men in the sixteenth century as in
the twentieth.

Election to the House of Commons became a common
experience for the lawyers and the leading gentry of the
Tudor period; they were the men who formed the backbone
of the commissions of the peace. In Kent in 1584 nearly all
the dignitaries had been returned to Parliament at least once,
and some thirty of the remaining members, approximately
fifty per cent. Many sat for a borough once or perhaps twice;
yet there were several cases of frequent re-election: John

Cobham, Michael Sondes, John Boys, Roger Manwood. Several secured election as knight of their shire—one of the evidences of eminence sought by the gentry of most counties largely for that reason. Robert Binge, Robert Rudston, and Thomas Willoughby all found seats outside the county. John Goldwell was chosen by Taunton three times and by Downton once. In the parliaments of the period of Lambarde's *Ephemeris* Kent J.P.s sat as follows:[1]

1572–83

Kent
  10 Sir Henry Sidney
  21 Sir Thomas Scott
Canterbury
  1562 William Lovelace
Maidstone
  66 Nicholas St. Leger
Queenborough
  29 John Cobham
Rochester
  58 William Partrige
Hythe
  1562 Thomas Honiwood
Lyme Regis
  30 John Astley
Plymouth
  39 John Hawkins
Sandwich
  12 Sir Roger Manwood
Weymouth
  32 Moyle Finch

Queenborough
  29 John Cobham
Bossiney
  E 78 John Leveson
Taunton
  52 John Goldwell

1586–7

Kent
  16 Sir Henry Cobham
  21 Sir Thomas Scott
Maidstone
  30 John Astley
  E 17 Thomas Randolph
Queenborough
  26 Sir Edward Hoby
  60 Michael Sondes
Rochester
  E 38 William Lewin
Taunton
  52 John Goldwell

1584–5

Kent
  Sir Philip Sidney
  Sir Edward Wotton
Maidstone
  E 17 Thomas Randolph
  60 Michael Sondes

1588–9

Kent
  16 Sir Henry Cobham
  Henry Brooke
Maidstone
  30 John Astley
  E 17 Thomas Randolph

[1] *Members of Parliament, 1213–1702* (Parl. Papers, 1878, vol. 62, pt. 1), *passim*; Browne Willis, *Notitia Parliamentaria* (3 vols., L., 1716–50), iii. 102. The numbers refer to the roster of 1584, the dates to another commission.

Queenborough
  60 Michael Sondes

Rochester
  E 38 William Lewin

Berkshire
  26 Sir Edward Hoby

Christchurch
  68 Justinian Champneys

Dover
  E 73 Thomas Fane, junior

Downton
  45 Richard Cosin

Hastings
  44 John Parker

Taunton
  52 John Goldwell

The voice of Kent must have been evident in St. Stephens. In the Kent commission for 1584 there were fifteen dignitaries, *ex officio*, or at least partly honorary, members. The men who are best described as courtiers, even though they included John Hawkins, numbered eleven. There were eight lawyers and six men whose status derived from the mercantile life of the City of London. Much the largest group were the thirty-six who were primarily gentry. Lambarde's *Ephemeris* mentioned three other justices: a City man, a lawyer, and a leading member of the gentry. A sample commission of the peace, these seventy-nine J.P.s provide one sort of guide to the many thousands who were justices between 1558 and 1640. With some exceptions they were a distinguished body of men.

NOTE TO PAGE 16

1 This roster is taken from British Museum Lansdowne MS. 747, ff. 141$^v$–3$^v$. In it and in other lists it has been convenient to give the place in the commission a number not found in the document and to use that number in the margin of the text as a key to the roster. It serves also as a subnumber in the footnotes for the citation of sources. Except when the text refers to important facts not included in a *DNB* article or in the *Complete Peerage*, no sources will be cited for men who are the subjects of *vitae* in those works. Various symbols indicate: mention in Lambarde's *Ephemeris* (E); membership in the quorum (q)—this is so shown in the original; enrolment in one of the universities (O or C); or in one of the inns of court (G, I, L, M, for Gray's Inn, Inner Temple, Lincoln's Inn, Middle Temple); and election to parliament (P). Further additions are the principal residence, approximate date of death, and notice in *DNB*. The usual square brackets enclose all other editorial additions to the manuscript. In order to minimize confusion it has seemed best to observe in general the uniformity of spelling which is now conventional, even in personal names. The Latin of most rosters has been translated.

5. J. E. Neale, *The Elizabethan House of Commons* (L., 1950), pp. 72, 214–21, 289, 290.

18. W. Bruce Bannerman (ed.), *The Visitations of Kent . . . 1530–1 and 1574 (A–H)* (Harl. Soc. Pub. lxxiv, L., 1923), p. 42; Edward Hasted, *A History of the County of Kent* (12 vols., Canterbury, 1797–1801), v. 64.

19. W. H. Shaw, *The Knights of England* (2 vols., L., 1906), ii. 66; *Arch. Cant.* xxiv

(1900), 197–9; *L. & P.* xixB, g166 (57); *A.P.C.*, *1575–6*, p. 107; ibid., *1577–8*, p. 385; *Cal. S.P. Dom. Eliz. Addenda*, *1565–79*, p. 79.

21. James Renat Scott, *Memorials of the Family of Scott* (L., 1876), pp. 86, 203–6, *et passim*; *DNB*: 'Reginald Scott'.
22. *DNB*: 'John Baker'; Hasted, *Kent*, iv. 375; ibid. v. 111; *Arch. Cant.* xxxviii (1926), 1–27.
23. *Visitations of Kent . . . 1530–1 and 1574*, pp. 56–7; Hasted, *Kent*, viii. 86; ibid. xi. 148–50; PCC 1568, 21 Holney; PCC 1587, 27 Drury.
24. Oswald Barron (ed.), *Northamptonshire Families* (L., 1906), p. 93; *L. & P.* xxiA, g717(3); W. C. Richardson, *History of the Court of Augmentations* (Baton Rouge, 1961), p. 43 *et passim*.
25. Hasted, *Kent*, ii. 545; PCC 1580, 19 Arundell; PCC 1587, 70 Spencer.
27. Hasted, *Kent*, v. 393; ibid. vi. 403, 451; W. Bruce Bannerman (ed.), *The Visitations of Kent . . . 1574 (I–Z) and 1592* (Harl. Soc. Publ. lxxv, L., 1924), pp. 32, 144; PCC 1592, 12 Nevill.
28. *DNB*: 'Edward Wotton', 'Henry Wotton', 'Thomas Wotton'.
29. Hasted, *Kent*, vi. 63.
31. Ibid., p. 87.
32. *DNB*: 'Thomas Finch'; Hasted, *Kent*, vii. 403–5.
33. Ibid. viii. 74; *DNB*: his son, 'Thomas Smith'.
34. Hasted, *Kent*, iii. 108, 109; W. P. Baildon (ed.), *The Records of the Honourable Society of Lincoln's Inn: The Black Books* (4 vols., L., 1897–1902), i. 254, 261, 291, 328, 368; ibid. ii. 23; PCC 1591, 27 Sainberbe.
35. Hasted, *Kent*, v. 314–15; Lansdowne MS. 737, f. 148.
36. Hasted, *Kent*, i. 492, 499; PCC 1604, 68 Harte.
37. Hasted, *Kent*, iii. 133, 220; PCC 1596, 53 Drake.
40. Hasted, *Kent*, v. 38; *Arch. Cant.* v (1863), 243.
41. Hasted, *Kent*, v. 339; PCC 1589, 12 Drury.
42. Hasted, *Kent*, iv. 304; Francis Blomefield, *An Essay towards a Topographical History of the County of Norfolk* (11 vols., L., 1805–10), v. 41 *et passim*; *A.P.C.*, *1590*, pp. 98, 173, 232–3; ibid., *1590–1*, p. 72; ibid., *1591–2*, p. 223.
43. Hasted, *Kent*, iv. 17, 22–3.
44. Ibid. ii. 172; ibid. ix. 267; H. P. Stokes, *Corpus Christi* (L., 1898), pp. 61–2; T. A. Walker, *A Biographical Register of Peterhouse Men* (2 vols., Camb., 1927–30), i. 226; W. K. Jordan, *Charities of Rural England* (L., 1961), p. 169; W. K. Jordan, *Social Institutions in Kent, 1480–1660* (vol. lxxv of *Arch. Cant.*, Ashford, 1961), p. 92.
47. *Northamptonshire Families*, pp. 89–95; Hasted, *Kent*, v. 516; ibid. vii. 106; PCC 1591, 28 Sainberbe.
48. Hasted, *Kent*, ix. 87–8.
49. Ibid. iii. 283; ibid. v. 11; *Visitations of Kent . . . 1530–1 and 1574*, p. 28.
50. *Visitations of Kent . . . 1574 and 1592*, p. 23; *Lincoln's Inn Black Books*, i. 261, 275, 305, 319, 322, 335, 355.
51. Hasted, *Kent*, vi. 196; *Visitations of Kent . . . 1530–1 and 1574*, p. 40.
52. Hasted, *Kent*, vii. 503, 504, 441; PCC 1599, 42 Rudd.
53. Lilian Boys Behrens, *Under Thirty-Seven Kings* (L., 1926), p. 44; Hasted, *Kent*, ix. 259–61.
54. Ibid. viii. 41; ibid. ix. 305; *Visitations of Kent . . . 1574 and 1592*, p. 130.
55. Hasted, *Kent*, vi. 426.
56. Ibid. vii. 280; P.R.O., Assize Rolls 35/26, 27; *Cal. S.P. Dom., Eliz. 1591–4*, p. 186; PCC 1595, 50 Scott; *DNB*: 'Albertus Mooreton'.
58. Hasted, *Kent*, iv. 61; ibid. ix. 279, 288; *Visitations of Kent . . . 1574 and 1592*, p. 18; PCC 1598, 62 Lewyn.

59. Hasted, *Kent*, vi. 403; PCC 1584, 32 Watson.
60. Hasted, *Kent*, v. 393; ibid. vi. 451; PCC 1592, 12 Nevill; *Visitations of Kent* . . . *1574 and 1592*, pp. 33, 146.
62. Hasted, *Kent*, ix. 22; *Arch. Cant.* xiv (1882), 61 ff.; *Visitations of Kent* . . . *1530–1 and 1574*, pp. 56–7.
63. Hasted, *Kent*, v. 468; PCC 1611, 39 Wood.
64. Cf. *infra*, pp. 33–4.
65. Hasted, *Kent*, v. 378–9; PCC 1585, 1 Brudenell.
66. *Arch. Cant.* xviii (1889), 20, 28; Hasted, *Kent*, viii. 405; *DNB*: 'Thomas Finch'.
67. Hasted, *Kent*, vi. 183; ibid. x. 53; PCC 1602, 29 Montague; G. E. Cokayne, *Complete Baronetage* (6 vols., Exeter, 1900–9), i. 77: 'William Monins'.
68. Hasted, *Kent*, ii. 174; ibid. viii. 74.
69. Ibid. v. 424; Lansdowne MS. 1218, f. 69$^v$; *Visitations of Kent* . . . *1574 and 1592*, p. 105.
70. Hasted, *Kent*, iii. 168; *Visitations of Kent* . . . *1574* and *1592*, p. 22.
71. J. J. Howard and G. J. Armytage (eds.), *The Visitation of London in the Year 1568* (Harl. Soc. Publ. i, L., 1869), p. 9; F. A. Blaydes (ed.), *The Visitation of Bedfordshire* . . . *1566, 1582, and 1634, etc.* (Harl. Soc. Publ. xix, L., 1884), p. 81; *Arch. Cant.* iv (1861), 208.
72. Hasted, *Kent*, v. 507; *Cal. S.P. Dom., 1581–90*, p. 618 *et passim*.
73. *Northamptonshire Families*, p. 94.
74. Hasted, *Kent*, v. 96 ff.
75. Ibid. viii. 106.
76. Ibid. vi. 305.
77. PCC 1584, 6 Watson; *Arch. Cant.* xiii (1880), 386 ff.
78. Cf. *infra*, p. 32–3.
79. Hasted, *Kent*, ii. 430 ff.; *Lincoln's Inn Black Books*, i. 436; ibid. ii. 105, 108, 118, 121.

# III

## CASE STUDIES OF J.P.s: DATA AND CATEGORIES

CASE studies and classification are devices which render abundant data amenable to analysis. Lambarde's *Ephemeris* has provided a key to a sample commission of the peace: Kent in 1584. Considered in some detail those J.P.s are seen to have been a very diverse body. If the materials for full biographical study are almost always wanting—even including the dignitaries at the head of the roster, fewer than a third have *vitae* in the *Dictionary of National Biography*, and only recently has Lambarde himself become the subject of a not very long book—it is clear that much evidence survives about most of the men who were justices. Were it feasible to work up those materials, a just assessment of a great many individuals could confidently be made, although the data would be massive, and proper assignments to categories might occasionally become rather less sure. The situation is well illustrated by a few case studies of J.P.s in several counties which indicate the degree of detail usually possible, the inferences which may rightly be drawn, and the hazards of classification.

Lambarde found that many of the Kent gentry were transplanted courtiers, lawyers, or merchants, and thus recognized four of the six categories—the other two are the dignitaries and the clergy—in terms of which some thirteen hundred J.P.s are best considered. But how should Lambarde himself be pigeonholed? The fortune of his merchant father made possible his entry into the ranks of the gentry, where he seems to have been truly welcome. He was known at Court. Yet it was his legal career, culminating in his appointment as a master in chancery, which was dominant. For statistical purposes he has here been made a lawyer. Similar problems of classification are encountered in the cases of other justices.

Sir John Leveson of Malling was a close friend of Lambarde. Both his grandfathers were Lord Mayors of London: Nicholas Leveson, an immigrant from Staffordshire, and Sir John Gresham, of a Norfolk family. Born in 1558, he was enrolled first in Queen's College, Oxford, and then in Gray's Inn. He married in turn a daughter of Sir Roger Manwood—notable citizen of Sandwich, baron of the Exchequer, and J.P. in Kent—and a daughter of Sir Walter Mildmay—Chancellor of the Exchequer. He was many times elected to parliament, originally from Bossiney as a colleague of Francis Drake, and finally as knight of the shire for Kent. A near neighbour, after 1585 he was frequently associated with Lambarde in the duties of the commission of the peace and later as co-executor under the will of Lord Cobham. He was knighted in 1589, became a deputy Lieutenant, and was included in 1597 in a commission appointed to exercise the office of Lord Lieutenant left vacant by Cobham's death.

Other records of the Privy Council demonstrate Leveson's diligence in the multifarious duties of local government. He was often concerned with the militia, and the proper care of Upnor Castle was his charge. In 1601 he constituted with three fellow justices—Sir Edward Wotton, Sir Thomas Walsingham, and Moyle Finch—the escort from Dover to London provided for a special envoy of the King of France (Baron Biron). Between 1600 and 1604, years for which the rolls survive, he was present at almost all the general sessions of the peace for west Kent. He happened to be staying at Lord Cobham's house in Black Friars at the moment of the Essex rebellion and participated in its suppression. As holder of the manor of Chadwell, Essex, he had formal charge of napery at the coronation of James I. These were tasks and privileges beyond the experience of most J.P.s.

Leveson was very wealthy. His will, probated in 1615, not only bequeathed rents worth £200 per year to his widow, generous legacies to younger sons, and £3,000 each to two granddaughters, but declared that £18,000 had been expended upon the litigation which he inherited from a distant cousin, Sir Richard Leveson, Vice-Admiral of England, whose possibly piratical exploits at sea gained him fame in his own day and much later the *vita* in the *Dictionary of National Biography* which Sir John did not win. If a significant file of his personal papers happens to survive, this ancestor of the Dukes of Sutherland would make the subject of an illuminating biography. To a life which must have been busy with private concerns, Sir John Leveson was able to add most of the diverse tasks—a term as sheriff is lacking—which were shouldered by his social class.[1] Should he be classified as a merchant, as a courtier, or as a member of the gentry?

Another pertinent figure was Sir John Boys. He was the fifth son of a family of gentry which had branches in several parts of Kent and included at least half a dozen J.P.s during the eight decades after the accession of Elizabeth. He won in legal and administrative capacities both wealth and prominence. He entered the Middle Temple in 1560, was called to the bar in 1570, served as reader a decade later, and was elected treasurer in 1589. There are further trivial details in the *Middle Temple Records*, but this is the outline of an unusually successful career. Knighted in 1603, he resided at St. Gregories on the outskirts of Canterbury. He was the owner of the manor of Betteshanger, not far from Nonington, and of a number of other properties, among them the Tudor house in Canterbury now called 'The Old Dutch House', which is thought to have been Dickens's model for the residence of Mr. Wickfield in *David Copperfield*. Boys served as Recorder of Canterbury, judge of the chancery court of the Cinque Ports, steward to successive Archbishops, and on different occasions M.P. for Sandwich, Midhurst, and Canterbury. In 1599 he established near his

---

[1] *H.M.C.*, *Salisbury MSS.* xi. 31, 32, 59–61; ibid. xvii. 226 *et passim*; *Arch. Cant.* v (1863), 253–6; ibid., xi (1877), 206–15; *Visitations of Kent . . . 1574 and 1592*, p. 5; Joseph Foster *Alumni Oxonienses* (4 vols., Oxford, 1891–2); Joseph Foster (ed.), *The Register of Admissions to Gray's Inn, 1521–1889* (L., 1889); Hasted, *Kent*, iii. 437; *Collections for a History of Staffordshire* (William Salt Archaeological Society, 1912), p. 34A; *V.C.H. Staffordshire*, v (1959), 80; *DNB*: 'Richard Leveson'; *A.P.C.*, *1596–7*, pp. 346, 377, 422; ibid., *1597*, pp. 109, 298; ibid., *1597–8*, pp. 29, 30, 307, 559; ibid., *1601–4*, pp. 190, 213, 257, 289, 294, 304, 316, 359, 384; *Cal. S.P. Dom.*, *Eliz.*, *1591–4*, p. 187; ibid., Jas. I, *1603–10*, pp. 24, 64, 81, 103, 253, 348, 394, 414; ibid., *1611–18*, p. 215; *Genealogist*, i (L., 1877), 386; PCC 1615, 97 Rudd; *A.P.C.*, *1599–1600*, pp. 94, 295.

home a hospital for the support of a dozen pious poor men
and women and for other charitable purposes. By his will
made in 1612 it was further endowed; as W. K. Jordan
suggests: 'No man could have left a finer monument.'[1] Was
he a member of the gentry, a lawyer, or a courtier?

Other counties provide equally apposite cases. William
Sheldon of Beoley, Worcestershire, was descended from a
family which migrated from Staffordshire in the fifteenth
century. From an uncle who supported Richard III against
Henry Tudor he inherited an estate forfeited and later
restored. Since the Inner Temple was one of the residences
specified in a pardon granted early in the reign of Mary, he
must have been a member of that society, but its records
are too scanty to provide any details with regard to his
experience there. As early as 1537 he was put in the commission of the peace, and in 1544–5 he was the grantee with
his brother of monastic lands to the extent of nearly £4,000.
In Edward's reign he received a life patent as Receiver of
the Court of Augmentations for a district which included
eight counties in the western Midlands and the Welsh
marches. As a member of two *ad hoc* commissions he participated in the collection of a tax granted by Parliament and
in a survey of the chantries in his county. If these several
activities are an explanation of the pardon, his stature in the
community seems also to be indicated by the fact that he was
a potential Knight of the Bath on the occasion of Mary's
marriage, securing an exemption 'in consideration of his
small abilitie and lyving'. In 1554 and again in 1555 he was
returned to Parliament, together with Sir John Bourne (the
principal Secretary), as knight for his shire. Three times he
served as sheriff. A J.P. through the reigns of Edward and
Mary, he was *Custos Rotulorum* from the accession of Elizabeth until his death in 1570.

Like other men of his time, Sheldon did not make his
religious position clear. In 1564 the Bishop of Worcester
included him among a considerable group who were

[1] Hasted, *Kent*, viii. 526; ibid. x. 44, 45; ibid. xi. 195, 390; *Middle Temple Records*,
i, *passim*; Behrens, *Under Thirty-Seven Kings*, pp. 83–5; Robert Hovenden (ed.),
*The Visitation of Kent, taken in the Years 1619–1621* (Harl. Soc. Publ. xlii, L., 1898),
*passim*; Jordan, *Social Institutions*, p. 45.

'indifferent or of no religion'. That he was a man of many parts must be indicated by the fact that he established on one of his estates the first tapestry-weaving enterprise in England; this, more than his wealth or his role in the life of the county, is the basis of what fame is now his, but in his own time he was known because his 'wysdom, estate and authority . . . equalled most of the gentlemen of England'.[1] Was he a courtier?

An answer to this question is best postponed. Meanwhile a comparison between Sheldon and Leveson is instructive. Each was rich, although the wealth of one came from City enterprise and the fortune of the other derived significantly from the suppressed monasteries. Each belonged to one of the inns of court; each married a daughter of a Baron of the Exchequer. One made a career on the outskirts of the metropolis, one in deeply rural England. Sheldon represents the middle years of the Tudor period; Leveson symbolizes the transition from Elizabeth to James. Both were men of great consequence in their society.

As his name suggests, Walter Jones had Welsh ancestors; he was distantly related to the Cecils. He was born in Witney, where his grandfather was a prosperous woollen merchant. He married Elinor Dorothy Pope, whose father was jeweller to the Queen and whose uncle was the founder of Trinity College, Oxford. Later he purchased from Robert Catesby— soon to be a principal figure in the Gunpowder Plot—the manor of Chastleton with its impressive Tudor mansion. In Oxfordshire, Chastleton is close to what was then an outlying part of Worcestershire. For his new home, tapestries incorporating his initials were woven at the Sheldon establishment. Had Ralph Sheldon, who succeeded his father in 1570 and lived until 1613, not been put out of the

[1] *V.C.H.*, *Worcestershire* (4 vols., L., 1901–24), iv. 14, 15; *Cal. Pat. Rolls, Edw. VI*, ii. 137; ibid. iii. 194, 199; ibid. v. 59, 317, 359; *Cal. Pat. Rolls, Mary, 1553–4*, p. 457; ibid., *1554–5*, pp. 76, 262; ibid., *1555–7*, p. 237; *A.P.C., 1554–6*, p. 50; ibid., *1580–1*, pp. 166, 214, 301–2; W. P. W. Phillimore (ed.), *The Visitation of the County of Worcester made in the Year 1569* (Harl. Soc. Publ. xxvii, L., 1888), p. 128; W. G. Thomson, *A History of Tapestry* (L., 1930), pp. 264–9; *L. & P.* xixA, g801 (50); ibid. xixB, g340 (9); ibid. xxB, g266 (7), 330; PCC 1571, 8 Holney; [T. R. Nash], *Collections for the History of Worcestershire* (2 vols., L., 1781–99), i. 66; E. A. B. Barnard, 'The Sheldon Tapestry Weavers', *Archaeologia*, lxxviii (1938), 255–314; Richardson, *Court of Augmentations*, p. 281.

commission of the peace because of his recusancy, the two men would have been colleagues on the bench.

Jones was called to the bar in Lincoln's Inn in 1584 and it may be inferred that he engaged in the practice of law in Worcester, for he owned a house there and was elected its burgess in four successive parliaments between 1584 and 1593. In 1602 the Garter King of Arms approved 'the pedigree and atchievement [sic] of the worshipful Walter Jones of Chastleton and of the City of Worcester'. In 1623 he received from the Crown the grant of an alms-room in Worcester Cathedral. He was appointed a J.P. not later than 1601 and remained a member of the commission until his death in 1632.

Since there are no letters addressed to him in the Privy Council register, Jones cannot have been a leading justice. There survive in the county archives, however, many recognizances and orders certified by him; there is no reason to suppose that he did not perform routine duties conscientiously. He is an excellent example of a man who was able to use wealth won in commerce—it is significant that in 1609 it was on his goods, not his lands, that he was assessed for the subsidy—coupled with training in the law, to rise to the magistracy and to establish a family who remained prominent in their county well into the twentieth century.[1] In which category does Jones fit?

A fifth justice who provides an interesting subject for study, James Clarke of Norton Fitzwarren, Somerset, presents no problem of classification—he was a lawyer— but he illustrates the importance of adequate data. From usual sources—specifically the *Middle Temple Records* and local history publications—it is apparent that he rose from a relatively humble background to achieve a successful career in the law. He was admitted to the Middle Temple, called to the bar, and later fined because he declined to serve as reader. Like most other members of the inn, his associations with men of his county were close, and he served as executor

[1] Margaret Dickins, *A History of Chastleton, Oxfordshire* (Banbury, 1938), pp. 22–6; *Lincoln's Inn Black Books*, i. 436; *Cal. S.P. Dom., Jas. I, 1619–23*, p. 483; Birmingham and Midland Institute, *Transactions*, xv (1888–9), 78 ff.; PCC 1632, 116 Audley.

of the wills of several prominent Somerset gentlemen. He was an overseer under that of Sir John Popham, for whom he also acted as agent in the purchase of Littlecote, Wiltshire, which became the Chief Justice's principal residence. Yet Clarke's son did not follow him on the bench, and the family was never prominent among the Somerset gentry. He seems to have been typical of a good many men who rose to the status of J.P. but made no greater mark in their society.

Had Clarke not happened to be involved in 1610 in a complicated series of suits arising out of the operations of rival grist-mills, which pitted him against Popham's grandson—Richard Warre—and several other J.P.s, no more would be known of his career. Because one episode produced great disorder during a formal legal enquiry, Clarke and Warre bandying such epithets as 'knave' and 'coxcombe', Clarke included an autobiographical sketch in a Star Chamber document. There it is disclosed that as a young man he became clerk to a rising lawyer from his county. While John Popham was reader, Clarke was admitted to the Middle Temple. In his new status he was still his sponsor's close associate, sharing chambers with a number of young men from the county who were in some sort the elder man's protégés, and undertaking such delicate tasks as the supervision of the conduct of those charges, among them Richard Warre. When Popham became a J.P., Clarke remained his collaborator and, after the busy lawyer became a judge and *Custos Rotulorum*, he secured for Clarke admission to the commission of the peace and made him deputy *Custos*. Manifestly Clarke was a much more important member of the bench than the usual records suggest.[1]

Another J.P. with regard to whom lawsuits are illuminating is Sir Thomas Posthumous Hoby. Among the subjects of these case studies he probably has been most widely noticed in historical writing—he figures in S. R. Gardiner's *History of England*. Both the picturesque name which announces his unusual relation with his father—the translator

[1] P.R.O., St. Ch. 8/163/26, 8/103/2; C. H. Hopwood (ed.), *Middle Temple Records* (4 vols., L., 1904–5), i. *passim*; Frederick Brown, *Abstracts of Somersetshire Wills* (ed. by F. A. Crisp) (6 vols., n. pl. 1887), vi. 73 *et passim*; *Somersetshire Archaeological and Natural History Society, Proceedings*, xcvii (1951), 157; *Wiltshire Archaeological Magazine*, iv. 220.

of Castiglione's *Courtier* who died while ambassador to France—and the fact that his mother, one of the talented daughters of Sir Anthony Cooke, was a sister-in-law of Sir William Cecil and of Sir Nicholas Bacon offer some explanation, though there is no *vita* in the *Dictionary of National Biography*. If his mother's importunities with Lord Burghley were no more successful than the more celebrated efforts of Francis Bacon, Hoby's advantages qualified him for marriage with Margaret Dakins, widow in succession of younger brothers of the Earl of Essex and Sir Philip Sidney, who was heiress of Hackness and other considerable properties in Yorkshire. Lady Margaret Hoby kept the earliest surviving diary written by a woman in English. It gives a vivid picture of the life of a Puritan household both while she was in residence in Hackness and on visits to London. The couple was childless, and after Sir Thomas's decease Hackness passed to his Sydenham cousins, who contributed many members to the Somerset bench.

'Posthumous' Hoby was educated at Trinity College, Oxford, and at Gray's Inn. He was knighted in 1593, made a member of the Council of the North through the support of Sir Robert Cecil in 1603, and was for many years a member of the commission of the peace for both the East and the North Riding of Yorkshire. He was elected to the House of Commons in almost every parliament between 1588 and 1629 for Appleby, Scarborough, or Ripon. For the Short Parliament he stood unsuccessfully for Scarborough against Sir Hugh Cholmeley of Whitby. He had long service as *Custos Rotulorum* of the North Riding, though at one time his conduct elicited a letter from the Privy Council requiring that he show more respect for the President of the Council of the North. Subsequently he was removed from the commission of the peace and from the Council, but was shortly restored to both. As Cholmeley wrote: 'having married a widow . . ., having a full purse, no children, and as it is thought not able [to] get one, [he] delighted to spend money and time in suits'.[1] Should Hoby be classified as a courtier?

---

[1] *DNB*: 'Thomas Hoby'; *Members of Parliament*, i. 455; *A.P.C.*, 1600–1, p. 488; Evelyn Fox, 'The Diary of an Elizabethan Gentle-woman', *Transactions of the Royal*

Hoby's best known litigation was the consequence of a hunting party in the late summer of 1600 headed by two very prominent J.P.s: Sir William Eure—heir of a Yorkshire peer who became Vice-President of the Council of the North in that year—and Richard Cholmeley—descendant of earlier J.P.s, formerly enrolled in Cambridge, knighted in 1603, father of Sir Hugh.[1] They reached the neighbourhood of Hackness at nightfall and invited themselves to be the guests of Hoby. Cards, drinks, obscene conversation, and boisterous laughter irked the reluctant host. A quarrel punctuated by references to a 'scurvy urchin' and a 'spindle-shanked ape' eventuated in a suit in Star Chamber and an informal court of reconciliation created by the Council of the North.[2]

Another suit which Hoby initiated happens to provide a vivid account of one quarter sessions. Since those meetings were major occasions in the lives of most justices, this episode merits attention; few such descriptions survive. It both illustrates the operation of the commission of the peace and contributes further data with regard to the classification of J.P.s.[3]

There were twenty-one justices present at Epiphany in 1616, twice the usual number in the East Riding at this period and more than were often assembled anywhere. In contrast to their usual practice Hoby's antagonists—Sir William Constable, Sir William Hilliarde, John Hotham, and John Legard—stayed until the end of the proceedings, constituting with their supporters a majority and thus appearing to pack the bench with 'popish sympathizers'. In his bill of complaint Hoby charged that they obstructed business by forcing votes on 'idle' matters. He further asserted that, with the support of the other three defendants and their 'associates', Constable, as *Custos Rotulorum*, adjourned the sitting

*Historical Society*, 3rd series, ii (L., 1908), 153–74; Dorothy M. Meads (ed.), *Diary of Lady Margaret Hoby, 1599–1605* (L., 1930); P.R.O., St. Ch. 5/H-22/21; St. Ch. 8/151/8; *Al. oxon.*; Neale, *House of Commons*, pp. 90–1 *et passim*; Samuel R. Gardiner, *History of England* (new edition, 10 vols., L., 1899), vi. 274.

[1] Hugh Cholmley, *The Memoirs of Sir Hugh Cholmley* (L., 1797), p. 20 *et passim*; *DNB*: 'Hugh Cholmeley'.

[2] Sir James Digby, *The Legards of Anlaby and Ganton* (L., 1926), pp. 30–3.

[3] St. Ch. 8/175/4.

for dinner and instructed the clerk of the peace to remove the records. Hoby declared this instruction to be clearly illegal, since the law provided that the *Custos* should ensure the presence of the records whenever two justices wished to hold a session. The contention was supported by Sir John [*sic*] Stanhope, Sir Francis Boynton, Sir William Ellis, who had delivered the charge to the jury at the opening of the proceedings, and by others. Another issue turned on the incidence of the obligation to repair a highway. Against Hoby's suggestion that the matter be left unsettled until the opinion of the justices of assize could be taken with regard to the law, his adversaries voted that the jury be instructed that responsibility rested on the hamlet in which the road lay, not on the whole parish. Finally, Hotham was accused of having entered the sessions late—while the charge was being given—of having taken Ellis's usual place, and of having seated himself upon the records, back to the public. Hoby urged that the four men be punished lest their conduct be a bad example to others.

In their answers to the interrogatories ordered by the court, Hotham, Legard, and their faction gave very different interpretations of the affair. Legard asserted that, as he had attended every sessions but one since he was sworn, his presence could not constitute packing; the majority vote about adjournment seemed reasonable. Hotham declared that he had had no intent to be rude to Ellis, that it was customary to adjourn for dinner, that he had no recusant friends, and that Hoby had preferred his bill out of malice. Hilliarde insisted that he had given the clergy and wardens in his division instructions to prosecute recusants. Constable affirmed that the removal of the records during the adjournment was proper, as it was to prevent Hoby and his adherents from holding a private sessions, and that the King's service was not injured. The depositions of the clerk and of Stanhope were in substantial support of Hoby. If he may have been an uncomfortable neighbour and colleague, he had his admirers.

Seven of Hoby's colleagues in the East Riding commission were named in this suit; like Hoby, Stanhope, Boynton, and Ellis were members of the North Riding commission also.

The group seems to have been a characteristic cross-section of a Yorkshire bench of that day. All except Stanhope and Sir William Ellis were of Yorkshire extraction. Stanhope, son of a Tudor adventurer, an adherent of Lord Protector Somerset, was a courtier who became a J.P. prior to 1596, in which year he was *Custos Rotulorum* of the North Riding, and a member of the Council of the North. Under James I he continued to be prominent, serving as a commissioner for the union with Scotland in 1603. When he was created Baron Stanhope in 1605, his promotion changed his place in the roster of the Yorkshire commissions, but it seems not to have been reflected in the style by which he was described by his colleagues on the bench. Ellis was, quite simply, a lawyer, a professional member of the Council of the North. Sir Francis Boynton—a member of a family long established in the county—was sheriff of Yorkshire in 1586 and joined the Council of the North in 1603. These men were Hoby's supporters. On the other side, John Legard belonged to a family well known in Yorkshire, though his father had migrated to London and prospered in the Haberdashers' Company. The son might be regarded as a member either of the gentry or of the mercantile group. Sir William Constable also came from a notable county family. An adherent of Essex in 1601, he lived long enough to be numbered among the regicides in 1649. John Hotham later gained much prominence as governor of Hull in the civil wars. Sir William Hilliarde was a Yorkshire squire who had many J.P. relatives in the three ridings. Thus there were included among the principal litigants in the Star Chamber suit—a group which was self-generated—men who may be assigned to five categories: dignitary, courtier, lawyer, merchant, gentry.[1] They formed a spectrum much like the other men here considered. In Yorkshire, as elsewhere, the county bench was diverse.

The number of case studies which might enhance this later *Eirenarcha* must be very large. Apposite data do in fact appear all through succeeding chapters and in the appendices;

---

[1] Cf. *infra*, p. 230, nos. 11, 23, p. 234, no. 36, p. 236, no. 19; Digby, *Legards of Anlaby and Ganton, passim*; *DNB*: 'William Constable'; Joseph Foster, *Pedigrees of the County Families of Yorkshire*, vol. ii: *North Riding* (L., 1874).

merely the rosters indicate a good deal. Such facts are available also in many works not explicitly concerned with J.P.s. For example, the more prominent Northamptonshire families have been accorded a special biographical volume in the *Victoria County History*. Likewise Miss M. E. Finch's book on *The Wealth of Five Northamptonshire Families* provides for a score of justices much more evidence than has here just been adduced with regard to men from other counties; many of those Northamptonshire J.P.s, however, satisfy the basic condition for present selection: no *vita* in *DNB* or in Mrs. Keeler's *Long Parliament*. The county's commission in 1626 included, moreover, numerous men who normally would not have been justices; yet an exhaustive search in Star Chamber and other records might well show that a few, like James Clarke of Somerset, enjoyed a contemporary esteem which was greater than now seems apparent. Varied Norfolk examples could be cited also. In the Bacon papers in the Folger Library are numerous documents concerned with, as one instance, Sir Nicholas Bacon's son-in-law, Sir Henry Woodhouse. He and other Norfolk justices appear in Alan Simpson's *The Wealth of the Gentry*. Thus all six counties could readily provide pertinent individuals. Where to stop?

That point has already been reached. The six relatively detailed case studies, supplemented by the group of men who were Hoby's colleagues, Sir Richard Cholmeley in particular, reflect the general nature of the commission, imply the levels of data commonly available, and provide the basis for a definition of the categories of J.P.s.

Half the men were knights, half mere esquires. The periods of office span the full interval between the accession of Elizabeth and the outbreak of the civil wars. Sheldon was a J.P. as early as 1537, while Hoby was still in the commission a century later. Richard Cholmeley was first appointed when hardly yet of age; Jones was close on eighty when he died. With a short interruption—removal and restoration were not uncharacteristic—Hoby served for nearly forty years. All but Clarke enjoyed such tenure that their names appear in more than one roster.

In ten cases the assessments for the subsidy are known

for 1609, a point near the middle of the whole period. The spread from £30 for Leveson and Boynton and £25 for Hoby to £10 for Jones and £6. 13s. 4d. for Sir William Hilliarde is considerable; all the other figures were £20. Such assessments are a very imperfect indication of wealth, but they do indicate both the affluence of Leveson and Boynton and the wide range among the men who were justices. At £100 Sir Nicholas Bacon—an extremely wealthy man—led all English J.P.s, while several inconspicuous men in impoverished counties were rated as low as £3.[1]

Available data suffice for little more than a skeletal outline of the lives of most J.P.s, and the traces of less routine details are largely capricious, frequently trivial, primarily related to the concerns of government. Yet, in spite of slender evidence, it can hardly be doubted that Leveson and Boys, Sheldon and Hoby exhibited qualities which would appear distinguished in almost any company. Jones and Clarke, likewise distinctive, were less impressive men. The six were a diverse group; so was each separate commission.

Since as deputy *Custos Rotulorum* he was a likely chairman of quarter sessions, even James Clarke played an important role in his county. Surely he was involved in numerous actions at law, and the apposite court records would unquestionably disclose additional, largely impersonal, facts of his career. Yet the *vita* which has just been sketched was possible only because he felt impelled to summarize his life in a Star Chamber document. In the most detailed history of Somerset he is unmentioned. Clarke represents those justices—surely a not inconsiderable number—who were in their time much more important men than the surviving evidence implies. Likewise the account of Walter Jones is essentially complete, though again the records of quarter sessions and of other courts would surely show his participation in various suits. The author of the *History of Chastleton*, who appears to have had access to family papers, could relate little more. For practical purposes all that can be known about either man can be set forth in a few paragraphs.

Evidence with regard to others is more extensive. *Custos Rotulorum*, Sheldon was the leading J.P. in his county,

---

[1] This matter is further discussed in Appendix G.

though he was never knighted. If he did not, who in his time would deserve attention in local history? Habington, Nash, and the *Victoria County History of Worcestershire* all give him appropriate consideration. No doubt the papers of the Court of Augmentations contain records of his many acts while he was Receiver for eight counties, but otherwise there survive—in addition to the same evidences as those of Clarke and Jones—only more numerous official instructions and papers relating to the management of land. In spite of the tapestry works at Beoley, William Sheldon remains a nebulous figure.

Hoby was more fortunate, as was Cholmeley; they figure in the autobiographical writing of relatives. Nearly a century later than Sheldon, and more prominent than Clarke and Jones, they also contributed more copiously to the classes of records which are preserved in official archives printed in part in calendars. An account of their public activities in fuller detail could easily be compiled. They are tangible personalities today.

Because Kent was close to London, among other reasons, the data with regard to Leveson and Boys are still more abundant. Moreover, each achieved a career which was little below the threshold of the *Dictionary of National Biography*. Boys was an outstanding citizen of Canterbury, well known in legal and political life in the metropolis. Leveson was the trusted colleague of eminent men, a pillar of local government in a major county. Legal and other public records, fortuitous documents in the surviving private papers of contemporaries, and numerous notices in Hasted's voluminous *History of the County of Kent* and in particularly full local history publications—*Archaeologia Cantiana*—all provide proof that Leveson and Boys were prominent among members of the Kent commission of the peace.

Such are the available and the potential evidences of the lives of selected justices. While wills and other personal data usually survive, in the absence of an extensive file of the private papers of its subject, not even a brief biography is possible. Mere sketches must suffice for them, for nearly thirteen hundred other men who were J.P.s in six counties at five moments, and for their counterparts elsewhere.

Yet certain conclusions are evident. Because they were in the commission of the peace, all these men were necessarily concerned with the law. They were often in court, usually as magistrates, occasionally as principal litigants. The episodes in which Clarke, Cholmeley, Hoby, and several of their colleagues participated were not unusual. The files of the Star Chamber are replete with cases of even more riotous affairs. The oath of office cannot have been considered in itself a binding obligation to keep the peace.

There were other avenues to legal knowledge. Most of the men—Cholmeley is an exception—were enrolled for a time in one of the inns of court and received there a measure of legal instruction. Jones was called to the bar, while Boys and Clarke were practising barristers. There can have been few J.P.s who were illiterate in the law. Cholmeley, moreover, was a member of a Cambridge college; Leveson and Hoby were up at Oxford. Five of the select group—Clarke is the odd man—were returned to the House of Commons at least once, while Leveson, Boys, Jones, and Hoby were perennially re-elected. This parliamentary experience—in 1636 approximately half the justices of the six counties were quondam members of the Commons—must have been fully as important as its better-known corollary of half the M.P.s being also J.P.s. During the growing crisis of the reign of Charles I the men who administered rural England had commonly studied in the inns of court and deliberated in Parliament. They were legislators as well as administrators and judges.

The problem of classification remains. In which category should each man properly be put? In some cases there is no doubt. Only the class of gentry fits Cholmeley, and Clarke was certainly a lawyer. Though Boys owned extensive real property and belonged to a family of gentry, he was a lawyer, not primarily a squire. Sheldon moved easily in the circle of established gentry, but it was his office in the Court of Augmentations that was the key to his fortune. On balance he must be regarded as a courtier. Jones likewise might qualify as a member of the gentry or—since he was a barrister—as a lawyer, but his estate derived from the profits of commerce; such at least is what the scanty evidence

suggests. Hoby and Leveson both had close connections
with the Court, and Leveson's wealth was inherited from
outstanding London merchants. Yet it is hard to regard
Hoby as other than a principal member of the Yorkshire
gentry, if Leveson's merchant status is less manifest. Classification is inevitably arbitrary at times.

The category of dignitaries is unambiguous: those men
whose place in the roster was not lower than the assize judges
—their names significantly do not appear in the lists of
assessments of justices in 1609. The courtiers are the men
who held appointments associated with the royal Court and
the central administration; lesser figures than the dignitaries,
they also had tangible ties with national affairs. The lawyers
are those who were called to the bar and seem to have made
a career in the law, although like Lambarde some were
certainly also active squires and may have been the descendants of merchants or of members of the gentry. Commerce
includes both the men who had themselves engaged in such
enterprises and their sons, who often did not follow a
mercantile life. If the sons were often primarily squires,
men not readily distinguishable among the gentry, they are
included in the commerce category because, unlike the
lawyers, there were few cases in which the man whose
mercantile fortune provided the basis for an appointment
to the commission of the peace actually became a J.P.
himself. Were the sons not put in this category, its numbers
would be too small to be significant. The clergy—a class
found chiefly after 1603—is relatively unambiguous.
Ecclesiastical administrators and experts in civil and canon
law belong here as well as ordained priests. The gentry,
finally, is an omnium gatherum. The J.P.s were presumed
by law to be landowners, and their duties were tantamount
in fact to the administration of rural England. This is the
class in which belong all those men not otherwise assigned.

# IV

## THE COMPLEXION OF THE
## COMMISSIONS OF THE PEACE

THE commission of the peace constituted an élite. Membership was not open to all who might aspire; an irregular but complicated procedure lay behind the selection. While the pertinent direct evidence is scanty and capricious, the nature of the process may be determined by an analysis of the results and some consideration of certain specific inclusions and exclusions. If difficult, generalization is not impossible.

In form, men became justices of the peace by appointment of the sovereign under the Great Seal. In fact, the Lord Chancellor or the Lord Keeper had responsibility for the commissions, which were drawn by his secretarial staff in accordance with his instructions. 'These [Lambarde wrote] be now at thys day appointed by the discretion of the Lord Chauncellor . . .'[1] As Lambarde surely knew, the custodian of the Seal could be acquainted with only a small fraction of the several thousand men whom he seemed to select during the decade, more or less, of his tenure of office. Often he followed the advice or suggestions of others—members of the Royal Court, the Lords Lieutenant, established J.P.s, justices of assize, personal friends, men who enjoyed influence, even the sovereign.

The law was explicit. By unrepealed statutes of 12 Richard II and 18 Henry VI it was specified that the commission of each shire should consist of six men who possessed lands worth twenty pounds a year. Yet, as Lambarde remarked, the numerical limitation was obsolete.

It was long since eluded by making of new commissions that had more justices thrust into them. And truelie it seemeth to me that (together with the like ambitious desire of bearing rule in some) the growing

---

[1] e.g. Huntington Library, Ellesmere MSS. 3165, 4124, 4613, 5434; Lambarde, *Eirenarcha* (L., 1581/2), p. 29.

number of the Statute laws committed to the charge of the Justices of the Peace hath bene the cause that they are now againe increased to the overflowing of each Shire at this day.

And he recognized that the property provision, too, no longer mattered.

Now although this portion of twenty pounds a yeare, be not at this day in account aunswerable to the charge and countenance fitte for a Justice of the Peace, yet who knoweth not, that at the making of this Lawe, it was far otherwise; And I do not doubt, but as the rate of all things is greatly risen since that time, so is there good care taken, that none be nowe placed in the Commission, whose livings be not increased in proportion.

In brief, fact did not accord with law.[1]

The Kent commission of the peace in 1584 has served as an introduction to the thirty rosters of J.P.s which form the core of the present study. The data, however, are so massive that the other rosters and their accompanying descriptions have been segregated in appendices where, though readily available, they do not impede analysis.

Included are characterizations of the several justices and surveys of the changing complexions of the commissions and of the differences between the counties. There are also statements about formal schooling, parliamentary experience, and other matters which parallel the data adduced with regard to Kent in 1584.

The following table summarizes statistics which the appendices make possible. The several columns show the total membership of the commissions, the division between dignitaries and the working group, the categories of the latter, the percentage which the dignitaries bore to the total, and the percentages which the various subgroups contributed to the working element. The process of compilation and the definitions upon which it is based have been explained in the last two chapters.[2]

In this summary analysis of the commissions of the peace of six counties at five periods, several trends are evident. There was a general growth in numbers, though most of it took place before 1608. Thereafter, except for a temporary

---

[1] Lambarde, *Eirenarcha*, pp. 35, 37–8.          [2] Cf. *supra*, p. 46.

| | Total | Dignitaries | % | Work. Com. | Court | % | Gentry | % | Law | % | Church | % | Commerce | % |
|---|---|---|---|---|---|---|---|---|---|---|---|---|---|---|
| **1562** | | | | | | | | | | | | | | |
| Kent | 56 | 12 | 21 | 44 | 12 | 27 | 23 | 52 | 7 | 16 | 0 | | 2 | 5 |
| Norfolk | 24 | 7 | 29 | 17 | 3 | 18 | 10 | 59 | 3 | 18 | 0 | | 1 | 6 |
| Northants. | 29 | 12 | 41 | 17 | 3 | 18 | 10 | 59 | 3 | 18 | 0 | | 1 | 6 |
| Somerset | 38 | 9 | 24 | 29 | 7 | 24 | 13 | 45 | 5 | 17 | 0 | | 4 | 14 |
| Worcs. | 28 | 9 | 32 | 19 | 4 | 21 | 12 | 63 | 2 | 11 | 0 | | 1 | 5 |
| N. Riding | 35 | 18 | 51 | 17 | 6 | 35 | 10 | 59 | 0 | | 1 | 6 | 0 | |
| | 210 | 67 | 32 | 143 | 35 | 24 | 78 | 54 | 20 | 14 | 1 | ·7 | 9 | 6 |
| **1584** | | | | | | | | | | | | | | |
| Kent | 76 | 15 | 20 | 61 | 11 | 18 | 36 | 59 | 8 | 13 | 0 | | 6 | 10 |
| Norfolk | 47 | 11 | 23 | 36 | 1 | 3 | 27 | 75 | 7 | 19 | 0 | | 1 | 3 |
| Northants. | 43 | 13 | 30 | 30 | 3 | 10 | 21 | 70 | 3 | 10 | 1 | 3 | 2 | 7 |
| Somerset | 49 | 10 | 20 | 39 | 3 | 8 | 26 | 67 | 7 | 18 | 0 | | 3 | 8 |
| Worcs. | 52 | 13 | 25 | 39 | 4 | 10 | 22 | 56 | 13 | 33 | 0 | | 0 | |
| N. Riding | 63 | 19 | 30 | 44 | 5 | 11 | 25 | 57 | 13 | 30 | 1 | 2 | 0 | |
| | 330 | 81 | 25 | 249 | 27 | 11 | 157 | 63 | 51 | 20 | 2 | 1 | 12 | 5 |
| **1608** | | | | | | | | | | | | | | |
| Kent | 110 | 13 | 12 | 97 | 16 | 16 | 52 | 54 | 12 | 12 | 5 | 5 | 12 | 12 |
| Norfolk | 59 | 7 | 12 | 52 | 3 | 6 | 39 | 75 | 10 | 19 | 0 | | 0 | |
| Northants. | 53 | 16 | 30 | 37 | 3 | 8 | 29 | 78 | 2 | 5 | 2 | 5 | 1 | 3 |
| Somerset | 57 | 12 | 21 | 45 | 1 | 2 | 32 | 71 | 8 | 18 | 1 | 2 | 3 | 7 |
| Worcs. | 45 | 11 | 24 | 34 | 1 | 3 | 25 | 74 | 7 | 21 | 0 | | 1 | 3 |
| N. Riding | 62 | 14 | 23 | 48 | 4 | 8 | 25 | 52 | 14 | 29 | 1 | 2 | 4 | 8 |
| | 386 | 73 | 19 | 313 | 28 | 9 | 202 | 65 | 53 | 17 | 9 | 3 | 21 | 7 |
| **1626** | | | | | | | | | | | | | | |
| Kent | 97 | 38 | 39 | 59 | 9 | 15 | 37 | 63 | 4 | 7 | 5 | 9 | 4 | 7 |
| Norfolk | 65 | 14 | 22 | 51 | 0 | | 34 | 67 | 12 | 24 | 3 | 6 | 2 | 4 |
| Northants.[1] | 78 | 24 | 31 | 54 | 6 | 11 | 36 | 67 | 7 | 13 | 5 | 9 | 0 | |
| Somerset | 56 | 16 | 29 | 40 | 2 | 5 | 25 | 63 | 7 | 18 | 4 | 10 | 2 | 5 |
| Worcs. | 41 | 12 | 29 | 29 | 0 | | 18 | 62 | 3 | 10 | 4 | 14 | 4 | 14 |
| N. Riding | 52 | 18 | 35 | 34 | 4 | 12 | 21 | 62 | 7 | 21 | 2 | 6 | 0 | |
| | 389 | 122 | 31 | 267 | 21 | 8 | 171 | 64 | 40 | 15 | 23 | 9 | 12 | 5 |
| **1636** | | | | | | | | | | | | | | |
| Kent | 85 | 22 | 26 | 63 | 3 | 5 | 38 | 60 | 16 | 25 | 4 | 6 | 2 | 3 |
| Norfolk | 62 | 10 | 16 | 52 | 0 | | 33 | 63 | 16 | 31 | 2 | 4 | 1 | 2 |
| Northants. | 57 | 18 | 32 | 39 | 4 | 10 | 25 | 64 | 7 | 18 | 2 | 5 | 1 | 3 |
| Somerset | 63 | 12 | 19 | 51 | 2 | 4 | 33 | 65 | 9 | 18 | 4 | 8 | 3 | 6 |
| Worcs. | 35 | 13 | 37 | 22 | 2 | 9 | 11 | 50 | 2 | 9 | 4 | 18 | 3 | 14 |
| N. Riding | 54 | 15 | 27 | 39 | 4 | 10 | 23 | 59 | 7 | 18 | 0 | | 5 | 13 |
| | 356 | 90 | 25 | 266 | 15 | 6 | 163 | 61 | 57 | 21 | 16 | 6 | 15 | 6 |

1 As is explained on pages 66, 176 ff., the Northamptonshire commission of 1626 was abnormal. The figures in the table are those of a commission diminished to correspond with the normal situation. The larger figures are:

The totals:

113   24 21%   89   6 7% 70 79%   7 8%   5 6%   1 1%

424   122 29%   302 21   7% 206 68%   40 13%   23 8%   10 3%.

great increase in Northamptonshire in 1626, there was a
tendency toward decrease which brought the size of the
working group nearly back to the figure of 1584. Comparison
with the commissions of the period before the accession of
Elizabeth shows that the over-all growth was moderate.
While the total for these six counties early in the reign of
Mary was exactly what it was in 1562 (210), this figure
was considerably smaller than that of May 1547 (282) or of
the later years of Henry VIII.[1] Some of the growth after
1558 must be considered to be a return to an earlier situation.

Yet these statistics also reflect the changing customs or
styles of English society. The proportion of the dignitaries
was highest in 1562 and in 1626, but the specific number
of the latter year was nearly double that of the former. The
Elizabethan percentage may be explained by the rather
small size of the total commissions, since the number of the
officers of state in Elizabeth's time did not diminish as much
as did the size of the whole body. The situation of 1626 was
clearly the consequence of the gift and sale of titles, honours,
and offices to which under Buckingham's influence James I
became so prone.[2] It is significant that in Kent, which was
close to the Court, this element nearly tripled between 1608
and 1626. The largest percentage of all was that of 1562 in
the North Riding, where quasi-feudal conditions, with a
sizeable aristocracy, still obtained. The Northamptonshire
figure of 1562 seems to have been at least partly fortuitous,
a reflection of an unusual concentration there of both titled
nobility and major officers of state, but the nobility were
self-perpetuating and the county's percentage of dignitaries
remained high. The large proportion in Worcestershire in
1636 may be explained by the small size of its total commission. The participation of the nobility in the commissions of
the peace will be further considered shortly.

The numbers of the lawyers are impressive. Perhaps the
large figure for Northamptonshire in 1562—which contrasts
with the relatively small ones of the subsequent periods—
reflected chance deviation, but the numbers in Worcestershire

---

[1] There are many commissions of the peace in *L. & P., passim*; *Cal. Pat. Rolls,
Ed. VI*, i. 85–92; *Cal. Pat. Rolls, Philip & Mary*, i. 17–26.
[2] Cf. Lawrence Stone, *The Crisis of the Aristocracy* (Oxford, 1965), Ch. III.

and the North Riding in 1584 must represent Elizabethan policy. The extra men were the professional members of the Councils of Wales and the North. Under the Stuarts these administrative agencies ceased to enjoy such imposing legal strength, and the change was reflected in the complexion of the commissions of the peace. Somerset and, even more, Norfolk developed strong legal traditions among the social group which fed their county benches. The number of their lawyers was consistently high. Under Charles the Kent commission included many barristers. In 1636 the combined percentage of lawyers for the six counties rose to the level which the policy of the Elizabethan government had produced in 1584. In the gathering crisis of 1640 not a few of these men were returned to the House of Commons.

Stuart policy is shown also by the increasing number of clergy who appeared in the working portion of all the commissions of the peace, particularly under Charles I. These men seem to have been commonly trained in the law at one of the universities and were not infrequently ecclesiastical administrators, although John Amy, who was a member of the commission for Worcestershire in 1608, was a student of the civil law rather than an ordained clerk. There must have been frequent occasions when the particular competence of these men was useful. Their presence among their lay associates cannot have been mere chance.

In 1621 the House of Commons in its general attack upon what appeared to be abuses in government, found time to complain about the excessive size of the county benches, the presence of so many lawyers, and, particularly for the palatine county of Durham, the number of clergy appointed.[1] Since a peak figure in the size of many county benches was reached in 1621, it appears that some regard was paid to these criticisms. Most commissions were reduced and, although it was temporary, there was a marked diminution in the numbers of the lawyers.

Other significant features are the diminishing element of the courtiers among the working group and the nearly constant percentage for the combined counties of the men

[1] Wallace Notestein, Frances Helen Relf, and Hartley Simpson (eds.), *Commons Debates, 1621* (7 vols., New Haven, 1935), iii. 113, 427, *et passim*; cf. *infra*, note 25.

who had a mercantile background. Stuart prodigality with titles of nobility which elevated the courtiers into dignitaries is part explanation of the former tendency. The increased number of merchants in 1608 may probably reflect the growing prosperity of the later Elizabethan era, while the high figure of 1636 derives from an increased but still small number of J.P.s with a mercantile background in Worcestershire and the North Riding.

The statistic which varied least was the percentage of the working group represented by the gentry. Even though the large size of this element provides a mathematical explanation of stability, the over-all increase from 78 in 1562 to 163 in 1636, or 202 in 1608, would have allowed a greater alteration in percentages than actually occurred. It was not a large change from the 54 per cent of the first year to the 61 per cent of 1636 or to the pinnacle of 64 per cent in 1626, when the legal element had been cut by nearly a half. Membership in the commission was a symbol of status among the gentry. Avoided perhaps occasionally by those whose position was evident, it was eagerly sought by men who were ambitious.

Efficient administration, however, required an adequate body of competent administrators, particularly when they were unpaid. It was often easier to secure a place in the commission if there were no veteran J.P. who lived near by. The office might even seek the man. As the size of the commissions grew, the ratio between the number of J.P.s and the area of the county necessarily diminished. Much the largest numbers of square miles per J.P. were in 1562: 124·7 for the working group in the North Riding and 120·8 in Norfolk. The highest figure for the total commission was 85·6 in Norfolk in the same year. The smallest figures in this year were 24·9 for the total commission in Worcestershire, and, for the working group, 34·7 for Kent and 36·7 for Worcestershire. The smallest figure of all was 8·1 for the total commission in the inflated state of the bench in Northamptonshire in 1626; for the working group it was 10·3. The low figure for what may be regarded as a normal working commission was 16·4 for Kent in 1608. Estimates of population are not sufficiently reliable to encourage mathematical use with regard to this period, yet Kent, with perhaps a hundred inhabitants per square mile, and Norfolk, with not quite ninety, were the most heavily peopled.[1] These statistics can give only a very imperfect indication of the responsibility of a J.P. Some justices were much more conscientious than others. The residences of even the active men were scattered in irregular fashion. Yet the averages show that Norfolk J.P.s in 1562, who were each entrusted with 120 square miles and 10,000 people, had a greater responsibility than that borne by many of their counterparts. Because of irregularities, geographical and human, any suggested norm must be purely hypothetical, but a characteristic Norfolk J.P., working in harness with colleagues, might have been concerned with as many as 50,000 people scattered over a roughly circular area of which the perimeter was twenty-five miles from his residence. He had a serious social obligation. Elsewhere and at other times the burden must have been lighter.

Included in the commissions of the peace were many members of certain clearly defined groups in society: bishops, secular lords, baronets.

In 1562 about three-fifths of the spiritual peers were justices. The Bishops of Chichester, Ely, Rochester, Coventry and Lichfield, Lincoln, Norwich, Chester, and Salisbury were not members of a commission issued under the Great Seal; the see of Gloucester was vacant; all the other prelates were members of at least one commission.[2]

Likewise the Earl of Derby and his heir (Lord Strange), Viscount Hereford, Lord Monteagle, Lord Vaux of Harrowden, Lord Latimer, Lord Cromwell, and Lord Hastings of Loughborough were included in no commission issued by the Lord Keeper. Lord Derby and Lord Strange may have been J.P.s in Lancashire, where Derby was Lord Lieutenant; its commission was the responsibility of the Chancellor of the Duchy and did not appear in the *libri pacis*. Lord Hastings, an ardent papist, was confined in the Tower. Lords Monteagle and Vaux were suspect, though Vaux was later included in the commission for Northamptonshire.[3]

[1] W. K. Jordan, *Philanthropy in England* (L., 1959), p. 27.
[2] Cf. *infra*, pp. 54–5.    [3] *DNB*: 'Edward Hastings'; S.P. 12/121, f. 23ᵛ.

Lord Hereford was still a young man. There is no easy explanation for the exclusion of Lords Latimer and Cromwell. Like the bishops nearly all the secular peers were justices in 1562.

In 1636 the Bishops of Bristol and St. David's were left out of all commissions, while among the secular peers the Earls of Sussex, Somerset, Carnarvon, and Middlesex, Viscount Conway, and Barons Audley, Vaux, Eure, Wharton, Gerard, Lovelace, Brudenell, and Savile were justices in no county. Somerset was never fully rehabilitated. Like their ancestors, Lords Monteagle and Vaux were Catholic recusants. In more or less overt fashion so were Lords Audley, Carnarvon, and Brudenell. Yet Vaux and Brudenell had been in the Northamptonshire commission in 1626, while the Catholic Earl of Exeter was both a J.P. and Lord Lieutenant in 1636. Lords Conway and Wharton, on the other hand, seem to have been of Puritan inclination. Lord Eure had sold most of his ancestral holdings and may probably have seemed unfit, while the Earl of Sussex was also financially embarrassed. Savile was certainly *persona non grata* to Wentworth, now President of the Council of the North. Thus there is a ready explanation in most cases where a peer was excluded. Probably a few lords quite simply did not wish to serve as J.P. If neither in 1562 nor in 1636 did the possession of a title of itself entail membership in a commission of the peace, a large majority of both ecclesiastical and lay lords were J.P.s.[1]

Much the same situation obtained at other times. Among the commissions in the years 1584, 1608, and 1626 (which have been discussed in detail), only those for Kent in 1584 and for Somerset in 1584 and 1626 were missing an expected episcopal member. In 1584 John Whitgift had only recently succeeded Grindal at Canterbury and had not yet joined the Bishop of Rochester on the Kent bench. The see of Bath and Wells was vacant in both years, but in 1626 the Bishop of Bristol was a J.P. in Somerset. In Worcestershire and in

---

[1] *DNB*: 'Philip Wharton', 'Robert Radcliffe', 'Robert Dormer', 'Thomas Savile', 'James Touchet', 'Robert Carr'; cf. *infra*, pp. 237–8; Godfrey Anstruther, *Vaux of Harrowden* (Newport, 1953), Ch. V; Joan Wake, *The Brudenells of Deene* (L., 1953), pp. 115–20.

the North Riding, as well as in Kent, there was often more than one mitred justice. In sum, the bishops were usually J.P.s; all the commissions included lay peers; and there were few cases in which a nobleman was not among the J.P.s of the county in which lay his principal properties.

Like the peers the baronets formed a sharply defined group whose members were likely candidates for the bench in the county in which they resided. The dignity had usually been secured by purchase and even as late as 1636 was commonly held by the original grantee. The baronets surely commanded estates which greatly exceeded the statutory floor of £20 and the much larger practical size which Lambarde had in mind. They were local magnates. Yet a few of them were not J.P.s.

Resident in Kent, for example, early in 1621 were ten baronets, and three more were created in the course of the year. The two senior baronetcies were held by men whose names do not appear in the *liber pacis* of that year, Sir Thomas Finch and Sir John Tufton. Finch was the third baronet, the heir of both his father and his elder brother; in 1634 he succeeded to the earldom of Winchelsea, which had been created for his mother in recognition of the services of her father—Sir Thomas Heneage. Finch became a J.P. only after he had inherited his peerage. In 1621 he was M.P. for Winchelsea, and in 1628 he was elected knight of the shire for Kent. It is not manifest why he was not a member of the commission of the peace in 1621 or in 1626. Sir John Tufton was the first baronet, the son of one Kentish J.P. and the father of two more. In 1621 he was elderly; perhaps that is why the family was represented on the bench by his two sons. The remaining baronets of 1621—Sir Samuel Peyton, Sir Henry Baker, Sir William Sedley, Sir William Twysden, Sir Edward Hales, Sir William Monins, Sir Adam Newton, Sir Thomas Roberts, Sir Thomas Palmer, Sir John Rivers, and Sir Isaac Sedley—were all in the commission. In 1626 and again in 1636 the situation in Kent was similar. Sir William Monins seems to have retired as J.P., although he did not die until 1643. Sir Thomas Peyton and Sir John Baker had succeeded their fathers but were still under age in 1626. Although Baker was sheriff in 1633–4, he seems not to have become a J.P. All other Kentish baronets were in the commission.[1]

In Northamptonshire Sir Erasmus Dryden and Sir Lewis Watson were among the J.P.s when the *liber pacis* of 1621 was compiled, while the name of Sir Baldwin Wake was interlined, presumably after he became a baronet in December of that year. Sir Lewis Tresham was a Catholic, the younger brother of the Gunpowder plotter, and he remained out of the commission. Sir Thomas Brudenell, likewise a Catholic, was not a J.P. in 1621, but he became one in 1626.[2] Other baronets in the swollen commission of the latter year were Sir Roland Egerton of Egerton in county Chester and of Farthinghoe in Northamptonshire, Sir John Hewett, and Sir Capell Bedell—both of Huntingdonshire— who had family connections in the neighbouring county and probably held property there. Save for the Treshams, the Brownes of Walcott were the only family of Northamptonshire baronets who before 1640 seem to have had no members in the commission of the peace.[3]

In the other four counties an incumbent of nearly all the baronetcies was a J.P. at some time in the period between 1621 and 1636. In Worcestershire Sir Thomas Littleton was included in 1626, although his membership of the bench lapsed while he travelled on the Continent during the thirties. Sir John Packington was a J.P. until his death in 1625. His heir was still a minor in 1636. In that year Sir Walter Devereux, Sir Edward Seabright, and Sir William Russell were all J.P.s. Likewise in Somerset the bench was graced at different moments by a Portman, a Powell, a Wake, and from Wiltshire a Ley and a Button, all baronets. In Norfolk the order was even more common, including the premier member, Sir Nicholas Bacon. Others who were J.P.s were Sir Philip Knyvett—in 1621 but not subsequently though he lived until 1655—Sir Lionel Tollemache, Sir John Hobart, Sir Thomas Woodhouse, Sir Lestrange Mordaunt, Sir Roger Townshend, Sir Richard Barney, Sir

---

[1] These data are based on a comparison of the Kent rosters for 1626 and 1636 with the whole body of names in Cokayne, *Baronetage*, i. Cf. also *Complete Peerage*: 'Wilchelsea', and *infra*, Appendix A.

[2] Cf. *infra*, p. 173.  [3] As above, note 1; cf. *infra*, Appendix B.

William Yelverton, and Sir John Corbett. Only Sir Edward Barkham of Southacre, who became a baronet in 1623 during the lifetime of his father (Lord Mayor of London in 1622), seems not to have been put in the commission of the county of his seat.[1] In Yorkshire the thirteen families of baronets were all in the commission in 1621, 1626, 1632, or 1636, but not all in the North Riding. In brief, sometimes either the abnegation of the man himself or the decision of the holder of the Great Seal kept a baronet off the bench, but such instances were not usual.

It is evident that with few exceptions the bishops, the temporal lords, and the baronets were included in one or more commissions of the peace. Membership was not quite a matter of course, but failure to appoint was even more clearly not a routine matter. Thus the social groups in which deliberate selection was commonly made were knights, clerical leaders who were not bishops, distinguished lawyers, and esquires. With the baronets they constituted the working commission. It is not possible to determine how many such men eligible for appointment, either technically as a matter of law or realistically as a matter of fact, were resident in any county at any moment, but certainly the number was larger than the total of those who actually were included in the commission. The Lord Keeper or Lord Chancellor must frequently have made conscious selections. In most cases there is no direct evidence to explain a choice, and it is dangerous to infer purpose from circumstantial evidence, but the situation need not remain unassayed.

There were no established procedures. As is manifest in the appendices which treat the several counties in detail, familiar names constantly occur. Once appointed to the bench, men commonly continued to serve until death. Very frequently their places on the bench, as well as their principal residences, were soon occupied by their heirs. In the families of the leading gentry, membership in the commissions was nearly as much a matter of heredity as it was with the nobility and the baronets.

Even in some cases of less prominent gentry, and certainly with regard to many leading lawyers, the Chancellor

[1] As p. 56, note 1, particularly 'Edmund Barkham'; cf. *infra*, Appendices A—F.

or Lord Keeper must have known the candidates personally. Some of the sources of such acquaintance are evident: residence in the same county; common membership in an inn of court, in a college at Oxford or Cambridge, in Parliament; close temporary domicile in Westminster or London; or family relationship by blood or marriage. Indeed, in a small number of cases, the putative J.P. was a close relative of the Keeper. For instance, Sir Nicholas Bacon appointed his eldest son, also named Nicholas, a justice in Suffolk and his second son, Nathaniel, a member of the bench in Norfolk. Likewise the name of John Egerton, destined to become first Earl of Bridgwater and Lord President of the Council of Wales, is among those of the justices for Cheshire in a *liber pacis* compiled in 1596 two months after his father (Sir Thomas Egerton) became Lord Keeper. And again two of Sir Thomas Coventry's sons were J.P.s in the counties of Worcester and Somerset during their father's custody of the Great Seal.[1] These are striking examples of the personal connections which existed between the custodians of the Great Seal and a not inconsiderable number of men who were put in the commission of the peace.

After 1580 a large and increasing proportion of those who became J.P.s had been for a time enrolled in one of the four inns of court. The holders of the Great Seal and the judges were always professional lawyers, and the inns were not large societies. It was a *milieu* in which apposite associations must have been a frequent occurrence. The records of the Middle Temple indicate the men with whom Sir Thomas Bromley must have been acquainted, but since his residence was not in any one of the six counties under present review, a more meaningful illustration of the range of such personal association is the circle of Somerset men with Chief Justice Popham at its centre which is considered in Chapter VI.[2]

Another way in which personal relationships affected the composition of the bench is shown in personal papers which happen to survive. In a day in which most appointments were secured by influence, gratuity, or purchase, the unpaid office of justice of the peace was not immune. The evidence of such pressures is considerable. Norfolk happens to furnish

[1] Cf. *infra*, pp. 198, 217.    [2] Cf. *infra*, pp. 92–3.

several convenient illustrations. In 1599 Sir Nicholas Bacon and Sir Bassingbourne Gawdy, both Norfolk J.P.s, recommended to Sir John Popham—as Lord Chief Justice he was close to the Lord Chancellor—that Henry Holdyche be put in the commission, 'there being none other within eight miles of his residence'. Within six months Holdyche was corresponding with Gawdy and others about J.P. business. Since both his father and grandfather had been in the commission, the appointment should not have presented great trouble, but the commendation seems to have been effective. A few years later Philip Gawdy wrote a number of letters to his brother Bassingbourne about other appointments to the bench. Evidently a good deal of manipulation which involved Lord Chief Justice Coke was in train.[1] Gawdy discovered that: 'There was a special restraint that afore the assize there should be no more put in all over England, for otherwise my Lord most willingly would have put him in, but he hath promised me after the assizes he shall be put in the commission'. And a little later: 'now my lord chancellor hath taken order that none shall come in but by means of the Justices of assize and they to receive commendation from two Justices of peace out of the county'.

That Lord Chancellor was Ellesmere, whose very extensive papers are now in the Huntington Library. In all these letters and memoranda there are few which deal with J.P.s—for the most part instructions to a clerk to renew the commission of some county or put a recent sheriff back in—and only one which is of more than routine nature. In May 1598 Roger Puleston of the county of Flint (kt. 1617, d. 1618) wrote to an unnamed friend clearly close to Lord Keeper Egerton (his style at that time):

I most earnestly crave a favour at your hands which is this. One Francis Wolrich of Dudnaston in the county of Salop, esq., hath married my wife's sister and my self by reason thereof and for many just respects, have cause to wish the advancement of his credit and reputation; and therefore do hereby intreat you for my sake to recommend him unto my lord to be put into the commission of the peace for that county. I do assure you that upon my credit (which I will not willingly blemish) he may for his living be placed in the very midst of

[1] I. H. Jeayes (ed.), *Letters of Philip Gawdy* (L., 1906), pp. 67, 69, 156–7.

all the justices of peace of that shire, very sound in Religion, and in [no] way to be touched with unhonest or evil practices in the whole course of his life, but a very honest gentleman, and well beloved in his country. Beside as I am informed there is not in the two hundreds next unto his dwelling any justice of peace but only my brother Bromley.[1]

Wolrich was probably put into the commission ere long; his name appears for Shropshire in the *liber pacis* of 1608. Perhaps Puleston's letter was timely, since by this year Ellesmere had become very scrupulous. In the Star Chamber he declared that:

he puts in few into the Commission but vpon Commendacyon from the lordes or Judges, whoe showlde Certifye vpon knowledge, & not informacyon; for in all partes the numbers are so increased that those that are the doers & beare the burden of the busynes can haue no place at the benche, nor hardelye gette into the Cowrte but as they are Called, for the number of new and younge knightes, that are Come in their braueryes & stande there lyke an Idoll to be gazed vpon, & doe nothinge, ys so greate & pressinge for place, Countenaunce & estimacyon . . .[2]

By themselves these episodes appear trivial; they lie in an area where the infinite extent of possible data makes generalization treacherous. Yet they illustrate the nature of the factors—recommendations by assize judges, and by personal friends, the aspirations of an individual, family prestige, perhaps county politics, and, possibly of greatest importance, the needs of the region—which operated in the appointment of justices.

If the commissions were to be the effective administrative agency which the national polity implied, their composition required systematic attention. Particularly in the earlier years of Elizabeth's reign such care was not wanting. There survive in the state papers two documents which reflect Cecil's concern with the complexion of their personnel. One is docketed in Latin in his holograph: 'Oct. 1569—Names of Justices and of others'. Together with the paper which

---

[1] Ellesmere MS. 50; cf. *supra*, p. 47, note 1.

[2] John Hawarde, *Les Reports del Cases in Camera Stellata*, ed. by W. P. Baildon (L., 1894), p. 368.

lies immediately ahead of it in the bound volume in the Record Office it shows the process by which commissions were then constructed, both new rosters of J.P.s and probably the special commissions of a more limited nature which constantly went to the gentry and particularly to the justices. The process started with a short list in the hand of a clerk. On this foundation names were added by Cecil's pen, few for some counties—Norfolk and Suffolk—many for others—particularly Kent and Northamptonshire. Then on another sheet of paper the clerk drew up a new basic list which included Cecil's additions. Finally Cecil entered still more names himself. He was ever a master of detail.[1]

Even more illuminating traces of official activity with regard to the commissions of the peace are found in two *libri pacis* now bound together as Lansdowne MS. 1218 in the British Museum. One has inscribed on its title-page in different hands '1562' and 'For the use of Lord Burghley'. Since internal evidence demonstrates that the correct date is November or December 1561, and, as Cecil was not then Baron Burghley, the latter note is manifestly a later addition. Yet its substantial accuracy is also evident, since it contains many annotations in what is clearly Cecil's holograph.

This *liber* is a base which was used in compiling the rosters of the new commissions which passed the Great Seal early in 1562 and were incorporated in the patent rolls. Attached to it is a memorandum headed: 'xvi° die ffebruarii Anno dom[inae] Reginae Elizabeth quarto. The names of the old shireffs and certayne others thought mete by the Justices of Assize to be put into the Commission of the peace and some omitted out'. At this time sheriffs were routinely removed from the bench upon the assumption of office and restored a year later. In this instance except for a few sheriffs not restored—in some cases they had died—all the changes indicated in the memorandum, both the inclusions and the exclusions, were incorporated in those patent-roll commissions which provided the initial rosters of Appendices A–F.[2] Clearly the assize justices played an important role in the process.

[1] S.P. 12/59/14, 15.
[2] Lansdowne MS. 1218, ff. 99–101; cf. *infra*, pp. 69–71.

So did Cecil. Scattered through the pages of both the *libri* in Lansdowne MS. 1218 are *marginalia* in his hand: words and figures. There are also several series of symbols— crosses, circles, triangles, squares—which indicate either approbation or disfavour. The circles and triangles are most informative and they are mutually exclusive. A careful survey of the justices whose names were thus distinguished leaves no serious doubt about the meaning of the marks. In the earlier book Cecil's glosses occur on many pages, but in the later one they are confined to the counties of Devon and Sussex, where they record the places of residence and the names of the father or of a brother of the wives of the several J.P.s. In the former the notes are partly indications of residence (Cumberland and Hampshire); partly names of men who were added to the commission; partly figures which must be assessments for the subsidy (Yorkshire). The incidence of the symbols—both the variety of sign and the frequency—varies considerably. The Welsh counties and a range in the north and west are untouched. Yorkshire, Northamptonshire, and Norfolk are liberally marked. The indications of disfavour are frequent in Yorkshire and wholly absent in Northamptonshire and Norfolk, with the gentry of which, because of their own residences, Cecil and Bacon respectively must have been particularly well acquainted. A *liber pacis* of 1573 also contains many circles—showing approbation—scattered through most counties. The significance of the symbols is further discussed in the next chapter in connection with the role of religion as a criterion of the fitness of J.P.s. Here it will suffice to note that these various glosses demonstrate that Cecil certainly—and Bacon inferentially—gave the personnel of the commissions of the peace careful and continuing attention. Such practice is consistent with their usual devotion to the affairs of the state, but the depth of detail is more than might be expected for men to whom so many time-consuming affairs were entrusted.[1]

---

[1] The judgement expressed in this paragraph is based on a careful study of the nature and incidence of the symbols, of what is known about the man in question, and on other evidence of Cecil's careful notes in Landsdowne MS. 1218 and in Egerton MS. 2345.

British Museum Lansdowne MS. 1218, a *liber pacis* of *c.* 1 January 1559. These folio of the North Riding show Sir William Cecil's marginal annotations which are discussed on p. 62.

A different kind of scrutiny of the commissions was described by John Hawarde in *Les Reportes del Cases in Camera Stellata* in 1595.

At the first sitting of the court, those Justices of the Peace who lived in and near London were ordered to appear, &c., by special order, and then the Lord Keeper, being Sir John Puckring, delivered an oration given in charge to him by the Queen herself . . . And for that the number of Justices of the Peace are growne allmoste infinite, to the hinderaunce of Justice, th'one trustinge so much vnto another that there are more Justicers than Justice, & as th'old saying is many times *multitudo imperatorum destruit exercitum*, & of these many insufficiente, vnlearned, negligente and vndiscreete. Her Mat<sup>ie</sup> therefore, like a good huswyfe looking vnto her household stuffe, tooke the booke in her handes, & in the sighte of vs, the Ld. Keeper and Tresorer, wente throughe & noted those Justices she would have Continue in Commission, & whome shee thoughte not meete, & willed vs Consyder of the reste, & that this audience showld knowe this, that she would not haue any to be in Commission of the peace to serue her that showlde retaine to any other man, & *ideo* th'old statute of 3 H. 7 shee woulde showld be narrowly looke unto. Nor any that doe not lyve w<sup>th</sup> in the County, or that have not of sufficiente lyving and Countenaunce, & they to remooue those that in discrecyon they thoughte not meete for the place . . .[1]

A later occasion when the over-all complexion of the commissions of the peace was certainly under scrutiny occurred in 1621. Under James I the pressures of ambition and personal influence grew so great that, in spite of what appear to have been Lord Chancellor Ellesmere's much more than perfunctory efforts to ensure competent commissions of the peace, the total numbers of justices grew until Kent had 135. Several other counties had nearly as many J.P.s, and the defects of the bench became the business of a parliament which accomplished the impeachment of Ellesmere's successor—Francis Bacon—and reached the impasse which induced the formal protestation of the House of Commons that was torn personally from the official journal by James I. In February, early in the session, one of the penalties proposed for the monopolist, Michell, who first incurred the ire of this angry assembly, was to 'put him out of the commission

---

[1] Hawarde, *Les Reportes*, pp. 19–21.

of the peace'. In April Sir Dudley Digges, a J.P. in Kent himself and destined to become Master of the Rolls, presented a petition and initiated a discussion which resulted in the appointment of a sizeable committee to draft legislation for the reform of the commissions of the peace. Grievances were several. The number of clergy in the commissions, particularly in County Durham, a palatine jurisdiction where the bishop had responsibility for the appointment of J.P.s, was stated to be larger than that of laymen. The extreme youth of some justices and the use of office for the professional advancement of budding lawyers were other faults. These were indicated by Digges in his

Report from the Committee for limitation of Justices, for nomber and for theire Condition, to sett downe somm competent proportion of estate. None too young. Now [*sic*] lawyers that have not ben Readers. No Clergy men but Bishops or somm of most gravvty of them. None under 20*l.* in the Kings bookes. And to consider somm dew limitation of the nomber.

In his account of the report and of the debate of May 1, John Pym added: 'It was Ordered, Mr. Secretarie, the Chancellor of the Exchequor, and Sir Ed Cooke to present our humble Peticion for the Reformacon of the Commission of the Peace'. Just what followed is not clear, but partly because of the press of business and the imminence of an adjournment, partly because of 'the ord[erly] government of the country which calls justices away especially at this time', no legislation was carried. In the late autumn Secretary Calvert reported at the opening of the second session of this parliament: 'That the King had given order that the justices of the peace might be put out of the commision that were unworthy, that his Majesty had taken order therin and it should be speedily amended'. However, many members of the House were J.P.s, and 'On behalfe of the Lawyers [it] was propownded That thowgh it be noe disgrace not to be a Justice of Peace, yet to bee excluded is a disgrace . . .' In January the Privy Council began making an expurgatory index of J.P.s and weeded out as many as twenty in some counties.[1]

---

[1] *Journals of the House of Commons*, i (L., 1803), 590–9; *Commons Debates, 1621*, ii. 432; ibid. iii. 111–12, 328; ibid. iv. 284; *Cal. S.P. Dom. Jas. I, 1619–23*, p. 332.

The problem of discipline among the justices of the peace was implied in the Commons both in the suggestion that Michell should be 'put out of the commission' and in the complaint of the lawyers that to be excluded was a disgrace. Inevitably many men who were unworthy must have received the appointment at one time or another. A significant portion of them must also have been eliminated, some by such action of the Chancellor as has been indicated, some by judgement of the Court of Star Chamber. It is quite impossible to determine how frequently incompetence or misfeasance or other personal deficiency was punished in this way. In the records of Star Chamber are the papers of many cases in which justices of the peace were involved in company with less distinguished gentry. The complaints ranged from the ridiculous to the extremely serious, from murder to slander,[1] from riot to the use of public position for personal purpose.[2] Frequently they reflected the rivalries of jealous neighbours.[3] Since the sentences of the court are not to be found in the files of its cases, this source helps little in evaluating the discipline exercised over the county benches either by the Chancellor or by the court. Hawarde, perhaps because he was himself a member of the commission in Surrey, seems to have been particularly interested in cases in which J.P.s were involved. Yet in the decade from June 1596 to November 1607 he reported only five cases in which the court ordered a J.P. to be dismissed from the bench.[4] Lambarde seems to confirm the implication that that punishment was not very common in the remark: 'I do remember that a J.P. was put out of the Commission of the Peace by order in the Star Chamber'.[5] More copious is the evidence of the use of such power for purposes of public policy, which will be considered in the next chapter. It is difficult not to conclude, however, that only infrequently were J.P.s dismissed from their office.

The fact that under the Stuarts justices who were removed for various reasons—personal quarrels, refusals to carry out

[1] e.g. St. Ch. 5/D26/6; St. Ch. 5/D5/19; St. Ch. 8/186/2.
[2] e.g. St. Ch. 8/272/28; St. Ch. 8/310/24; St. Ch. 8/209/8.
[3] e.g. St. Ch. 8/152/12.
[4] Hawarde, *Les Reportes*, pp. 68, 108–9, 268, 330, 354–6.
[5] Lambarde, *Eirenarcha* (L., 1581/2), p. 87; cf. *supra*, p. 43.

royal policy, persistent opposition to the Court—were often soon restored to the bench suggests that in practice the Chancellor did not have much discretion, at least when major members of the gentry were involved. Sir Francis Hastings, Sir Thomas Wentworth, and more than one member of the Knightley family of Northamptonshire were dismissed for various reasons—these are examples that emerge in the detailed study of the rosters upon which this work is based—but almost all of them were soon restored. Since much of their activities concerned, not public policy, but routine, relatively petty, crime, provided they were not corrupt, J.P.s were unlikely to be obnoxious in their official capacities. It must have seemed less awkward to grant them the usual symbol of their actual status than to suffer the inconveniences which prominent squires had it in their power to introduce into the desirable functioning of rural government.

Likewise the extraordinary situation in the Northamptonshire commission in 1626 suggests that the Crown possessed in fact little discretion. Whatever the explanation of the sudden inflation of the county's bench from 62 in 1625 to 113 in 1626 and its reduction again in 1627 to 54, there must be revealed a normal size of about sixty. Special conditions—probably the acute rivalry among the county's leading families—induced this unparalleled increase in the commission.[1] Clearly in this county there was a reserve pool of gentry who might receive appointment in special circumstances. When these conditions no longer obtained, the justices who inherently lacked merit, so it would seem, were just as quickly taken off the bench.

Like water the commission here and presumably elsewhere had a natural level. With few exceptions it included almost all but also only those members of the gentry, able and willing to assume the office, whose very prominence dictated their appointment. Both the size and the complexion reflected the general social conditions and the governmental institutions of England. If good health, an adequate estate, decent conduct, and the wish to be a justice were present, the appointment was within the grasp of the

[1] Cf. *infra*, Appendix C, pp. 177–8.

aristocracy and substantial gentry. Particular individuals might be denied by the royal administration, but not many. These men were the leaders of the county. While a few specific men might be excluded, there was no alternative administration.

# V

## RELIGION AND POLITICS

UNDER Elizabeth I and the first two Stuarts the justices of the peace were the principal organ of local government. Because they were unpaid, amateur administrators only lightly subject to discipline, coherent national policy required that, by and large, they be in sympathy with the position taken by the sovereign on major matters. In the time of Elizabeth religion was the chief concern. In the seventeenth century that problem persisted, while questions of taxation and the liberty of the subject also created divisions within the body politic. All were issues over which dissident J.P.s might be removed from the commission.

The recurrent religious upheavals of the middle years of the Tudor period created a situation in which by modern notions orderly administration was barely possible. Men of stature do not alter their faith to suit the whims of a new and perhaps transient regime. Much as the want of replacements required that the bulk of the clergy should continue in their cures, so a threat of anarchy necessarily inhibited a wholesale remodelling of the commissions of the peace. The problems of Church and State were parallel and related.

In the early months of Elizabeth's reign the Council of Trent had not yet defined Roman doctrine on important points and the English position was not at all clear; Philip II hoped to marry the new queen. As Sir John Neale has shown, no one expected that the impending religious settlement would take the form which in actuality has lasted so long.[1] Some sort of religious clairvoyance would have been required for a reconstitution of the commissions in accord with an ecclesiastical order which had not yet been legislated.

The degree to which the composition of the commissions

[1] J. E. Neale, *Elizabeth I and her Parliaments, 1559–1581* (L., 1953), pt. 1.

of the peace was affected by these conditions is not easily determined. If the rosters for the last months of Mary's reign were available, a comparison of them with those in the earlier *liber* in Lansdowne MS. 1218 would quickly reveal the amount of change in the first two months after Elizabeth's accession. However, the *liber* does show that there was much continuity among the prominent members of the commission whose religious convictions were least likely to be hidden from the Queen, the Lord Keeper, and the principal Secretary.

Not only were most of the surviving bishops retained as J.P.s—Archbishop Heath in Middlesex and the three Ridings of Yorkshire, Bonner of London likewise in the former as well as in Hertfordshire and Essex—but also such eminent laymen as William Roper (Sir Thomas More's faithful son-in-law), Sir Thomas Tresham (prior of the reconstituted Hospital of St. John), Sir John Bourne (Cecil's predecessor as principal Secretary), and Edmund Plowden (noted lawyer). Evidence that religion was not decisive at this time is provided also by the nobility. Among the few peers who were not included in this *liber* were the Earl of Northumberland, Lord Vaux, and Lord Hastings of Loughborough. But Northumberland, who rebelled in 1569, was a member of the commissions for Northumberland and the three Ridings of Yorkshire in 1562, and Vaux, who turned out to be a devoted Romanist, was included in that for Northamptonshire not later than 1569, only to be dismissed in 1580 for his complicity with Edmund Campion. On the other hand, Lord Hastings, who was removed from the commission and confined in the Tower in 1561 because of his ardent Catholicism, was a J.P. in 1559.[1] It is clear that potential loyalty to Rome did not in itself then disqualify a man as a J.P.

Between the compilation of the first Elizabethan *liber* and its presumed supersession by a later one—no longer extant —probably in July 1559, annotations indicate many modifications of the county benches. They show a developing

---

[1] Lansdowne MS. 1218; *DNB*: 'William Vaux', 'Edward Hastings', 'Thomas Percy'; Anstruther, *Vaux*, pp. 103–27; *Huntington Library Quarterly*, xviii (1954–5), 169–77; ibid. xxii (1958–9), 301–12.

situation which seems to argue that, though doubtless there were changes, they may have been little if any more numerous than those induced by such a constant as human mortality. Sir Thomas Tresham's name was stricken from the rosters for Middlesex and for his native Northamptonshire; he died in March 1559. Bonner's name was crossed off the list for Middlesex while Heath's remained untouched; Bonner was deprived of his see in May but Heath lasted until July. Apparently they ceased to be justices when they were no longer bishops. Conversely, Puritan Peter Wentworth, later a most vehement but loyal critic of Elizabeth, is shown in this *liber pacis* to have been briefly a J.P. in Oxfordshire. His name appears in no other list of J.P.s. More significant are the symbols of favour—circles and the squares which were clearly their earlier equivalent—and of disfavour—triangles —and the names in Cecil's holograph added to the rosters of many counties.

It would be instructive if it were possible to decide that the root of the disfavour was religious. Bishop Bonner's name received a triangle in Essex. Plowden was given that mark in Berkshire. In the North Riding there were many glosses: a dozen names added by Cecil's pen; figures indicating assessments; a number of circles and squares, some beside names in Cecil's hand; and eleven triangles, one of which adorned a name added by Cecil—Francis Salwyn. The other ten to whom triangles were given were Sir George Conyers, Sir Christopher Danby, Sir Edward Gower, Leonard Dacre, Robert Mennell, Richard ('Old') Norton, John Sayer, Robert Trystram, James Fox, and James Strangways. All except Danby, Dacre, Mennell, and Sayer had been eliminated from the commission by the time of the compilation of the second *liber pacis* in Lansdowne MS. 1218. On the other hand some of the names which bore a circle had also disappeared. Neither symbol can have indicated a judgement which by itself was decisive for continued membership in the commission. If the sentiments of Dacre and Norton became clear when they joined the rising in the north in 1569, the triangles suggest that Cecil suspected their reliability in 1559. Yet Dacre remained in the commission, as did Danby and Sayer, whom Archbishop

Young depicted in 1564, along with Dacre, Michael Wandesforde, Thomas Rokeby, and Anthony Caterick, all J.P.s in 1562, as 'no favorers of religion'. Likewise Edmund Plowden, who was given a triangle in 1559, was still a J.P. in Berkshire in 1562. In Buckinghamshire Lords Windsor, Mordaunt, Paget, and Hastings received triangles. Hastings was soon confined in the Tower, but the others remained in the commission. Lord Mordaunt, a Henrician courtier nearly 80 years old, was a J.P. in Northamptonshire as well, where, amidst many circles, his name was bare of symbol. In Worcestershire Sir John Bourne likewise won no symbol and soon ceased to be a J.P. Viscount Montagu had voted against the Act of Supremacy in 1559, but he continued to be a justice in Surrey and in Sussex.[1]

It seems evident that the composition of the commissions of the peace received continuing and careful scrutiny, but that religious faith by itself was not decisive. Probably it was not accident that for the counties which Cecil and Bacon knew best—Northamptonshire, Rutland, and Lincolnshire in one case, Norfolk and Suffolk in the other—the only triangles were a very few in Lincolnshire (Lindsey) and in Suffolk. A number of the Northamptonshire, Worcestershire, and North Riding J.P.s who had not found favour in the eyes of their bishops continued to hold their office. Continuity is important.[2]

In the crisis of 1569 the Privy Council ordered all justices, present and past, to take an oath to observe the Act of Uniformity. The compliance of the counties—or in some cases their subdivisions—was reported slowly. Most men carried out the instructions; Cecil himself subscribed in Northamptonshire. Some whose religious position had been suspect to their bishops in 1564 caused no trouble, and a few men generally reputed to be papists signed. Those who have been mentioned here are Lord Vaux and Sir John Bourne. William Roper and Edmund Plowden, however, refused to take the oath but entered bonds pledging their good behaviour. The difference between Catholic and non-

---

[1] Lansdowne MS. 1218; Mary Bateson, 'A Collection of Original Letters from the Bishops to the Privy Council, 1564', in *The Camden Miscellany*, ix (L., 1895), 71.
[2] Lansdowne MS. 1218; Bateson, 'Original Letters', 6, 36, 72.

Catholic did not always seem so sharp as it sometimes looks today. The fittest J.P.s were not easily determined.[1]

In 1587 an even greater crisis approached. Again an inquiry into the state of the commissions of the peace was undertaken. If John Strype is hardly an unbiased judge of the matter, his must be a sound opinion that 'none might be entrusted with that weighty charge, but such gentlemen as might be assured to be hearty men, jealous in the Queen's affairs and true to the government established'. In *Annals of the Reformation* he published the replies which the bishops made to an instruction similar to that of 1564. The Bishop of Norwich requested Burghley to keep his report confidential 'because the knowledge of such information is offensive'; in some cases it was difficult to judge, since men feigned conformity. A few justices were suspect: Thomas Lovell, Henry Doyley, Thomas Townshend, William Rugg, Nicholas Hare, Clemens Paston. The Bishop's standard must have been high: Lovell, Doyley, Rugg, and Hare were still listed in later *libri pacis*. The returns in other counties were comparable. There is also a paper from Burghley's office which shows clearly that the commissions were under careful review—a list of 'Justices left out of the C. of P. for their wives' recusancy'. On the eve of the Armada a J.P.'s wife had to be above suspicion. Presumably unreliable husbands were also excluded.[2]

In the Stuart period there continued to be concern over recusancy in the commissions of the peace. The matter was discussed in the House of Commons, and James I regarded it as cause for exclusion from the bench. None the less, some overt Catholics, such as Lords Exeter and Vaux in Northamptonshire and Lords Morley and Monteagle in Somerset, remained in office.[3] The Puritans were especially alert to this as to other aspects of the Catholic threat. Yet the growing conflict over politics and religion progressively estranged them from the royal administration and they became liable themselves to disciplinary or criminal process.

[1] S.P. 12/59/37; S.P. 12/60/47.

[2] John Strype, *Annals of the Reformation* (4 vols., L., 1709–31), iii, pt. 2, 459; P.R.O., S.P. 13/Case F, no. 11, f. 25ᵛ; S.P. 12/206, no. 8.

[3] Cf. *infra*, pp. 172, 179, 190, 193.

The threat, however, seems to have been more serious than the actuality. In 1605 a petition in support of non-conforming ministers was met by the temporary removal from the Northamptonshire commission of Sir Richard and Sir Valentine Knightley, Sir Edward Montagu, Sir William Lane, and Erasmus Dryden. Sir Francis Hastings, who had joined with them, was dismissed in Somerset. Earlier, in 1589, discipline in the guise of a fine by the Star Chamber had been visited upon the elder Knightley because the Marprelate press had been traced to Fawsley. On that occasion, too, he was deprived also of his Deputy Lieutenancy. As before he was now soon restored, and, except for Hastings, his fellows with him.[1]

In August 1607 there was a rumour that Puritan parliament men were to be put out of the commission of the peace. This gossip reached the pen of a man—Dudley Carleton—who had access to official circles, but no names were given. Reference to the proceedings in the previous session of Parliament, however, suggests that Hastings and Valentine Knightly, together with Sir Edwin Sandys, Sir Anthony Cope, Sir Richard Spencer, Sir Francis Barrington, Sir William Strode, Sir Robert Wingfield, Sir George Moore, and Nicholas Fuller, were the most likely candidates for such retaliation. Yet Cope, Spencer, Strode, Wingfield, and Moore were all members of the commissions of their counties in 1608. Sandys was probably not yet a J.P. though he was in the commission in Kent in the reign of Charles I. Barrington, who had been a J.P. as early as 1596, was not listed in the Essex roster in the *liber pacis* in 1608, but he was included among the Deputy Lieutenants of the county. He was again a justice in 1621. Fuller had a major role in the *cause célèbre* over prohibitions just at this time, but probably he was never a J.P. If Carleton believed that Puritan members of parliament were to be disciplined by being removed from the bench, that punishment seems in fact to have been inflicted on very few men. In 1622 a similar, also apparently unsubstantiated, rumour followed the dissolution of an even more unruly parliament. The absence of all pertinent evidence argues that the Puritans

[1] Cf. *infra*, pp. 170–1.

as such were not systematically excluded from the county benches.[1]

Secular politics, however, clearly did provoke punitive measures, for justices were expected to be examples of pre-eminent loyalty. After the dissolution of Parliament in 1614 without the grant of a subsidy, James hoped to receive a benevolence in its stead. The response of the counties varied, but many J.P.s were not the desired models for their fellow subjects. Particularly in Devon and in Somerset was there reluctance to contribute. A circular letter from the Privy Council on 4 July was followed in Somerset by a longer one on 17 September. Five days later many Somerset J.P.s responded, as their Devon associates had done earlier, that there were no precedents for such gifts. On 2 November a summons was sent to Sir Maurice Berkeley, Sir Nicholas Halswell, and John Paulet—and four days later to Sir George Speke, Sir Francis Heale, Sir Francis Popham, and Edward Rogers—to appear at the Council board not later than 20 November for reasons which would there be explained. Their very prompt appearance led the Council on 15 November to address to the whole bench in Somerset a further justification of the procedure:

> whereof as of the rest then delivered the gentlemen then presente can give yow further and more particular satisfaction, . . . in contemplacion whereof the said gentelmen then presente did then acknowledg the error which yow and they together had by mistaking committed therein . . . wee are to lett yow knowe that it is acknowledged before us by some of your nomber, that, speaking with sundry persons of good ability of the limittes wherein they serve as Justices of that county, they did finde many of them to answere that they were willing of their free good will to contribute, if they might have any example given them by the Justices themselves, and by those of the cheifest rancke and worth of the contry . . .

It is not evident how effective were these rather drastic steps, but the total sums realized by the benevolence hardly

---

[1] David Harris Willson (ed.), *The Parliamentary Diary of Robert Bowyer 1606–1607* (Minneapolis, 1931), *passim*; *Journals of the House of Commons*, i. 314–92; Gardiner, *History of England*, i. 324–54; ibid. ii. 36–40; *Cal. S.P. Dom., Jas. I, 1603–10*, p. 368; S.P. 14/33, *passim*; C. 193/13; George Roberts (ed.), *Diary of Walter Younge, esq.* (Camden Soc. Publ. no. xli, L., 1848), p. 50.

encouraged its early repetition. Apparently these Somerset justices suffered no further discipline. They were not put out of the commission and they were, indeed, notably diligent in their attendance at quarter sessions. Years later Popham was a leader of the parliamentary party in the Long Parliament, while Paulet, then Baron Paulet, was a royalist.[1]

Other examples of apparent punishment for political activity are found in Yorkshire. Sir Thomas Hoby, who had become a J.P. at the turn of the century, a member of the Council in the North in 1603 and *Custos Rotulorum* of the North Riding in 1621, was dismissed from the Council in 1622 and put off the bench. The cause seems to have been a quarrel with Lord Scrope, the Lord President of the Council, which evoked an admonition from the King. After 1630 Hoby was restored both to the commission and to the Council. In 1626 Sir Thomas Wentworth, whose personal antagonist, Sir John Savile, was then in high favour, received the calculated indignity of being dismissed as J.P. and as *Custos Rotulorum* of the West Riding. Earlier he had been forced to serve as sheriff in order to prevent his election to the Commons.[2]

Much the most important cases in which justices were coerced to comply with royal policy sprang from the dissolution of Parliament in 1626 without a grant of taxes. First followed an effort to obtain a 'free gift'. A general reluctance to contribute doomed the scheme, but opposition in Somerset—in spite of, or because of, the experience of 1614—was particularly strong. The ringleaders this time were Sir Robert Phelips, John Symes, and Hugh Pyne. Phelips, a vehement critic of Buckingham, was one of the men eliminated from this parliament by his appointment as sheriff. Symes and Pyne campaigned vigorously against the gift. All three were removed from the commission of the peace. In the next year, after his attack on the forced loan—Charles I's more serious effort to extract from the country the money

---

[1] Godfrey Davies, *The Early Stuarts* (Oxford, 1959), p. 18; *A.P.C., 1613–14*, pp. 491–6, 557–9, 611, 614, 628–31; A. H. A. Hamilton, *Quarter Sessions from Queen Elizabeth to Queen Anne* (L., 1878), pp. 491–6.

[2] Cf. *supra*, p. 38, and *infra*, pp. 235, 237; *Cal. S.P. Dom., Jas. I, 1619–23*, p. 168; C. V. Wedgwood, *Thomas Wentworth, First Earl of Strafford, 1593–1641, a Revaluation* (N.Y., 1962), p. 56.

which parliament did not grant—Pyne was held in prison and prosecuted in King's Bench. His legal practice, worth possibly £2,000 per annum, seems to have been ruined. It was thought at the time that the antipathy of Lord Paulet was an element in his disgrace. Yet his unrestrained attack on Buckingham—'It can never be well with England until there be means made that the Duke's head may be set [let?] fall from his shoulders'—offers an alternative explanation. In other counties a dozen J.P.s were removed from the bench because of the roles they played in connection with the gift.

The aftermath is instructive. Symes was pricked for sheriff in November 1626 to follow Phelips. Since there was no prospect of another parliamentary election, the labour and considerable incidental expenses of the office were the only punitive effect at that time. If not eagerly sought, the position was one which only the leading gentry commonly held. It was not without prestige, and the King made a choice between three candidates. Both Phelips and Symes were restored to the commission by 1628, and in 1629, shortly after Hugh Pyne's death, his son succeeded him on the county bench as well as in his estates. Justices were occasionally disciplined for political reasons by being put out of the commission, but the exclusion was often temporary.[1]

Resistance to the forced loan was not confined to Somerset. Better-known opponents were Sir Thomas Wentworth, Sir John Eliot, and the five men—Sir Thomas Darnell, Sir John Corbett, Sir Walter Erle, Sir John Heveningham, and Sir Edmund Hampden—who brought *habeas corpus* proceedings for release from their confinement. The five knights had all been J.P.s, Corbett and Heveningham in Norfolk, Darnell in Lincolnshire, Erle in Dorset, and Hampden in Northamptonshire. The western part of the last county, indeed, exhibited a most determined hostility toward enforced generosity.[2]

Clearly there was excitement in the air when the assizes

---

[1] R. F. Williams (ed.), *The Court and Times of Charles the First* (2 vols., L., 1848), i. 295; *Cal. S.P. Dom., Chas. I, 1625–6*, p. 436; ibid. *1627–8*, p. 312; Thomas Garden Barnes, *Somerset 1625–1640* (Camb., 1961), p. 153; Gardiner, *History of England*, vi. 131; Davies, *Early Stuarts*, p. 37; cf. Somerset roster, 1636, nos. 43, 51, *infra*, p. 199.     [2] Davies, *Early Stuarts*, p. 37.

met in Northampton in February 1627. Early in the sitting Dr. Robert Sibthorpe, himself a J.P., preached before the justices on obedience, 'showing the Duty of Subjects to pay Tribute and Taxes to their Prince'. Just what immediate reception the speaker's remarks received is not known, but the sermon, brought to the attention of the King, was licensed for publication by Laud after Archbishop Abbot had been suspended from the exercise of his authority because he refused to grant the licence. Even before the assizes met, sixteen members[1] of the county's exceptionally large commission, together with several neighbouring gentlemen, had appeared at the Council board and been ordered not to depart from Westminster. Commendation was sent, meanwhile, to the eastern division of the county, specifically to Lords Westmorland, Montagu, and Mordaunt.

Yet the manipulation of the commission in the previous year had not induced subservience.[2] The Puritan J.P.s from the western side firmly resisted unparliamentary taxation. On 31 January Sir William Chauncey, a commissioner for the loan, appeared at the Council board a second time.

Hee was tolde by the Erle of Dorset that hee did owe more to the Crowne than many others, for if the Crowne had bene as harde towardes him as hee is now towards it hee had not bene in so good a plight. Whereupon in a bolde and arrogant manner he said to the Erle of Dorset, 'I am as free as yourself, Sir,' and shewed by his gesture to brave a Counsellor at the Boarde. In which regarde of insolence towardes a peere and member of the Boarde, as also of his unreverent caryage in that place their Lordships thought fit to commit him to the prison of Newgate.

Later five more J.P.s from Northamptonshire—Sir Erasmus Dryden, Sir William Wilmer, Thomas Elmes, Richard Knightley, and Hampden—and a number from other counties joined Chauncey in confinement. In July, while the famous *habeas corpus* proceedings were pending, they were among the nearly fifty men who were exiled to places of 'house arrest' away from their own counties. Was there

---

[1] Sir William Chauncey, Sir John Danvers, Sir Erasmus Dryden, Sir Edmund Hampden, Sir Anthony Haselwood, Sir John Pickering, Sir Richard Samwell, Sir William Wilmer, John Blincoe, John Breton, Thomas Elmes, Richard Kenricke, Richard Knightley, Francis Nicolls, William Pargiter, John Wyrley.

[2] Cf. *infra*, pp. 176–9.

intentional humour in the petition of the sheriff of Oxford-shire on behalf of Elmes that because of intolerable living conditions he be permitted to remove from Nettlebed—in fact to Henley? In January 1628, just before the election of the parliament which adopted the Petitition of Right, these doughty men—except the deceased Hampden—were all released from restraint. Even though the Northampton-shire commission was now much reduced, at least half the sixteen became J.P.s again.[1]

Altogether there were seventy men, not all of them J.P.s, who accepted loss of liberty rather than comply with the King's demand. Beside a total group of approximately sixteen hundred justices in the working commissions in all England, the number is not impressive. From the six counties herein treated there were Sir Thomas Wentworth and George Radcliffe from the North Riding and Sir John Corbet and Sir John Heveningham from Norfolk in addition to the men from Northamptonshire. They suffered a much more severe form of coercion than removal from the county bench. Even without the loss of life, martyrdom works its influence beyond all relation to the number of individuals involved.

When next there arose a conflict over royal policy which closely concerned the J.P.s the experience of the forced loan was not forgotten. It is a curious fact that historians have given to most of the controversy over ship money hardly more attention than they have accorded the details of the five knights and the forced loan. Much the most informative treatment is Barnes's *Somerset, 1625–1640*, where the chapter on ship money follows one which discusses in detail the effort under the Book of Orders to provide vigorous administration of the Poor Law subject to central direction.[2] In each innovation the royal government embarked on a policy to which there was serious opposition among the

---

[1] *A.P.C., Jan.–Aug. 1627*, pp. 15, 42 (quotation), 51, 395, 449, 507; ibid., *Sept. 1627–June 1628*, pp. 217–18; *Cal. S.P. Dom., Chas. I, 1627–8*, pp. 15, 157–8; cf. *infra*, pp. 179–80.

[2] Gardiner, *History of England*, Chs. 74, 77, 82; Davies, *Early Stuarts*, pp. 84–5; Barnes, *Somerset*, Chs. VII, VIII; M. D. Gordon, 'The Collection of Ship Money in the Reign of Charles I', *Transactions of the Royal Historical Society*, 3rd Series, iv (L., 1910), 141–62.

gentry. Both failed. With regard to the relief of poverty the law was explicit. The king had no discretion. It was the justices of the peace who had the task of supervising the work of parish overseers. There was no such statutory authority nor prescribed agency for the collection of ship money. After careful consideration it was decided not to follow the precedent of the loan of 1626–7—special commissioners who were in fact almost always justices—but to impose the task upon the sheriffs and, beneath them, the local constables. The J.P.s would be bypassed.

Had the whole scheme been more successful and longer lived, there might have developed an administrative system in which the sheriff was restored to something like his medieval prominence. He would have ceased to be subordinate in effect to the county bench and become again the king's chief local agent. He might conceivably have won a status not unlike that of the *intendants* upon whom Richelieu was at the moment constructing an autocratic monarchy. Yet in fact it was impossible to displace the gentry with the justices at their head. They were the principal propertyholders, the men who had to pay a significant part of any tax that was fairly assessed, unless like the French nobility they were given exemption from important imposts. Moreover the sheriffs were in fact chosen from the ranks of the principal gentry. Between 1634 and 1639—the effective period of the experiment with ship money—in the six counties all thirty-one sheriffs except three were drawn from the men with whom this study is concerned: baronets, knights, gentry who were themselves J.P.s at some time, or members of families which staffed the commissions.

The three exceptions were Charles Cockayne and Philip Holman in Northamptonshire, and Henry Hodges in Somerset.[1] Cockayne was the only son of a well-known Mayor of London who married a daughter of the sixth Earl of Thomond and was thus a cousin by marriage of Sir Barnaby Bryan, a member of the county commission. The fact that he was sheriff in 1636 may be the actual reason why his name was not included in the roster of that year. Philip Holman and Henry Hodges seem to have had such

[1] *Complete Peerage*: 'Cullen'; Barnes, *Somerset*, p. 132 *et passim*.

slight prominence that, had they been justices, they would
here have been described as obscure gentry. The experiment
with ship money had been too sudden and too brief. In spite
of the royal intent, the key figures in its collection came from
the group of J.P.s. There was not time for the development
of an alternative county administration.

Since most of the J.P.s were prominent landholders, the
details of the story of ship money inevitably involve many of
them. Only a few, however, are apposite here. That there
were more disputes in Somerset and Northamptonshire
than in other counties was presumably the consequence of
their earlier experience with enforced generosity. In Somerset Sir Robert Phelips had a reputation as well as great
authority. It may have been the memory of his opposition to
the forced loan which led to a prompt summons to appear
before the Council in the presence of the King himself after
the Bishop of Bath and Wells had not succeeded in adjusting
a dispute between Phelips and the town of Ilchester over
the proper assessment of Northover. Judgement was in
favour of Phelips.[1] In Northamptonshire the focal dispute
over the fair assessment of Burton Latimer reflected the
rivalry between the east and west divisions of the county
which had festered for more than a decade. Again there was
adjudication by the Council after clerical referees—Dr.
Robert Sibthorpe and Sir John Lambe (a Northamptonshire
J.P. and Dean of the Arches)—had proved ineffectual. Nor
can it have been a surprise when the sheriff reported to the
Council that 'Mr. Knightley still endeavours to nourish
contention'. Payment was resisted even by the Earl of Peterborough, the former Lord Mordaunt, who had loyally
supported the forced loan. When the sheriff proposed to
distrain a mare and a cow, Sir William Wilmer, who had
been incarcerated in 1627, announced he would himself
rescue Peterborough's cattle. This was 1637, the year of the
case of John Hampden, a Buckinghamshire J.P., whose
uncle had been a fellow victim with Wilmer.[2]

[1] Barnes, *Somerset*, pp. 216–18; *Cal. S.P. Dom., Chas. I, 1635–6*, p. 189; ibid., *1637*,
pp. 98, 133.
[2] Ibid., *1635–6*, pp. 229–30, 348–9; ibid., *1636–7*, pp. 127, 405, 471–4, 526, 538;
ibid., *1637*, pp. 333–4, 395–6.

Such conduct was the background against which an order in council was addressed to all sheriffs. It declared that the King had taken into consideration the growing prejudice to his service of refusals to pay ship money except under distraint. All sheriffs, Deputy Lieutenants, and justices of the peace who forbore payment were to be discharged from their offices. The sheriffs were instructed to certify to the Council the names of such as had 'expressed their averseness to this so great and necessary service'. It was an emphatic and certainly not a secret threat to coerce the J.P.s by the undoubted power of dismissal. In the year of the ship-money case, the order might well have been followed by numerous exclusions. In fact the state papers seem to contain no single certificate from a sheriff. The threat was not carried out.

In the next year another one of the Northamptonshire men confined for refusal to make a loan in 1627, Sir Richard Samwell, was described to Sir John Lambe as 'a man so venomous against ecclesiastical jurisdiction . . . [that] his head standing upon Puritan shoulders, neither will obedience be performed nor truth extracted'. Yet he was still a J.P. some months later when Sibthorpe again wrote to Lambe: 'There is no new commission come down although . . . the Lord Keeper . . . had given a warrant to put out Sir Richard'.[1] Why was no effective suasion used against J.P.s in connection with ship money?

The evidence with regard to dismissals from the commissions of the peace for broad reasons of general policy shows that on occasion such action was taken. Twice in Elizabeth's reign inquiry was made of the bishops about the faith of their fellow justices. Once all J.P.s were required to take an oath to support the established church. Although some Romanists were eliminated at those times, none of the purges seems to have been really thorough. A formal and outward conformity sufficed for the most part. If certain Catholics were removed at those times of crisis, others were displaced at other moments. A loyal bench was desired, but the influences which narrowed the choice of J.P.s to the leaders of the county were so strong that considerable aberration had to be tolerated. In the Stuart period it was political

---

[1] *Cal. S.P. Dom., Chas. I, 1636–7*, p. 181; ibid., *1637–8*, pp. 191, 536.

opposition on particular questions rather than notorious religious dissent which invited retribution. Public if limited use was made of the power of discipline. In almost all cases the victims—or heroes—were soon restored to their office. There was a limited group of men who were well qualified for appointment as J.P.s. Leaders of the county, they were an indispensable element in social organization. National and royal policy could not well nor long be at odds with their sentiments.

# VI

## THE EDUCATION OF J.P.s

THAT the nobility and leading gentry of Tudor England came increasingly to seek for their sons the education offered at Oxford, Cambridge, and the inns of court has become an accepted historical dictum. No study which examines in detail the lives of such men could fail to show many cases of entrance into those societies. Thus twenty-two among the sixty-one men, including Lambarde, who composed the working part of the Kent commission in 1584 had been admitted to one of the inns, while ten had attended a university. Was the Kent bench a characteristic group? Just how usual was such training in the country as a whole, and what bearing did it have upon the conduct of justices? Doubtless many future J.P.s were enrolled in the inns, but how diligently did most of them study? Since the usual age of residence at Oxford and Cambridge was significantly lower than it is today, may it be assumed that the study was not very important? These are matters about which generalities have not often been supported by detailed data. In the thirty groups of justices of the present study there is the basis for a confident statement with regard to the formal, institutionalized training of 'the most important class of men in England'.

In 1562, among the men who composed the commissions of the peace in the six counties, only a few had been enrolled in either a university or an inn. Of the fifty-six men in the Kent commission, for example, five had been students at Cambridge: Archbishop Parker, Lord Cobham (Warden of the Cinque Ports), John Cobham, Lord Keeper Bacon, and Sir Richard Sackville, both the latter having gone on to become barristers at Gray's Inn. Sixteen others had been enrolled at some one of the inns, nine having been called to the bar. Finally, there were twenty-nine knights and esquires who had attended neither a university nor an inn. Among the eleven barristers were the Lord Keeper of the Great

Seal, an under-treasurer of the Exchequer, the Attorney-General, two future judges, and two serjeants. The commission divides rather sharply into professional men and relatively uneducated gentry.

Comparable situations obtained in other counties. Thus, of Worcestershire's twenty-eight J.P.s, only ten—Lord Keeper Bacon, Bishop Sandys, two assize judges, the chief justice of Chester, Sir William Sheldon (administrator), Thomas Hoby (courtier and ambassador), two members of the gentry (Sir Thomas Russell and William Cokesey), and one lawyer (Richard Smyth)—seem to have been enrolled in either a university or an inn. Similarly, only ten of Norfolk's twenty-four justices, fifteen of Somerset's thirty-eight, and twelve of the North Riding's thirty-five were formally 'educated'.

In sharp contrast was the situation in 1636. At that time only eleven of Kent's eighty-five justices, ten of Worcestershire's thirty-five, nine of Northamptonshire's fifty-seven, and eight of Somerset's sixty-three were never students in either a university or an inn. Three-quarters of a century had witnessed changes in much more than the total number of J.P.s.

The details of this transformation in the formal training of the men who became justices of the peace deserve summary and interpretation. The following table (pp. 86-8) contains the essential facts. In its compilation it was necessary to make some assumptions which should be made explicit. Where the identity of a student in either a university or an inn was not certain (a condition encountered chiefly in the earlier years), that which seemed to be the more probable situation was assumed to be the case. Thus the data may include a few men who were not in actuality the future J.P.s. If the totals may thus be a trifle magnified, there are surely some cases— again largely in the earlier years—where defective records have not disclosed the enrolment of a future justice. It seems not unlikely that the two types of error are approximately in balance and that the statistics are very nearly true. Another problem of definition is the considerable number of instances where a man of distinction was awarded a degree by decree rather than for conventional academic achievement, or was admitted to one of the inns when of decidedly mature age. These men cannot have had the same sort of experience as their fellows, although after their admission to an inn, they may have participated actively in the life of the society. Such enrolments have not been included in the data in the table. Likewise the frequent incorporation of graduates of one university in the other and the less usual membership of a man in more than one inn have been ignored. These duplications and honorary enrolments, however, attest the esteem in which both the universities and the inns were held and tend to confirm the importance of the conventional admissions which are tabulated.

Under each county and in the summary totals are two columns which represent the division into dignitaries and working commission which was recognized at the time and has here been followed in general. The figure at the head of each column at each date is the total number of men in that particular group. For the inns of court there are usually two figures, the first being the number of men admitted to the inn, the second the number called to the bar. At the end of each section 'Both' shows the number of justices who were enrolled in both a university and an inn of court; 'None' describes the men who attended neither kind of institution.[1]

The copious data summarized in the table imply matters of great moment. There is reflected a transformation in the usual experience of the English gentry and aristocracy. From a group which received its training primarily in the skills of a feudalistic society, and its literary education largely at an elementary level and perhaps at home, it became one whose members commonly enrolled for study at the universities or the inns of court and not infrequently at both. Several recent studies have examined this 'cultural revolution' from varied points of view: small segments of the aristocracy and gentry, the personnel of the House of Commons, the influence of humanism, the changing curricula and student bodies of the universities. All these facets are important with regard to the office of justice of the peace. Nor is the fact irrelevant that the colleges of Oxford and Cambridge, which were one medium of the cultural change, and the inns of court, which

---

[1] The data are all derived from the sources indicated below in Appendices A–F.

| | Total* | North Riding | Worcs. | Som. | Nthts. | Norf. | Kent |
|---|---|---|---|---|---|---|---|
| **1562** | 49 / 143 | 18 / 17 | 9 / 19 | 9 / 29 | 12 / 17 | 7 / 17 | 12 / 44 |
| Ox. | 2 / 3 | 1 / 2 | 0 / 0 | 1 / 1 | 0 / 0 | 0 / 0 | 0 / 0 |
| Cam. | 12 / 4 | 2 / 0 | 3 / 1 | 2 / 0 | 6 / 1 | 2 / 1 | 4 / 1 |
|  | 14 / 7 | 3 / 2 | 3 / 1 | 3 / 1 | 6 / 1 | 2 / 1 | 4 / 1 |
| M.T. | 7-6 / 10-7 | 1-1 / 0-0 | 2-2 / 3-2 | 1-1 / 6-4 | 2-2 / 1-1 | 2-1 / 0-0 | 0-0 / 0-0 |
| I.T. | 1-1 / 5-2 | 0-0 / 0-0 | 0-0 / 1-0 | 1-1 / 1-0 | 0-1 / 0-0 | 0-0 / 1-1 | 0-0 / 2-1 |
| Gray's | 7-4 / 15-3 | 2-2 / 3-0 | 1-1 / 1-0 | 2-1 / 1-0 | 3-1 / 3-0 | 2-1 / 1-1 | 3-3 / 6-2 |
| Linc's | 2-2 / 14-8 | 0-0 / 2-1 | 0-0 / 0-0 | 0-0 / 2-1 | 1-1 / 1-1 | 0-0 / 3-1 | 1-1 / 6-4 |
|  | 17-13 / 44-20 | 3-3 / 5-1 | 3-3 / 5-2 | 4-3 / 10-5 | 6-4 / 5-2 | 4-2 / 5-3 | 4-4 / 14-7 |
| Both | 7 / 2 | 1 / 0 | 2 / 0 | 2 / 1 | 5 / 1 | 2 / 0 | 2 / 0 |
| None | 25 / 94 | 13 / 10 | 5 / 13 | 4 / 19 | 5 / 12 | 3 / 11 | 6 / 29 |
| **1584** | 61 / 246 | 19 / 44 | 13 / 39 | 10 / 39 | 13 / 30 | 11 / 36 | 15 / 61 |
| Ox. | 7 / 10 | 2 / 0 | 1 / 3 | 4 / 3 | 2 / 1 | 2 / 1 | 2 / 4 |
| Cam. | 24 / 47 | 7 / 17 | 6 / 3 | 4 / 3 | 6 / 4 | 6 / 14 | 4 / 6 |
|  | 31 / 57 | 9 / 17 | 7 / 6 | 8 / 6 | 8 / 5 | 8 / 15 | 6 / 10 |
| M.T. | 4-3 / 23-11 | 1-1 / 1-1 | 1-1 / 5-3 | 2-2 / 12-5 | 3-2 / 4-1 | 1-1 / 0-0 | 1-1 / 2-1 |
| I.T. | 7-6 / 21-10 | 0-0 / 1-2 | 1-1 / 7-4 | 1-1 / 2-0 | 1-0 / 1-0 | 2-2 / 8-4 | 5-5 / 2-0 |
| Gray's | 7-1 / 45-13 | 2-0 / 12-5 | 1-0 / 3-2 | 2-0 / 4-1 | 5-1 / 8-2 | 1-0 / 6-3 | 1-0 / 13-0 |
| Linc's | 4-4 / 25-12 | 2-2 / 9-4 | 2-2 / 4-3 | 0-0 / 1-1 | 0-0 / 1-0 | 2-2 / 5-1 | 0-0 / 5-3 |
|  | 22-14 / 114-46 | 5-3 / 23-12 | 5-4 / 19-12 | 5-3 / 19-7 | 9-3 / 14-3 | 6-5 / 19-8 | 7-6 / 22-4 |
| Both | 12 / 35 | 4 / 13 | 3 / 2 | 4 / 4 | 6 / 4 | 5 / 9 | 3 / 4 |
| None | 20 / 110 | 9 / 17 | 4 / 16 | 1 / 18 | 2 / 15 | 2 / 11 | 5 / 33 |

| | Kent | Norf. | Nthts. | Som. | Worcs. | North Riding | Total |
|---|---|---|---|---|---|---|---|
| **1608** | 13 · 97 | 7 · 52 | 16 · 37 | 12 · 45 | 11 · 34 | 14 · 48 | 56 · 311 |
| Ox. | 2 · 15 | 0 · 1 | 1 · 4 | 1 · 11 | 1 · 6 | 3 · 5 | 8 · 41 |
| Cam. | 5 · 24 | 3 · 30 | 7 · 3 | 3 · 5 | 3 · 1 | 5 · 22 | 21 · 85 |
| | 7 · 39 | 3 · 31 | 8 · 7 | 4 · 16 | 4 · 7 | 8 · 27 | 29 · 126 |
| M.T. | 0–0 · 9–4 | 0–0 · 3–0 | 0–0 · 5–2 | 2–1 · 12–3 | 2–2 · 7–1 | 1–1 · 2–1 | 5–4 · 38–11 |
| I.T. | 3–2 · 5–1 | 2–2 · 8–3 | 3–3 · 1–1 | 2–2 · 4–0 | 1–1 · 7–3 | 2–1 · 4–1 | 8–6 · 29–7 |
| Gray's | 1–0 · 18–3 | 1–1 · 7–2 | 4–1 · 8–0 | 0–0 · 7–1 | 2–1 · 0–0 | 4–1 · 16–3 | 11–3 · 56–9 |
| Linc's | 2–2 · 16–4 | 1–1 · 16–5 | 4–1 · 2–0 | 2–2 · 7–4 | 1–1 · 5–2 | 1–1 · 6–6 | 2–2 · 52–21 |
| | 6–4 · 48–12 | 4–4 · 34–10 | 11–5 · 16–3 | 6–5 · 30–8 | 6–5 · 19–6 | 8–4 · 28–11 | 26–15 · 175–48 |
| Both | 2 · 19 | 1 · 23 | 5 · 4 | 1 · 12 | 1 · 4 | 3 · 19 | 10 · 81 |
| None | 2 · 29 | 1 · 10 | 2 · 18 | 3 · 11 | 2 · 12 | 2 · 12 | 11 · 91 |
| **1626** | 38 · 59 | 14 · 51 | 24 · 54† | 16 · 40 | 12 · 29 | 18 · 34 | 79 · 265 |
| Ox. | 14 · 14 | 4 · 0 | 7 · 14 | 8 · 17 | 9 · 13 | 8 · 1 | 34 · 59 |
| Cam. | 10 · 23 | 3 · 27 | 9 · 15 | 2 · 3 | 1 · 2 | 3 · 19 | 19 · 88 |
| | 24 · 37 | 7 · 27 | 16 · 29 | 10 · 20 | 10 · 15 | 11 · 20 | 53 · 147 |
| M.T. | 3–1 · 5–1 | 2–2 · 2–1 | 3–1 · 8–1 | 3–1 · 10–2 | 3–2 · 6–2 | 2–2 · 3–1 | 7–2 · 34–8 |
| I.T. | 2–2 · 7–1 | 3–2 · 8–4 | 2–1 · 3–1 | 2–2 · 1–1 | 2–2 · 9–1 | 1–1 · 4–2 | 6–5 · 32–10 |
| Gray's | 2–0 · 15–1 | 1–0 · 8–3 | 3–1 · 8–2 | 0–0 · 4–0 | 0–0 · 1–0 | 4–2 · 11–3 | 5–1 · 47–9 |
| Linc's | 3–1 · 2–0 | 1–0 · 9–4 | 3–1 · 2–0 | 3–2 · 6–4 | 3–2 · 2–1 | 1–1 · 5–1 | 8–2 · 26–10 |
| | 10–4 · 29–3 | 7–4 · 27–12 | 11–4 · 21–4 | 8–5 · 21–7 | 8–6 · 18–4 | 8–6 · 23–7 | 26–10 · 139–37 |
| Both | 8 · 21 | 5 · 16 | 10 · 12 | 6 · 9 | 7 · 8 | 5 · 13 | 21 · 79 |
| None | 12 · 14 | 5 · 13 | 7 · 16 | 4 · 8 | 1 · 4 | 4 · 4 | 21 · 58 |

| | Kent | Norf. | Nthts. | Som. | Worcs. | North Riding | Total |
|---|---|---|---|---|---|---|---|
| 1636 | 22 63 | 10 52 | 18 39 | 12 51 | 13 22 | 15 39 | 64 266 |
| Ox. | 11 20 | 4 1 | 5 13 | 6 24 | 8 11 | 5 5 | 26 74 |
| Cam. | 5 23 | 5 34 | 9 15 | 3 4 | 1 0 | 5 14 | 18 90 |
| | 16 43 | 9 35 | 14 28 | 9 28 | 9 11 | 10 19 | 44 164 |
| M.T. | 2-2 9-3 | 2-2 2-1 | 2-1 9-4 | 3-1 18-5 | 2-2 3-0 | 2-2 2-1 | 8-5 43-14 |
| I.T. | 1-1 14-6 | 3-2 5-3 | 3-2 3-1 | 1-1 3-1 | 2-2 4-1 | 3-2 5-2 | 7-5 34-14 |
| Gray's | 5-2 21-7 | 0-0 12-5 | 3-1 9-2 | 1-1 2-0 | 1-1 0-0 | 2-1 16-4 | 8-5 60-18 |
| Linc's | 0-0 3-2 | 0-0 13-7 | 0-0 0-0 | 2-2 10-4 | 1-1 2-1 | 0-0 6-0 | 3-3 34-14 |
| | 8-5 47-18 | 5-4 32-16 | 8-4 21-7 | 7-5 33-10 | 6-6 9-2 | 7-5 29-7 | 26-18 171-60 |
| Both | 6 34 | 5 24 | 6 17 | 5 17 | 5 5 | 4 14 | 18 111 |
| None | 4 7 | 1 9 | 2 7 | 1 7 | 3 5 | 2 5 | 12 42 |

* The totals are not mere additions of the preceding columns: duplications are eliminated—e.g. the Lord Chancellor was a J.P. in every county, but is counted only once. There are four cases of men who appear as dignitaries in one county and as working J.P.s in another. They are counted twice, once in each capacity: 1562, Sir Henry Sidney in Kent and Wors.; 1526, John Welshe in Som. and N.R.; 1584, Francis Gawdy in Kent and Norf.; 1608, Sir Edward Phelips in Som. and N.R.

† The figures for Northamptonshire in 1626 are those of the 'diminished' commission. The figures for the full commission are:

| | | | | | | |
|---|---|---|---|---|---|---|
| Ox. | 19 | M.T. | 13-1 | Both | 20 |
| Cam. | 22 | I.T. | 8-1 | None | 31 |
| | 41 | Gray's | 11-2 | | |
| | | Linc's | 5-0 | | |
| | | | 37-4 | | |

were the locus for study of the common law, were both, like the J.P.s themselves, institutions peculiar to England.[1]

Fritz Caspari, in *Humanism and the Social Order in Tudor England*, demonstrates that a 'thorough reversal of the upper-class attitude toward learning took place. The ideal of the learned, responsible gentleman who devotes himself to the tasks of government . . . became the model of an increasingly active and powerful gentry.'[2] The university aspect of the development is cogently analysed, although without such statistical support as has just been adduced, in Mark Curtis's *Oxford and Cambridge in Transition 1558–1642*. He shows how the colleges provided—largely beyond the statutory instruction of the universities—an education which was often consciously designed to fill the needs of the men who became the governors of England.[3]

The universities, not being 'class' schools, brought the sons of the gentry and nobility into contact with young men of other social groups. Yeomen's sons and earls' sons, merchants' sons and the heirs of the landed gentry were all bred together in learning. All received the same slant on things.

Frequently they came only for one or two years before they went down to read at the Inns of Court, to travel abroad, or to return to their homes and estates ... Only the light-minded among them spent all their leisure in hunting, bear-baiting, dicing, wenching, and tippling. The more purposeful and thoughtful ones ... turned their attention to other subjects: sometimes to learning which would have practical application in their future lives. . . .

In the second generation of the sixteenth century . . . a cultural revolution had taken place. The English aristocracy in general, and not just occasional members of it, had accepted the precepts of the humanists.

---

[1] J. H. Hexter, 'The Education of the Aristocracy in the Renaissance', *Journal of Modern History*, xxii (1950), 1–20; Fritz Caspari, *Humanism and the Social Order in Tudor England* (Chicago, 1954); Mark H. Curtis, *Oxford and Cambridge in Transition, 1558–1642* (Oxford, 1959); Neale, *House of Commons*, pp. 302–3; A. L. Rowse, *The England of Elizabeth* (L., 1950), Ch. XII; Keeler, *Long Parliament*, pp. 27–8; Joan Simon, *Education and Society in Tudor England* (Camb., 1966), pp. 355–60; Kenneth Charlton, *Education in Renaissance England* (L., 1965), Chs. V, VI.

[2] Curtis, *Oxford and Cambridge*, p. 64, citing Caspari, *Humanism and the Social Order*, pp. 136, 151.

[3] Curtis, *Oxford and Cambridge*, pp. 269, 127, 81; there is a different judgement in Charlton, *Education*, Ch. V.

One pertinent facet of this process Curtis does not explore. There are evident in the statistics in the table tendencies toward regional and group cohesion which are well known in the twentieth century in England, in the United States, and elsewhere. Doubtless at first because of relative propinquity, but thereafter also because of established ties, young men from Somerset and from Worcestershire were much more likely to attend Oxford than Cambridge, while those from Norfolk were enrolled even more uniformly in the colleges on the banks of the Cam. Indeed, in the working part of the Norfolk commission, there was at none of the five dates more than one old Oxonian. The preferences of the other three counties were more nearly in balance, though it was always Cambridge which was favoured, except in Kent in 1636. Then the plurality of Cantabrigian resident gentry was insufficient to outweigh the Oxonians among the nobles and officers of state, which included the Bishop of Oxford and Archbishop Laud, who was Chancellor of the university. It is impossible to specify just what was the influence which their common membership in one university may have had over colleagues on a county bench who were also more or less close neighbours, but all university men and women know that in more recent times such mutual loyalties may be important.

Although the statistics show—and the fact is generally known—that rather more future justices attended the inns of court than were resident in Oxford and Cambridge, this 'third university' awaits a study comparable to Curtis's book. However, hidden among many tedious, routine entries in the *Middle Temple Records* are ample traces of the lively, urban environment which must have excited young men whose earlier experience had been profoundly rural. Again a few sentences must suffice.[1]

None shall play at dice or cards within this House, neither in the Hall, nor in the chambers, at any time of year, on pain of expulsion. No outcries in the night shall be made, nor chambers broken open, as by the Lord of Candlemas night or such like disorder, on pain of being put out of commons.

[1] *Middle Temple Records*, i. 272, 379.

If the inns included in their membership a group of high-spirited young men, and if their instruction was in part moral and religious, they were primarily schools of law. This was their peak period as teaching institutions, and the regulations with regard to attendance at readings, moots, and bolts[1] were severe. Absence was punished by fines which were systematically levied. The fees for admission and the fines were significant sums. Men do not spend such money for nothing. There can be no question that most of the future J.P.s really studied law.

Much as Curtis's words about the universities best serve to describe conditions there, so does Sir William Holdsworth's account of the practices of the inns of court provide the aptest survey of legal education.[2]

The education, the discipline, the whole life of the Inns of Court was collegiate in the best sense of the word . . . We are not therefore surprised to find that they attracted students who had no thought of becoming professional lawyers . . . They gave first-rate technical training in the law; and, in this litigious age, such a training was absolutely necessary to those who had property to protect . . . 'The members lived to a great extent in community. In the Hall they met for breakfast, dinner, or supper, as well as for lectures or disputations. In the Chapel they assembled for common prayer and the Holy Communion. At Christmas and sometimes at other seasons they shared both in the labour and the expense of presenting masques and plays in the Inn or at Court.'

More tangible are the consequences of a pattern of admissions to the inns of court comparable to those of the universities. In the Somerset group of 1562, among the ten working members of the bench who had been enrolled in any inn, six had been members of the Middle Temple. In 1584 it was twelve among nineteen, and in 1636 eighteen among thirty-three. With sixteen in thirty-four in 1608, Norfolk men showed a parallel partiality for Lincoln's Inn, while the men from Kent tended to favour Gray's Inn, though in 1608 a nearly equal number had been at Lincoln's Inn. From Northamptonshire and from the North Riding, Gray's Inn

---

[1] Bolts or boltings were less formal than moots; both were practice arguings of points of law.

[2] Holdsworth, *History of English Law*, ii. 506–10; again a different point of view is found in Charlton, *Education*, Ch. VI.

drew the largest enrolment, while among Worcestershire men the Inner Temple was most popular. By 1636 the numbers and the proportions had both risen sharply. With seventy-five per cent—forty-seven among sixty-three—Kent was ahead. The smallest ratio was that of Worcestershire: forty-one per cent. For the six counties together not quite sixty-five per cent of the J.P.s were members of the inns of court.

In the records of the Middle Temple some of the process which produced these choices is manifest. In order to secure admission each man had not only to pay a fee but also to persuade a current member to bind himself as surety for the payment of the applicant's obligations. Usually chambers in the inns were shared. In the case of the Middle Temple, the names of the sureties and of the established occupants of the chambers were commonly a part of the record of admission. In a great many cases they indicated men from the same county, sometimes a brother or a cousin, possibly a father, but more usually merely a countryman, perhaps a neighbour, presumably a friend. It is apparent that there was at work a process inherent in human society, a quite natural reliance on friendship and kinship when young men leave home.

In the case of the Somerset men in the Middle Temple, the county's most distinguished lawyer during the time of Elizabeth, John Popham, clearly played a major role in the arrangements.[1]

9 Feb. [1596] Mr. George, second son of Thomas Malett, late of Enmore, Somerset, esq., deceased, specially, fine only 40s., at the instance of Sir John Popham, Chief Justice of England. Bound with Messrs. Richard and Thomas Warre.

4 Nov. [1600] Mr. Tristram, fourth son of Thomas Horner of Cloverd, Somerset, esq., specially, no fine at the instance of John Popham, knt. Chief Justice. Bound with Messrs James Clarke and Richard Warre.

22 Apr. [1594] Rich. Warre, John Horner, Thos. Hannam, and Thos. Warre to the chamber late Mr. Rosse's over the door or gate of the Middle Temple, gratis, at the instance of John Popham.

Except for Clarke and Rosse, who were professional associates of Popham, all the men mentioned in the foregoing

[1] *Middle Temple Records*, i. 342, 361, 408.

passages were in some fashion family connections of the Chief
Justice. He had one son, Francis, who was a member of the
Middle Temple and for many years a Somerset J.P. He also
had five daughters who married Sir John Mallett, Roger
Warre, Thomas Hannam, Thomas Horner, and Edward
Rogers. Hannam came to be a serjeant-at-law and a J.P. in
Dorset. Popham's other sons-in-law all came from families
of Somerset justices, and Mallett, Rogers, and Horner sat
on the county bench themselves.

A reader who is acquainted with the personnel of the
commissions of the peace or with the history of Somerset
will find familiar names on every page of the records of the
Middle Temple parliament. Nearly a third—52 among 166
—of the men who were Somerset J.P.s in the sixty years
after 1580 were connected with that society. Contiguous to
the entries about future Somerset justices are parallel traces
of their associates in other counties, just as the men themselves lived in adjacent rooms. Similarly in Lincoln's Inn
Humphrey Wyndham, a barrister who was a member of the
commission in Somerset in 1584 and 1608, shared chambers
—perhaps even a bed—with William Lambarde as late as
1580.[1] Shortly he married the widow of Lambarde's brother.
If the records of the other inns are not so full as those of the
Middle Temple, life within them must have been almost
identical. Clearly they were a locale in which friendships
must constantly have been formed.

The influence of the inns upon the lives of their members
is not tangible, but some gauge may be found in certain
attendant circumstances. During these decades the inns
grew in size, but the average membership of each inn was
rather more than 200, including perhaps 20 benchers or
readers, 50 (utter) barristers, and about 150 men whose
membership was of more recent date.[2] A standard period of
active association cannot be determined, nor would a figure
reached by statistical procedure be meaningful. Clearly most
newly admitted students did not take their privilege so

[1] Wyndham, *Family History*, pp. 108–9.
[2] The most informative accounts of the educational system of the inns of
court are in the prefaces to their published records: *Pension Book of Gray's Inn*, I.
ix–lii; *Lincoln's Inn Black Books*, I, i–xi; ibid. II, i–xli; *Middle Temple Records*, i,
1–49; Inderwick, *The Inner Temple*, pp. lxxviii–lxxxi.

seriously as to fit themselves for a call to the bar. Probably more than half the new members forfeited their chambers for inadequate participation within the seven or eight years which usually preceded the call to the bar of the men whose legal training was diligently pursued. Each inn was not unlike an Oxford or Cambridge college. Some of the education came from direct instruction, some was the consequence of mere residence in a society devoted to the pursuit of the law.

No man equalled Edward Coke. Many must have learned relatively little law. But membership in such a society surely left some impress on the minds of most young men, as it does today on students in universities all over the world. Though the residual knowledge of the law possessed by the members of the several county benches of 1636 may sometimes have been minimal, can it be doubted that residence for several months in each of three or five or ten years in a lively society of two hundred men was an experience which made its mark? Because this is an intangible matter, it is not the less significant. In 1640 almost all the men who administered English local government had resided for a time in the capital as a member of a legal college. They were personally acquainted with many of their counterparts not only in their home counties but also in all sections of the land. They did not always exhibit great sophistication, but they were men of a world larger than their native county.

More tangible than the effect of mere membership in an inn is the incidence of serious legal study. All through the eight decades after the accession of Elizabeth there were in the commission of each county several men who had been called to the bar. In 1562 Kent with four barristers among the dignitaries and seven in the working group led the other five counties. There were fewest in Worcestershire and the North Riding, two and one respectively in the resident or working portion. In the one case these men were the chief justice of Chester and a professional member of the Council of Wales (Richard Smyth), and, in the other, serjeant Mennell, a professional member of the Council of the North. In neither county was there a barrister who held no other office. Thereafter the numbers of barristers grew markedly. In

1636 Kent had eighteen among the sixty-three members of the working group, Somerset ten in fifty-one, Norfolk sixteen in fifty-two. For the six counties the total was sixty, nearly a quarter of the whole number. One aspect of the increased legal experience of the J.P.s is considered in the context of their official activity in the next chapter. Here it may be suggested that it is a part—the parallel rise in membership in the two universities and in Parliament are others —of the growing sophistication of a characteristic J.P.

# VII

## THE BURDEN OF THE COMMISSION

I F the justices of the peace were indeed 'the most influential class of men in England', they earned that eminence by their activity even more than by their identity. As a group they were wealthy, well educated, ambitious, in reasonable accord with national policy both religious and political, much more than the mere creatures of the royal administration; in brief, they were the leaders of their counties. Comprehensive as were the functions assigned by statute and by the terms of the commission, the J.P.s, in fact, filled a still wider part in English life. The commission of the peace set them apart and gave them the authority which was the foundation of their peculiar role in society. It was the central fact in their public life, but, the basis of local government in Tudor and Stuart England, its limits were yet too narrow. To the J.P.s there came from Westminster a stream of particular commissions: from the Privy Council, from the major officers of state, from the central courts. Varying between routine, almost trivial, instructions and weighty matters of state, these special assignments fell to the justices because of their role in society. Since such tasks technically did not pertain to the office, they were largely ignored by Lambarde and the authors of like manuals and seem to be underestimated also in more recent studies.[1]

How important such extra responsibilities might be is apparent in a letter written to Nathaniel Bacon in September 1576 when he was not quite thirty years old and had just been put in the commission. The writer was the Lord Keeper of the Great Seal.[2]

[1] e.g. Tanner, *Tudor Constitutional Documents*; Holdsworth, *History of English Law*; Rowse, *England of Elizabeth*; cf. G. E. Aylmer, 'Attempts at Administrative Reform', *English Historical Review*, lxii (1957), 231–3.

[2] Folger MSS. L. d. 140.

To my sonne Nathaniell Bacon at Cockthorpe near Stiffkey in Norfolk geve this.

Sonne I send you A letter from the lords of the Counsell of such effect as may appear unto you upon the perusing of it. This matter being wisely and discretely handled may breed you credit amongst my lords and the rest of the counsell, and so may it in the country also, by the trust that is committed to you. The best advise that I can give you is, first to send for my son Woodhouse [Henry Woodhouse who married Ann Bacon] and to apprehend as many of the offenders and to stay their ships and goods in them according to the tenor of the Counsell's letter, lest else if you should fall to examination before their apprehension it is possible they will start aside.

The second degree is to examine men of the best credit that you can get, whereby their offenses may be proved and the offenders also. You are particularly to examine to see what by their confessions may be understanded as how many prizes they have taken, where, when, and of whom, and to whom they have made sale. And by whom they have been victualled etc. as you shall thinke most meet. Albeit the principals will not confess all, yet perchance by their mariners and servants you shall find the rest.

After you understand the cause and the quantity and quality of the offences, then are you to take bonds for their appearance, of such before the counsell as by their letters you are appointed. And therein you are to give them such day as by that time your certification of your examinations and proceedings may be there also. . . . If you come not up, then shall it be well done, that besides your letter and certification to the counsell you send me a copy of both. I doubt that I shall not be at the court with the Counsell before the end of the progress, which I think will not take end till after Michaelmas. And therefore it were best you came yourself up, by me and with my letters to go to the Counsell. The charges that you shall sustain by this journey I will bear myself. Besides you shall do well to use the matter so as if any more pryces [prizes] be brought in by Hubberd or any other by Carewe's commission of such like that they may be stayed as the rest. Which cannot be done without care taken that they shall have no warning of this proceeding.

In your choice of justices to assist you, it shall be well done that you call those that be wise and willing also, whose hands you are to have to your examinations.

What my son Woodhouse will think that he is not joined with you in this letter I know not, but you by your discretion are to salve that as you may. Albeit I have given you such advices as has been before remembered, yet you are to do in all things as occasion shall serve.

And this with my hearty commendations to my daughter and God's blessing to your children. I bid you fare well from my house at Gorhambury this XXVIIIth of August 1576. Your father
N. Bacon

I send you all the letters written to me
from my L. Admiral because you should understand
all I know to be done in this cause.

The full circumstances of this case which involved elements of piracy are not clear. That they were out of the ordinary is evident from the concern which was shown by Sir Nicholas Bacon. Even if he may have felt a father's desire that a son meet a first major test with credit, in a trivial situation he would hardly have urged a trip so costly as to suggest the need for paternal subsidy. Nor would there have been a danger of the jealousy of a brother-in-law over an inconsequential assignment. Nathaniel Bacon may not have visited Westminster. In any event, nearly a month after the initial letter, the Lord Keeper wrote about the business again, and the Privy Council simultaneously sent to Sir Christopher Heydon, Sir William Butt, and Ralph Sheldon, as well as to the younger Bacon, a letter of further instructions, which in contrast to the first one is recorded in its register. The case was adjudicated in the Court of Admiralty, the vessel was impounded in the charge of Bacon and others, and members of the crew were convicted of a degree of piracy which led to their imprisonment. Later they secured a pardon, the cost of which they were able to meet only by the earnings of a fishing trip to Iceland after their special release under bond. Whatever the merit which Bacon may have won in this matter, he soon became a leading Norfolk justice.[1]

The case illustrates the operation of Tudor government admirably. The impetus came from the Council. The local agents were all members of the county bench, and their legal authority derived implicitly from the terms of the commission of the peace. Characteristic was a later instruction in the case which was addressed to Henry Woodhouse and Francis Wyndham—serjeant-at-law and Recorder of Norwich, soon to become judge of the Common Pleas—as well as to Butt and Bacon. All were J.P.s, while any two were empowered

[1] *A.P.C.*, *1575–7*, pp. 203, 256; ibid., *1577–8*, pp. 314–15; ibid., *1578–80*, p. 98.

to act. It was a flexible system which blended local initiative and a measure of central control. From their special status under the comprehensive terms of the commission of the peace the justices were expected to act spontaneously in many cases, but when appropriate they received orders which might be addressed to one, to two, to a few, or to the whole bench as circumstances might require.

Yet the flexibility entailed a dangerous latitude, as another letter in the Bacon papers indicates. In 1609 the Council concluded that,

although there be many in the Commission of the peace . . . of great integrity and discretion and of special desert for their diligence and care in their places of services, yet we find it so prejudicial to the success of all causes to leave them to the care of many wherein the rule seldom faileth which common experience hath made so certain that those duties which concern all men are neglected of every man, as we think it high time to prevent the growing evils which may ensue for lack of good distribution in causes that concern public services which are often carried so confusedly or executed so remissly as the vulgar sort of people will in time get a custom of disobedience. And therefore seeing the state is so composed as so many things as are here resolved by his Majesty or his council must take their effect afterwards from the care and good endeavours of the Justices of peace amongst whom (instead of due performance) many directions are posted over from one to another . . . we have thought good to move you . . . to select by mutual consent among yourselves some three or four or more . . . to whose peculiar care you may at the beginning of every year commend the execution and dispatch of such directions as you received . . .[1]

So multifarious were the functions of the justices of the peace, dealing as they were with such a combination of matters of national and local concern, of the particular and the general, that one may wonder if an executive committee could in fact have provided an adequately coherent plan for the commission. In any event the scheme seems to have been still-born; there is no evidence that the proposal was carried out in Norfolk or elsewhere. Instructions from the central authority continued to be addressed individually to diverse members of the local élite.

[1] H. W. Saunders (ed.), *The Official Papers of Sir Nathaniel Bacon of Stiffkey, Norfolk* (Camden Soc., 3rd Series, vol. xxvi, L., 1915), pp. 24–5.

Neither in the nature of the tasks imposed, nor in the identities of the men upon whom they were laid, was there a logical pattern such as might provide a basis for straight-forward analysis. Simple and satisfactory generalization is impossible. Even a perusal of both Lambarde's *Ephemeris* and the fullest collection of printed papers—those of Nathaniel Bacon—can hardly give an adequate impression of the labours of a J.P. A few illustrations of specific tasks assigned to certain justices which suggest the character of their function and the manner in which their duties were carried out will serve, however, as an introduction to more tangible evidence about the operation of the commission of the peace.

An example of an apparently routine commission was the chancery writ—the particular matter in dispute was trivial—whose execution in Taunton in 1610 led to some disorder. There followed a Star Chamber suit which evoked the auto-biographical sketch used in the brief *vita* of James Clarke in Chapter III. Almost all the men involved were J.P.s, either present or future. The chancery writ was addressed to Sir Nicholas Halswell, a leading member of the Somerset bench and to two barristers, both young men, who were soon to follow their fathers in the commission of the peace—William Francis and Richard Warre, a grandson of Chief Justice Popham. One litigant in the chancery suit, Clarke's son-in-law Robert Cuffe, had already begun the career as J.P. which lasted until 1639, while his opponent, Sir Henry Hawley, was the grandson and nephew of earlier justices and was himself later a member of the commission in Somerset. Thus a dispute about grist-mills on a river bank required the issue of a chancery writ which in turn dragged six members of the social group of the J.P.s into the toils of Star Chamber.[1]

Other cases which likewise involved members of the commissions of the peace show further variety in those extra tasks. Six months after the defeat of the Armada Sir Henry Cobham, William Lambarde, John Leveson, and William Sedley must surely have carried out willingly an instruction that they arrange lodging for men travelling to Greenwich to serve under Sir John Norris and Sir Francis

[1] P.R.O., St. Ch. 8/103/2; St. Ch. 8/163/26.

Drake.[1] In November 1613 Sir Nathaniel Bacon, Sir Henry Spelman, Sir Hamond Lestrange, and five less well-known Norfolk justices—Sir Ralph Hare, Sir Henry Bedingfield, Thomas Hewar, Thomas Oxborough, and Thomas Athowe —were directed by the Privy Council to set men at work repairing the dykes along the rivers Wisbech and Ouse and to meet the cost from voluntary local contributions.[2] In the next month five prominent Yorkshire justices—Sir William Constable, Sir William Eure, Sir Thomas Hoby, Sir Henry Griffith, and Sir William Alforth—were instructed to search out and to restore to the owners the pilfered goods of some shipwrecked Scots merchants.[3] Six months later in Kent Sir Richard Sondes and Sir Nicholas Gilborne were expected to prevent the export of ordnance—twenty-five 'pieces of bastard culverin'.[4]

Superficially more important and surely less frequent than the commissions just cited were those addressed to large numbers of justices. For example, an order for an inquiry concerning lands held by recusants in Kent in November 1627 was directed to the sheriff and twenty justices. Even larger was the group who dealt with the tangled affairs of Sandwich grammar school in 1633. The school had been established by a distinguished judge, Roger Manwood, and it was now contended that his heirs were withholding moneys properly belonging to the school. The issue was submitted to a commission headed by Archbishop Abbot and the Bishop of Rochester which totalled fifty-six, nearly fifty of whom were among the sixty-odd members of the working group of Kent J.P.s of that day.[5] In effect this was an extra task laid on the commission of the peace.

Sometimes Council orders were addressed to the whole commissions of several counties. Twice in the autumn of 1614 the justices of Surrey, Kent, Essex, Middlesex, and London received instructions to undertake a survey of housing, both buildings newly constructed since the accession of James I and those divided into more numerous units in the

---

[1] *A.P.C.*, *1588–9*, pp. 11–12.  [2] Ibid., *1613–4*, pp. 265–7.
[3] Ibid., pp. 298–9.  [4] Ibid., p. 487.
[5] William Boys, *Collections for a History of Sandwich in Kent* (Canterbury, 1792), p. 216.

same period.[1] It was the justices of all three Yorkshire Ridings who were expected to provide relief for Hull in 1637 because of the plague. The J.P.s were jointly men of all work.[2] Perhaps half the pages of the *Acts of the Privy Council* record instructions sent to them, although commonly the status of the recipients is not indicated.

Sometimes their tasks may have seemed unworthy; sometimes they were very grim. An example of the first sort is the instruction issued during the height of the campaign for the forced loan in July 1627 to the J.P.s of Middlesex, Huntingdonshire, Bedfordshire, and Northamptonshire. They were required to arrange lodgings at Barnet, St. Albans, Dunstable, Bedford, and Wellingborough for the Queen while she travelled for her health. 'And whereas considering the immoderate heat and the dustiness of those high wayes, being very greate roads, her Majesty cannot without much annoyance and hazard to her health travaile those wayes, it is therefore thought fit that the most commodious wayes and passages that may be found should be made through the fields from place to place.'[3] A very special and grim duty was that performed by at least four—and probably many more—members of the Northamptonshire bench when they witnessed the execution of Mary Stuart.[4]

It would be futile to cite further, inevitably capricious, examples of the extremely diverse labours of the justices of the peace. They were the key figures in a flexible administrative machine and they carried out both special and general commissions of which the commission of the peace was merely the most regular and the most important. Any classification is contrived, as the efforts of students from Lambarde onwards indicate. His was a lawyer's perspective, though he did deal with the sundry administrative responsibilities of the commission in which there was a potential breach of the peace. The four books of his manual for J.P.s —I, a general survey of the office of justice of the peace; II, the cases which a single justice may handle; III, cases

---

[1] *A.P.C., 1613–4*, pp. 589–91, 622.
[2] *Cal. S.P. Dom., Chas. I, 1637–8*, p. 225.
[3] *A.P.C., 1627–8*, pp. 407–8.
[4] *Cal. S.P. Scotland*, ii. p. 272; cf. Garrett Mattingly, *The Armada* (Boston, 1959), Ch. I.

appropriate to two or more justices—culminated by IV, Quarter Sessions.[1] If the essence of the social function which the J.P.s fulfilled is its amorphous nature, the central role of quarter sessions is none the less clear. And for quarter sessions at least there are tangible data.

There the justices certified—filed the formal record of— many of the acts which they had performed either singly or in concert with one or two fellows. There those acts might be confirmed or disallowed. There might be laid a rate which would finance one of the responsibilities of local government. There the more weighty criminal actions were adjudicated. At the sessions much of the business of the county was delegated to selected members of the bench for action. Except for the assizes, when the judges were present also, the quarter sessions were the most formal, the most authoritative, and the most important element in the operation of the commission of the peace.

The varied physical and social conditions of the various counties are the probable explanation of the differences which had developed in the organization of the quarter sessions.[2] In Somerset there was a regular cycle—Epiphany sessions at Wells, Easter sessions at Ilchester, Midsummer at Taunton, and Michaelmas at Bridgwater. Any departure from this pattern was very unusual. In Kent there was the division of the county into the East and West parts, with the sessions alternating between Maidstone and Canterbury. So distinct was this pattern that during the four and a half years between January 1601 and July 1604 the only deviation was the sessions of Michaelmas 1602 held in Canterbury with thirteen present, while a meeting of five J.P.s occurred simultaneously in Maidstone. Likewise there were only two

---

[1] William Lambarde, *Eirenarcha* (L., 1588); cf. G. R. Elton, *The Tudor Constitution* (Cambridge, 1960), pp. 451–6, and Barnes, *Somerset*, Ch. III.

[2] The discussion in this and the next few paragraphs is based upon these sources, the computations being my own: Kent Archives Office, Quarter Sessions Records, i–iv; *Quarter Sessions Records of the County of Somerset*, vol. i (ed. by E. H. Bates, vol. xxiii of Somerset Record Society, 1907), *passim*; ibid., vol. ii (ed. by E. H. Bates-Harbin, vol. xxiv of Somerset Record Society, 1908), *passim*; *Worcester County Records: Calendar of the Quarter Sessions Papers*, ed. by J. W. Willis-Bund (2 vols., Worcester, 1899–1900), *passim*; The North Riding Record Society, *Quarter Sessions Records*, ed. by J. C. Atkinson, i–iv (L., 1884–6), *passim*; *Cal. S.P. Dom. Jas. I, 1611–18*, p. 218.

men who attended any sessions in the other part of the county: Nicholas Gilborne, who lived at Charing midway between Canterbury and Maidstone, was once present at Maidstone in April 1600, and Samuel Boys, who lived at Hawkhurst in the extreme south of the county, was present in January 1602 at Canterbury. In the North Riding, except for the Easter sessions at Thirsk, there were commonly two, and occasionally more, segments of the sessions in different parts of the Riding at different times. Technically the later meetings were adjourned sessions, but except for one or two stalwarts the J.P.s present were not the same men. In Northamptonshire most sessions met at Northampton, but some were held at Kettering.

The records of the sessions—the rosters of those present and the file of recognizances or other documents deposited with the clerk of the peace—provide concrete evidence of the weight which the duties of a J.P. constituted for individual justices. In the matter of attendance the records of several of the counties here considered—and there can be no question that in this regard these counties were representative—show that regularity was not judged to be essential by most justices, even if those meetings were the keystone of the whole structure.

The sessions rolls for Kent survive for the period from January 1601 to July 1604. For Somerset they begin in January 1614 and except for a few defects they are continuous from that point. The records for the North Riding commence in April 1605 and again save for slight lapses are thereafter continuous. For Worcestershire there have survived from this period no records of sessions as such, but recognizances and other papers which were certified at sessions do exist, and in this regard the printed records of Worcestershire are more complete than those of any of the other five counties. Few official records for the period before the Civil War have been available for Norfolk or Northamptonshire. These several series demonstrate the functioning of the sessions and shed much light on the whole activity of J.P.s.

Beside superficial uniformity there was important diversity. Over the whole period for which records survive there seems to have been a sessions of some sort in each county at each of the four seasons specified by statute: Epiphany, Easter, Midsummer, and Michaelmas. But attendance varied greatly both in regard to numbers and to quality. In Kent the high figure was twenty-five from a 'working' membership of about sixty in July 1602, and the low figure that of the following year—three. The average was 12·5. In Somerset the high figure was twenty-four for the sessions at Wells in 1620, when the total number of working J.P.s was about fifty-five. The low number was the seven who were present at Ilchester in 1635. For the whole series of sessions from 1614 to 1638, save for a few gaps, the average was about 13·5. For the North Riding the data are not fully comparable because of the multiple meetings which constituted the Epiphany, Midsummer, and Michaelmas sessions. Yet the numbers were somewhat less than in Kent or Somerset. Not only was the size of the commission smaller; distances were great and roads were rough. In 1609 fifteen justices assembled at Thirsk; seventeen were present in 1637. The working part of the bench, including the professional members of the Council of the North, who very seldom attended, numbered just under forty. Thus in each of these counties what may be regarded as standard attendance was approximately a quarter of the working commission.

No less revealing than statistics of maximum, minimum, and average attendance are those of frequency of individuals. In the series of fifteen Kentish sessions there were sixty-four different justices who attended at least one sessions.[1] This is almost the number of working J.P.s at the time. However, the roster of the commission was frequently altered, and there were twenty working justices who attended no sessions during these years; the changes in the membership of the commission balanced the persistent absences. It was noted earlier that Lambarde attended almost all the Maidstone sessions during the years of his *Ephemeris*. His was an active role, since he commonly gave the charge to the jury which initiated the major work of the meeting. This task he continued to fulfil until the year of his death (1601), for which there survives a draft text endorsed 'not used'.[2] There were

---

[1] Kent Archives Office, Quarter Sessions Records, i–iv; cf. *infra*, Appendix A.
[2] Read, *William Lambarde*, pp. 56, 145–9.

other conscientious justices. Matthew Hadd missed only one of the eleven Canterbury sessions, while Sir John Boys, Sir Michael Sondes, Peter Manwood, and Henry Finch each missed two. An even better record was set at Maidstone by Sir Thomas Fludd, who was present at all nine meetings, while Sir John Leveson and Samuel Boys were absent only once. Few meetings were missed by Nicholas Gilborne, Lawrence Washington, or Sir Thomas Wilford. Probably more significant is the fact that among these eleven regulars Sir John Boys, Matthew Hadd, Henry Finch, and Lawrence Washington were four trained lawyers. In the group of sixty-four there were ten barristers; their diligence was distinctly superior to that of their less learned brethren. There was at least one barrister at each of the sessions, and the average number was 2·6. Thus Sir John Boys, Matthew Hadd, Henry Finch, and Moyle Finch were commonly present at Canterbury, while William Lambarde, William Sedley, Lawrence Washington, and Zachary Scott were usually in attendance at Maidstone to lend to the bench their by no means insignificant knowledge of the law. If the Kent commission was composed of a majority of amateurs, it had a strong leavening of experts in its roster.

The more ample records of Somerset make possible an analysis of the longer period from 1614 to 1638.[1] Much as Somerset resembled Kent in the total number of men who attended quarter sessions, so was there a likeness in the fact that a rather small group of stalwarts, particularly a few barristers, accepted responsibility for the duties which were carried on there. Sir Edward Hext and Robert Cuffe, who were already in the commission in 1608, together with Thomas Southworth, William Bull, and John Harington provided for the sessions a backbone which must have contributed greatly to its effective operation. Hext, who died early in 1624, attended all twelve of the meetings of 1614, 1615, and 1616. Between 1617 and 1622 he was present three times in each year, except perhaps 1620, when a defective record credits him with only two sessions. Cuffe, who had been a J.P. as early as 1604 and lived until 1639, was present at forty-four sessions in the twenty-four years from

[1] *Quarter Sessions Records of Somerset,* i, ii, *passim*; cf. *infra*, Appendix D.

1614 to 1638, an average of nearly two per year. Thomas Southworth, Recorder of Wells, who, because he was added to the commission after 1608 and died before 1626, did not appear in the roster of either year, had an equally impressive performance. In the forty-five meetings between January 1614 and January 1625, he was absent from only seven, and in the years between 1618 and 1621 he was present at thirteen consecutive sessions. William Bull's name is found in the records of twenty-four of the forty sessions of the years from 1629 to 1638. John Harington attended no fewer than thirty-eight of the forty-eight sittings between January 1627 and October 1638, a proud performance even for the chairman of sessions.

Other barristers were far less regular. Thus Humphrey Wyndham, a close associate of Lambarde, who probably practised law in London, was present only once after the records begin—Midsummer 1614—although he lived until 1622. Rice Davies, who joined the commission in 1621 and may in some sense have taken Wyndham's place, attended all four meetings in 1622 and thereafter once or twice a year until 1633, after which he was not present although he lived until 1649. These records are samples of varied performances; to detail more cases would add little to an understanding of the operation of the commission.

Very significant, however, must be the fact that almost always there were several barristers present at quarter sessions. At no meeting between January 1614 and July 1620 were there fewer than three barristers on the Somerset bench, and there were four occasions on which six were in attendance. At a characteristic sitting a quarter of the justices consisted of men who had been called to the bar, while the ratio of one to three sometimes occurred and twice there were four of them among ten J.P.s. After 1620 the Ilchester sessions commonly counted only two barristers, and at Wells in January 1627 a single trained lawyer was present. Eight years later, also at Wells, there occurred the only sessions without any barrister, though the Bishop of Bath and Wells and John Coventry, *Custos Rotulorum* and son of the Lord Keeper of the Great Seal, may have provided compensatory distinction if less legal skill.

There is no means of knowing the influence which these lawyers exercised over the proceedings, but it is only reasonable to suppose that the legal knowledge which they must have possessed decidedly raised the level at which the court operated. In Norfolk, and in Kent at most times, the proportion of barristers in the commission was as high as in Somerset. There, and perhaps also in Northamptonshire, their legal competence presumably had like importance. In Worcestershire and the North Riding the councillors in the commission gave it a notably different complexion.

The attendance of the non-barrister members of the Somerset commission varied greatly. Sir Nicholas Halswell, whose father had long been a J.P., came regularly until 1622. He was removed from the commission in 1625 when he was outlawed for financial delinquency. John Symes, present at forty-four sessions between 1614 and 1638, showed an over-all devotion nearly identical to Cuffe's. Sir Francis Popham was certainly a major figure in the life of the county, but he was present at quarter sessions on only six occasions in these same years. Sir John Wyndham, who lived on to 1645, attended about once a year until 1621 and then not at all. George Luttrell of Dunster, who died in 1629, usually came to the Bridgwater sessions until 1621; his son, Thomas, was equally regular between 1633 and 1638 but at Taunton. Edward Lancaster was present at seventeen consecutive meetings between April 1621 and April 1626. In contrast Sir George Speke was a member of the commission from as early as 1596 until his death in 1637, but he was never present after the records began in 1614. There is also no evidence of the presence of Sir Edward Gorges, Samuel Norton, or Humphrey Sydenham, although they were in the commission for a considerable period from the date of the earliest surviving roll. If among the non-barrister J.P.s the more assiduous ones were usually the relatively recent arrivals in their social group, the non-lawyer element in the commission exhibited wide divergence with regard to attendance at quarter sessions.

Several special conditions in the North Riding make an exact comparison with Kent and Somerset impractical: the longer run of surviving records, the extra element in its commission of the members of the Council of the North, and the fact that except for the Easter sessions at Thirsk there were usually held what amounted to parallel sessions for different sections of that rugged area. Yet, like all others, its commission was one in which there was both considerable stability of personnel and frequent minor change.[1] It, too, had a few justices who after several years of particularly conscientious service ceased to attend sessions although they remained members of the commission. It seems best to assay the evidence for the North Riding by describing the situation at the moments, broadly understood, of three *libri* which have herein been used for analysis.

In the years 1607, 1608, and 1609 there was a total of twenty-one sessions. The attendance figures for the Easter sessions at Thirsk, commonly the largest of the year, probably because there were then no 'adjourned' meetings, were thirteen in 1607, seven in 1608, and (as has been shown) fifteen in 1609. The smallest group was that which met at Richmond in January 1607—technically an adjourned sitting—when only three justices were present, while in July and October 1607 and in January 1608 there were sessions with only four present. This constituted a considerable range in attendance, but seven or eight from a working group of forty-eight would be not unrepresentative. This is a somewhat smaller proportion than in the other counties.

Among the working members of the bench thirty-six justices—three-quarters of the whole body—were present at least once. Twenty-two attended two or three times, while several showed marked diligence. Of the four lawyers who were not members of the Council of the North, one (Robert Hungate) was present on ten occasions, while the others were in attendance at seven, six, and four sessions.[2] The records of the non-lawyers were: one man, eleven; three, ten; two, nine; four, eight. Sir Henry Bellasis (8) and Sir Conyers Darcy (8) were members of families of much note, but Sir Richard Vaughan (11), Thomas Norcliffe (10), and Richard Darley (9) were parvenus. Sir Timothy Whittingham (10) was the son of an eminent Dean of Durham. It was a mixed group.

[1] North Riding Records Soc., *Quarter Sessions Records*, i–iv, *passim*; cf. *infra*, Appendix F.    [2] Robert Briggs, Sir Henry Jenkins, and Walter Bethell in order.

At all the primary sessions and at most of the adjourned sessions there was at least one barrister present, while there were five barristers at Thirsk in April 1609 and four on three other occasions. There were only a few cases in which any man attended both the main and the adjourned meeting, but Thomas Davile (9) showed particular devotion by his presence at both Malton and Richmond in October 1608 and at Thirsk and Richmond in July 1609.[1] Among the members of the Council of the North practice varied, with the Yorkshire notables, Sir Henry Bellasis (8), Sir Francis Boynton (2), Sir Thomas Lascells (2), and Sir William Bamburgh (6), not scorning quarter sessions, although none of the titled members was ever present in these years. Among the professional councillors four were consistently absent,[2] but Sir Cuthbert Pepper and Sir John Gibson each graced two meetings.

In the period between January 1625 and July 1627 (when the record becomes defective) there was a similar situation with regard to the series of seventeen meetings. The maximum attendance was the fifteen at Helmsley in July 1625— two more than at Thirsk the previous April—and the smallest the three who were present at the adjourned sessions at Richmond in January 1626. Among a working bench of only thirty-four justices, twenty-seven different men were present for at least one sessions. The highest figure was the ten of Roger Gregory, though Roger Wyvell had nine, while Sir Thomas Bellasis (created Baron Fauconberg in 1627) and Matthew Jobson had seven each. Sir Richard Darley and the barrister Sir Thomas Norcliffe were both present at six sessions. Outstanding was the record set in 1625 by a new member of the bench, Thomas Best of Middleton Querow, who was present at six sessions, both the initial and the adjourned meetings in January, July, and October. Son of a London scrivener, though apparently of a Yorkshire background, he was not listed in the *liber pacis* of 1626, but was restored to the commission and is to be found in the roster of 1636.

---

[1] In addition to those named in the text: John Gibson jr. (10), Charles Layton (8), Adam Midlam (8).

[2] Sir Charles Hales, Sir John Bennett, Sir Richard Williamson, Sir John Ferne.

Among the members of the Council of the North, Sir David Foulis (a Scots favourite who was shortly to fall into great disfavour), Sir Thomas Fairfax, Sir John Gibson, and John Wilson, Dean of Ripon, were present at least once, but at this time most of the Councillors, including even the lawyers, were consistently absent.[1] Among the non-councillors there were six justices who were present at no sessions.[2] At this period general attendance fell low and there were a few sessions with no barristers present.

For the years 1636 to 1639 the records show twenty-four sessions. There were thirty-nine members of the working commission, of whom only twenty-two attended any sessions. The largest attendance was seventeen—at Thirsk in 1637. Among the seventeen who were consistently absent nine were members of the Council of the North, two being Yorkshire magnates, Sir Edward Osborne and Sir Thomas Hoby, rather than professional members. Christopher Wandesford likewise came from a distinguished county family and was Wentworth's deputy in Ireland, a responsibility which explains his absence from sessions in the North Riding. The two members of the Council who did attend sessions were Sir John Hotham—six meetings—and Sir John Gibson— two. Among the twenty-two men whose presence is recorded for at least one sessions, twelve attended six or more times. Some belonged along with Hotham to the established élite of Yorkshire: Henry Bellasis (heir apparent of Lord Fauconberg) (6), Sir Hugh Cholmeley (7), Sir Thomas Gower (6), John Dodsworth (11), and Roger Wyvell (7). George Metcalfe (12) and William Caley (8) were relative parvenus. John Legard of Ganton (6), whose name was not in the *liber pacis* of 1636, was probably the son of a man who had figured in the fracas at the quarter sessions in the East Riding in 1616.[3] Matthew Hutton was the son of the distinguished

---

[1] Lawyers: Sir Henry Tankard, Sir Thomas Tildesley, Sir John Lowther, Sir Thomas Ellis, Sir William Ellis. Sir William Ellis, however, delivered the charge to the jury at an East Riding sessions in 1616. St. Ch. 8/175/4; cf. *supra*, p. 40.

Others: Sir Thomas Wentworth, Sir Marmaduke Wyvell, Sir Richard Cholmeley, Sir Arthur Ingram. It was during a West Riding sessions in 1626 (cf. *supra*, p. 75). that Wentworth received the order which removed him from the bench.

[2] Sir Thomas Dawnay, Sir Timothy Whittingham, Sir William Sheffield, William Mallory, Henry Griffin, Thomas Gilby.

[3] Cf. *supra*, p. 40.

judge, Sir Richard, who was among the dignitaries in the commission. Two lawyers, Thomas Heblethwayte and John Wastell, were both present thirteen times. Aside from the law members of the Council of the North, Robert Barwicke, present at only two sessions, was the sole other barrister in this commission. Heblethwayte and Wastell must have concerted a plan of their attendance at quarter sessions; four times only did both appear at a meeting and six times only were both absent. The lack of any barrister on the bench at some sessions is not surprising in view of the reduction in the number of lawyers in the group who were not of the Council of the North and the failure of any of the legal members of that council to attend the sessions.

In sum, among these three counties there were both similarities and differences. A large majority of the justices attended quarter sessions at least occasionally, though an important minority were not present for a good many years. There was a group of some ten or a dozen men who carried the burden of the office. Some of these stalwarts were parvenus; some were the descendants of generations of gentry. There were trained lawyers and men with little or no legal education. The lawyers were significantly more numerous in Kent and in Somerset than in the North Riding; in all three counties the lawyers were decidedly more diligent in their participation in quarter sessions. It seems reasonable to infer from the records that there was some at least informal concert to ensure if possible the presence of one or two men who had been called to the bar.

In addition to their attendance at quarter sessions the best index of the activity of J.P.s is the record of the acts which they took outside. Official records are the file of recognizances which they were expected to 'certify' at the assizes or the quarter sessions. Here the record for Worcestershire is unique among the six counties at hand.[1] Just as attendance at sessions was not at all uniform, so was there variation in the occasions when individual justices took action. In the dozen last years of the reign of Elizabeth—1591 to 1603—the largest number of recognizances and orders filed with the clerk of the peace by any one justice was

[1] Willis-Bund, *Worcester Quarter Sessions Papers*, II, xx–xxi, xxviii–xxix.

twenty, a record shared by William Lygon (knighted in 1603) and Gervase Babington, Bishop of Worcester. Edmund Colles, Francis Dingley, William Savage, and Edmund Harwell followed with nineteen, eighteen, seventeen, and sixteen respectively. Six J.P.s signed between nine and five papers and the rest of the commission fewer. Surely the surviving files are not complete.

The larger files for the reigns of James I and Charles I still do not suggest a very burdensome task for most J.P.s. In the former period Dingley had the highest total, 136, for the years between 1609 and 1625. He was followed by Sir John Bucke with 103 for the same years. The next figure was the 90 of Sir Richard Grevis, whose first surviving paper is dated 1607; but Edward Cookes certified 23 in a single year, 1625. For Dingley, Bucke, and Grevis the average numbers per year were approximately nine, eight, and seven. Walter Jones, who was encountered in Chapter III, signed twenty-nine between 1604 and 1625, an average of little more than one per year. In the time of Charles I much the same condition obtained. Sir John Bucke filed 327 of the total of 1,499 for the county during the whole reign. Dr. John Charlett, canon of Worcester, was next with 113 and Edward Cookes followed with 110. The yearly averages were 27 for Bucke, 8 for Charlett, and 10 for Cookes; the number of years of their service was not uniform.

Other data are found in Lambarde's *Ephemeris* and in a similar diary kept intermittently between 1608 and 1622 by Bostock Fuller of Tandridge Court, Surrey.[1] Fuller's activity appears to have been erratic—there are long lapses, which may indicate that he simply did not keep the diary, and during other months there were only one or two entries—but his largest numbers were the thirteen in October 1615 and the twelve in May 1608. 1615 was the year of most consistent work; for it the diary had an average of some three entries a month. As it was recorded in his *Ephemeris*, Lambarde's work as a justice required his attention with much the same frequency. Although there was considerable variation from month to month, the averages year by year ran at

---

[1] Granville Leveson-Gower, 'Note Book of a Surrey Justice', *Surrey Archaeological Collections*, ix (1888), 161–232.

the rate of two or three episodes a month, with the largest figure being that for 1585, when there were thirty-six recorded actions, eight being in March.[1] Further data about an active J.P. may be found in the papers of Sir Nathaniel Bacon. Since they are arranged in print in topical form, the frequency with which Bacon carried out any one of the multifarious tasks of a county magistrate is not immediately apparent, but the ratio between the total numbers of papers and the years of service is compatible with the evidence derived from the archives of Worcestershire and from the diaries of Lambarde and Fuller.

These several sources appear to be complementary. There can be no doubt that William Lambarde and Sir Nathaniel Bacon were unusually conscientious justices of the peace. Lambarde's *Ephemeris* was clearly kept as an aid in the performance of his official duties. Therein he entered all the instances—and a good deal else—in which he took an action which must be certified at quarter sessions. The largest total was eight in a single month. The testimony of Bostock Fuller's diary and the file of the official papers of Nathaniel Bacon are consistent with this level of activity. Even the heaviest annual file of the Worcestershire justices—the twenty-three of Edward Cookes in 1625—is less. If it is likely that some of Worcestershire papers may not ever have been filed or have subsequently been lost, it is unlikely that any J.P. much exceeded the level of work of this sort which Lambarde recorded in March 1585.

This reckoning makes no allowance for the undoubted burden of other sorts of duty, such as the administration of the Poor Law and the frequent special commissions, with regard to which there is little pertinent evidence beyond the Bacon papers. Any estimate of the frequency with which a representative justice might be given an onerous extra task can be only a guess. Probably Barnes is right that under Charles I the extra tasks imposed by the Book of Orders to implement the Poor Law and the collection of such unwonted taxes as ship money rendered the work of J.P.s so heavy that for the first time since the accession of Elizabeth, many members of the gentry were reluctant to bear their

---

[1] Read, *William Lambarde*, pp. 36–41.

sovereign's commission.[1] They were unpaid, in a sense amateur, basically volunteer, certainly not professional, civil servants. Yet, except for the meetings of quarter sessions which often lasted for three days, there cannot have been many weeks in which even a diligent J.P. devoted to his labours more than one day.

Such a level of activity is sufficient to explain Lambarde's lament about the stacks of statutes piled on the J.P.s and the other indications of arduous duty, but clearly it did not deter most of the recognized leaders of the county. Nor was the time spent in official labours the only burden which the office entailed. No less real because now incalculable must have been such matters as the cost of clerical help, the increased chance of incurring the hostility of neighbours, the danger, the expense, and the discomfort of travel, the ever present possibility of a summons to the Privy Council board. If the load was not light, the intangible rewards must have been commensurate. Honour and prestige, influence and power, the opportunity and the recognition of service are compensation in most societies and for most men—not least for the gentry of Tudor and Stuart England—and may elicit devoted performance. Doubtless the motives and the behaviour of many justices were far from exemplary. Star Chamber cases leave no doubt that many J.P.s were self-seeking, even corrupt, individuals. Yet there is also adequate evidence that the system functioned effectively. Manifestly pleasant festivities attended the quarter sessions and, presumably, often the petty sittings which were held by as few as two men. These must have provided as great satisfactions as do the conventions and even the committees attended by men of all callings in the society of the twentieth century. The records of the barrister and other leading members of several commissions imply that in some degree their attendance was not unarranged. Many of the justices took their duties very seriously. Jointly they gave England what must have been the cheapest—and perhaps for its day the best—local government in the world.

# VIII

## THE HISTORICAL STATURE OF
## THE J.P.s

RULERS of the countryside in Tudor and Stuart England, the justices of the peace were a remarkable group
of men. Their signal achievement is evident though
not readily defined. Like their analogues on the Continent,
they carried out sundry tasks implicit in post-feudal society.
Procedures were diverse and the merest hint of comparison
is suggestive.

Neither the *intendants* whom Richelieu instituted in
France, nor the barons who misgoverned the Papal States
bore much resemblance to the English J.P.s. Social origins,
educational experience, personal wealth, political authority,
all were different. With amateur officials neither the abso-
lutist regime of Louis XIV nor the nepotistic theocracy of
baroque Italy could have functioned. The J.P.s were little
like the *hidalgos* of Habsburg Spain; still less do they suggest
the petty nobility of Germany. The authority of a legislative
assembly increased in the seventeenth century only in England, and the close association between local administration
and national parliament was without parallel. It was their
peculiar combination of prominent but private status with
major public function which gave the J.P.s their cardinal role.

A just assessment of this dual estate has been the basic
purpose of the present study. Implicit or explicit through all
its pages, both text and appendices, two features stand out:
the formulation of a fit standard to gauge this large body of
men, and the judgements which then become possible. The
yardstick is essential; only with its use, to be specific, could
the data about the complexion of the commissions of the
peace and the education of J.P.s have been assembled. It
should prove helpful for cognate studies of other counties or
in detailed investigations in the same six shires. Doubts with
regard to the fortunes of the gentry might yet be stilled. Here

findings have been made about the recruitment and tenure of J.P.s, the relation of religious and of political problems to the staffing of the commissions of the peace, and the fashion in which the multiform duties were carried out.

The commissions of 1562 indicate the situation at the beginning of the reign of Elizabeth; the simultaneous commissions of all counties are readily available in the *Calendar of the Patent Rolls*. The effect of the new regime is evident. Data from six counties show that in local administration as in other concerns—for example, the formulation of a national religious policy—Elizabeth and her immediate advisers moved with caution. There was no wholesale purging of the commissions of the peace. The new dispensation represented a notable change, but there was no abrupt overturn.

The complexion of the county benches had been significantly altered by the middle of the reign. Lambarde's *Ephemeris* complements the roster of Kent in 1584 to demonstrate much more fully than could either document by itself the nature and the operation of a particularly instructive commission. An efficacious and sophisticated political and social institution is disclosed. Men whose experience, wealth, and reputation rendered them competent to manage their rural communities had the authority and the will to fulfil their responsibility. By implication that was also the situation elsewhere, and the data with regard to other counties—the eminence of Northamptonshire J.P.s, the number of lawyers in Norfolk, the dual roles of the members of the Councils of Wales and the North—infer that Kent, though much affected by its proximity to London, was not truly exceptional.

Again in 1608 an independent document—the list of assessments of the men who formed the working part of the bench—lends an increased meaning to the bare rosters of the commissions. Evidence with regard to wealth is available for a large but not unmanageable group of gentry distinguished by the processes of their own society. The Ellesmere survey in Appendix G provides, moreover, rosters of the commissions of all counties—much as does the *Calendar of the Patent Rolls* in 1562. Comparisons may easily be made at a point nearly midway between the accession of Elizabeth I and the beginning of the civil wars. The working groups at that moment seem to have been larger and more varied than at other times.

And in 1608 the altered atmosphere of the Stuart period is manifest. There had been a striking proliferation of formal dignities. The smaller numbers of lawyers in the commissions of Yorkshire and of the counties in the marches of Wales illustrate the ominous decline in the technical competence of Stuart administration.

The penetration by members of the Anglican clergy into secular aspects of English life is shown clearly in the commissions of 1626. The special conditions of Northamptonshire in that year happen also to provide persuasive evidence that the J.P.s were an élite whose membership was in large degree the consequence of forces in society which, not capable of nice definition, were so much a part of the life of the community that their effect was self-generating. An individual situation induced a great but a brief inflation of the bench. Charles I and his Council had in fact a narrowly restricted initiative with regard to the personnel upon whom all local government depended.

The rosters of the last surviving *liber pacis* before 1640 prove the stability of the commissions and show the independence of the country gentry. While the Council threatened to dismiss both J.P.s and other officers who did not willingly pay ship money, they did not resort to such discipline. Lawyers were again abundant. In the gathering crisis these were phenomena of major import.

The notion is hardly novel that the English civil wars, with their background in the preceding reigns, were the birth-labour of modern political institutions and democratic principles. Yet, during the past quarter-century varied studies of the period after the accession of Elizabeth I, some of deep penetration, have revealed a temper, complexity, and meaning which escaped earlier students. This social achievement was the work of a not very large group of men. As members of the central—royal—administration, political, military, and ecclesiastical, there can have been at any moment no more than one hundred ranking officials who exercised policy-making responsibility. The major 'intellectuals'—talented poets, playwrights, musicians, artists, prominent clergy, inspired dons, scientists, cartographers, historians—were hardly more numerous. Greater but still not very large was the body of leading merchants and innovating artisans. One hundred men, more or less, were gathered together in the upper chamber when Parliament was in session, and some 450 in the House of Commons. If to these categories there be added both certain leading lawyers and those justices who belonged to none of these categories, the full tale has been told of the men who gave English society its only conscious direction. The sum is not large; perhaps half those men were J.P.s.

That the justices were indeed leaders of English society in a broad sense is shown by the heterogeneous accomplishments which won notice in the *Dictionary of National Biography* for many. Samuel Norton of Somerset was an alchemist. His colleague Thomas Hughes was primarily a lawyer, but such fame as he has rests on his drama *The Misfortunes of Arthur*. The courtier Francis Crane became the director in the seventeenth century of a tapestry works which rivalled the earlier Sheldon enterprise. Sir Thomas Smyth and Sir Ferdinando Gorges were major figures in the development of the American colonies. John Hawkins and Francis Drake are mentioned in these pages. Stephen Proctor (not in *DNB*) made himself so unpopular in London and in Yorkshire for his unscrupulous activity that he attracted attention in the House of Commons. Sir Arthur Ingram was both more important and more scrupulous, but he, too, left a not wholly savoury reputation. Leading figures in both the Cobham Plot and the Gunpowder Plot have appeared appropriately. Wyatt's rebellion, the rising of the northern earls, and the execution of Mary Stuart are each mentioned. Since the convention of the day made them at least nominal justices in several counties, particularly in Kent, all the principal figures in public life are in the rosters of justices. The father of John Pym and the uncle of John Hampden were J.P.s. The major lawyers have been encountered: Coke, Popham, Hobart, every custodian of the Great Seal after 1558 except Francis Bacon. Traces of the Gresham family are found in four counties—all except Worcestershire and Northamptonshire. The author of *Patriarcha* entered quietly as a member of the Kent commission. Sir Henry Spelman, famous for his historical writing, was a diligent member of the Norfolk bench for many years. Even literature of the first water is represented by John Donne, a J.P. in Kent in 1621. Except that he lived in the borough of Stratford, Shakespeare might almost have been made a J.P. after he returned to Warwickshire. Trevelyan's dictum must be inverted. The influential men in England were J.P.s.

Much the largest category of working justices—rather more than three-fifths—were county gentry. They owned many broad acres, much inherited, some purchased. Not a small amount was former monastic holdings; an important portion of these fortunes came from the earnings of commerce. In Kent many J.P.s were the heirs of City men. On the Norfolk bench there sat the beneficiaries of fortunes made in the commerce and industry of Norwich, King's Lynn, and Great Yarmouth. In Somerset also there were J.P.s whose wealth had been won in the woollen trades and in the commerce of the county's leading towns. Nor were men of equivalent backgrounds unrepresented at the quarter sessions of Northamptonshire, Worcestershire, and the North Riding. The particular circumstances of these several shires were etched in the characteristics of their justices. Often they were men whose local prominence required their appointment to the commission of the peace.

Doubtless the justices were not uniformly or even usually self-sacrificing servants of their society. The records of Star Chamber show that they were involved in much litigation. Very few men of prominence, even those charged with the enforcement of the law, remained untouched by some fracas which came before the courts. J.P.s were antagonists and rivals as well as friends and colleagues. Yet the patterns of attendance at quarter sessions and other evidence make it clear that many, particularly the considerable group of justices who had been called to the bar, regarded their responsibilities very seriously.

The law was a dominant element in the lives of the members of this élite. Since their paramount task was judicial, this was an appropriate fact. Yet the analogous French development—the division of social roles between the nobility of the robe and an increasingly parasitical nobility of the sword—demonstrates that no particular social and political organization was inherent in the decay of feudalism.[1] It can hardly have been foreordained that in England the successors of the feudal nobility should have been a class of gentry/aristocracy who combined judicial and administrative responsibilities as the incumbents of appointive offices which were unsalaried but eagerly sought. Hardly less fateful than the development from medieval origins which came to Parliament during the Tudor century—and surely not unrelated—was the emergence of this extraordinary social group.

Not only did a powerful class—wherever their homes—have an experience which like the law was common to all counties, but in the universities and the inns of court they established bonds with their peers from other shires. Thus was born a national élite who might become a coherent body. In the early months of the Long Parliament Charles I had few supporters, Strafford and Laud virtually none. If a schism within the class made the civil wars possible, after the Restoration England was managed by the J.P.s. Centuries later their counterparts, now sometimes called 'the Establishment', constitute a phenomenon which to observers familiar with less compact lands seems to be peculiar to Great Britain.

Even more important was indoctrination in the principles of the common law. More perhaps than any other revolution the great English rebellion showed respect for established legal forms. One of the striking aspects of the Long Parliament was the reluctance of many members to adopt measures logically inherent in the situation. They believed themselves to be the defenders of legality against the illegal acts of the King's ministers. Even after the success of the parliamentary armies and the execution of Charles Stuart, many of the forms of English government were little disturbed. Commissions of the peace continued to be issued much as before, and, though there were marked changes among the dignitaries

[1] Cf. John P. Dawson, *A History of Lay Judges* (Camb., 1960), pp. 293, 299–301, *et passim*.

at the head of the roster, there was, particularly in eastern and southern counties, considerable stability of personnel. Only in the period of the Nominated Parliament were there important legal innovations. The quasi-monarchy of Cromwell simulated return to the old order, and the Restoration was a conscious effort to turn the clock back. The *libri pacis* resumed their *ante-bellum* form. All this is known.

It has been less commonly recognized that the qualified lawyers, the members of the House of Commons, and the J.P.s in Elizabethan and Stuart England were so closely intertwined that they were essentially different embodiments of a single social entity. And, as Holdsworth suggested in the passages quoted in earlier chapters,[1] the legal experience of J.P.s was a matter of great moment. From this education may well have sprung the instinct to act in accordance with the simple phrases but complex notion variously called the rule of law and due process. Nor can it be mere accident that English-speaking societies have known so little internal violence; like the English civil wars the American Revolution was based upon an appeal to law and was remarkably law-abiding.

Close to the heart of the democratic institutions which Anglo-American society owes to its legacy from the Stuart era is a legalistic attitude toward social administration. In England, in the United States, and in the nations of the Commonwealth many functions of local government are still performed by men, essentially amateurs, who, if not always trained in the law, have an instinctive respect for orderly process. They are the successors of men of impressive stature in Elizabethan and early Stuart society. In a resplendent heritage no less important than the better-known manifestation which is Parliament is the more constant and more pervasive feature which is the commission of Justice of the Peace.

[1] Cf. *supra*, pp. 1, 91.

# APPENDIX A

# KENT

1562[1]

| | | | | | | | | |
|---|---|---|---|---|---|---|---|---|
| 1 | | q | Matthew [Parker], Archbishop of Canterbury | C | | | 1575 | DNB |
| 2 | | q | Nicholas Bacon, knight, lord keeper | C | G | P | 1579 | DNB |
| 3 | | q | William [Paulet], Marquess of Winchester [lord treasurer] | | | P | 1572 | DNB |
| 4 | | q | Henry [Fitzalan], Earl of Arundel [lord steward] | | | | 1580 | DNB |
| 5 | | | William [Herbert], Earl of Pembroke | | | | 1570 | DNB |
| 6 | * | | Henry [Neville], Lord Burgavenny [Abergavenny] | | | P | 1587 | |
| 7 | * | q | William [Brooke], Lord Cobham, warden of the cinque ports [lord lieutenant] | C | | | 1597 | |
| 8 | r | | William [Burgh], Lord Borough [Burgh] | | | | 1584 | |
| 9 | * | q | Henry [Carey], Lord Hunsdon | | | P | 1596 | DNB |
| 10 | r | q | Richard Sackville, knight, undertreasurer of the exchequer | C | G | P | 1566 | DNB |
| 11 | | q | Ranulph Cholmeley, serjeant-at-law | | L | P | 1563 | |
| 12 | | q | Gilbert Gerard, attorney-general | | G | P | 1593 | DNB |

| | | | | | | | | | |
|---|---|---|---|---|---|---|---|---|---|
| 13 | r | q | Percival Harte, knight | Lullingstone | | | | 1580 | |
| 14 | * | q | Henry Sidney, knight | Penshurst | | | P | 1586 | DNB |
| 15 | | q | Martin Bowes, knight | North Cray | | | P | 1566 | DNB |
| 16 | | | Maurice Dennys, knight | Sutton-at-Hone | | | | 1564 | |
| 17 | | | William Damsell, knight | Wye | | | P | 1582 | |
| 18 | | | Henry Crispe, knight | Birchington | | | P | 1575 | |
| 19 | | | Thomas Kempe, knight | Wye | | | P | | |
| 20 | r | | Thomas Finch, knight | Eastwell | | | | 1563 | DNB |
| 21 | | | George Howard, knight | | | | P | 1575 | |
| 22 | * | | Thomas Cotton, knight | Oxenhoath | | | | 1585 | |
| 23 | * | | Christopher Alleyn, knight | Ightham | | | P | 1590 | |
| 24 | * | | Henry Cheyney, knight | Shurland | | | P | 1587 | |
| 25 | * | q | Thomas Wotton [custos rotulorum] | Boughton Malherbe | | | | 1587 | DNB |
| 26 | * | q | Warham St. Leger | Leeds Castle | | | | 1597 | DNB |
| 27 | * | | Richard Baker | Sissinghurst | | | P | 1594 | |
| 28 | * | | John Cobham | Newington | C | | P | 1594 | |
| 29 | s | | Nicholas Crispe | Birchington | | | P | 1564 | |
| 30 | * | | Thomas Scott | Smeeth | | I | P | 1594 | DNB |
| 31 | | q | William Isley | East Farleigh | | | | | |
| 32 | r | q | Humphrey Hales | Dungeon | | G | | 1571 | |
| 33 | * | | William Cromer | Tunstall | | G | P | 1598 | |
| 34 | * | q | John Lennard | Chevening | | L | | 1590 | |
| 35 | | | Anthony Weldon | Swanscombe | | | | 1573 | |
| 36 | | | Thomas Stanley | Wilmington | | | P? | | |
| 37 | * | | Robert Rudston | Boughton Monshelsea | | | P | 1589 | |
| 38 | * | | Thomas Walsingham | Chislehurst | | L | | 1584 | |
| 39 | | q | Nicholas Barham | Maidstone | | G | P | 1577 | DNB |
| 40 | | q | Thomas Watton | Addington | | | | 1579 | |
| 41 | * | q | Roger Manwood | Sandwich | | I | P | 1592 | DNB |
| 42 | | q | William Lovelace | Canterbury | | G | P | 1577 | |
| 43 | | q | Thomas Lovelace | Kingsdown | | G | | 1578 | |
| 44 | | q | Ralph Bossevile | Bradbourne | | L | | 1581 | |

| | | | | | | | |
|---|---|---|---|---|---|---|---|
| 45 | * q | Robert Binge | Northfleet | | P | 1595 | |
| 46 | q | Thomas Doyle | | | | | |
| 47 | q | John Beyer | Dartford | L | | 1572 | |
| 48 | * q | Robert Richers | Wrotham | L | P | 1588 | |
| 49 | | Hugh Cartwright | West Malling | L | P | 1572 | |
| 50 | * | Thomas Henley | Otham | | | 1591 | |
| 51 | * q | George Moulton | Ightham | | | 1588 | |
| 52 | r | George Fane | Badsell | G | | 1572 | |
| 53 | * | Thomas Hales | Thannington | | | 1583 | |
| 54 | r | Thomas Honiwood | Charing | | P | | |
| 55 | | Hugh Darrell | Northfleet | | | | |
| 56 | | John Sybell | Eynsford | | | 1574 | |

The following names are found in the *liber pacis* of 1559:

| | | | | | | | |
|---|---|---|---|---|---|---|---|
| 57 | r q | Anthony St. Leger, knight | Ulcombe | C G | | 1559 | *DNB* |
| 58 | | George Somerset, knight | Wickhambrook, Suffolk | | | 1560 | |
| 59 | | Rowland Clerke, knight | Well Court | | | | |
| 60 | q | Thomas Harlackenden | Woodchurch | | | 1558 | |
| 61 | | Thomas Townshend | | | | | |
| 62 | q | John Tufton | Hothfield | | | 1567 | |
| 63 | q | John Tooke | Great Chart | | | 1565 | |
| 64 | * q | Thomas Sackville | Buckhurst | I | P | 1608 | *DNB* |
| 65 | r | Francis Binge | | | | | |
| 66 | q | Robert Brente | Willesborough | | | 1570 | |
| 67 | r | Edmund [Thomas?] Walsingham | Chislehurst | | | 1549 | [1584] |
| 68 | | John Meyney | Biddenden | | | 1566 | |
| 69 | | Hugh Catlin | | | | | |
| 70 | | George Clerke | Wrotham | | | 1559 | |

Dignitaries 12; Court 12; Gentry 23; Law 7; Church 0; Commerce 2.

The general character of the Kent commission of the peace at the outset of the reign of Elizabeth was much like that of 1584, which was considered in detail in Chapter II. Indeed twenty-two members of the commission of 1562 were still J.P.s two decades later, and seven were the fathers of men whose names are in the later roster; no further comment is needed. (In this list the symbols of the asterisk—the same man—and the letter 'r'—a relative—refer to a roster of later rather than earlier date.) With one exception the presence in the commission of the dignitaries at the head requires no explanation; either their role was *ex officio* or they were men of such eminence that their membership derived naturally from some connection in the county. Sir Richard Sackville was a prominent lawyer, a cousin of the Queen, who had acquired very extensive monastic lands. Two men further down the roll were likewise magnates who happened to have an interest in Kent. Sir George Howard was a brother of Henry VIII's fifth queen, Master of the Armoury, and a figure at the royal Court. Thomas Stanley, who held the manor of Wilmington, seems to have been a cadet member of the family of the Earls of Derby. None of these men can have been an active J.P. in Kent.

Three knights and one esquire played a significant part in national affairs in addition to possessing Kentish lands. Sir Martin Bowes was 15 a former Lord Mayor of London of Yorkshire background who had entered the royal service. Sir Maurice Dennys, who came of a good 16 Gloucestershire family, had been a servant of Henry VIII and Receiver-General of the Hospital of St. John of Jerusalem. Sir William Damsell was Receiver-General of the Court of Wards and 17 Liveries. Anthony Weldon was Clerk of the Green Cloth. 35

There were four prominent lawyers in the commission. William Lovelace, Recorder of Canterbury, and Nicholas Barham were both 42, 39 serjeants-at-law. Ralph Bossevile, Clerk of the Court of Wards and 44 Liveries, and Hugh Cartwright were barristers in Lincoln's Inn. 49

Leading gentry of the county were also in the roster. Sir Henry Crispe—whose son was his colleague—'was a man of great name and of 18, 29 singular estimation for his discretion and weight in the management of the county as well as for his hospitality'. His ancestors had held much of the Isle of Thanet for more than a century. Sir Thomas Kempe 19 likewise came of a family long established in the county; he was knight of the shire in 1559. William Isley had been involved with his father 31 in Wyatt's rebellion, but after their pardon much of their lands had been restored, and as early as 1559 he had followed his forebears as J.P. Thomas Watton, head of a family which had ranked among the 40 gentry for generations, seems to have been involved in very extensive dealings in land. Thomas Lovelace, a cousin of serjeant William, 43 belonged to a family of local eminence.

The remaining members of the commission of 1562 were minor gentry, some so obscure that their identity is not readily established. Thomas Honiwood and Hugh Darrell may even have been clerical 54, 55 errors for Robert Honiwood and George Darrell. The probability that there were such mistakes is strengthened by the fact that one entry in the roster in the *liber pacis* of 1559 is clearly erroneous. 'Edmund Walsingham' cannot be correct; the well-known Lieutenant 67 of the Tower died in 1549. It is easy to imagine that a clerk might write the given name of the father in place of his relatively obscure son, Thomas. 38

There were a number of other names in the 1559 *liber pacis* which do not occur in the Kent bench as disclosed by the patent roll. None of them represents a type of man not found in 1562 or in 1584, and the changes in the rather fluid commission for Kent do not seem to imply the problem with regard to the religious convictions of J.P.s that is considered in Chapter V. Sir Anthony St. Leger was the father 57 of Warham; Thomas Sackville, then Lord Buckhurst, was a J.P. in 64 1584. Thomas Harlackenden, John Tooke, Robert Brente, and John 60, 63, 66 Meyney were all Kentish gentry of some note. Sir George Somerset, 68, 58 second son of the Earl of Worcester, married a daughter of Sir Walter Henley and like the Fane family acquired some Kentish lands which had once been monastic property. Such may also have been the earlier status of the land in which Watton dealt, but the spoliation of the monks did not lie at the root of the prosperity of the gentry of Kent to the degree which obtained in other counties. In 1562, as when Lambarde wrote, the City, the law, the royal Court, and established county families were the backgrounds of the justices of the peace in Kent. If the number of former members of the universities and of the inns of court was still small, more than half the men listed in the patent-roll commission were elected to the Commons at least once.

## 1608[2]

| No. | | | | Name | Place | | | | | Year | |
|---|---|---|---|---|---|---|---|---|---|---|---|
| 1 | | | q | Richard [Bancroft], Archbishop of Canterbury | | | C | | | 1610 | DNB |
| 2 | | | q | Thomas [Egerton], Lord Ellesmere, chancellor of England | | | | L | P | 1617 | DNB |
| 3 | * | | q | Thomas [Sackville], Earl of Dorset, treasurer of England | | | | I | P | 1608 | DNB |
| 4 | | | q | Charles [Howard], Earl of Nottingham, lord great admiral | | | | | | 1624 | DNB |
| 5 | | | q | Henry [Howard], Earl of Northampton, warden of the cinque ports | | | C | | P | 1614 | DNB |
| 6 | | s | q | Robert [Sidney], Viscount Lisle | | | O | | P | 1626 | DNB |
| 7 | | | q | William [Barlow], Bishop of Rochester | | | C | | | 1613 | DNB |
| 8 | | s | q | Robert [Sackville], Lord Buckhurst | | | O | I | P | 1609 | DNB |
| 9 | | | q | Edward [Neville], Lord Burgavenny [Abergavenny] | | | | | P | 1622 | |
| 10 | | s | q | Edward [Wotton], Lord Wotton [lord lieutenant] | | | C | | P | 1626 | DNB |
| 11 | | | q | John [Stanhope], Lord Stanhope, vice-chamberlain | | | C | G | P | 1621 | DNB |
| 12 | | | q | Thomas Walmesley, knight, justice of common pleas | } assize | | | L | P | 1612 | DNB |
| 13 | | | q | John Croke, knight, justice of king's bench | | | | I | P | 1620 | DNB |
| 14 | | s | q | Francis Fane, knight | Badsell | 30 | C | L | P | 1628 | DNB |
| 15 | | s | q | Henry Neville, knight | Birling | 20 | C | | P | 1641 | |
| 16 | | | q | Roger Aston, knight | Cranford, Middx. | 66 | | | P | 1612 | |
| 17 | | s | q | George Fane, knight | Burston | 20 | C | L | P | 1640 | DNB |
| 18 | | s | q | Peter Manwood, knight | Hackington | 20 | | I | P | 1625 | DNB |
| 19 | | | q | Thomas Vavasor, knight, marshall of the household | | 40 | | | P | 1620 | |
| 20 | | | q | Edward Hoby, knight [*custos rotulorum*] | Queenborough Castle | 40 | O | | P | 1617 | DNB |
| 21 | * | | q | Moyle Finch, knight | Eastwell | 60 | | G | P | 1614 | |
| 22 | | | q | Henry Palmer, knight | Beaksbourn | | | | | 1611 | DNB |
| 23 | | | q | Thomas Wilford, knight | Kingston | 20 | | L | | 1611 | |
| 24 | * | | q | John Scott, knight | Smeeth | 30 | O | | P | 1618 | DNB |
| 25 | * | | q | John Leveson, knight | Halling | 30 | O | G | P | 1615 | |
| 26 | | | q | Robert Mansell, knight | | 20 | O | | P | 1656 | DNB |
| 27 | | | q | Thomas Waller, knight | Dover Castle | | | | P | 1613 | |
| 28 | | s | q | Thomas Walsingham, knight | Chislehurst | 20 | | G | P | 1630 | DNB |
| 29 | * | | q | Michael Sondes, knight | Throwley | 30 | | L | P | 1617 | |
| 30 | | s | q | Anthony Meyney, knight | Biddenden | 25 | C | I | P | 1611 | |
| 31 | | s | q | William Lovelace, knight | Bethersden | 10 | | G | P | 1628 | |
| 32 | | | q | Henry Lindley, knight | Middleham, Yorks. | | | G | | 1610 | |
| 33 | | | q | Oliph Leigh, knight | Addington, Surrey | 20 | O | L | | 1612 | |
| 34 | | s | q | Percival Harte, knight | Lullingstone | 20 | O | | P | 1642 | |
| 35 | r | | q | Nicholas Tufton, knight | Hothfield | 20 | O | L | P | 1631 | |

| | | | | | | | | | |
|---|---|---|---|---|---|---|---|---|---|
| 36 | | q | Walter Chute, knight | Bethersden | 26 | O | G | P | 1618 |
| 37 | | q | Edward Darcy, knight | Dartford | 20 | C | | P | 1612 |
| 38 | s | q | John Smyth, knight | Ostenhanger | | | | P | 1609 |
| 39 | | q | Maximilian Dalison, knight | Halling | 20 | | G | P | 1631 |
| 40 | * | q | Thomas Palmer, knight | Wingham | 5 | | G | P | 1626 | *DNB* |
| 41 | s | q | Thomas Baker, knight | Sissinghurst | 20 | O | | P | 1625 |
| 42 | | q | Anthony Dering, knight | Surrenden | 20 | | | | 1635 |
| 43 | | q | Thomas Peyton, knight | Knowlton | 24 | | G | | 1611 |
| 44 | s | q | Richard Sondes, knight | Throwley | 20 | C | | P | 1633 |
| 45 | | q | John Trever, knight | Oatlands, Surrey | 10 | | | P | 1630 |
| 46 | s | q | Thomas Smyth, knight | Sutton-at-Hone | 25 | | | P | 1625 | *DNB* |
| 47 | r | q | Edward Hales, knight | Woodchurch | 20 | | G | P | 1654 | K |
| 48 | | q | Christopher Parkins, knight | Westminster | | | O | P | 1622 | *DNB* |
| 49 | | q | Robert Edolphe, knight | Hinxhill | 20 | | M | | 1617 |
| 50 | | q | Nicholas Gilborne, knight | Charing | 20 | | I | | 1632 |
| 51 | | q | George Chowne, knight | Wrotham | 20 | | L | P | 1616 |
| 52 | | q | William Barnes, knight | Woolwich | 20 | | | P? | 1619 |
| 53 | | q | Edward Filmer, knight | East Sutton | 20 | C | | | 1629 |
| 54 | | q | Thomas Harfleete, knight | Chequers | 20 | | | | 1617 |
| 55 | s | q | Richard Smyth, knight | Leeds Castle | 20 | | | P | 1628 |
| 56 | | q | Timothy Lowe, knight | Bromley | 20 | | L | | 1617 |
| 57 | r | q | Ralph Bossevile, knight | Bradbourne | 20 | | L | | 1635 |
| 58 | s | q | Robert Bossevile, knight | Eynsford | | | L | | 1623 |
| 59 | s | q | Samuel Lennard, knight | West Wickham | 20 | C | L | P | 1618 |
| 60 | | q | William Withens, knight | Eltham | 20 | | | | 1632 |
| 61 | | q | William Steede, knight | Harrietsham | 20 | O | | | 1633 |
| 62 | | q | Thomas Engham, knight | Goodneston | 20 | | | | 1622 |
| 63 | s | q | Ralph Weldon, knight | Swanscombe | 20 | | | | 1609 |
| 64 | * | q | John Boys, knight | Canterbury | 20 | | M | P | 1612 |
| 65 | | q | Norton Knatchbull, knight | Boxley | 20 | C | M | P | 1636 |
| 66 | s | | Edward Boys, knight | Nonington | 20 | C | | | 1635 |
| 67 | | q | Adam Spratling, knight | St. Lawrence | 10 | | | | 1615 |
| 68 | r | q | Charles Hales, knight | Thannington | 12 | | | | 1623 |
| 69 | r | q | Thomas Honiwood, knight | Elmsted | 20 | | G | | 1622 |
| 70 | | | Peter Buck, knight | Rochester | 12 | | | | 1625 |
| 71 | | q | William Page, knight | Shorne | 20 | | M | | 1625 |
| 72 | * | q | William Sedley, knight | Aylesford | 30 | O | L | | 1618 |
| 73 | | q | George Rivers, knight | Chafford | 20 | C | M | P | 1630 |
| 74 | | | George Pawle, knight | Lambeth, Surrey | 20 | | | P | 1635 |
| 75 | | q | Thomas Neville, Dean of Canterbury | | | C | | | 1615 | *DNB* |
| 76 | | | Thomas Blague, Dean of Rochester | | | C | | | 1611 | *DNB* |
| 77 | | q | Adam Newton, Dean of Durham | Charlton | | | | | 1630 | *DNB* |
| 78 | r | q | Charles Brooke | Temple Combe, Soms. | 20 | | | | 1610 |
| 79 | | q | Charles Fotherby, Archdeacon of Canterbury | | 8 | C | | | 1619 |
| 80 | | q | George Newman, doctor of laws | Canterbury | 8 | C | | P | 1627 |
| 81 | s | q | Thomas Scott | Smeeth | 40 | O | | P | 1611 |
| 82 | * | | Richard Hardres | Upper Hardres | 20 | | G | | 1613 |
| 83 | | q | George Waller | Groombridge | 20 | | | | |
| 84 | | q | Edmund Stile | Beckenham | 20 | | | | 1617 |
| 85 | * | q | Robert Honiwood | Charing | 5 | | G | | 1627 |
| 86 | | q | Lawrence Washington | Maidstone | 20 | O | G | P | 1620 |
| 87 | * | | Thomas Potter | Westerham | 20 | | | | 1610 |
| 88 | | q | Richard Wilkinson | Wateringbury Place | 20 | | | | 1622 |
| 89 | s | q | William Monins | Waldershare | 20 | C | | | 1643 |
| 90 | | q | Matthew Hadd | Canterbury | 12 | C | L | | 1617 |

| 91 | q | Bartholomew Mann | Rochester | 5 | | M | P | 1616 |
|----|---|------------------|-----------|---|---|---|---|------|
| 92 | s | Henry Finch | Canterbury | 10 | C | G | P | 1625 |
| 93 | q | George Wyatt | Boxley | 15 | | G | | 1624 |
| 94 | s | Henry Heyman | Selling | 10 | C | G | | 1613 |
| 95 | q | Zachary Scott | Halden | 10 | | L | | 1609 |
| 96 | q | William Beswick | Spelmonden | 20 | | L | | 1637 |
| 97 | q | William Campion | Goudhurst | 20 | C | L | P | 1615 |
| 98 | s | George Binge | Wrotham | 20 | C | | | 1617 |
| 99 | q | Michael Berresforde | Wrotham | | | | | 1608 |
| 100 | | Henry Hall | Maidstone | 12 | | M | | 1622 |
| 101 | | Samuel Boys | Hawkhurst | 16 | C | M | | 1627 |
| 102 | q | John Herdson | Folkstone | 20 | | | | 1622 |
| 103 | | Henry Paramore | St. Nicholas, Thanet | 20 | C | | | 1620 |
| 104 | q | Stephen Theobald | Seal | 20 | C | I | | 1619 |
| 105 | | Robert Cranmer | Chevening | 20 | | I | | 1619 |
| 106 | | John Grymes | | 20 | | | | 1645 |
| 107 | | Henry Snelgrave | Beckenham | 20 | | | | 1640 |
| 108 | | Robert Barkley | Canterbury | 15 | | | P? | 1614 |
| 109 | | Nicholas Kempe | Islington, Middx. | 20 | | M | | 1624 |
| 110 | | Edward Hendon | Biddenden | 10 | O | G | P | 1644 |

Dignitaries 13; Court 16; Gentry 52; Law 12; Church 5; Commerce 12.

This roster—and the five others of 1608—has an extra column showing for the working part of the commission the assessments which appear in the memorandum in the Ellesmere papers which is in Appendix G. The asterisks indicate that the J.P. had been a member of an earlier commission, while 's' shows a son and 'r' another relative. The 'K' beside the name of Sir Edward Hales is the first example of a symbol which indicates a sketch in Mrs. Keeler's *The Long Parliament*.

In 1608 the Kent commission had several striking features. Since 1584 its size had grown from 76 to 110; this is the largest body which is here given detailed consideration, although a *liber pacis* of 1621, compiled just before a systematic pruning of the commissions, listed 135 J.P.s for Kent. If the thirteen dignitaries at the head of the roster were slightly fewer, the number of knights in the working commission had mushroomed from 11 to 61. Much of this increase in Kent was part of the general growth of formal distinctions which followed the advent of the Stuarts. Some was due to the proximity of Kent to London and Westminster, which already in 1584 had given its bench an unusual number of government officials, professional lawyers, and City men. Finally there was the element of prominent non-episcopal clergy which was pleasing to the first James and to his son.

In contrast to the unusual continuity of personnel in the Kent commission between 1562 and 1584, there was a large change between 1584 and 1608; inevitably many of the men who had already served so long died in the decade after 1584. Indeed, only three of the men who did survive until 1608 were omitted from that roster: Sir Henry Cobham, now the unfortunate eighth Baron who was held in the

Tower because of his role in the plot of 1603; John (now Sir John) Parker, who was a J.P. in Surrey; and (Sir) Martin Barnham. Moreover, most of the new names which appeared in a roster of 1596 were still present in 1608. There was much greater continuity between the two reigns than the ten 'hold-overs' from 1584 until 1608 suggests. Many sons and other relatives of former justices stood in the places of men who had died. Clearly there had been no displacement of the conventional leaders of the county.

The sixteen J.P.s who were associated with the Court included close relatives of peers whose major estates were in the county, men who enjoyed middle-rank posts at Court, the holders of responsible though not major offices in government. The connections of the aristocracy were: Sir Francis Fane, who later became Earl of West- 14 morland; Sir George Fane, his brother; Sir Henry Neville, heir of 17, 15 Lord Abergavenny; Charles Brooke, who was now the effective head of 78 the house of Cobham even though his residence remained in Somerset. Sir Peter Manwood, son of the late Chief Baron of the Exchequer, 18 might be classified as a member of the gentry did his name not stand among the courtiers at the head of the roster. Court positions were held by Sir Roger Aston, Marshall of the Wardrobe, and Sir Thomas 16 Vavasor, Marshall of the Household. Sir Edward Hoby was Constable 19, 20 of Queenborough Castle and Sir Thomas Waller was Lieutenant of 27 Dover Castle. There were three naval officials: Sir Henry Palmer, 22 Comptroller; Sir Robert Mansell, Treasurer and later Vice-Admiral; 26 and Sir Peter Buck, Clerk of the Check. Sir John Trever was Steward 70, 45 of the Works at Windsor. Sir Ralph Weldon followed his father as 63 Clerk of the Green Cloth. Sir Christopher Parkins was Master of 48 Requests. Finally Richard Wilkinson, descended on his mother's side 88 from the Darrell family of Scotney, was one of the clerks of chancery.

The twelve lawyers included two veterans—Sir John Boys and Sir 64 William Sedley—and two sons of earlier justices—Sir Samuel Lennard, 72, 59 who was a bencher of Lincoln's Inn, and Henry Finch, a leading 92 member of Gray's Inn, who became a serjeant in 1616. Three barristers were double readers and treasurers of their inns: Bartholomew Mann and Henry Hall both in the Middle Temple, and Matthew 91, 100 Hadd (who was also J.P. for Canterbury and Steward of the Cinque 90 Ports) at Lincoln's Inn. Nicholas Kempe of the Middle Temple 109 suffered a fine for declining to be a reader. For Edward Hendon a 110 barony of the exchequer in 1639 was the climax of a long career at the bar. Stephen Theobald won no greater distinction than a call to the 104 bar at the Inner Temple. Lawrence Washington—whose name is more 86 familiar in the United States than in England—was a barrister of Gray's Inn and became Registrar of the Court of Chancery. Zachary Scott, a relative with a bar sinister of the family of Scott's Hall in 95

Smeeth, was called to the bar in Lincoln's Inn and became Protonotary of the Court of Common Pleas, a position which had earlier been held
53 by the father of his colleague Sir Edward Filmer. This Kent bench had remarkable legal talent.
77    Some legal knowledge must have been possessed by Adam Newton, tutor to Prince Henry and Dean of Durham, who was a member of
80 Gray's Inn but also an official of the Church. George Newman clearly studied canon and civil law; he was an advocate who became chancellor
75, 76 of the diocese of Canterbury. Thomas Neville, Thomas Blague, and
79 Charles Fotherby followed more orthodox clerical careers. Yet the appointment of these men to the commission of the peace was symptomatic of the growing interpenetration of secular and ecclesiastical life.

Twelve members of this commission had City backgrounds. Sir
25 John Leveson, now a Deputy Lieutenant, has already been considered. Sir John, Sir Thomas, and Sir Richard Smyth were sons of 'Customer' Smyth who must have inherited much of his talent as well as his
46 fortune. Thomas, first Governor of the East India Company, had a
38 prominent career in commerce and in politics. John was the progenitor
55, of the Viscounts Strangford. Richard, also a wealthy man, purchased
52 Leeds Castle from Sir Warham St. Leger. Sir William Barnes was the
73 grandson and son of Lord Mayors, while Sir George Rivers could claim
60 only a father who had held that honour. Sir William Withens, his
50, 56 brother-in-law Sir Nicholas Gilborne, Sir Timothy Lowe, William
96, 97 Beswick, and William Campion owed to the commerce of London the
106 fortunes which they inherited. John Grymes, son of a London haberdasher and a Surrey heiress, was only briefly a Kent J.P. before he settled in Suffolk. In these men the transformation of merchants into gentry is illustrated. Nine of the dozen were knighted. Several married daughters of gentlemen. Five were enrolled at one of the inns of court and two attended Cambridge. All owned considerable estates.

Most of the remaining fifty-two members of this commission were Kentish gentry of not very great standing. Some belonged to families which had been known in the county for centuries; others were
32 relatively parvenu. A few invite comment. Sir Henry Lindley was knighted in Ireland in 1599, and committed to prison briefly for complicity in the Essex rebellion; although he had been a member of the county bench as early as 1596, he does not appear to have held any
102 considerable estates in Kent. John Herdson was the holder of the manor of Folkstone and as much a citizen of that town as a Kentish squire.
93 The inclusion of George Wyatt, a son of the conspirator, in the county
74 commission marks the rehabilitation of the family. Sir George Pawle
42 was the author of a life of John Whitgift. Sir Anthony Dering was a member of an established county family which with him first reached

an eminence matched by few. If this was a large commission, it was a group of exceptional men.

The justices who had received some training in one of the universities, in one of the inns of court, or in both, now exceeded seventy per cent. While parliamentary experience remained at much the level of 1584, not quite half the total group securing election to the Commons for at least one parliament, the closer connection of the Kent bench with the royal administration and with the life of the capital must be indicated by the presence in Westminster of twenty Kent J.P.s in the Commons of the Parliament which sat between 1604 and 1610:

| | |
|---|---|
| 24, 25 | Kent: Sir John Scott, Sir John Leveson |
| 14 | Maidstone: Sir Francis Fane |
| 20, 28 | Rochester: Sir Edward Hoby, Sir Thomas Walsingham |
| 64 | Canterbury: Sir John Boys |
| 29 | Queensborough: Sir Michael Sondes |
| | Cinque Ports: |
| 27, 98 | Dover: Sir Thomas Waller, George Binge |
| 47 | Hastings: Sir Edward Hales [from October 1605] |
| 38, 65 | Hythe: Sir John Smyth, Sir Norton Knatchbull [from October 1609] |
| 17 | Sandwich: Sir George Fane |
| 8 | Sussex: Lord Buckhurst |
| 45 | Bletchingley: Sir John Trever |
| 19 | Boroughbridge: Sir Thomas Vavasor |
| 26 | Co. Carmarthen: Sir Robert Mansell |
| 30 | Cirencester: Sir Anthony Meyney |
| 11 | Newtown, Isle of Wight: Lord Stanhope |
| 18 | Saltash: Sir Peter Manwood |

Some of these M.P.s were associated with the Court, but most of them were emphatically residents of the county. The gentry of Kent showed an unusual interest in national politics.

## 1626[3]

| | | | | | | | |
|---|---|---|---|---|---|---|---|
| 1 | George [Abbot], Archbishop of Canterbury | O | | | 1633 | DNB |
| 2 | Sir Thomas Coventry, lord keeper | O | I | P | 1640 | DNB |
| 3 | James [Ley], Earl of Marlborough, lord treasurer | O | L | P | 1629 | DNB |
| 4 | Henry [Montagu], Earl of Manchester [lord president] | C | M | P | 1642 | DNB |
| 5 | Edward [Somerset], Earl of Worcester [lord privy seal] | | | | 1628 | DNB |
| 6 | George [Villiers], Duke of Buckingham | | | | 1628 | DNB |
| 7 | William [Herbert], Earl of Pembroke | O | | | 1630 | DNB |
| 8 | Philip [Herbert], Earl of Montgomery | O | | P | 1650 | DNB |

| No. | | Name | Place | | | | | | |
|---|---|---|---|---|---|---|---|---|---|
| 9 | s | Edward [Sackville], Earl of Dorset | | O | | P | 1652 | DNB | |
| 10 | | William [Cecil], Earl of Salisbury | | C | G | P | 1668 | | |
| 11 | | John [Egerton], Earl of Bridgewater | | | | P | 1649 | DNB | |
| 12 | * | Robert [Sidney], Earl of Leicester | | O | | P | 1626 | DNB | |
| 13 | | James [Hay], Earl of Carlisle | | | | | 1636 | DNB | |
| 14 | | Henry [Rich], Earl of Holland | | C | | P | 1649 | DNB | |
| 15 | * | Francis [Fane], Earl of Westmorland | | C | L | P | 1629 | DNB | |
| 16 | | William [Knollys], Earl of Banbury | | | | P | 1632 | DNB | |
| 17 | | George [Carew], Earl of Totnes | | O | | P | 1629 | DNB | |
| 18 | | Sir George Hay, knight, chancellor of Scotland | | | | | 1634 | DNB | |
| 19 | | Thomas [Erskine], Earl of Kelley | | | | | 1639 | DNB | |
| 20 | | Henry [Carey], Viscount Rochford | | | | | 1666 | | |
| 21 | | Henry [Cary], Viscount Falkland | | O | | | 1633 | DNB | |
| 22 | | Oliver [St. John], Viscount Grandison | | O | L | P | 1630 | DNB | |
| 23 | | John [Buckeridge], Bishop of Rochester | | O | | | 1631 | DNB | |
| 24 | | Edward [Conway], Lord Conway | | | | P | 1631 | DNB | |
| 25 | s | Mildmay [Fane], Lord le Despenser | | C | | P | 1666 | DNB | |
| 26 | * | Henry [Neville], Lord Abergavenny | | C | | P | 1641 | | |
| 27 | r | Richard [Lennard], Lord Dacre | | | | | 1630 | | |
| 28 | * | Edward [Wotton], Lord Wotton | | C | | P | 1626 | DNB | |
| 29 | | John [Roper], Lord Teynham | | | | | 1627 | | |
| 30 | | Fulke [Greville], Lord Brooke | | C | | P | 1628 | DNB | |
| 31 | | Dudley [Carleton], Lord Carleton | | O | | P | 1632 | DNB | |
| 32 | | Sir Thomas Edmondes, knight | | | | P | 1639 | DNB | |
| 33 | | Sir John Suckling, knight | London | | G | P | 1627 | | |
| 34 | | Sir Robert Naunton, knight | Westminster | C | | P | 1635 | DNB | |
| 35 | | Sir John Coke, knight | Hall Court, Herts. | C | | P | 1644 | DNB | |
| 36 | | Sir Richard Weston, knight | | | M | P | 1635 | DNB | |
| 37 | | Sir Julius Caesar, knight | | O | I | P | 1636 | DNB | |
| 38 | | Sir Humphrey May, knight | | O | M | P | 1630 | DNB | |
| 39 | * | Sir George Fane, knight | Burston | C | L | P | 1640 | DNB | |
| 40 | * | Sir Nicholas Tufton, baronet | Hothfield | O | L | P | 1631 | | |
| 41 | s | Sir John Sedley, baronet | Southfleet | O | I | | 1638 | | |
| 42 | s | Sir William Twysden, baronet | East Peckham | C | G | P | 1628 | | |
| 43 | | Sir Edward Hales, knight & baronet | Woodchurch | | G | P | 1654 | | K |
| 44 | * | Sir Adam Newton, baronet | Charlton | | | | 1630 | DNB | |
| 45 | | Sir Thomas Roberts, knight & baronet | Cranbrook | | G | | 1628 | | |
| 46 | s | Sir John Rivers, baronet | Chafford | O | I | | 1651 | | |
| 47 | r | Sir Isaac Sedley, knight & baronet | Great Chart | | | | 1627 | | |
| 48 | | Sir Francis Cottington, baronet | | | | P | 1652 | DNB | |
| 49 | s | Sir Edward Scott, knight | Smeeth | O | | P | 1643 | | |
| 50 | | Sir Dudley Digges, knight | Chilham | O | | P | 1639 | DNB | |
| 51 | | Sir Robert Heath, knight, attorney-general | Brasted | C | I | P | 1649 | DNB | |
| 52 | * | Sir Robert Mansell, knight | Greenwich | O | | P | 1656 | DNB | |
| 53 | * | Sir Thomas Walsingham, knight | Chislehurst | | G | P | 1630 | DNB | |
| 54 | s | Sir Francis Barnham, knight | Maidstone | C | G | P | 1646 | DNB | K |
| 55 | | Sir Edwin Sandys, knight | Northbourne | O | M | P | 1629 | DNB | |
| 56 | * | Sir Percival Harte, knight | Lullingstone | O | | P | 1642 | | |
| 57 | | Sir William Selby, knight | Ightham | C | G | | 1637 | | |
| 58 | * | Sir Maximilian Dalison, knight | Halling | | G | P | 1631 | | |
| 59 | * | Sir Anthony Dering, knight | Surrenden | | | | 1635 | | |
| 60 | * | Sir Richard Sondes, knight | Throwley | C | | P | 1633 | | |
| 61 | * | Sir Nicholas Gilborne, knight | Charing | | I | | 1632 | | |
| 62 | r | Sir Thomas Gresham, knight | Titsey, Surrey | O | | P | 1630 | | |
| 63 | * | Sir Edward Filmer, knight | East Sutton | C | | | 1629 | | |
| 64 | * | Sir Richard Smyth, knight | Leeds Castle | | | P | 1628 | | |
| 65 | * | Sir William Withens, knight | Eltham | | | | 1632 | | |

| 66 | * | Sir Norton Knatchbull, knight | Boxley | C | M | P | 1636 | |
|---|---|---|---|---|---|---|---|---|
| 67 | * | Sir Edward Boys, knight | Nonington | C | | | 1635 | |
| 68 | | Sir Edward Duke, knight | Aylesford | C | I | | 1640 | |
| 69 | | Sir John Hippesley, knight | Dover | | | P | 1655 | K |
| 70 | s | Sir Thomas Wilford, knight | Kingston | | | P | 1646 | |
| 71 | s | Sir Thomas Walsingham, knight | Chislehurst | C | | P | 1669 | K |
| 72 | * | Sir George Newman, knight | Canterbury | C | | P | 1627 | |
| 73 | r | Sir Edward Gilborne, knight | Shoreham | C | I | | | |
| 74 | * | Sir Henry Snelgrave, knight | Beckenham | | | | 1640 | |
| 75 | s | Sir Henry Palmer, knight | Bekesbourne | | | | | |
| 76 | s | Sir Henry Bossevile, knight | Eynsford | | | | 1639 | |
| 77 | | Sir Robert Lewkener, knight | Acryse | C | | | 1636 | |
| 78 | | Sir Henry Grimston, knight | Boxley | C | G | | 1645 | |
| 79 | r | Sir Humphrey Stile, knight | Beckenham | O | I | | 1659 | |
| 80 | s | Sir John Honiwood, knight | Elmsted | C | G | | 1652 | |
| 81 | r | Sir Robert Darrell, knight | Little Chart | C | G | | 1645 | |
| 82 | | Sir Christopher Mann, knight | Canterbury | | G | | 1638 | |
| 83 | | Isaac Bargrave, Dean of Canterbury | | C | | | 1643 | *DNB* |
| 84 | | Walter Balcanquall, Dean of Rochester | | C | | | 1645 | *DNB* |
| 85 | | John Bancroft, D.D. | Univ. Coll., Oxford | O | | | 1640 | *DNB* |
| 86 | | Francis Rogers, D.D. | Canterbury | C | | | 1638 | |
| 87 | | John Simpson, D.D. | Aldington | O | | | 1630 | |
| 88 | * | George Waller | Groombridge | | | | | |
| 89 | r | Edward Chute | Bethersden | | G | | 1640 | |
| 90 | * | Samuel Boys | Hawkshurst | C | M | | 1627 | |
| 91 | | John Walter | Fawkham | | G | | 1626 | |
| 92 | | Thomas Seyliard | Brasted | | | | 1650 | |
| 93 | | Henry Dixon | Tonbridge | O | G | | 1645 | |
| 94 | r | Edward Boys | Nonington | C | M | P | 1646 | K |
| 95 | | Richard Parker | Northfleet | O | M | | 1647 | |
| 96 | | Joshua Downing | Chatham | | | | | |
| 97 | s | Thomas Paramore | St. Nicholas, Thanet | C | G | P | 1638 | |

Dignitaries 38; Court 9; Gentry 37; Law 4; Church 5; Commerce 4.

In 1626 the Kent commission was paradoxically both swollen and contracted. Even more than in other counties Stuart prodigality with honours was evident. From a total of 97 there were only 10 men who could boast no title or degree save esquire. The dignitaries now constituted roughly forty per cent of the whole body. The working part had been reduced from the 97 of 1608 to 59. Inevitably there were fewer men in almost all its categories.

Among the magnates the usual great officers of state had been joined by the Lord President of the Council, the Lord Privy Seal, the favourite (Buckingham), and by other English peers as well as by several Scottish courtiers; Kent was close to the usual residence of the sovereign, and they must be regarded as supernumerary members of the commission. Two men invite comment. The heir on his mother's side to a title of impressive antiquity, Lord Dacre was 27 descended from Kentish families, Sackvilles, Bakers, and Lennards, as well as from peers on the Scottish border. Lord Teynham was the 29 head of the county family of Roper—descendants of Sir Thomas More

—whose Catholicism had kept them out of the commission of the peace in the past.

The proximity of the capital is the explanation likewise of the
24  numerous lesser officials: the three secretaries of state (Lord Conway,
33, 35  Sir John Suckling, Sir John Coke), the Master of the Rolls (Sir Julius
37  Caesar), the Chancellor of the Duchy of Lancaster (Sir Humphrey
38, 36  May), the Chancellor of the Exchequer (Sir Richard Weston), the
34  Master of the Court of Wards (Sir Robert Naunton), and diplomatist
32  Sir Thomas Edmondes. Members of the commission in other counties
as well as in Kent, their presence here was like that of most of the
peers. A few of the dignitaries had already been justices in 1608; a
few were relatives of earlier J.P.s.

At the head of the working part of the bench came the holders of the
fifteen-year-old order of baronet. With two exceptions—Sir Francis
Cottington and Sir Adam Newton—they were members of Kentish
44  families. Though still Dean of Durham, Newton is best placed with
48  Cottington, who had also had a close association with the King in the
72  past, and with Sir George Newman, who did not find a knighthood
inconsistent with important ecclesiastical position. Two other courtiers
69  were Sir John Hippesley, a protégé of Buckingham and Lieutenant of
96  Dover Castle, and Joshua Downing, a naval administrator. While he
happened to come from a Kentish background, Attorney-General
51  Heath must be regarded as a member of the royal Court.

As in 1608, there was a clerical phalanx of five men who divided
the knights from the esquires. Four professional lawyers—the barristers
80, 93, 95  Sir John Honiwood, Henry Dixon, and Richard Parker and a master in
50  chancery, Sir Dudley Digges—were all native sons of the county. A
73  second Gilborne brother (Sir Edward) was the only recruit whose
fortune derived from the commerce of London. These were the men
whose presence in the Kent commission invites comment.

More significant than obscure J.P.s were men who were not
included in the list. There were no assize judges; this is the only
commission herein considered in detail which had no judicial member
in addition to the holder of the Great Seal. Still alive were several
men who had been J.P.s in 1608 but were no longer in the commission,
and a larger number who had been justices in 1621 and had likewise
been removed. John Donne is the most famous of the latter. Some
bases for elimination may be surmised. Sir William Lovelace, Sir
William Steede, Sir George Rivers, and Robert Honiwood were old
men; the sons of two, Sir John Rivers—already a baronet in his
father's lifetime—and Sir John Honiwood, had taken their places.
Sir Humphrey Stile was some sort of surrogate for his uncle, Edmund.
Sir John Trever and Sir George Pawle both lived in Surrey, and John
Grymes had moved to Suffolk. Edward Hendon was a very busy

lawyer who had become a serjeant; he soon returned to the Kent bench. Sir William Monins had become a baronet, but in his case as in those of Sir Ralph Bossevile and William Beswick there is no easy explanation for disappearance from the commission of the peace.[4]

The number of courtiers in the Kent commission is the explanation of a change in the parliamentary representation of the county. Although the proportion—about fifty-five per cent—of Kent J.P.s who were returned to the House at least once was rather greater than in the past, half the eighteen men who sat in 1626 were courtiers; the number of distinctively Kentish men had declined from 14 to 8. This was the situation:

> Kent: Sir Edward Hales, Sir Edward Scott
> Canterbury: Sir John Finch, James Palmer
> Maidstone: Sir George Fane, Sir Francis Barnham
> Queenborough: Roger Palmer, Robert Pooley
> Rochester: Henry Clerke, Sir Thomas Walsingham

All but Pooley and Clerke bore a surname which is found in the roster of the county's bench. The courtier J.P.s found seats outside Kent.

The commission of 1626 saw a striking increase in the dignitaries and holders of lesser offices. Although there were thirteen fewer members than in 1608, the number of squires was not much changed. The pruning of 1621 affected particularly the men of the City and of the law. The elimination of local lawyers brought Kent to a level lower than that in any of the six counties except Worcestershire. During the next decade, however, they came back.

## 1636[5]

| | | | | | | | |
|---|---|---|---|---|---|---|---|
| 1 | | q | William [Laud], Archbishop of Canterbury, primate of all England | O | | | 1644 *DNB* |
| 2 | * | q | Thomas [Coventry], Lord Coventry, lord keeper | O | I | P | 1640 *DNB* |
| 3 | | q | William [Juxon], Bishop of London, lord treasurer | O | | | 1663 *DNB* |
| 4 | * | q | Henry [Montagu], Earl of Manchester, lord keeper of the privy seal | C | M | P | 1642 *DNB* |
| 5 | * | q | Philip [Herbert], Earl of Pembroke and Montgomery, chancellor of the household, *custos rotulorum* [lord lieutenant] | O | | P | 1650 *DNB* |
| 6 | | q | Theophilus [Howard], Earl of Suffolk, lord warden of cinque ports | O | | P | 1640 *DNB* |
| 7 | * | q | Edward [Sackville], Earl of Dorset, chamberlain of the queen | O | | P | 1652 *DNB* |
| 8 | * | q | William [Cecil], Earl of Salisbury | C | G | P | 1668 |
| 9 | s | q | Robert [Sidney], Earl of Leicester | O | G | P | 1677 |
| 10 | * | q | Mildmay [Fane], Earl of Westmorland | C | | P | 1666 *DNB* |
| 11 | * | q | Henry [Carey], Earl of Dover | | | P | 1666 |
| 12 | s | q | Thomas [Finch], Earl of Winchelsea | C | | P | 1639 |
| 13 | s | q | John [Tufton], Earl of Thanet | | | | 1676 |

| | | | | | | | | | | |
|---|---|---|---|---|---|---|---|---|---|---|
| 14 | | q | John [Warner], Bishop of Rochester | | O | | | 1666 | DNB | |
| 15 | * | q | John [Bancroft], Bishop of Oxford | | O | | | 1640 | DNB | |
| 16 | * | q | Francis [Cottington], Lord Cottington, chancellor of exchequer | | | | P | 1652 | DNB | |
| 17 | * | q | Thomas Edmondes, knight, treasurer of the household | | | | P | 1639 | DNB | |
| 18 | | q | Henry Vane, knight, comptroller of the household | | O | G | P | 1655 | DNB | K |
| 19 | * | q | Dudley Digges, knight, master of the rolls | | O | | P | 1639 | DNB | |
| 20 | s | q | John Finch, knight, chief justice of common pleas | | | G | P | 1660 | DNB | |
| 21 | | q | Francis Crawley, knight, a justice of common pleas | | C | G | | 1649 | DNB | |
| 22 | | q | Richard Weston, knight, a baron of exchequer | | | M | | 1652 | DNB | |
| 23 | * | q | George Fane, knight | Burston | C | L | P | 1640 | DNB | |
| 24 | | q | Richard Spencer, esq. | Orpington | O | G | P | | | |
| 25 | s | q | Roger Twysden, knight & baronet | East Peckham | C | G | P | 1672 | DNB | |
| 26 | * | q | Edward Hales, knight & baronet | Woodchurch | | G | P | 1654 | | K |
| 27 | s | q | Walter Roberts, knight & baronet | Cranbrook | | | | | | |
| 28 | * | q | John Rivers, baronet | Chafford | O | I | | 1651 | | |
| 29 | * | q | John Sedley, knight & baronet | Southfleet | O | I | | 1638 | | |
| 30 | s | q | Edward Dering, knight & baronet | Surrenden | C | M | P | 1644 | DNB | K |
| 31 | * | q | Humphrey Stile, knight & baronet | Beckenham | O | I | | 1659 | | |
| 32 | r | q | Thomas Stile [baronet] | Wateringbury | O | M | | 1637 | | |
| 33 | | q | John Bankes, knight, attorney-general | Corfe Castle | O | G | P | 1644 | DNB | |
| 34 | | q | Edward Littleton, knight, solicitor-general | | O | I | P | 1645 | DNB | |
| 35 | | q | Ralph Whitfield, knight, king's serjeant | Bennenden | | G | P | | | |
| 36 | s | | George Sondes, knight | Throwley | C | M | P | 1677 | DNB | |
| 37 | r | q | William Brooke, knight | Cooling | C | M | P | 1643 | | |
| 38 | * | q | Robert Mansell, knight | Greenwich | O | | P | 1656 | DNB | |
| 39 | * | q | Percival Harte, knight | Lullingstone | O | | P | 1642 | | |
| 40 | * | q | Edward Boys, junior, knight | Nonington | C | M | P | 1646 | | K |
| 41 | * | q | Edward Duke, knight | Aylesford | C | I | | 1640 | | |
| 42 | s | q | Humphrey Tufton, knight | Hothfield | O | I | P | 1659 | | K |
| 43 | s | q | Francis Leigh, knight | Addington, Surrey | C | I | P | 1644 | | |
| 44 | | q | Timothy Thornhill, knight | Wye | | G | | | | |
| 45 | * | | Thomas Wilford, knight | Kingston | | | P | 1646 | | |
| 46 | * | q | Thomas Walsingham, knight | Chislehurst | C | | P | 1669 | | K |
| 47 | * | q | Robert Darrell, knight | Little Chart | C | G | | 1645 | | |
| 48 | * | q | Edward Osborne [i.e. Gilborne], knight | Shoreham | C | I | | | | |
| 49 | * | q | Henry Snelgrave, knight | Beckenham | | | | 1640 | | |
| 50 | * | q | Henry Palmer, knight, comptroller general of the royal navy | Bekesbourne | | | | | | |
| 51 | * | | Henry Bossevile, knight | Eynsford | | | | 1639 | | |
| 52 | * | q | Robert Lewkener, knight | Acryse | C | | | | | |
| 53 | s | q | Robert Filmer, knight | East Sutton | C | L | | 1653 | DNB | |
| 54 | * | q | John Honiwood, knight | Elmsted | C | G | | 1652 | | |
| 55 | | q | John Howell, knight | Wrotham | | | | 1641 | | |
| 56 | * | q | Henry Grimston, knight | Boxley | C | G | | 1645 | | |
| 57 | * | q | Edward Hendon, serjeant-at-law | Biddenden | O | G | P | 1644 | | |
| 58 | * | q | Robert Heath, knight, serjeant-at-law | Brasted | C | I | P | 1649 | DNB | |
| 59 | | q | Henry Clarke, serjeant-at-law | Rochester | | M | P | | | |
| 60 | * | q | Isaac Bargrave, Dean of Canterbury | | C | | | 1643 | DNB | |
| 61 | * | q | Walter Balcanquall, Dean of Rochester | | C | | | 1645 | DNB | |
| 62 | * | q | Francis Rogers, S.T.D. | Canterbury | C | | | 1638 | | |
| 63 | | q | Thomas Jackson, S.T.D. | Canterbury | O | | | | | |
| 64 | | q | Thomas Gardiner, esq., Recorder of London | | | I | | 1652 | DNB | |
| 65 | s | q | Thomas Digges | Chilham | O | G | | 1687 | | |

| 66 | * | q | Edward Chute | Bethersden | | G | | 1640 | |
|----|---|---|--------------|------------|---|---|---|------|---|
| 67 | | q | Lancelot Lovelace | Sittingbourne | | G | | 1640 | |
| 68 | | q | Edward Hadd | Canterbury | | L | | | |
| 69 | | q | Thomas Denn | Kingston | | I | P | 1655 | |
| 70 | | | Reginald Edwards | | | I | | | |
| 71 | | | Samuel Shorte | Tenterden | C | G | | | |
| 72 | * | | Thomas Seyliard | Brasted | | | | 1650 | |
| 73 | * | q | Thomas Paramore | St. Nicholas, Thanet | C | G | P | 1638 | |
| 74 | * | | Henry Dixon | Tonbridge | O | G | | 1645 | |
| 75 | | q | James Franklyn | Wye | O | M | | | |
| 76 | | q | John Porter | Lamberhurst | O | I | P | 1652 | |
| 77 | | q | Richard Lee | Delce Magna | | I | P | 1652 | K |
| 78 | * | q | Richard Parker | Northfleet | O | M | | 1647 | |
| 79 | | q | John Hendon | Biddenden | | G | | | |
| 80 | | q | John Colepeper | Hollingbourne | O | M | P | 1660 | K |
| 81 | | | George Stroode | Westerham | O | G | | 1663 | |
| 82 | | | William Boys | Hawkhurst | C | G | | | |
| 83 | | q | Thomas Blunt | Charlton | O | G | | | |
| 84 | | | Thomas Godfrey | Lydd | C | | P | | |
| 85 | | | Thomas Bletchenden | Aldington | | G | | | |

Dignitaries 22; Court 3; Gentry 38; Law 16; Church 4; Commerce 2.

Between 1626 and 1636 the Kent commission shrank further to 85 in total size. There were 39 veterans of the rosters of 1608 and 1626; there were 13 sons of earlier justices and a number of more distant relatives. A few men who had been eliminated in the pruning of 1621 had been restored. None the less there were important differences from the bench of a decade before. The dignitaries had further decreased to 22. The working group had grown by a mere 4, but there had taken place a striking increase in the men who had been called to the bar.

Among the dignitaries all the Scots favourites and most of the holders of minor positions at Court had disappeared. There remained four great officers of state, but the other secular peers were almost all men who enjoyed some patent connection with Kent. There were four judges; the two men assigned to the Kent circuit and two who were sons of the county: Sir Dudley Digges, Master of the Rolls, and [19] Sir John Finch, Chief Justice of the Common Pleas. The Attorney- [20, 33] General and the Solicitor-General appear to have been present because [34] of their office rather than their local eminence, but there were four serjeants-at-law (all so designated in the *liber pacis*) who held Kent properties. Sir Robert Heath, a man who had been Attorney-General [58] and Chief Justice of the Common Pleas until he was dismissed because of his Puritan sympathies, remained in the Kent commission. Each of the inns of court had a sometime reader and treasurer, all with Kent connections: Thomas Gardiner, Recorder of London, Lancelot Love- [64, 67] lace, Recorder of Canterbury, Edward Hadd, and James Franklyn. [68, 75] Two other benchers were Samuel Shorte and John Porter. Thomas [71, 76]

69 Denn was a reader of the Inner Temple, while Sir John Honiwood,
Henry Dixon, Richard Parker, Reginald Edwards, and Robert Filmer
53 were barristers. Though not published until 1680, Filmer's *Partriarcha*
was written at this time. Including the Lord Chancellor and the Lord
Privy Seal there were thus 23 trained lawyers in a commission of 85;
the 18 in the working group constituted nearly thirty per cent.
Four other men invite comment: John Colepeper, Thomas Jackson, and the two City men. Since there are no traces of another likely
80 man who bore the name, Sir John of Hollingbourne and Wigsell, knight
of the shire in the Long Parliament and later first Baron Colepeper, is
presumably the Kentish J.P., but why did his name appear so far down
the roster? A clerical error is the least implausible explanation. Like
63 the other clergy, Thomas Jackson, who held several Kentish cures,
81 was a protégé of Laud's. George Stroode was an intruder in Kent.
Of a Somerset background and with commercial experience in Bristol
and London, he purchased an estate in Westerham and became a
83 Kentish squire. Thomas Blunt also had a City background. At a
moment when the lawyers had become a major component of the
Kent bench the commercial life of London had markedly receded.

Along with the growth in numbers of men who had had legal
studies there was an increase in those who had had experience at the
universities. Forty members of this commission had enjoyed both kinds
of training, and there were only 11 who had had neither. Election to
the House of Commons was again at the level of approximately fifty
per cent, but there were only eleven Kent J.P.s who were returned to
the parliaments of 1640: Sir George Fane, Sir Roger Twysden, and
John Porter sat in the Short Parliament; Sir Edward Dering, Sir
Humphrey Tufton, Sir John Colepeper, and Richard Lee were
elected to the Long Parliament; Sir Henry Vane, Sir Edward Hales,
Sir Edward Boys, and Sir Thomas Walsingham were chosen twice in
that year. Each time Queenborough accepted one member from the
Court circle; otherwise all Kent M.P.s were local men. In the Long
Parliament, Vane excepted, they were reformers in 1640. Some
remained true to the cause of Parliament and Vane abandoned the
King, but Dering, Colepeper, and Hales faltered and were deprived
of their seats. Other J.P.s who were reformers in sentiment in 1640
must have ceased to support Parliament, since they, too, were subject
to the sequestration of their estates and to fine during the next
decade.[6]

The Kent J.P.s who have been considered during the years from
1558 to 1636 numbered 342. Among the 85 who were justices in
1636 some 20 were lineal descendants of men who had been in the
commission in 1562 or in 1584. In a number of cases a male succession
had failed but heirs in the female line were on the bench. The Finches

now possessed the estate of Sir Thomas Moyle; Sir John Rivers had inherited from his mother the lands of Thomas Potter; Robert Binge's daughter married Sir John Smyth. Frequently the property, when it was purchased, seemed to carry with it membership in the commission of the peace. John Goldwell sold Bexley to Sir William Withens, who in turn sold it to Sir John Tufton. Sir Christopher Alleyn's estate at the Mote in Ightham now belonged to Sir William Selby. George Clifford's manor of Bobbing was held in 1636 by Sir Humphrey Tufton. Land as well as family conferred status.[7]

The J.P.s included the leading squires of the county with a few exceptions. Sir Francis Barnham, Sir Peter Heyman, and Edward Partrige, for example, all members of the Long Parliament, were heirs of J.P.s of 1584 but were not in the commission of 1636. None the less the Kent commission of the latter year bore a marked resemblance to its Elizabethan antecedent. At both times the list was headed by great officers of state, by bishops, and by members of the nobility resident in the county. The largest group were the principal gentry. In their midst were men whose status depended upon fortunes derived from the trade of London. Even more striking were the lawyers. As Lambarde noted, Kent attracted courtiers, lawyers, and merchants who mingled with the gentry.

## NOTES TO APPENDIX A

1. In this and in the other rosters in the appendices there are three symbols which were not used for the commission in Kent in 1584—cf. *supra*, p. 16. An asterisk shows that the same man was a member of a commission already discussed; 's' indicates a son of a J.P. in the same county, sometimes in the same commission; 'r' signifies a father, a grandson, a nephew, or a cousin of another justice. *Cal. Pat. Rolls, Eliz.* ii (1560–3), 438; Lansdowne MSS. 1218, ff. 16ᵛ–17ᵛ.

*1562 roster:*

6. Cf. Kent, 1584 roster, no. 4, *supra*, p. 16.

7. Ibid., no. 5.

11. *Lincoln's Inn Black Books*, i. 263, 304, 318, 324, 339, *et passim*; PCC 1563, 23 Chayre.

13. Hasted, *Kent*, ii. 544, 545; PCC 1580, 19 Arundell.

16. Hasted, *Kent*, ii. 302, 346, 352; PCC 1564, 1 Morrison; Jordan, *Social Institutions*, p. 92.

17. Hasted, *Kent*, vii. 353, 356; *A.P.C.*, 1571–5, p. 19; Joel Hurstfield, *The Queen's Wards* (L., 1958), pp. 115, 203, 205, 212.

18. Hasted, *Kent*, x. 297; PCC 1575, 41 Pyckering.

19. Hasted, *Kent*, vii. 348, 349; ibid. viii. 340; *Arch. Cant.* xxi (1895), 228; ibid. xxviii (1909), 314.

21. Gerald Brenan and E. P. Statham, *The House of Howard* (2 vols., L., 1907), ii. 341–5.

22. Cf. Kent, 1584 roster, no. 18.

23. Ibid., no. 19.

24. Ibid., no. 9.

25. Ibid., no. 28.
27. Ibid., no. 22.
28. Ibid., no. 29.
29. Hasted, *Kent*, viii. 511, 512.
31. Ibid. iv. 379; ibid. vii. 59, 121.
32. Ibid. xi. 149.
33. Cf. Kent, 1584 roster, no. 31.
34. Ibid., no. 34.
35. Hasted, *Kent*, ii. 411; PCC 1573, 5 Martyn.
36. Hasted, *Kent*, ii. 332, 333.
37. Cf. Kent, 1584 roster, no. 41.
38. Ibid., no. 77.
40. Hasted, *Kent*, iv. 546; *Arch. Cant.* lix (1946), 296.
42. Hasted, *Kent*, ii. 479; ibid. vii. 489, 493; ibid. xii. 249; *Arch. Cant.* x (1876), 184–220.
43. Hasted, *Kent*, ii. 487; ibid. vi. 157; PCC 1578, 11 Bakon.
44. Hasted, *Kent*, iii. 83–4; *Visitations of Kent . . . 1530–1 and 1574*, p. 31; Hurstfield, *Queen's Wards*, pp. 39, 210, 228.
45. Cf. Kent, 1584 roster, no. 49.
47. Hasted, *Kent*, ii. 312; Jordan, *Social Institutions*, p. 39.
48. Cf. Kent, 1584 roster, no. 50.
49. Hasted, *Kent*, ii. 316; ibid. iv. 509; *Lincoln's Inn Black Books*, i. 273, 285, *et passim*.
50. Cf. Kent, 1584 roster, no. 47.
51. Ibid., no. 40.
52. Hasted, *Kent*, ii. 353; cf. Kent, 1584 roster, no. 24.
53. Ibid., no. 62.
54. Hasted, *Kent*, v. 425; Lansdowne MSS. 1218; P.R.O., Assize Rolls 35/2, 3.
55. *Arch. Cant.* xvii (1887), 38 ff.; ibid., xviii (1889), 18; Egerton MSS. 2345; Assize Rolls 35/6.
56. Hasted, *Kent*, ii. 533; *Arch. Cant.* xxvi (1904), 79 ff.; PCC 1574, 40 Martyn.
57. *DNB*: 'Anthony St. Leger'.
58. Hasted, *Kent*, vii. 105; Barron, *Northamptonshire Families*, p. 95.
59. Shaw, *Knights of England*, ii. 62; *Cal. Pat. Rolls, Eliz., 1560–3*, xi. 423; Hasted, *Kent*, vi. 138.
60. *Arch. Cant.* xiv (1882), 352, 360; Hasted, *Kent*, vii. 231, 232.
61. I have been unable to identify Thomas Townshend.
62. Hasted, *Kent*, vii. 517, 518.
63. Ibid. ix. 422; *Visitation of Kent . . . 1574 and 1592*, i. 60; *Arch. Cant.* xxvi (1904), 97–8.
64. *DNB*: 'Thomas Sackville'.
65. Cf. no. 45 *supra*.
66. Hasted, *Kent*, vii. 570; *Cal. Pat. Rolls, Philip and Mary*, i (1553–4), 20–1.
67. *DNB*: 'Edmund Walsingham'.
68. Hasted, *Kent*, vii. 132.
69. I have been unable to identify Hugh Catlin.
70. Hasted, *Kent*, iv. 346.

2. P.R.O., S.P. 14/33, ff. 33–6; Barnes and Smith, 'Justices of the Peace', *Bull. Inst. Hist. Research*, xxxii (1959), 238.

*1608 roster:*
15. *Complete Peerage*: 'Abergavenny'.
16. *Alum. oxon.*; PCC 1615, 50 Cope.
19. Cokayne, *Baronetage*, ii. 61.

21. Hasted, *Kent*, vii. 404.
23. Ibid., p. 99; ibid. ix. 343; Shaw, *Knights of England*, ii. 87, 143.
24. Scott, *Family of Scott*, p. 214 *et passim*.
25. Cf. *supra*, p. 32.
27. Hasted, *Kent*, iii. 289, 290; ibid. ix. 519; PCC 1613, 123 Capell; *DNB*: 'William Waller'.
29. Hasted, *Kent*, vi. 451.
30. Ibid. iv. 367; Jordan, *Social Institutions*, p. 50.
31. Hasted, *Kent*, xi. 171.
32. Shaw, *Knights of England*, ii. 96; *A.P.C., 1600–1*, p. 160; PCC 1610, 42 Wingfield.
33. *Alum. oxon.*; PCC 1612, 24 Fenner; Hasted, *Kent*, ii. 198.
34. Ibid. ii. 544, 545.
35. Cokayne, *Baronetage*, i. 70; *Complete Peerage*: 'Nicholas Tufton'.
36. Hasted, *Kent*, v. 541; *Visitation of Kent . . . 1619*, p. 96; Gardiner, *History of England*, ii. 249.
37. Hasted, *Kent*, ii. 297.
38. Ibid. vii. 529.
39. Ibid. iii. 382, 384; *Arch. Cant.* xv (1883), 402.
40. Cf. Kent, 1584 roster, no. 57.
41. *Visitation of Kent . . . 1619*, p. 64; Hasted, *Kent*, vii. 100, 101.
42. Ibid. pp. 466–7.
43. Ibid. x. 90, 91; PCC 1611, 32 Cope.
44. Hasted, *Kent*, vi. 452.
45. *Cal. S.P. Dom., Jas. I, 1603–10, passim*.
49. Hasted, *Kent*, vii. 561.
50. Ibid., p. 430; ibid. i. 449.
51. Ibid., v. 24.
52. Ibid. i. 450; H. H. Drake, *Hasted's History of Kent; the Hundred of Blackheath* (L., 1880), p. 160.
53. Hasted, *Kent*, ii. 376; ibid. v. 379.
54. Ibid. iii. 364; ibid. ix. 199, 200; *Arch. Cant.* xl (1928), 105 ff.
55. Hasted, *Kent*, v. 486; ibid. viii. 340.
56. Drake, *Hasted's History*, p. 269.
57. Hasted, *Kent*, iii. 84.
58. Ibid., pp. 84, 91; PCC 1623, 72 Swann.
59. Hasted, *Kent*, iii. 109.
60. Ibid. i. 478.
61. *Ibid.*, p. 449; Jordan, *Social Institutions*, p. 57.
62. Hasted, *Kent*, ix. 242 ff.
63. Ibid. ii. 412.
64. Cf. Kent, 1584 roster, no. 64.
65. Hasted, *Kent*, iv. 399; ibid. vii. 596; Jordan, *Social Institutions*, p. 84.
66. Behrens, *Under Thirty-Seven Kings*, pp. 43–5; Hasted, *Kent*, ix. 259–61.
67. Ibid. x. 388, 389.
68. Ibid. ix. 23; ibid. xii. 146.
69. Ibid. viii. 37, 38.
70. *Visitation of Kent . . . 1574 and 1592*, p. 86; *Visitation of Kent . . . 1619*, p. 26; PCC 1625, 68 Clarke.
71. Hasted, *Kent*, iii. 451.
72. Cf. Kent, 1584 roster, no. 79.
73. Hasted, *Kent*, iii. 251; ibid. v. 191.
74. Shaw, *Knights of England*, ii. 142; PCC 1635, 35 Sadler; he was the author of *Life of Whitgift* (L., 1612).

75. *Som. Arch. Soc., Proceedings*, xlv (1899), ii. 12; Trevor-Roper, *Gentry*, p. 14.
79. Hasted, *Kent*, ix. 337; ibid. xi. 403; ibid. xii. 13–15.
80. Ibid. ix. 519; ibid. xi. 230.
81. Scott, *Family of Scott, passim*.
82. Cf. Kent, 1584 roster, no. 54.
83. Cf. *supra*, no. 27.
84. Hasted, *Kent*, i. 542 ff.; *Arch. Cant.* iii (1860), 194.
85. Cf. Kent, 1584 roster, no. 69.
86. *Alum. cantab.*; PCC 1620, 3 Soame.
87. Cf. Kent, 1584 roster no. 70.
88. Hasted, *Kent*, v. 111.
89. Cokayne, *Baronetage*, i. 77.
90. Hasted, *Kent*, v. 536; ibid. xii. 61.
91. A. R. Ingpen, *The Middle Temple Bench Book* (L., 1912), 165.
92. Hasted, *Kent*, xi. 54; ibid. xii. 114.
93. Ibid. iv. 336, 341; ibid., vii. 257.
94. Ibid. viii. 309.
95. *Visitation of Kent . . . 1574 and 1592*, p. 110; *Lincoln's Inn Black Books*, i. 441, and ii. 3, 127.
96. Hasted, *Kent*, v. 315; ibid. vii. 77; PCC 1637, 17 Goare.
97. Hasted, *Kent*, vii. 81.
98. Ibid. v. 11.
99. Ibid. viii. 502; *Visitation of Kent . . . 1619*, p. 172; PCC 1608, 28 Windebanck
100. Hasted, *Kent*, vii. 297, 301, 361.
101. *Alum. cantab.*; PCC 1627, 115 Skynner.
102. Hasted, *Kent*, viii. 93, 150, 160, 185; *Arch. Cant.* x (1876), xlvii, cxxii, cxxiii.
103. Hasted, *Kent*, ix. 592; ibid. x. 242; *Arch. Cant.* xii (1878), 400.
104. Hasted, *Kent*, iii. 55.
105. Ibid., p. 118; ibid. viii. 224; *Arch. Cant.* xvi (1886), 116.
106. *Collectanea Topographica et Genealogica* (8 vols., L., 1834–43), iii. 155; *A.P.C.*, *1613–14*, p. 158.
107. Hasted, *Kent*, i. 531; PCC 1640, 19 Coventry; *A.P.C. 1615–16*, pp. 92, 208, 279; ibid., *June–Dec. 1626*, p. 199.
108. *Arch. Cant.* xiv (1882), 208; PCC 1616, 129 Cope.
109. *Middle Temple Records*, i. 235, 308, *et passim*; PCC 1624, 74 Byrde.
110. Hasted, *Kent*, iv. 311; Reginald J. Fletcher (ed.), *The Pension Book of Gray's Inn* (2 vols., L., 1901–10), i. 208.

3. P.R.O., C193/12.

*1626 roster:*

33. Hasted, *Kent*, x. 173; cf. *DNB*: 'Sir John Suckling', his son.
39. Cf. Kent, 1608 roster, no. 17.
40. Ibid., no. 35.
41. This Sir John Sedley was the son of Sir William Sedley of Aylesford (Cokayne, *Baronetage*, i. 73: cr. 1611).
42. J. R. Twisden, *The Family of Twysden and Twisden* (L., 1939), *passim*.
43. Jordan, *Social Institutions*, p. 29.
45. Cokayne, *Baronetage*, i. 157: cr. 1620; Hasted, *Kent*, vii. 107.
46. Cokayne, *Baronetage*, i. 169: cr. 1621; Hasted, *Kent*, iii. 251; ibid. v. 191.
47. Cokayne, *Baronetage*, i. 173: cr. 1621.
49. Scott, *Family of Scott*, pp. 209–12 *et passim*.
55. Jordan, *Social Institutions*, p. 97.
56. Cf. Kent, 1608 roster, no. 34.

57. Hasted, *Kent*, v. 42, 43; Jordan, *Social Institutions*, p. 88.
58. Cf. *Kent*, 1608 roster, no. 39.
59. Ibid., no. 42.
60. Ibid., no. 44.
61. Ibid., no. 50.
62. Hasted, *Kent*, iii. 177; W. Bruce Bannerman (ed.), *The Visitation of the County of Surrey* (Harl. Soc. Publ., xliii, L., 1899), p. 78; *Surrey Archaeological Collections*, xxxiii (1920), 11.
63. Cf. *Kent*, 1608 roster, no. 53.
64. Ibid., no. 55.
65. Ibid., no. 60.
66. Ibid., no. 65.
67. Ibid., no. 66.
68. Hasted, *Kent*, v. 576.
70. Ibid. ix. 343; ibid. xi. 55.
72. Cf. *Kent*, 1608 roster, no. 80.
73. *Visitation of Kent . . . 1619*, p. 192.
74. Cf. *Kent*, 1608 roster, no. 107.
75. *DNB*: 'Henry Palmer', his father.
76. Sir G. J. Armytage (ed.), *The Visitation of . . . Kent . . . 1663, etc.* (Harl. Soc. Publ., liv, L., 1906), p. 17.
77. Hasted, *Kent*, viii. 99, 102; ibid. x. 389.
78. *Visitation of Kent . . . 1663*, p. 101; Walter C. Metcalfe (ed.), *The Visitations of Essex* (Harl. Soc. Publ. xiii, xiv, L., 1878–9), i. 207; *Arch. Cant.* xviii (1889), 66.
79. Cokayne, *Baronetage*, i. 259: cr. 1624; *Arch. Cant.* iii (1860), 194.
80. Hasted, *Kent*, viii. 38.
81. Ibid. vii. 458, 459; *Arch. Cant.* xvii (1887), 38 ff.
82. Hasted, *Kent*, xi. 183, 238.
86. Ibid. viii. 141; ibid. xi. 233; ibid. xii. 9.
87. *Alum. oxon.*
88. Cf. *Kent*, 1608 roster, no. 83.
89. Hasted, *Kent*, v. 541; ibid. vi. 109; *Arch. Cant.* xviii (1909), 55 ff.
90. Cf. *Kent*, 1608 roster, no. 101.
91. Hasted, *Kent*, ii. 448.
92. Ibid. iii. 198; Cokayne, *Baronetage*, iii. 217 ('John Seyliard', his son): cr. 1661.
93. Hasted, *Kent*, v. 222; *Arch. Cant.* xx (1893), 36.
95. *Middle Temple Bench Book*, p. 188.
96. *Cal. S.P. Dom.,1627–8*, pp. 4, 5, 8, *et passim.*
97. Hasted, *Kent*, x. 239; *A.P.C., Jan.–June 1627*, pp. 194–5, 395, 441.

4. Cf. *Kent*, 1608 roster, nos. 31, 61, 73, 85, 84, 45, 74, 106, 110, 89, 57, 96; P.R.O., C193/13, f. 53.

5. Barnes and Smith, 'Justices of the Peace', *Bull. Inst. Hist. Research*, xxxii (1959), 239; P.R.O., S.P. 16/405, ff. 32ᵛ–5.

*1636 roster:*
18. Hasted, *Kent*, v. 24.
23. Cf. *Kent*, 1608 roster, no. 17.
24. Hasted, *Kent*, ii. 107.
27. Cokayne, *Baronetage*, i. 151: cr. 1620.
28. Cf. *Kent*, 1626 roster, no. 46.
29. Ibid., no. 41.

31. Ibid., no. 79.
35. Hasted, *Kent*, vii. 180; ibid. viii. 260; *Pension Book of Gray's Inn*, i. 326.
37. Hasted, *Kent*, iii. 415; *Complete Peerage*: 'Cobham'.
39. Cf. Kent, 1608 roster, no. 34.
41. Cf. Kent, 1626 roster, no. 68.
43. Hasted, *Kent*, ii. 197–8.
44. Ibid. vi. 7, 9; ibid. vii. 349; ibid. ix. 403, 404.
45. Cf. Kent, 1626 roster, no. 70.
47. Ibid., no. 81.
48. Ibid., no. 73.
49. Cf. Kent, 1608 roster, no. 107.
50. Cf. Kent, 1626 roster, no. 75.
51. Ibid., no. 76.
52. Ibid., no. 77.
54. Ibid., no. 80.
55. Hasted, *Kent*, v. 22.
56. Cf. Kent, 1626 roster, no. 78.
57. Cf. Kent, 1608 roster, no. 110.
59. *Middle Temple Bench Book*, p. 186; Hasted, *Kent*, vi. 220; ibid. iv. 61, 62.
62. Cf. Kent, 1626 roster, no. 86.
63. Hasted, *Kent*, xi. 228; ibid. xii. 65.
65. Ibid. vii. 275.
66. Cf. Kent, 1626 roster, no. 89.
67. *Pension Book of Gray's Inn*, pp. 187, 271; Hasted, *Kent*, ii. 478; ibid. xii. 611.
68. *The Records of the Honorable Society of Lincoln's Inn: Admissions* (2 vols., L., 1896), i. 111; *Lincoln's Inn Black Books*, ii. 56, 208, 275, 298, 310, 450.
69. Hasted, *Kent*, ix. 345; ibid. xii. 611.
70. *Students admitted to the Inner Temple, 1547–1660* (L., 1877), p. 126.
71. *Pension Book of Gray's Inn*, i. 228, 258; Hasted, *Kent*, vii. 206, 207.
72. Cf. Kent, 1626 roster, no. 92.
73. Ibid., no. 97.
74. Ibid., no. 93.
75. *Middle Temple Bench Book*, p. 185; Hasted, *Kent*, vii. 351.
76. *Masters of the Bench of the Honourable Society of the Inner Temple, 1450–1883, and Masters of the Temple, 1540–1883* (L., 1883), p. 34; Hasted, *Kent*, v. 300.
78. Cf. Kent, 1626 roster, no. 95.
79. Hasted, *Kent*, iv. 356.
81. Ibid. iii. 166; *Som. Arch. Soc., Proceedings*, xxx (1884), 72.
82. *Alum. cantab.*
83. Hasted, *Kent*, iv. 241; *Alum. oxon.*
84. Hasted, *Kent*, viii. 311, 426, 427, 436, 453.
85. Ibid., p. 322; ibid. x. 138, 140.

6. Keeler, *Long Parliament*, pp. 52, 53.

7. Hasted, *Kent*, vii. 503; ibid. v. 42, 43; ibid. vi. 199.

# APPENDIX B

# NORFOLK

## 1562[1]

| | | | | | | | | |
|---|---|---|---|---|---|---|---|---|
| 1 | q | Nicholas Bacon, knight [lord keeper] | | C | G | P | 1579 | DNB |
| 2 | q | William [Paulet], Marquess of Winchester [lord treasurer] | | | | P | 1572 | DNB |
| 3 | q | Thomas [Howard], Duke of Norfolk, earl marshal | | | | | 1572 | DNB |
| 4 | q | Henry [Fitzalan], Earl of Arundel [lord steward] | | | | | 1580 | DNB |
| 5 | | Thomas [Radcliffe], Earl of Sussex | | C | G | P | 1583 | DNB |
| 6 | q | Robert Catlyn, knight, chief justice of the queen's bench | | | M | | 1574 | DNB |
| 7 | q | Anthony Brown, a justice of the common pleas | | | M | P | 1567 | DNB |
| | | | | | | | | |
| 8 | q | William Woodhouse, knight [custos rotulorum] | Hickling | | | P | 1564 | |
| 9 | q | Edmund Wyndham, knight | Felbrigg | | | | 1569 | |
| 10 | q | Christopher Heydon, knight | Baconsthorpe | | | P | 1579 | |
| 11 | q | William Butt, knight | Thornage | | | | 1583 | |
| 12 | | Thomas Woodhouse, knight | Waxham | | L | P | 1572 | |
| 13 | | Nicholas Strange [Lestrange], knight | Hunstanton | | | P | 1580 | DNB |
| 14 | | Thomas Lovell, knight | East Harling | | | P | 1567 | |
| 15 | q | Richard Fulmerston, knight | Thetford | | | P | 1567 | |
| 16 | q | John Blennerhassett | Frenze | | | P | 1573 | |
| 17 | q | Osbert Moundford | Feltwell | | | | 1580 | |
| 18 | | Thomas Steninge | Earl Soham, Suff. | | | | | |
| 19 | | Thomas Gibbons [Guybon] | King's Lynn | | | | 1570 | |
| 20 | | William Paston | Oxnead | | C | | 1610 | DNB |
| 21 | | Edmund Beaupre | Outwell | | L | | 1568 | |
| 22 | q | Henry Reppes | West Walton | | L | | 1566 | |
| 23 | q | Thomas Gawdy, the elder | Redenhall | | I | P | 1589 | DNB |
| 24 | | William Yelverton, the elder | Rougham | | G | P | 1587 | |

The following names are found in the *liber pacis* of 1559:

| | | | | | | | | |
|---|---|---|---|---|---|---|---|---|
| 25 | q | Gilbert Gerard, attorney-general | | | G | P | 1593 | DNB |
| 26 | q | James Boleyn, knight [custos rotulorum, 1559] | Blickling | | | | 1561 | |
| 27 | | Thomas Tyndall, knight | Hockwold | | | P? | 1584 | |
| 28 | | Roger Woodhouse, knight | Kimberley | | L | | 1560 | |
| 29 | | Thomas Knyvett, knight | Buckenham | | | P | 1569 | |
| 30 | q | Robert Holdyche | Ranworth | | | | 1558 | |
| 31 | | Henry Hubberd [Hobart] | Hales | | | | 1561 | |
| 32 | | John Appleyard | Bracon Ash | | L | P | 1569 | |
| 33 | | Francis Thursby | Gaywood | | | | | |
| 34 | | Robert Barney | Gunton | | | | 1559 | |
| 35 | q | John Eyer | Narborough | | | | 1561 | |
| 36 | | Robert Coke | Mileham | | L | | 1561 | |
| 37 | q | Thomas Gawdy, junior | Harleston | | | | | |
| 38 | q | John Barney of Langley | | | | | 1559 | |
| 39 | | William Cockett | Besthorpe | | | | 1579 | |
| 40 | | William Brampton | Norwich | | G | | 1563 | |

Dignitaries 7; Court 3; Gentry 10; Law 3; Church 0; Commerce 1.

Only twenty-four in number, the Norfolk commission of the peace in 1562 is the smallest with which this study is concerned in detail.

1   Among the magnates the Lord Keeper (Sir Nicholas Bacon) and
3   England's sole Elizabethan duke (Norfolk) were county as well as national figures. Another feature was the absence of the local bishop; perhaps his ultra-Protestant notions made John Parkhurst suspect. The eight knights included both parvenus and men whose families had long been prominent. Descendants of generations of gentlemen
8   the Woodhouses acquired extensive monastic lands. Sir William and
12  Sir Thomas were brothers, and Sir William's son—heir to his uncle as well as to his father and a J.P. in 1584—married a daughter of Lord
13  Keeper Bacon. Sir Nicholas Strange (later spelled Lestrange) was likewise the heir of an ancient family which profited from Tudor opportunities. Son of a henchman of Thomas Cromwell, he had
11  fought in Ireland. Sir William Butt's father had been Henry VIII's
14  chief physician, and Sir Thomas Lovell was the heir of an earlier, notorious, Thomas who had received important offices under Henry VII and Henry VIII. Both families now held much monastic spoils. The descendant of notable fifteenth-century lawyers, Sir Christopher
10  Heydon's grandfather (Sir John) had been a prominent member of the
9   Court of Henry VII. Sir Edmund Wyndham belonged to a family which had risen during the fifteenth and sixteenth centuries from the ranks of Norwich merchants to such prominence both at Court and in the county that they qualified for marriages with ancient gentry,
15  even with the house of Howard. Sir Richard Fulmerston, of yet more humble background, was one of the very largest of all beneficiaries of monastic expropriation. In 1562 the leading Norfolk J.P.s were a splendid cross-section of Tudor society.

The esquires were also diverse. There were two interlopers, John
16  Blennerhassett of a family long prominent in Cumberland, who married in succession daughters of a Suffolk and a Norfolk gentleman,
18  and Thomas Steninge of Somerset background, who acquired a considerable estate in Suffolk and by his marriage to a widowed daughter of the Earl of Oxford became the step-father of the Duke of Norfolk. Prominent in both the fifteenth and the sixteenth centuries, the family
20  of gentry of which young William Paston was the head is probably better known to later students than to his contemporaries. Likewise the heir of a good tradition and the possessor of monastic spoils,
21  Edmund Beaupre was a barrister as well as a Norfolk squire. William
24, 23 Yelverton, an ancient of Gray's Inn, and Thomas Gawdy, treasurer of the Inner Temple, were members of Norfolk families which
19  produced many eminent lawyers. Thomas Gibbons came from a family of burghers in King's Lynn. In sum, if the Norfolk bench of 1562 included a larger proportion of members of established families

than was the case in other counties, there were also several men of recent prominence: burghers, lawyers, courtiers, and newly risen gentry.

The considerable modification of the Norfolk roster between the commission as it appears in a *liber pacis* of the spring of 1559 and that on the patent roll in February 1562 presents the interesting problem that is discussed in Chapter V, but here it is germane to consider some of these extra men in the context of the others. The Attorney-General 25 and the Queen's great uncle (Sir James Boleyn) are figures whose status 26 is obvious. Sir Thomas Tyndall, Sir Roger Woodhouse, Sir Thomas Knyvett, and Francis Thursby were all well-established gentry. Tyndall was descended from a Northamptonshire family which 27 achieved some prominence in the fifteenth century and migrated to Norfolk in consequence of marriage with an heiress. Woodhouse was 28 the head of the senior line of his family, only a distant cousin of Sir Thomas and Sir William. The Knyvett fortune was started by a 29 fourteenth-century Lord Chancellor. Thursby had a fifteenth-century 33 mayor of King's Lynn in his ancestry, but he married a daughter of Lord Abergavenny. John Eyer and Robert Coke were successful 35, 36 lawyers with Norfolk connections. Eyer was a master in chancery and receiver-general for the Crown in Norfolk and other East Anglian counties. Coke, the father of the famous Lord Chief Justice, was a bencher of Lincoln's Inn. Robert Holdyche, who had been a J.P. as 30 early as 1538, was a steward of the Duke of Norfolk. The ancestry of the brothers Robert and John Barney has been traced back—perhaps 34, 38 fictitiously—to the late twelfth century. Both were members of the army which went to France in 1544, and Robert was a juror at the trial of the Duke of Norfolk in 1546. The remaining men were gentry of no great prominence from families of varied antiquity. At least half these justices had died prior to February 1562. Sheriff in that year, Tyndall was ineligible for the commission. Whether their religious views explain the elimination of Knyvett, Brampton, and Cockett is not clear. As a group they were much like the men in the patent-roll commission.

The major source of recruitment for the Norfolk bench in the early years of Elizabeth was the gentry, old or new, sometimes with Norfolk burghers in the background. There were no cases of London merchants turned Norfolk squire or returned to a native county. There were in 1562 two professional lawyers in the working part. Two-thirds of the group held monastic land which was granted to the present holder or to his ancestor in the male line. If the wealth of these justices varied widely—the Duke of Norfolk and Fulmerston must have enjoyed very large incomes—no man can have been less than well-to-do. They were an affluent group of men and an influential one.

## 1584[2]

| | | Name | Place | | | | | |
|---|---|---|---|---|---|---|---|---|
| 1 | | Thomas Bromley, knight, lord chancellor of England | | O | M | P | 1587 | DNB |
| 2 | | William [Cecil], Lord Burghley, lord treasurer of England | | C | G | P | 1598 | DNB |
| 3 | s | Philip [Howard], Earl of Arundel | | C | | | 1595 | DNB |
| 4 | r | Henry [Radcliffe], Earl of Sussex | | | | P | 1593 | DNB |
| 5 | | Edward [Freake], Bishop of Norwich | | C | | | 1591 | DNB |
| 6 | | Edward [Parker], Lord Morley | | C | | | 1618 | |
| 7 | | Henry [Cromwell], Lord Cromwell | | | | | 1592 | |
| 8 | | Christopher Wray, knight, chief justice | | C | L | P | 1592 | DNB |
| 9 | | Edmund Anderson, knight, chief justice [of common pleas] | | O | I | | 1605 | DNB |
| 10 | * | Thomas Gawdy, knight, justice of queen's bench | | | I | P | 1589 | DNB |
| 11 | s | Francis Wyndham, justice of common pleas | | C | L | P | 1592 | DNB |
| | | | | | | | | |
| 12 | | Arthur Heveningham, knight | Hockwold | | | | 1630 | |
| 13 | | Edward Clere, knight | Blickling | | I | P | 1607 | |
| 14 | * | William Paston, knight | Oxnead | C | | | 1610 | DNB |
| 15 | s | Thomas Knyvett, knight | Buckenham | | | P | 1594 | |
| 16 | s | Nicholas Bacon, knight | Redgrave, Suff. | C | G | P | 1624 | DNB |
| 17 | s | Henry Woodhouse, knight | Hickling | C | | P | 1625 | |
| 18 | r | Roger Woodhouse, knight | Kimberley | | | P | 1588 | |
| 19 | | Drew Drury, knight [custos rotulorum] | Riddlesworth | C | | P | 1617 | |
| 20 | s | William Heydon, knight | Baconsthorpe | | L | | 1594 | |
| 21 | r | Francis Gawdy, serjeant-at-law | Wallingford | | I | | 1606 | DNB |
| 22 | | Edward Flowerdew, serjeant-at-law | Hethersett | | I | P | 1586 | DNB |
| 23 | r | Clemens Paston | Oxnead | | | | 1597 | |
| 24 | * | William Yelverton | Rougham | | G | P | 1587 | |
| 25 | | Thomas Farmer | East Barsham | | | P | 1621 | |
| 26 | s | Nathaniel Bacon | Stiffkey | C | G | P | 1622 | DNB |
| 27 | | Henry Doyley | Shotesham | | L | | 1597 | |
| 28 | | John Palgrave [Pagrave] | Barningham | C | I | | 1611 | |
| 29 | | Thomas Townshend | Bracon Ash | C | | P | 1590 | |
| 30 | | William Gresham | Intwood | O | G | P | 1624 | |
| 31 | r | Thomas Gawdy | Harleston | | | | | |
| 32 | r | Bassingbourne Gawdy | West Harling | C | I | P | 1590 | |
| 33 | | John Peyton | Outwell | | | P | 1630 | DNB |
| 34 | | Thomas Hogan | Bradenham | | | | 1586 | |
| 35 | | Nicholas Hare | Stow Bardolph | C | I | P | 1597 | |
| 36 | s | Henry Gawdy | Claxton | C | I | P | 1620 | |
| 37 | | William Rugg | Felmingham | C | G | | 1616 | |
| 38 | | Thomas Barroughe | Shipdham | | G | | 1590 | |
| 39 | | Thomas Hewar | Emneth | | | | 1585 | |
| 40 | s | Martin Barney | Gunton | | I | | 1600 | |
| 41 | r | Miles Hobart | | C | L | | | |
| 42 | r | William Blennerhassett | Frenze | | | | | |
| 43 | | Thomas Sidney | Little Walsingham | | | | 1585 | |
| 44 | | Robert Kemp | Gissing | | L | P? | 1595 | |
| 45 | | John Walpole | Houghton | | L | P | 1588 | |
| 46 | s | John Holdyche | Ranworth | C | | | 1589 | |
| 47 | | John Steward | Martham | C | | | 1605 | |

Dignitaries 11; Court 1; Gentry 27; Law 7; Church 0; Commerce 1.

Still in the Norfolk commission in 1584 were all three surviving members of the bench of 1562. Twice as large as before, it was now of a size consistent with usual Tudor and Stuart practice. In the group of dignitaries note may be made of the inclusion of the Bishop of

Norwich—in contrast to 1562—and of Lord Morley, who must have 5, 6
owned lands in Norfolk as well as in the eight other counties where he
was a J.P. Nearly half the remaining justices were sons or more distant
relatives of former members of this bench.

Much the most notable feature of the roster was the number of
judges, present and future. In addition to the two men assigned to the
Norfolk circuit—Wray and Anderson—there were Sir Thomas
Gawdy and Francis Wyndham, who served other circuits, and the two 10, 11
serjeants-at-law Edward Flowerdew and Francis Gawdy, who were 22, 21
elevated to the judicial bench in 1584 and 1588 respectively. An
interlineation in this roster was Edward Coke, and Henry Hobart
was added to the bench at some moment prior to 1597; each became
in time Attorney-General and Justice of the Common Pleas. Except
for Wray and Anderson all were sons of Norfolk. Less eminent but
also learned in the law were five other prominent barristers: William
Yelverton, Robert Kemp, John Palgrave, Nicholas Hare, and William
Rugg. Hare, the son of a London mercer and the nephew of a man 35
who had been Master of the Rolls and Speaker of the Commons in
1529, was Recorder of King's Lynn; the other four had Norfolk
backgrounds. In the later years of Elizabeth there was an abundance
of legal talent and experience in the Norfolk commission.

Three knights were men of some note. Sir Arthur Heveningham 12
was the head of a family which can be traced back to the thirteenth
century; he owned extensive property in both Norfolk and Suffolk.
Sir Edward Clere, the son of a man who had been J.P. in the time of 13
Henry VIII, was descended from a family of minor Norfolk gentry.
Much more significant is the fact he had married the heiress of the
vast Fulmerston estate. He travelled widely, contracted a great debt,
and was forced to sell much of his wife's inheritance. Blickling was
purchased by Henry Hobart. Sir Drew Drury was descended from a 19
family very prominent in East Anglia, though his father had maintained
his principal seat in Buckinghamshire. A man of much consequence
at Court, he was co-custodian of Mary Stuart and Lieutenant of the
Tower. He married a Norfolk heiress, controlled very extensive lands
in East Anglia, and was *Custos Rotulorum*.

Among the esquires three were rather more than simple county
gentry. William Gresham was the grandson of a Lord Mayor of 30
London, and the cousin and heir of the founder of the royal exchange.
Owner by inheritance of an estate in Surrey, he was a J.P. in Kent,
but his family came from Norfolk and acquired there much monastic
property. After 1584 he commonly resided at Intwood near Norwich,
was knight of the shire in 1586, and frequently acted with Sir William
Heydon, Sir Arthur Heveningham, Thomas Townshend, and Thomas
Farmer on special commissions dispatched by the Privy Council.

33 John Peyton was the second son of a Kentish knight—his elder brother was a J.P. in Kent in 1608—and married a Norfolk coheiress, Dorothy, a daughter of Edmund Beaupre and widow of the late Chief Baron Sir Robert Bell. He had an interesting career. Knighted by Leicester in the Netherlands, he succeeded Drury as Lieutenant of the Tower and later became Governor of Jersey. He was M.P. for King's Lynn, Middlesex, and Weymouth. His wife's property is the likely explanation of his membership of this commission. Thomas

43 Sidney, the son of a man who acquired a modest estate in monastic lands in Little Walsingham, was customer of Lynn and a brother-in-law of Sir Francis Walsingham. He was a cousin of Sir Henry Sidney of Penshurst, and, when his son died in 1612 without direct heirs, the Norfolk estate passed to the Kent branch of the family.

Three other esquires in this commission bore surnames which were
27 to become more famous in subsequent years. Henry Doyley was the head of a family which Blomefield traces back to the Conquest, but he acquired his estate at Shotesham by his marriage with its heiress. He held considerable other property and was twice sheriff. Thomas
29 Townshend was a cadet member of the East Raynham family estab-
45 lished by a fifteenth-century judge. John Walpole—son of Lucy Robsart, cousin and heiress of Leicester's tragic wife—was a not very prominent county gentleman who had as twin sons a notable Jesuit and the ancestor of the future Prime Minister.

Parallel to the increase in legal skill the Norfolk bench experienced growth in membership in the universities and in Parliament. Among the working portion of the commission rather more than half were at some time enrolled in Cambridge, one of the inns of court, and the House of Commons. In 1572 six Norfolk justices were sent to Westminster, while in 1584 there were four. More than half the seats represented by Norfolk J.P.s were in that county, but Sir Nicholas Bacon was knight of the shire for Suffolk, while John Peyton was returned by Lyme Regis and Nicholas Hare by Horsham. Norwich regularly elected its own aldermen, who were not county J.P.s, and Yarmouth also was not partial to local gentry. Led by the Gawdys and the Bacons, the Norfolk commission of 1584 was an impressive body of men.

1608[3]

| 1 | q | Thomas [Egerton], Lord Ellesmere, chancellor of England | L | P | 1617 | *DNB* |
| 2 | q | Thomas [Sackville], Earl of Dorset, treasurer of England | I | P | 1608 | *DNB* |
| 3 | q | Thomas [Howard], Earl of Suffolk, chamberlain of the household | C | | 1626 | *DNB* |

| # | | | q | Name | Place | N | | | | Year | | |
|---|---|---|---|------|-------|---|---|---|---|------|-----|---|
| 4 | | s | q | Robert [Radcliffe], Earl of Sussex | | | | | | 1629 | DNB | |
| 5 | | | q | John [Jegon], Bishop of Norwich | | | C | | | 1618 | DNB | |
| 6 | | s | q | Edward Coke, knight, chief justice of common pleas | assize | | C | I | P | 1634 | DNB | |
| 7 | | | q | William Daniel, knight, justice of common pleas | | | | G | | | | |
| 8 | * | | q | Henry Gawdy, knight | Claxton | 25 | C | I | P | 1620 | | |
| 9 | | s | q | Ralph Hare, knight | Stow Bardolph | 20 | C | I | P | 1623 | | |
| 10 | * | | q | Arthur Heveningham, knight | Hockwold | 20 | | | | 1630 | | |
| 11 | * | | q | William Paston, knight | Oxnead | 40 | C | | | 1610 | DNB | |
| 12 | | r | q | Thomas Knyvett, knight | Ashwellthorpe | 20 | | M | P | 1617 | | |
| 13 | * | | q | Nicholas Bacon, knight | Redgrave, Suff. | 100 | C | G | P | 1624 | DNB | |
| 14 | * | | q | Henry Woodhouse, knight | Hickling | 5 | C | | P | 1625 | | |
| 15 | * | | q | Drew Drury, knight [custos rotulorum] | Riddlesworth | | C | | P | 1617 | | |
| 16 | * | | q | John Peyton, knight | Outwell | 50 | | | P | 1630 | DNB | |
| 17 | | s | q | Philip Woodhouse, knight | Kimberley | 20 | C | L | P | 1623 | | |
| 18 | | | q | Robert Mansell, knight | | 20 | O | | P | 1656 | DNB | |
| 19 | | | q | Charles Cornwallis, knight | Brome Hall, Suff. | 30 | C | | P | 1629 | DNB | |
| 20 | | s | | Thomas Woodhouse, knight | Kimberley | 6 | C | L | P | 1658 | | K |
| 21 | | s | q | Henry Clere, knight | Blickling | 20 | | | | 1622 | | |
| 22 | | s | | Henry Sidney, knight | Little Walsingham | 18 | C | L | | 1612 | | |
| 23 | | r | q | Henry Hobart, knight, attorney-general | Blickling | | C | L | P | 1625 | DNB | |
| 24 | | | | James Calthorpe, knight | Cockthorpe | 10 | C | L | | 1615 | | |
| 25 | | r | q | Thomas Barney, knight | Gunton | 20 | | L | | 1616 | | |
| 26 | | s | q | Edmund Moundford, knight | Feltwell | 20 | | I | | 1617 | | |
| 27 | | s | q | Clypsby Gawdy, knight | Little Wenham, Suff. | 20 | C | I | P | 1619 | | |
| 28 | | r | | Henry Wyndham, knight | | 10 | | L | | 1628 | | |
| 29 | | | q | Anthony Browne, knight | Elsing | 20 | | | | | | |
| 30 | | s | q | Hamond Lestrange, knight | Hunstanton | 20 | C | | P | 1654 | | |
| 31 | | | q | Henry Spelman, knight | Congham | 20 | C | L | P | 1641 | DNB | |
| 32 | * | | q | Nathaniel Bacon, knight | Stiffkey | 30 | C | G | P | 1622 | DNB | |
| 33 | | s | q | Edward Blennerhassett, knight | Frenze | 20 | | | | 1618 | | |
| 34 | | s | q | Thomas Hewar, knight | Emneth | 20 | | | | 1630 | | |
| 35 | | s | | Robert Gawdy, knight | Claxton | | C | I | P | 1638 | | |
| 36 | | | q | Robert Houghton, serjeant-at-law | Norwich | 20 | | L | P | 1624 | DNB | |
| 37 | | | q | Robert Redman, doctor of laws | Norwich | 20 | C | | | 1625 | | |
| 38 | | | | Thomas Corbett | Sprowston | 20 | C | L | P | 1617 | | |
| 39 | * | | q | John Palgrave | Barningham | 20 | C | I | | 1611 | | |
| 40 | | s | q | William Yelverton | Rougham | 16 | C | G | | 1631 | | |
| 41 | * | | q | William Rugg | Felmingham | 8 | C | G | | 1616 | | |
| 42 | | s | | Philip Knyvett | Buckenham | 10 | C | L | | 1655 | | |
| 43 | | | | Lestrange Mordaunt | Little Massingham | 20 | | | | 1627 | | |
| 44 | | s | | Edmund Doyley | Shotesham | 25 | | | | 1612 | | |
| 45 | | | q | John Richers | Swannington | 20 | | | | | | |
| 46 | | s | q | John Reppes | West Walton | 15 | C | L | | 1612 | | |
| 47 | | | | Thomas Oxborough | King's Lynn | 10 | | L | P | 1623 | | |
| 48 | | r | q | Robert Kemp | Gissing | 15 | | L | | 1612 | | |
| 49 | | | | Elias Brantingham | Norwich | 8 | | G | | | | |
| 50 | | | | Thomas Athowe | Beechamwell | 8 | C | G | | 1630 | | |
| 51 | | | q | Richard Gwynn | Fakenham | 5 | | I | P | 1630 | | |
| 52 | | | | Gregory Pratt | Hockwold | 12 | | | | 1609 | | |
| 53 | | | | James Scamler | Hickling | 20 | | G | P | 1633 | | |

| 54 | | q | Richard Jenkinson | Tunstall | 20 | C | | | 1624 | |
| 55 | | q | Bartholomew Cotton | Starston | 20 | | M | | 1613 | |
| 56 | | q | Nicholas Hearne | Arminghall | 10 | C | L | | 1612 | |
| 57 | | q | Thomas Richardson | Norwich | 20 | C | L | P | 1635 | *DNB* |
| 58 | s | q | Henry Holdyche | Ranworth | 20 | C | I | | 1618 | |
| 59 | r | | John Kemp | Antingham | 20 | C | M | | 1610 | |

Dignitaries 7; Court 3; Gentry 39; Law 10; Church 0; Commerce 0.

More striking than the modest increase in the total size of the Norfolk commission after the accession of James I was the growth in the number of the knights to thirty. Most of these men were either veterans of the commission of 1584 or relatives of earlier justices. Three of the surviving members of the Elizabethan bench had been omitted: Lord Morley, whose principal estates were elsewhere; William Gresham, who had squandered his heritage and moved back to Surrey; and Thomas Farmer, who had been forced to part with much of his Fulmerston inheritance. There was much continuity.

There were three members of the royal administration. Sir Robert
18 Mansell, Vice-Admiral and Treasurer of the Navy, notorious monopolist in glass, who was considered under Kent, had been added to the Norfolk bench probably because of his marriage with a daughter of
19 Lord Keeper Sir Nicholas Bacon. Sir Charles Cornwallis, resident ambassador in Spain and after 1610 Treasurer of the Household of the Prince of Wales, had his principal seat in Suffolk but in 1604 he had
28 been chosen as knight of the shire for Norfolk. Sir Henry Wyndham, related in a junior line to the more prominent family of Felbrigg, held a post in the customs service and thus served as a civil servant as well as a J.P.

Although the lawyer members of this commission now included
36 only two future judges—Robert Houghton, who had been Recorder of Norwich since 1595 and was elevated to the King's Bench in 1613,
57 and Thomas Richardson, successively Recorder of King's Lynn and of Norwich, Chief Justice of the Common Pleas, and finally of the King's Bench—there were six men of lesser distinction who made a
37 profession of the law. Dr. Robert Redman was chancellor of the diocese of Norwich. Two Lincoln's Inn barristers were Thomas
47 Oxborough, who was born in the county and was related to several of
56 his fellow justices, and Nicholas Hearne who became Clerk of the Crown and acquired extensive properties in Norfolk and Suffolk.
49, 50 Elias Brantingham and Thomas Athowe were also Norfolk men, but it was Gray's Inn in which they were chosen as readers. The Inner
51 Temple was the society in which Richard Gwynn of Welsh background found a career which led to a serjeanty in 1623. If the group did not have quite the eminence of their predecessors, they brought much legal talent to the bench.

The commission included three members of the gentry who deserve mention. Sir James Calthorpe came from a family which provided for 24 the heralds' visitation a pedigree over fifteen generations. Sir Henry Spelman's family is traced back to the eleventh century by Blomefield, 31 but though at different times sheriff and knight of the shire he is best known as a learned and diligent antiquarian and a historian of consequence. Sir Thomas Woodhouse was not only a scion of a large and 20 distinguished family, but he was now beginning a period of service which lasted through the civil wars and included membership in the Long Parliament down to its dissolution.

The Norfolk commission in 1608 was much like that of 1584 in spite of a twenty-five per cent increase in size. Educational experience at Cambridge and the inns of court was more common. Election to the Commons was a little less frequent. Only six members of this commission sat in the Parliament which was elected in 1604, all for Norfolk constituencies except Sir Robert Mansell. Nearly all Norfolk J.P.s were native sons, lawyers sometimes, usually gentry of greater or lesser prominence. Headed by Sir Edward Coke, including several Gawdys and Bacons, embellished by the learning of Sir Henry Spelman, it was again a very unusual group of men.

## 1626[4]

| | | | | | | | | | |
|---|---|---|---|---|---|---|---|---|---|
| 1 | | Sir Thomas Coventry, knight, lord keeper | | O | I | P | 1640 | DNB | |
| 2 | | James [Ley], Earl of Marlborough, lord treasurer | | O | L | P | 1629 | DNB | |
| 3 | | Henry [Montagu], Earl of Manchester [lord president] | | C | M | P | 1642 | DNB | |
| 4 | | Edward [Somerset], Earl of Worcester [lord privy seal] | | | | | 1628 | DNB | |
| 5 | | George [Villiers], Duke of Buckingham | | | | | 1628 | DNB | |
| 6 | * | Robert [Radcliffe], Earl of Sussex | | | | | 1629 | DNB | |
| 7 | s | Theophilus [Howard], Earl of Suffolk | | O | | P | 1640 | DNB | |
| 8 | | Robert [Rich], Earl of Warwick | | C | I | P | 1658 | DNB | |
| 9 | | Thomas [Savage], Viscount Savage | | | | | 1635 | | |
| 10 | | Samuel [Harsnett], Bishop of Norwich | | C | | | 1631 | DNB | |
| 11 | | Sir Thomas Edmondes, knight | | | | P | 1639 | DNB | |
| 12 | | Sir John Suckling, knight | | | G | P | 1627 | | |
| 13 | | Sir Humphrey May, knight | | O | M | P | 1630 | DNB | |
| 14 | | Sir Thomas Trevor, knight | | | I | P | 1656 | DNB | |
| | | | | | | | | | |
| 15 | s | Sir Edmund Bacon, knight & baronet | Redgrave, Suff. | C | G | P | 1649 | | |
| 16 | | Sir Lionel Tollemache, knight & baronet | Helmingham, Suff. | | | P | 1640 | | |
| 17 | s | Sir John Hobart, knight & baronet | Blickling | | L | P | 1647 | | |
| 18 | * | Sir Thomas Woodhouse, knight & baronet | Kimberley | C | L | P | 1658 | | K |
| 19 | * | Sir Lestrange Mordaunt, baronet | Little Massingham | | | | 1627 | | |
| 20 | r | Sir Roger Townshend, baronet | East Raynham | | L | P | 1637 | | |
| 21 | s | Sir Richard Barney, baronet | Gunton | | I | | 1668 | | |
| 22 | * | Sir William Yelverton, baronet | Rougham | C | G | | 1631 | | |
| 23 | | Sir Henry Jerningham, baronet | Cossey | C | | | 1646 | | |

| 24 | s | Sir John Corbett, baronet | Sprowston | | | L | P | 1628 | | |
|----|---|---------------------------|-----------|---|---|---|---|------|---|---|
| 25 | * | Sir Charles Cornwallis, knight | Brome Hall, Suff. | C | | | P | 1629 | DNB | |
| 26 | * | Sir Thomas Richardson, knight | Norwich | C | | L | P | 1635 | DNB | |
| 27 | | Sir Thomas Jermyn, knight | Rushbrooke, Suff. | C | M | | P | 1645 | | K |
| 28 | * | Sir Arthur Heveningham, knight | Hockwold | | | | | 1630 | | |
| 29 | s | Sir William Woodhouse, knight | Hickling | | | | P | 1639 | | |
| 30 | s | Sir John Heveningham, knight | Hockwold | C | I | | P | 1633 | | |
| 31 | r | Sir Anthony Drury, knight | Besthorpe | C | | | P | 1638 | | |
| 32 | | Sir William de Gray, knight | Merton | | | | | 1632 | | |
| 33 | * | Sir Hamond Lestrange, knight | Hunstanton | C | | | P | 1654 | | |
| 34 | * | Sir Henry Spelman, knight | Congham | C | | L | P | 1641 | DNB | |
| 35 | s | Sir Augustine Palgrave, knight | Barningham | C | I | | | 1639 | | |
| 36 | * | Sir Robert Gawdy, knight | Claxton | C | I | | P | 1638 | | |
| 37 | r | Sir Thomas Hearne, knight | Haveringland | | | G | P | 1638 | | |
| 38 | r | Sir Thomas Southwell, knight | Woodrising | | | L | | 1643 | | |
| 39 | | Sir Robert Bell, knight | Outwell | C | | | P | 1639 | | |
| 40 | | Sir Thomas Dereham, knight | West Dereham | C | I | | | 1645 | | |
| 41 | s | Sir John Hare, knight | Stow Bardolph | | | | P | 1638 | | |
| 42 | | Sir Charles Le Groos, knight | Crostwick | C | G | | P | 1650 | | K |
| 43 | * | Thomas Athowe, serjeant-at-law | Beechamwell | C | G | | | 1630 | | |
| 44 | * | Richard Gwynn, serjeant-at-law | Fakenham | | I | | P | 1630 | | |
| 45 | r | Edmund Suckling | Norwich | C | | | | 1628 | | |
| 46 | | Andrew Byng, D.D. | Norwich | C | | | | 1652 | DNB | |
| 47 | | Clemens Corbett, LL.D. | Norwich | C | | | | 1652 | DNB | |
| 48 | | Drew Drury | Riddlesworth | C | | | P | 1632 | | |
| 49 | | Miles Hobart | London | C | | L | | 1639 | | |
| 50 | r | Framlingham Gawdy | Harling | | | G | P | 1654 | DNB | K |
| 51 | r | Anthony Hobart | Hales Hall | | | | | | | |
| 52 | | John Smyth | Thetford | | | | | 1638 | | |
| 53 | | Owen Sheppard | Kirby Bedon | | | | | | | |
| 54 | | John Jermy | Gunton | | M | | | 1631 | | |
| 55 | | Thomas Holl | Heigham | C | | | | 1628 | | |
| 56 | | John Potts | Mannington | | | | P | 1673 | | K |
| 57 | r | Adam Scamler | Hevingham | C | I | | | 1645 | DNB | |
| 58 | s | Edmund Moundford | Feltwell | C | | | P | 1643 | | K |
| 59 | | Francis Mapes | Rollesby | | | | | 1638 | | |
| 60 | | Francis Parlett | King's Lynn | C | | L | | | | |
| 61 | r | Charles Suckling | Woodton | | | | | 1644 | | |
| 62 | * | Elias Brantingham | Norwich | | | G | | | | |
| 63 | | Edmund Reeve | Aylsham | C | | G | | 1647 | DNB | |
| 64 | r | Charles Lovell | East Harling | | | | | 1641 | | |
| 65 | r | [Edmund] Doyley | Shotesham | | I | | | 1638 | | |

Dignitaries 14; Court 0; Gentry 34; Law 12; Church 3; Commerce 2.

The Norfolk commission of the peace in 1626, like those of other counties, reflected sharply the inflation of honours which had occurred during the reign of James I. In a total of sixty-five men, only eighteen were mere esquires. Four prominent members of the royal Court were the Duke of Buckingham, Sir Thomas Edmondes, Sir John Suckling, and Sir Humphrey May, who were J.P.s in other counties and have

12  been considered under Kent. Suckling, whose brothers Edmund and Charles were his fellows on the Norfolk bench, had a Norwich back

13  ground, while May seems to have held Norfolk property once parcel of the lands of Carrow Priory. Dignitaries whose presence in this roster

8  invites explanation were the second Earl of Warwick and Viscount

Savage. Warwick was heir to extensive properties spreading out from    9
Essex, where he was Lord Lieutenant. Savage, son of a wealthy
Cambridgeshire mother, married a Suffolk heiress, and must have
controlled lands which made appropriate his appointment to the
Norfolk bench. Though lacking a fellow judge in this roster, Sir
Thomas Trevor served the Norfolk circuit.                              14
  While there were thirteen members of this commission who were
veterans of 1608, and the usual large number of sons and more distant
relatives of former J.P.s, seven surviving members of the earlier bench
had been omitted. Sir Edward Coke, who now resided in Buckinghamshire, was hardly *persona grata* at Court; this was the year in which he
was forced to serve as sheriff so that he would be ineligible for election
to the Commons. As Governor of Jersey, Sir John Peyton had for
many years not in fact been able to perform the duties of a Norfolk
J.P. Death had deprived Sir Robert Mansell of the wife whose estate
had given him status in the county. Sir Philip Knyvett had dissipated
his inheritance; later he sold Buckenham Castle. Sir Anthony Browne
was a Suffolk gentleman. It is not clear that Sir Henry Wyndham was
still alive. There is no ready explanation for the elimination of Sir
Thomas Hewar and James Scamler. The unusual break in continuity
of service, however, seems to have been unplanned.
  Most of the baronets and knights were veterans or heirs of earlier
justices, though three baronets and four knights invite comment.
Descended from a prominent Suffolk family, Sir Lionel Tollemache    16
was a Privy Councillor. Sir Roger Townshend, the better-known cousin   20
of an earlier J.P., built at East Raynham a mansion designed by Inigo
Jones. Sir Henry Jerningham, grandson of an important official of the   23
Court of Queen Mary, came from a Norfolk family which can be
traced back well before the Tudor period. Like their fellows these
baronets were influential as well as wealthy. Among the knights Sir
Thomas Jermyn, whose ancestry can be distinguished as far back as    27
the reign of John, became a Privy Councillor and Comptroller of the
Household later in the reign of Charles I. Sir William de Gray,      32
whose family Blomefield traced back to the Conquest, and Sir Charles
Le Groos, who had Paston and Cornwallis forebears, were prominent    42
Norfolk gentlemen.
  The legal strength of the Norfolk commission was kept at a high
level both by the inclusion of the surviving lawyers—three serjeants,
Richardson, Athowe, and Gwynn, and one barrister, Brantingham—
and by the appointment of one future judge, Edmund Reeve (previ-    63
ously Recorder of Great Yarmouth), one Middle Temple reader, John
Jermy, and six barristers: Sir Augustine Palgrave, Sir Thomas South-   54
well, Sir Thomas Dereham, Francis Parlett (Recorder of King's
Lynn), Miles Hobart, and Adam Scamler.

45    The clerical members of this commission included Edmund Suck-
46 ling, Dean of Norwich and son of a former mayor, Dr. Andrew Byng,
Archdeacon of Norwich and a collaborator in the Authorized Version
47 of the Bible, and Dr. Clemens Corbett, professor at Cambridge,
chancellor of Chichester, and vicar-general of Norwich. Suckling and
Corbett were members of well-known county families.
53    Three other justices require mention. Owen Sheppard was a
receiver-general for a Howard Earl of Northampton who after the
death of his patron became established among the gentry. Thomas
55, 59 Holl and Francis Mapes were Norwich burghers whose landed wealth
allowed them to enter the ranks of the squirearchy.
   The educational experience of the members of the Norfolk commission of 1626 was much like that of the bench of 1608. Only
thirteen men had never been enrolled at either a university or an inn of
court. Ten Norfolk J.P.s found seats in the Parliament of 1626;
Sir Humphrey May at Leicester, Sir John Hobart at Brackley, Sir John
Hare at Evesham, Sir Thomas Jermyn at Bury St. Edmunds, and
Sir Charles Le Groos at Orford. Sir John Suckling, Sir John Corbett,
Sir Thomas Hearne, Sir Robert Bell, and Framlingham Gawdy were
for Norfolk constituencies.

## 1636[5]

| | | | | | | | | | | |
|---|---|---|---|---|---|---|---|---|---|---|
| 1 | * | q | Thomas [Coventry], Lord Coventry, lord keeper | | O | I | P | 1640 | DNB | |
| 2 | | q | William [Juxon], Bishop of London, lord treasurer | | O | | | 1663 | DNB | |
| 3 | * | q | Henry [Montagu], Earl of Manchester, keeper of privy seal | | C | M | P | 1642 | DNB | |
| 4 | r | q | Thomas [Howard], Earl of Arundel and Surrey, earl marshal [lord lieutenant] | | C | | | 1646 | DNB | |
| 5 | * | q | Theophilus [Howard], Earl of Suffolk, warden of cinque ports | | O | | P | 1640 | DNB | |
| 6 | * | q | Robert [Rich], Earl of Warwick | | C | I | P | 1658 | DNB | |
| 7 | | q | Matthew [Wren], Bishop of Norwich | | C | | | 1667 | DNB | |
| 8 | s | q | Henry [Howard], Lord Maltravers [custos rotulorum] | | | | P | 1652 | DNB | |
| 9 | | q | John Bramston, knight, chief justice of king's bench | | C | M | | 1654 | DNB | |
| 10 | | q | George Crooke, justice of king's bench | | O | I | P | 1642 | | |
| 11 | s | q | Thomas Richardson, knight | Honingham | C | L | P | 1643 | | |
| 12 | * | q | Edmund Bacon, knight & baronet | Redgrave, Suff. | C | G | P | 1649 | | |
| 13 | * | q | John Hobart, knight & baronet | Blickling | | L | P | 1647 | | |
| 14 | * | q | Lionel Tollemache, knight & baronet | Helmingham, Suff. | | | P | 1640 | | |
| 15 | * | q | Thomas Woodhouse, knight & baronet | Kimberley | C | L | P | 1658 | | K |
| 16 | * | q | Roger Townshend, baronet | East Raynham | | L | P | 1637 | | |
| 17 | * | q | Richard Barney, baronet | Gunton | | I | | 1668 | | |
| 18 | * | q | Henry Jerningham, baronet | Cossey | C | | | 1646 | | |
| 19 | | q | John Holland, baronet | Quidenham | C | | P | 1700 | | K |
| 20 | r | q | Miles Hobart, knight | Plumstead | | | P | 1639 | | |
| 21 | * | | William Woodhouse, knight | Hickling | | | P | 1639 | | |
| 22 | * | q | Anthony Drury, knight | Besthorpe | C | | P | 1638 | | |

| | | | | | | | | | | |
|---|---|---|---|---|---|---|---|---|---|---|
| 23 | | q | John Wentworth, knight | Somerleyton, Suff. | C | L | P | 1652 | | |
| 24 | * | q | Hamond Lestrange, knight | Hunstanton | C | | P | 1654 | | |
| 25 | * | q | Henry Spelman, knight | Congham | C | L | P | 1641 | DNB | |
| 26 | * | q | Augustine Palgrave, knight | Barningham | C | I | | 1639 | | |
| 27 | * | q | Robert Gawdy, knight | Claxton | C | I | P | 1638 | | |
| 28 | * | q | Thomas Hearne, knight | Haveringland | | G | P | 1638 | | |
| 29 | * | q | Thomas Southwell, knight | Woodrising | | L | | 1643 | | |
| 30 | * | q | Robert Bell, knight | Outwell | C | | P | 1639 | | |
| 31 | * | q | Thomas Dereham, knight | West Dereham | C | I | | 1645 | | |
| 32 | * | q | John Hare, knight | Stow Bardolph | | | P | 1638 | | |
| 33 | * | q | Charles Le Groos, knight | Crostwick | C | G | P | 1650 | | K |
| 34 | | | Owen Smyth, knight | Burgh, Suff. | C | G | | 1636 | | |
| 35 | s | q | Robert Kemp, knight | Gissing | | G | | 1647 | | |
| 36 | | q | William Denny, knight, one of king's counsel learned in law | Norwich | C | G | P | 1642 | | |
| 37 | * | q | Edmund Moundford, knight | Feltwell | C | | P | 1643 | | K |
| 38 | | q | Francis Astley, knight | Melton Constable | C | G | | 1638 | | |
| 39 | * | q | Edmund Reeve, serjeant-at-law | Aylsham | C | G | | 1647 | DNB | |
| 40 | * | q | Andrew Byng, S.T.D. | Norwich | C | | | 1652 | DNB | |
| 41 | * | q | Clemens Corbett, LL.D. | Norwich | C | | | 1652 | DNB | |
| 42 | s | | William Heveningham | Hockwold | C | | P | 1678 | DNB | K |
| 43 | * | q | Miles Hobart | London | C | L | | 1639 | | |
| 44 | * | | Framlingham Gawdy | Harling | | G | P | 1654 | DNB | K |
| 45 | r | q | John Spelman de Narborough | | C | M | P | 1662 | | |
| 46 | | | John Spelman | Congham | C | G | | 1643 | DNB | |
| 47 | * | q | Anthony Hobart | Hales Hall | | | | | | |
| 48 | s | q | Thomas Knyvett | Ashwellthorpe | C | | | 1658 | | |
| 49 | * | | Francis Mapes | Rollesby | | | | 1638 | | |
| 50 | * | q | John Smyth | Thetford | | | | 1638 | | |
| 51 | * | | John Potts | Mannington | | | P | 1673 | | K |
| 52 | * | q | Adam Scamler | Hevingham | C | I | | 1645 | DNB | |
| 53 | r | | Thomas Wyndham | Felbrigg | O | L | | | | |
| 54 | | | John Buxton | Tibenham | | G | | 1660 | | |
| 55 | | q | William Barnes | East Winch | | | | | | |
| 56 | | | Thomas Talbott | Wymondham | C | L | | | | |
| 57 | s | | John Athowe | Beechamwell | C | G | | 1638 | | |
| 58 | s | | Francis Jermy | Gunton | C | M | | | | |
| 59 | * | | Francis Parlett | King's Lynn | C | L | | | | |
| 60 | | | Robert Wilton | Topcroft | C | | P | | | |
| 61 | | q | Miles Corbett | | C | L | P | 1662 | DNB | K |
| 62 | | | William Buckworth | Wisbech, Cambs. | C | L | | | | |

Dignitaries 10; Court 0; Gentry 33; Law 16; Church 2; Commerce 1.

The high degree of stability in the Norfolk commission in the reign of Charles I is shown by the small number of men—a mere ten in the working group—who were neither veterans of 1626 nor relatives of men whose names had appeared in earlier rosters. Moreover, among the surviving resident J.P.s, only Charles Suckling and Charles Lovell were not still on the bench ten years later.

The remarkable legal competence of the working group had also been maintained. If three serjeants in the earlier commission had died, Edmund Reeve had now become a serjeant, and ten new barristers had joined the six who were still alive (Palgrave, Southwell, Dereham,

Reeve, Scamler, Parlett), three of them lawyer sons of lawyers—Sir
Thomas Richardson, John Athowe, and Francis Jermy—one, Miles
Corbett, a lawyer scion of a well-known county family who was
destined to become a regicide, two others likewise relatives of earlier
Norfolk J.P.s: Miles Hobart and Thomas Wyndham. Four bore
names new to the county bench: Sir William Denny, son of a Suffolk
yeoman, was a Gray's Inn reader who became Recorder and M.P. for
Norwich, Francis Astley, descended from gentry, Thomas Talbott, son
of a clerical lawyer, and William Buckworth of Cambridgeshire. Thirty
per cent were men who had been called to the bar; it was a bench
rich in legal experience even if there were fewer judges than in 1584.

Only one baronet and two knights are not accounted for. Sir John
Holland was the son of a man who seems to have owed his position at
least in part to services for the Earl of Arundel. Sir John Wentworth
and Sir Owen Smyth were Suffolk gentry who owned lands in Norfolk
and had close connections with its leading families.

There were only ten men in the whole commission who had never
been enrolled at either an inn or a university. Slightly more than half
this commission served at some time as members of the House of
Commons. Eight (whose names are marked by 'K') were elected to
the Long Parliament at its beginning, and Sir John Hobart and John
Spelman were later returned in by-elections. Except for Sir Charles
Le Groos's seat at Orford the constituencies were in the county. All
these men were reformers. Norfolk remained staunchly loyal to the
parliamentary cause, not least the justices of the peace. The records
of the committee for the advance of money and that for compounding
show that only Bishop Wren, Lord Maltravers, Sir John Bramston,
and seven working justices—Sir Lionel Tollemache, Sir Richard
Barney, Sir Miles Hobart, Sir Hamond Lestrange, Sir Charles Le
Groos, Sir Robert Kemp, and John Buxton—were fined for anti-
parliamentary action. Few counties matched this record.

In summary, it is clear that the bulk of the Norfolk J.P.s all through
the period from the accession of Elizabeth to the outbreak of the civil
wars were county gentry, most of them the heads of leading families.
In 1562 and again in 1608 there were three men who can best be
termed courtiers. In Elizabeth's time and after 1625 there were a few
whose close backgrounds were the commerce of the chief towns of the
region. Under Charles I in Norfolk as elsewhere a few leading clergy
were among the working members of the bench. What really distinguished the Norfolk commission was the number of its members who
had been called to the bar and frequently reached even higher distinction. Was it accident that the Norfolk bench combined men who had
had professional legal experience and those who were to remain in
Parliament after the open rupture with the King?

11, 57, 58
61
43, 53
36
38, 56
62

19
23
34

# NOTES TO APPENDIX B

1. *Cal. Pat. Rolls, Eliz.* ii (1560–3), 440; Lansdowne MS. 1218, ff. 23, 23ᵛ.

*1562 roster:*

8. Blomefield, *Norfolk,* ix. 352–3; Walter Rye (ed.), *The Visitation of Norfolk . . . 1563 [and] . . . 1613* (Harl. Soc. Publ. xxxii, L., 1891), pp. 320–1; *L. & P.* xxa, g620(27); ibid. xxiA, g1166(44).

9. *Visitation of Norfolk,* p. 324; H. A. Wyndham, *A Family History, 1410–1688* (L., 1929), *passim,* esp. pp. 90–6.

10. *Visitation of Norfolk,* p. 152; Blomefield, *Norfolk,* vi. 505–7; *L. & P.* xxa, g1081(48); ibid. xxiB, g648(62); Trevor-Roper, *Gentry,* p. 19.

11. Blomefield, *Norfolk,* vii. 164; *DNB*: 'William Butts'; *L. & P.* xxa, g125(12).

12. Cf. no. 8, *supra.*

13. *Visitation of Norfolk,* p. 272; Blomefield, *Norfolk,* x. 319; *L. & P.* xvi, g379(10), *et passim.*

14. Blomefield, *Norfolk,* i. 324; Hurstfield, *Queen's Wards,* pp. 242, 243; *L. & P.* xxa, g1081(53).

15. Blomefield, *Norfolk,* ii. 57; *L. & P.* xiiiA, no. 1520; ibid. xivA, g651(46); ibid. xxiB, no. 712.

16. Blomefield, *Norfolk,* i. 141; *Visitation of Norfolk,* p. 39.

17. Blomefield, *Norfolk,* ii. 193; *Visitation of Norfolk,* p. 201.

18. W. A. Coppinger, *The Manors of Suffolk* (7 vols., L., 1905–11), ii, 358–9; *Complete Peerage,* ix. 621.

19. Blomefield, *Norfolk,* viii. 538–9.

21. *Visitation of Norfolk,* pp. 34, 216; Blomefield, *Norfolk,* vii. 459; *L. & P.* xvii, g443(45); ibid. xixA, g610(10), g1383(81).

22. *Visitation of Norfolk,* p. 230; Blomefield, *Norfolk,* ix. 135.

23. Ibid. v. 370; H.M.C., Gawdy MSS. (10th rpt., App. ii), p. 21; *DNB*: 'Thomas Gawdy'.

24. *DNB*: 'Christopher Yelverton'.

26. Blomefield, *Norfolk,* vi. 289; PCC 1561, 25 Loftus.

27. Blomefield, *Norfolk,* ii. 180–1.

28. Ibid., p. 540; Simpson, *Wealth,* p. 57.

29. Blomefield, *Norfolk,* i. 379.

30. *L. & P.* xiii, g1519(20); ibid. xxB, 734; Blomefield, *Norfolk,* ii. 230.

31. *Visitation of Norfolk,* pp. 164–5; Blomefield, *Norfolk,* viii. 19.

32. *Visitation of Norfolk,* p. 6; Blomefield, *Norfolk,* v. 84.

33. Ibid. viii. 421.

34. Ibid., p. 120; *Visitation of Norfolk,* p. 15; *L. & P.* xixA, no. 273; ibid. xxiB, no. 697; ibid. xvi, g305(68).

35. Blomefield, *Norfolk,* vi. 159.

36. *Lincoln's Inn Black Books,* i. 287, 325.

37. Cf. no. 23, *supra.*

38. Blomefield, *Norfolk,* x. 150; cf. no. 34, *supra.*

39. Blomefield, *Norfolk,* i. 498; *Visitation of Norfolk,* pp. 80–1.

40. Blomefield, *Norfolk,* i. 243–5; ibid. vi. 431; *Visitation of Norfolk,* pp. 46–53.

2. Lansdowne MS. 737, ff. 19ᵛ–20ᵛ.

*1584 roster:*

12. Blomefield, *Norfolk,* v. 94; Alfred Suckling, *The History and Antiquities of the County of Suffolk* (2 vols., L., 1846–7), ii. 384, 388–9; *L. & P.* xxa, no. 102.

13. Blomefield, *Norfolk,* ii. *passim;* ibid. vi. 395.

15. Ibid. i. 379.

16. Cf. *DNB*: 'Nicholas Bacon', his father.
17. Blomefield, *Norfolk*, ii. 353.
18. Ibid. pp. 540 ff.
19. Arthur Campling, *The History of the Family of Drury* (L., n.d.), Ch. VII; Blomefield, *Norfolk*, i. 278.
20. Ibid. vi. 508.
23. *DNB*: 'William Paston'.
24. Cf. Norfolk, 1562 roster, no. 24.
25. Blomefield, *Norfolk*, vii. 56–7.
27. Ibid. v. 506.
28. *Alum. cantab.; Students admitted to the Inner Temple*, p. 8.
29. *Visitation of Norfolk*, p. 291; Blomefield, *Norfolk*, v. 84; ibid. vii. 134, 199; *Norfolk Archaeology*, xxiii (1929), 95; *A.P.C. 1590–1*; pp. 72, 308.
30. *DNB*: 'Thomas Gresham'; *Visitation of Norfolk*, pp. 136–7; *Alum. oxon.*
31. Blomefield, *Norfolk*, v, 370.
32. *Visitation of Norfolk*, pp. 125–7; Blomefield, *Norfolk*, i. 306.
34. G. A. Carthew, *A History . . . of the Parishes of West and East Bradenham* (Norwich, 1883), pp. 104–14; Blomefield, *Norfolk*, vi. 136.
35. *Alum. cantab.; Students admitted to the Inner Temple*, p. 4.
36. Cf. *DNB*: 'Thomas Gawdy'.
37. Blomefield, *Norfolk*, viii. 151–2; ibid. xi. 36; *Pension Book of Gray's Inn*, i. 499.
38. *Norfolk Archaeology*, v, supplement, p. 114; Blomefield, *Norfolk*, ix. 122.
39. *Norfolk Archaeology*, v, supplement, p. 150; Blomefield, *Norfolk*, ix. 150; PCC 1586, 18 Windsor.
40. Blomefield, *Norfolk*, viii. 120; PCC 1605, 50 Hayes.
41. Blomefield, *Norfolk*, vii. 244.
42. Ibid. i. 141.
43. Ibid. ix. 280; PCC 1585, 17 Brudenell.
44. Blomefield, *Norfolk*, i. 178.
45. *DNB*: 'Edward Walpole'; Blomefield, *Norfolk*, vii. 108; Walter Rye, *The Later History of the Family of Walpole* (Norwich, 1920), p. 9.
46. Blomefield, *Norfolk*, ii. 230.
47. Ibid. vii. 384.

3. P.R.O., S.P. 14/33, ff. 46–7ᵛ.

*1608 roster:*

7. *Pension Book of Gray's Inn*, i. 28, 77, 94.
8. Cf. Norfolk, 1584 roster, no. 36.
9. Blomefield, *Norfolk*, vii. 442.
10. Cf. Norfolk, 1584 roster, no. 12.
12. Blomefield, *Norfolk*, v. 153 ff.
13. Cf. Norfolk, 1584 roster, no. 16.
14. Ibid., no. 17.
15. Ibid., no. 19.
17. Blomefield, *Norfolk*, ii. 534; Cokayne, *Baronetage*, i. 51 (cr. 1611).
21. Blomefield, *Norfolk*, vi. 395.
22. Ibid. ix. 280.
24. *Visitation of Norfolk*, pp. 65–6; Blomefield, *Norfolk*, ix. 217; ibid. vii. 57.
25. Ibid. xi. 128.
26. Ibid. ii. 191.
27. *Alum. cantab.; Students admitted to the Inner Temple*, p. 140.
28. Wyndham, *Family History*, pp. 87, 113, 140, 149–56.

29. Blomefield, *Norfolk*, viii. 201–2; A. W. Hughes Clarke and Arthur Campling (ed.), *The Visitation of Norfolk . . . 1664* (2 vols., Harl. Soc. Publ. lxxxv, lxxxvi, L. 1933, 1934), i. 38.
30. Blomefield, *Norfolk*, x. 319.
31. F. M. Powicke, *Sir Henry Spelman and the Concilia* (L., [1930]), *passim*.
33. Blomefield, *Norfolk*, i. 141.
34. *Norfolk Archaeology*, v, supplement, p. 150; PCC 1630, 101 Scroope.
35. Blomefield, *Norfolk*, x. 116.
37. *Alum. cantab.*
38. Blomefield, *Norfolk*, x. 458–60.
39. Cf. Norfolk, 1584 roster, no. 28.
40. Cokayne, *Baronetage*, i. 146 (cr. 1620).
41. Cf. Norfolk, 1584 roster, no. 37.
42. Blomefield, *Norfolk*, i. 380; Cokayne, *Baronetage*, i. 24 (cr. 1611).
43. Blomefield, *Norfolk*, ix. 17; Cokayne, *Baronetage*, i. 61 (cr. 1611).
44. Blomefield, *Norfolk*, v. 508.
45. *Visitation of Norfolk, 1563 and 1613*, p. 233; Blomefield, *Norfolk*, x. 304–5; Hasted, *Kent*, v. 8; *Miscellanea Genealogica et Heraldica*, 5th Series vi (1926–8), 425; PCC 1625, 19 Clarke.
46. Blomefield, *Norfolk*, ix. 137.
47. *Lincoln's Inn Black Books*, i. 400, 422, 440; ibid. ii. 428; PCC 1624, 3 Byrde.
48. Blomefield, *Norfolk*, i. 178.
49. *Pension Book of Gray's Inn*, i. 65, 100, 171, 218.
50. Ibid., pp. 71, 129, 137, 175, 181, 182, 211; *Alum. cantab.*
51. *Masters of the Bench of the Inner Temple*, p. 20.
52. Blomefield, *Norfolk*, viii. 395.
53. Ibid. xi. 299; *Visitation of Norfolk, 1563 and 1613*, p. 241; cf. *supra*, p. 155.
54. Blomefield, *Norfolk*, xi. 120.
55. Ibid. v. 346; PCC 1613, 74 Capell.
56. Blomefield, *Norfolk*, v. 421; PCC 1612, 51 Fenner.
58. Blomefield, *Norfolk*, xi. 113.
59. Ibid. i. 178.

4. P.R.O., C 193/12.

*1626 roster:*

12. Cf. Kent, 1626 roster, no. 33.
15. Cokayne, *Baronetage*, i. 2 (cr. 1611).
16. Ibid., p. 18 (cr. 1611); *Suffolk Institute of Archaeology and Natural History, Proceedings*, viii (1894), 200–1.
17. *DNB*: 'Henry Hobart'; Blomefield, *Norfolk*, vi. 398–9.
19. Cf. Norfolk, 1608 roster, no. 43.
20. Cokayne, *Baronetage*, i. 111 (cr. 1617).
21. Blomefield, *Norfolk*, xi. 128.
22. Cf. Norfolk, 1608 roster, no. 40.
23. Blomefield, *Norfolk*, ii. 415.
24. Ibid. x. 458–60.
28. Cf. Norfolk, 1608 roster, no. 10.
29. *Visitation of Norfolk, 1563 and 1613*, p. 321.
30. Blomefield, *Norfolk*, v. 94.
31. Campling, *Family of Drury*, p. 90; Blomefield, *Norfolk*, i. 498.
32. Ibid. ii. 306.
33. Cf. Norfolk, 1608 roster, no. 30.
35. *Alum. cantab.*

36. Cf. Norfolk, 1608 roster, no. 35.
37. Blomefield, *Norfolk*, viii. 228.
38. Ibid. x. 277.
39. Ibid. vii. 459.
40. Ibid., p. 324; *Students admitted to the Inner Temple*, p. 126.
41. Blomefield, *Norfolk*, vii. 442.
42. Ibid. xi. 10–11.
43. Cf. Norfolk, 1608 roster, no. 50.
44. *Masters of the Bench of the Inner Temple*, p. 20.
45. *Alum. cantab.; Visitation of Norfolk, 1563 and 1613*, p. 274.
48. Cokayne, *Baronetage*, ii. 13 (cr. 1627).
49. Cf. no. 17, *supra*.
51. Blomefield, *Norfolk*, viii. 18, 19.
52. *Visitation of Norfolk, 1563 and 1613*, pp. 253–8; *Visitation of Norfolk, 1664*, ii. 201; Blomefield, *Norfolk*, ii. 93.
53. Ibid. v. 456, 477, *et passim*; *Visitation of Norfolk, 1563 and 1613*, p. 248.
54. *Middle Temple Bench Book*, p. 171; Blomefield, *Norfolk*, viii. 120.
55. Ibid. iii. 371.
59. Ibid. xi. 185; *Visitation of Norfolk, 1664*, ii. 131.
60. *Lincoln's Inn Black Books*, i. 120; *Alum. cantab.*
61. Blomefield, *Norfolk*, x. 190.
62. Cf. Norfolk, 1608 roster, no. 49.
64. Blomefield, *Norfolk*, i. 324.
65. Ibid. v. 508.

5. P.R.O., S.P. 16/405, ff. 47ᵛ–9.

*1636 roster:*
10. *Masters of the Bench of the Inner Temple*, p. 19.
11. Cf. *DNB*: 'Thomas Richardson', his father.
12. Cf. Norfolk, 1626 roster, no. 15.
13. Ibid., no. 17.
14. Ibid., no. 16.
16. Ibid., no. 20.
17. Ibid., no. 21.
18. Ibid., no. 23.
20. *Gentleman's Magazine*, 190 (1851, pt. II), 383; Shaw, *Knights of England*, i. 163; Blomefield, *Norfolk*, vii. 244.
21. Cf. Norfolk, 1626 roster, no. 29.
22. Ibid., no. 31.
23. *Alum. cantab.*
24. Cf. Norfolk, 1608 roster, no. 30.
26. Cf. Norfolk, 1626 roster, no. 35.
27. Cf. Norfolk, 1608 roster, no. 35.
28. Cf. Norfolk, 1626 roster, no. 37.
29. Ibid., no. 38.
30. Ibid., no. 39.
31. Ibid., no. 40.
32. Ibid., no. 41.
34. Blomefield, *Norfolk*, i. 408; ibid. vi. 324–5.
35. Ibid. i. 178; Cokayne, *Baronetage*, ii. 163 (cr. 1642).
36. *Pension Book of Gray's Inn*, i. 260, 279, 285.
38. Ibid. pp. 236, 310; Blomefield, *Norfolk*, ix. 420.
43. Cf. Norfolk, 1626 roster, no. 17, and *supra*, no. 20.

45. Blomefield, *Norfolk*, vi. 153.
47. Cf. Norfolk, 1626 roster, no. 51.
48. Blomefield, *Norfolk*, v. 157; Bertram Schofield (ed.), *The Knyvett Letters, 1620–1644* (Norfolk Record Soc., vol. xx, 1949), pp. 19–28 *et passim*; Blomefield, *Norfolk*, ii. 503.
49. Cf. Norfolk, 1626 roster, no. 59.
50. Ibid., no. 52.
53. Wyndham, *Family History*, pp. 190–3; R. W. Ketton-Cremer, *Felbrigg, The Story of a House* (L., 1962), pp. 34–44.
54. Blomefield, *Norfolk*, i. 260, 263, 264; ibid. v. 283; *Visitation of Norfolk, 1664*, i. 45.
55. Ibid., p. 13.
56. *Lincoln's Inn Black Books*, ii. 145, 274, 339; *Alum. cantab.*; Blomefield, *Norfolk*, ii. 503.
57. Ibid. vii. 288.
58. Ibid. viii. 120.
59. Cf. Norfolk, 1626 roster, no. 60.
60. Blomefield, *Norfolk*, i. 360, 363, 364.
62. *Lincoln's Inn Black Books*, ii. 141, 149.

# NORTHAMPTONSHIRE

## 1562[1]

| | | | | | | | | |
|---|---|---|---|---|---|---|---|---|
| 1 | q | Nicholas Bacon, knight [lord keeper] | | C | G | P | 1579 | *DNB* |
| 2 | q | William [Paulet], Marquess of Winchester [lord treasurer] | | | | P | 1572 | *DNB* |
| 3 | q | William [Parr], Marquess of Northampton | | | | | 1571 | *DNB* |
| 4 | q | Henry [Fitzalan], Earl of Arundel [lord steward] | | | | | 1580 | *DNB* |
| 5 | q | Francis [Russell], Earl of Bedford | | C | G | P | 1585 | *DNB* |
| 6 | q | Edmund [Scamler], Bishop of Peterborough | | C | | | 1594 | *DNB* |
| 7 | | George [Zouche], Lord Zouche | | | | | 1569 | |
| 8 | q | John [Mordaunt], Lord Mordaunt | | | | | 1562 | |
| 9 | q | William Cecil, knight [*custos rotulorum*] | | C | G | P | 1598 | *DNB* |
| 10 | q | James Dyer, knight | | | M | P | 1582 | *DNB* |
| 11 | q | Edward Saunders, knight, chief baron of the exchequer | | C | M | P | 1576 | *DNB* |
| 12 | q | William Bendlowes, serjeant-at-law | | C | L | P | 1584 | *DNB* |
| 13 | q | Walter Mildmay, knight | Apethorpe | C | G | P | 1589 | *DNB* |
| 14 | | Valentine Knightley, knight | Fawsley | | | P | 1566 | |
| 15 | q | John Spencer, knight | Althorp | | | P | 1586 | |
| 16 | | William Fitzwilliam, knight | Milton | | | P | 1599 | *DNB* |
| 17 | | Nicholas Throckmorton, knight | Paulerspury | | | P | 1571 | *DNB* |
| 18 | | Robert Lane, knight | Horton | | G | P | 1585 | |
| 19 | | Thomas Andrews, knight | Cherwelton | | | | 1564 | |
| 20 | | John Farmer, knight | Easton Neston | | | P | 1571 | |
| 21 | q | Edward Griffin | Dingley | | L | | 1570 | |
| 22 | | Thomas Wattes | Blakesley | | | | 1593 | |
| 23 | | Thomas Lovett | Astwell | | | | 1586 | |
| 24 | | Thomas Spencer | Little Everdon | | G | | 1576 | |
| 25 | q | Francis Saunders | Welford | | M | | 1585 | |
| 26 | | Edmund Elmes | Lilford | | | | 1602 | |
| 27 | | George Lynne | Southwick | | | | 1593 | |
| 28 | | Thomas Mulsho | Finedon | | | | 1562 | |
| 29 | | Thomas Catesby of Wyshton | Whiston | | | | 1571 | |

The following names are found in the *liber pacis* of 1559:

| | | | | | | | | |
|---|---|---|---|---|---|---|---|---|
| 30 | q | John [Williams], Lord Williams | Thame, Oxon. | | | P | 1559 | *DNB* |
| 31 | | Thomas [Tresham, knight] prior of St. John of Jerusalem | Rushton | | | P | 1559 | |
| 32 | | Humphrey Stafford, knight | Blatherwycke | | | | 1575 | |
| 33 | q | Edward Montagu | Boughton | | | | 1602 | |
| 34 | | Edmund Brudenell | Dene | | | | 1585 | |
| 35 | | John Butler | Aston-le-Walls | | | | 1559 | |
| 36 | | Thomas Wake | Market Deeping | | | | 1567 | |
| 37 | q | Giles Isham | Pytchley | | M | P | 1559 | |
| 38 | q | Reginald Conyers | Wakerley | | | | 1560 | |
| 39 | q | Robert Wingfield | Upton | | | | 1576 | |
| 40 | q | John Mershe | Delapré Abbey | | | P | 1560 | |
| 41 | | Richard Cave | Stanford | | | | 1560 | |
| 42 | | [William] Chauncey | Edgcote | | M | P | 1585 | |
| 43 | | Francis Quarles | Ufford | | | | 1576 | |

Dignitaries 12; Court 3; Gentry 10; Law 3; Church 0; Commerce 1.

The striking feature of the Northamptonshire commission in the reign of Elizabeth I is the number—and the proportion—of the names which are well known today. Pre-eminent was William Cecil, while after him there came in 1562 not only the Lord Keeper, the Lord Treasurer, the Lord Steward, but also the Marquess of Northampton, the Earl of Bedford, Sir Walter Mildmay, and others. There is no manifest explanation of this intriguing concentration of eminence.

Brother of Queen Katherine Parr, the Marquess of Northampton  3 was a leading Henrician official whose chief estates lay in the county. The vast and scattered domain inherited by the second Earl of Bedford  5 included important holdings in Northamptonshire, and his seat at Woburn Abbey was only fifteen miles across the boundary in Bedfordshire. Lords Zouche and Mordaunt were peers whose estates were in  7, 8 Northamptonshire in large part.

Sir William Cecil, Sir Walter Mildmay, Sir Nicholas Throckmorton, and Sir William Fitzwilliam were all major figures in Tudor public affairs; they can have had little time for their duties as J.P.s here or in other counties. This is not the context for a discussion of their careers, but it is appropriate to note that they all held extensive lands in this county, Cecil and Fitzwilliam partly by inheritance, Mildmay and Throckmorton through their own efforts. Nor was their membership in the commission nominal. Cecil's signature appears beside those of his colleagues in 1569 on the formal acceptance of the existing religious settlement. During the interval between his terms as Lord Deputy, Fitzwilliam served as governor of Fotheringhay, where Mary Stuart found her last tragic residence. All four men resided at their seats for periods which occasionally were prolonged.

Only somewhat less well known were several other knights. Sir John Spencer came of a family of graziers who by skilful husbandry  15 and wise purchase acquired very great wealth. 'Alone perhaps, among English nobility, the Spencers owed their riches and their rise . . . to successful farming.' His grandfather, the first Sir John, was sheriff of Northamptonshire in 1511 and a J.P. in Warwickshire in 1515. He was a nephew of the notorious Richard Empson and arranged for his children two marriage alliances with the Knightley family and another with Sir Richard Catesby of Ashby St. Legers. The younger Sir John secured as a wife a daughter of a wealthy London merchant and gave the family the base upon which his son was elevated to the peerage in 1603. Sir John Farmer also had a connection with Richard Empson,  20 from whom his father, a very successful merchant of the staple, purchased the manor of Easton Neston. Grandson on his mother's side of a Lord Mayor of London, he married a daughter of Lord Vaux and thus entered the nexus of personal relationships which embraced most of the men in the commission of the peace. Throckmorton had a

Vaux grandmother. Family ties likewise bound Cecil to the Wing-
fields, the Fitzwilliams, and the Caves. Scion of a family long established
14 at Fawsley and Upton, Sir Valentine Knightley was the possessor, in
addition to his ancestral holdings, of considerable lands which he
inherited from a lawyer brother, Edmund, a serjeant who had purchased extensive monastic property. Even though not of the quorum,
he must have been a very active justice; his was a family which was
never ennobled but long remained among the leaders in county society.
It was a close society.

Three lawyer members of this commission belonged to county
11 families. The Saunders forebears of the Chief Baron of the Exchequer
had lived at Harrington for a century, and his mother was a Cave.
25, 21 A cousin, Francis Saunders, was also a barrister. Edward Griffin rose
through the ranks of barrister and bencher in Lincoln's Inn to become
Solicitor-General in 1545 and Attorney-General in 1553. A very
wealthy man, his estates were acquired by inheritance, by purchase,
and by grant from the Crown. All the other members of the commission
are best classed as gentry; some had greater, some lesser, prominence.

With this group of J.P.s there should be considered fourteen men
whose names were listed in a *liber pacis* of the early months of 1559
and were certainly associated with them on the bench. Sir Thomas
31 Tresham, lay prior of the recently recreated order of the Knights of
St. John of Jerusalem, was the head of an eminent county family
notable for its loyalty to the Roman Church. After his death there
were no Treshams in the commission until a less devoted cousin
30 received an appointment early in the Stuart period. Lord Williams of
Thame, perhaps a relative of Thomas Cromwell, had been an official
in the Court of Augumentations who retained the favour of both
Mary and Elizabeth, dying at Ludlow in 1559 while Lord President
of the Council of Wales. The name and the family of Sir Humphrey
32 Stafford were much more distinguished than either Tresham or
Williams, but, although he owned an estate in the county which
explains his presence in the commission, he was not himself so prominent nor was he primarily a Northamptonshire magnate.

Edward Montagu, Edmund Brudenell, and Giles Isham owed their
status to success at the bar. Montagu and Brudenell were descendants
37 of Chief Justices. Isham, likewise a member of a family of some local
note, acquired at the Middle Temple a knowledge of the law which
34 qualified him to become steward for the Earls of Bedford. Brudenell
33 was the ancestor of the Earls of Cardigan, and Montagu was the progenitor of both the Dukes of Manchester and the Earls of Sandwich.
Isham's younger brother, John, who was later a J.P., sought his
fortune as a member of the Mercers' Company in London and, though
his descendants achieved only the degree of baronet, they likewise have

long been county notables. Another mercer was John Mershe, who 40 had a minor appointment at Court and joined with other mercers in extensive dealings in monastic lands. His membership in the Northamptonshire commission must have been based upon his brief possession of the former Delapré monastery just outside Northampton which was much later to become the headquarters of the Northamptonshire Record Society. The other justices were all minor gentry.

These were the men who executed the office of J.P. in the early years of Elizabeth I; their status among the gentry came from the profits of recent achievement in the law, in government service, in commerce, or in farming. The legal and political careers were more numerous than those in trade or in agriculture. Some fifteen owed their prosperity to success at the bar, about the same number to the rewards of service in the middle or upper ranks of the Tudor state, and seven or eight to the inheritance of lands which had been possessed by their families for as long as a century. Only eight of the surnames borne by forty-three justices are not found in Henrician commissions of the peace; all these men except Throckmorton, Thomas Spencer, Lynne, and Isham were sons of earlier justices or had themselves been commissioned before 1559. Very nearly all owned lands which the records calendared in *Letters and Papers of Henry VIII* show to have been monastic property.

There seems to be no indication that religion is the explanation for the disappearance from the commission in 1562 of the fourteen men whose names were listed in the *liber pacis* of 1559. Half of them had died. Stafford was not truly a Northamptonshire man. The estates of Chauncey and Wingfield lay in the Soke of Peterborough, in the separate commission of which they were later included. Brudenell and Montagu were subsequently J.P.s in the county. Wake was a black sheep in his family, which in a cadet line long remained very prominent. Quarles may have wished to bear the burden of the commission no longer.

In education and parliamentary experience Northamptonshire was much like other counties at this time. Nearly half the members of the full commission were enrolled in either a university or an inn; the same proportion were elected to the Commons at least once. Among the men in the *liber pacis* of 1559 there were fewer who had been members of any of those bodies.

## 1584[2]

| | | | | | | | | |
|---|---|---|---|---|---|---|---|---|
| 1 | | q | Thomas Bromley, knight, lord chancellor of England | O | M | P | 1587 | *DNB* |
| 2 | * | q | William [Cecil], Lord Burghley, lord treasurer of England | | | | | |
| | | | [*custos rotulorum*] | C | G | P | 1598 | *DNB* |

| No. | | | | Name | Residence | | | | Date | DNB |
|---|---|---|---|---|---|---|---|---|---|---|
| 3 | * | | q | Francis [Russell], Earl of Bedford | | C | G | P | 1585 | DNB |
| 4 | | | q | Robert [Dudley], Earl of Leicester | | | | P | 1588 | DNB |
| 5 | * | | q | Edmund [Scamler], Bishop of Peterborough | | C | | | 1594 | DNB |
| 6 | | s | q | Edward [Zouche], Lord Zouche | | C | | | 1625 | DNB |
| 7 | | | q | William [Sandys], Lord Sandys | | | | | 1623 | |
| 8 | | s | q | Louis [Mordaunt], Lord Mordaunt | | | M | P | 1601 | |
| 9 | | | q | Henry [Compton], Lord Compton | | | G | P | 1589 | |
| 10 | | | q | Christopher Hatton, knight, vice-chamberlain | | O | I | P | 1591 | DNB |
| 11 | * | | q | Walter Mildmay, knight, chancellor of the exchequer | | C | G | P | 1589 | DNB |
| 12 | | | q | Thomas Meade [justice of the common pleas] | | | M | | 1585 | |
| 13 | | | q | Robert Shute [baron of the exchequer] | | C | G | P | 1590 | DNB |
| 14 | | s | q | Thomas Cecil, knight | Burghley | C | G | P | 1623 | DNB |
| 15 | * | | q | John Spencer, knight | Althorp | | | P | 1586 | |
| 16 | * | | q | William Fitzwilliam, knight | Milton | | | P | 1599 | DNB |
| 17 | * | | q | Robert Lane, knight | Horton | | G | P | 1585 | |
| 18 | * | | q | Edmund Brudenell, knight | Dene | | | | 1585 | |
| 19 | | s | q | Richard Knightley, knight | Fawsley | | | P | 1615 | DNB |
| 20 | * | | q | Edward Montagu, knight | Boughton | | | | 1602 | |
| 21 | | s | q | Anthony Mildmay | Apethorpe | C | G | P | 1617 | DNB |
| 22 | | s | q | Edward Griffin | Dingley | | L | | 1625 | |
| 23 | | s | q | William Fitzwilliam | Milton | | G | P | 1618 | |
| 24 | | | q | James Ellis | Peterborough | C | | | 1596 | |
| 25 | | r | q | Roger Cave | Stanford | | M | | 1586 | |
| 26 | | s | | George Farmer | Easton Neston | | | | 1612 | |
| 27 | * | | | Edmund Elmes | Lilford | | | | 1602 | |
| 28 | * | | q | William Chauncey | Edgcote | | M | P | 1585 | |
| 29 | | | q | Christopher Yelverton | Easton Maudit | | G | P | 1612 | DNB |
| 30 | | s | | Valentine Knightley | Fawsley | O | G | P | 1618 | |
| 31 | | | q | Bartholomew Tate | Delapré | | | P | 1601 | |
| 32 | | | | Edward Cope | Canons Ashby | C | G | | 1620 | |
| 33 | | r | q | John Wake | Salcey Forest | | | | 1621 | |
| 34 | | s | q | Thomas Mulsho | Finedon | | M | | 1608 | |
| 35 | * | | | George Lynne | Southwick | | | | 1593 | |
| 36 | | s | | Thomas Andrews | Cherwelton | | | | 1594 | |
| 37 | | | | Michael Harcourt | Leckhampstead, Bucks. | | | P | 1597 | |
| 38 | | | q | Michael Lewis | Gray's Inn | | G | | 1585 | |
| 39 | | r | q | John Isham | Lamport | | | | 1596 | |
| 40 | | | q | Edward Watson | Rockingham Castle | | | | 1584 | |
| 41 | | | q | Thomas Kirton | Thorpe Mandeville | I | | | 1606 | |
| 42 | | | | William Clarke | Watford | | | P | 1604 | |
| 43 | | | | Francis Barnard | Little Brington | | M | | 1602 | |

Dignitaries 13; Court 3; Gentry 21; Law 3; Church 1; Commerce 2.

In the Northamptonshire commission in 1584 the large number of veterans and relatives of earlier justices assured a comparable continuity in character. Two major figures at Court who came to possess important estates in the region were the Earl of Leicester and Sir Christopher Hatton. The Earl was so greatly favoured by the Queen that his presence in any commission can occasion no surprise, but in fact he was a J.P. in few counties and his connection with Northamptonshire may be explained by the proximity of Kenilworth to the county boundary. Hatton, a descendant of an undistinguished county family, purchased the unfinished Kirby Hall from Sir Humphrey Stafford's

heir. Equally suited for the commission was the head of the Compton 9
family, already established at Compton Wynyates and destined to
retain it and other major holdings for centuries. Descended from the
fourth Earl of Shrewsbury as well as from a soldier and servant of
Henry VIII, married to a daughter of the Queen's cousin (the Earl of
Huntingdon), Compton's fitness is manifest. Lord Sandys was likewise 7
prominent at Court and presumably held property in the county. Three
active and important lawyers were Christopher Yelverton, Michael 29
Lewis, and Francis Barnard. A reader and treasurer of Gray's Inn, 38, 43
Yelverton was Recorder of Northampton. Lewis and Barnard were
barristers who had county interests. Dr. James Ellis was chancellor of 24
the diocese of Peterborough. Two J.P.s whose fortunes derived from
the commerce of London were John Isham and Thomas Kirton. 39, 41
Michael Harcourt, the third son of a prominent Oxfordshire knight, 37
married an heiress whose estate at Leckhamstead was very close to the
county boundary. The remaining members of the commission were
minor gentry. Edward Watson, the tenant of Rockingham Castle, 40
which he made the seat of a family that long remained notable, was
the son of a ward of Thomas Cromwell who had become surveyor for
the Bishop of Lincoln and steward of the abbot of Peterborough.

The stability of the Elizabethan commission in Northamptonshire
is indicated further by the fact that in 1584 it included all but four
of the surviving justices of the early years of the reign. William Bendlowes, a serjeant-at-law formerly associated with the Midlands circuit,
lived in Essex and may have died already. The deaths of Thomas
Lovett in 1586 and Francis Saunders in 1585 suggest that advancing
age and ill health may be the explanation for their being put out of the
commission. Religious persuasion is another possibility, since in 1564
Bishop Scamler had judged Lovett to be 'a great letter of religion' and
Saunders to be 'indifferent'. Yet Saunders, like Thomas Wattes, whom
the Bishop considered to be an 'earnest furtherer of religion', was still
a justice in 1573. In the *liber pacis* of that year, however, appears in
Burghley's hand beside Wattes's name the notation *nil valet*. Apparently his means were too slender to enable him to the discharge responsibilities of a J.P.[3] A few men were put out of the Northamptonshire
commission.

As in Kent and Norfolk the number of the working J.P.s who had
attended a university (5) or an inn of court (14) had increased markedly
since 1562. Not quite half the justices were at some time members of
the Commons, and Northamptonshire was represented in 1584 by
Sir Christopher Hatton and Sir Walter Mildmay, while Sir Thomas
Cecil was knight of the shire for Lincolnshire and Anthony Mildmay
for Wiltshire. The younger Fitzwilliam represented Peterborough,
and Sir Richard Knightley sat for Northampton, while Valentine

Knightley found a seat at Tavistock and William Clarke at Saltash. The county was ably represented at Westminster.

## 1608⁴

| No. | ✶ | s/r | q | Name | Place | Val | | | P | Year | DNB |
|---|---|---|---|---|---|---|---|---|---|---|---|
| 1 | | | q | Thomas [Egerton], Lord Ellesmere, chancellor of England | | | | L | P | 1617 | DNB |
| 2 | | | q | Thomas [Sackville], Earl of Dorset, treasurer of England | | | | I | P | 1608 | DNB |
| 3 | | | q | Henry [Howard], Earl of Northampton, warden of the cinque ports | | | C | | P | 1614 | DNB |
| 4 | ✶ | | q | Thomas [Cecil], Earl of Exeter, lieutenant of the aforesaid county [custos rotulorum] | | | C | G | P | 1623 | DNB |
| 5 | | | q | Thomas [Dove], Bishop of Peterborough | | | C | | | 1630 | DNB |
| 6 | ✶ | | q | Edward [Zouche], Lord Zouche | | | C | | | 1625 | DNB |
| 7 | | s | q | Henry [Mordaunt], Lord Mordaunt | | | | | | 1609 | |
| 8 | | s | q | William [Compton], Lord Compton | | | O | L | | 1630 | |
| 9 | | s | q | William [Russell], Lord Russell | | | | L | P | 1613 | |
| 10 | | | q | Thomas [Gerard], Lord Gerard | | | C | G | P | 1618 | |
| 11 | | s | q | Robert [Spencer], Lord Spencer | | | | | P | 1627 | DNB |
| 12 | | | q | John [Stanhope], Lord Stanhope, vice-chamberlain of the household | | | C | G | P | 1621 | DNB |
| 13 | | | q | Edward Coke, knight, chief justice of common pleas | | | C | I | P | 1634 | DNB |
| 14 | | | q | Peter Warburton, knight, justice of common pleas, assize | | | | L | P | 1621 | DNB |
| 15 | | | q | Thomas Foster, knight, justice of common pleas, assize | | | | I | | 1612 | |
| 16 | ✶ | | q | Christopher Yelverton, knight, justice of king's bench | | | | G | P | 1612 | DNB |
| 17 | | s | q | Richard Cecil | Burghley | | C | G | P | 1633 | |
| 18 | | | q | Edmund Carey, knight | | 50 | | | P | 1637 | |
| 19 | ✶ | | q | Anthony Mildmay, knight | Apethorpe | 40 | C | G | P | 1617 | DNB |
| 20 | ✶ | | q | Edward Griffin, knight | Dingley | 60 | | L | P? | 1625 | |
| 21 | ✶ | | q | Richard Knightley, knight | Fawsley | 20 | | | P | 1615 | DNB |
| 22 | ✶ | | q | George Farmer, knight | Easton Neston | 30 | | | | 1612 | |
| 23 | | r | q | Arthur Throckmorton, knight | Paulerspury | 20 | O | | P | 1626 | |
| 24 | | s | q | William Lane, knight | Horton | 20 | | | P | 1616 | |
| 25 | | | q | Robert Osborne, knight | Kelmarsh | 20 | | | | | |
| 26 | ✶ | | q | William Fitzwilliam, knight | Milton | 30 | | G | P | 1618 | |
| 27 | | s | q | Edward Watson, knight | Rockingham | 20 | | | P | 1617 | |
| 28 | | r | q | Robert Wingfield, knight | Upton | 20 | | G | P | 1609 | |
| 29 | | s | q | Walter Montagu, knight | Monmouthshire | 20 | | | P | 1615 | |
| 30 | | r | q | Euseby Isham, knight | Pytchley | 20 | | M | | 1626 | |
| 31 | | s | q | Euseby Andrews, knight | Cherwelton | 20 | | | | 1619 | |
| 32 | | | q | Richard Chetwood, knight | Chetwode, Bucks | 20 | | | | 1633 | |
| 33 | | | q | John Needham, knight | Lechborough | 26 | | G | | 1618 | |
| 34 | | s | q | Tobias Chauncey, knight | Edgcote | 20 | | M | | 1609 | |
| 35 | | | q | William Samwell, knight | Upton | 20 | | | | 1628 | |
| 36 | | | | Edward Onley, knight | Catesby | 30 | O | G | | 1638 | |
| 37 | | | | Henry Longvill, knight | Wolverton, Bucks | 40 | | | | 1618 | |
| 38 | | s | q | William Tate, knight | Delapré Abbey | 20 | O | M | P | 1617 | |
| 39 | | | q | Henry Hickman, master in chancery | Peterborough | 8 | C | | P | 1618 | |
| 40 | | | q | William Pritherough, doctor of laws | Doctors Commons | | O | | | 1616 | |
| 41 | ✶ | | q | John Wake | Salcey Forest | 20 | | | | 1621 | |
| 42 | ✶ | | q | Thomas Mulsho | Finedon | | | M | | 1608 | |
| 43 | | | q | Francis Morgan | Kingsthorpe | 5 | | M | | 1617 | |
| 44 | | | q | Roger Dale | Tekesore, Ruts. | 8 | | I | | 1623 | |
| 45 | | | | Thomas Burnaby | Watford | 20 | | G | | 1609 | |

| 46 | q | James Pickering | Titchmarsh | 8 | | 1612 |
| 47 | | John Freeman | Great Billing | 20 | | 1615 |
| 48 | q | Arthur Brooke | Great Oakley | 20 | | 1628 |
| 49 | r | Thomas Tresham | Newton | 20 | | 1637 |
| 50 | r | William Saunders of Hadden | | 20 | G | 1623 |
| 51 | | Tobias Houghton | Kelthorpe, Ruts. | 6 | | 1625 |
| 52 | | William Belcher | Nortoft | 20 | | 1609 |
| 53 | | John Rand | Northampton | 3 | L | |

Dignitaries 16; Court 3; Gentry 29; Law 2; Church 2; Commerce 1.

The Northamptonshire commission of 1608 reflected earlier than those in the other counties the inflation of honours and dignities which followed hard upon the death of Elizabeth. There were only thirteen men in a total of fifty-three who did not enjoy some recorded distinction. Yet the favourites of the new king came from Scotland or had their residences in other counties; the commission lacked the galaxy of statesmen and courtiers which had adorned it in the past. All but three of the survivors from the commission of 1584 were still members. Lord Sandys seems never to have had a close connection with the county, and (Sir) Edward Cope appears to have made his principal residence at his estate in Suffolk. Valentine Knightley—knighted in 1603—had been removed from office because of his support of a Puritan petition.[5]

Lord Stanhope of Harrington, Master of the Posts and Vice- 12 Chamberlain of the Household, and Sir Christopher Yelverton, now 16 justice of the King's Bench, both had clear connections with the county. Lord Gerard and Lord Chief Justice Coke, whose principal 10, 13 estates were in neighbouring counties, presumably owned lands in Northamptonshire, which explains their membership in its commission. Such is probably the case also with Sir Edmund Carey, third son of the 18 Earl of Hunsdon, who was a J.P. in Hertfordshire and Oxfordshire as well. Two other members of the Court circle were Sir John Need- 33 ham, gentleman pensioner to Elizabeth I, who married a daughter of Sir Edward Watson of Rockingham Castle, and Sir William Samwell, 35 auditor to Elizabeth, who purchased an estate at Upton.

There were two ecclesiastical lawyers and two leading barristers in this commission. Dr. Henry Hickman was a master in chancery and 39 chancellor of the diocese of Peterborough. Dr. William Pritherough of 40 Doctors Commons was lay rector of Maidwell St. Mary. Francis Morgan and Roger Dale were readers in their inns of court. 43, 44

Comment seems appropriate on two other members of this bench. John Rand was so obscure that confident identification is not possible. 53 He probably belonged to a family of Northampton burghers. John Freeman, who owned a considerable estate at Great Billing and made 47 an interesting will in which he made an important bequest to Clare College and established an alms house for indigent men and women, serves as a good example of the inter-connections of the gentry in the various counties. He married his daughters to Sir Robert Osborne of Kelmarsh, Northamptonshire, Sir Edward Gorges of Somerset, and James Scamler of Norfolk, who all appear in these pages.

In the Stuart period not only did Northamptonshire cease to have its remarkable group of national figures, but it fell behind other counties in the proportion of its justices who received the training of the universities and the inns of court. In the working commission there were 16 men who had been enrolled in an inn and only 3 barristers. 13 among 37 were at some time elected to the House of Commons, none of them a simple esquire. In the first Stuart parliament Sir Richard Cecil was returned for Peterborough and Sir Edmund Carey was chosen by Calne in Wiltshire in a by-election. Northamptonshire was represented by Sir Valentine Knightley and Sir Edward Montagu, who were both removed from the commission in 1605. If the county's bench continued to exhibit special qualities, they had a different nature.

## 1626[6]

|    |   | Name | Place | | | | Date | |
|----|---|------|-------|---|---|---|------|---|
| 1  |   | Thomas Coventry, knight, lord keeper |  | O | I | P | 1640 | DNB |
| 2  |   | James [Ley], Earl of Marlborough, lord treasurer |  | O | L | P | 1629 | DNB |
| 3  |   | Henry [Montagu], Earl of Manchester [lord president] |  | C | M | P | 1642 | DNB |
| 4  |   | Edward [Somerset], Earl of Worcester [lord privy seal] |  |   |   |   | 1628 | DNB |
| 5  |   | Francis [Manners], Earl of Rutland |  |   |   |   | 1632 | DNB |
| 6  |   | William [Cecil], Earl of Salisbury |  | C | G | P | 1668 |   |
| 7  |   | William [Cecil], Earl of Exeter [lord lieutenant] |  |   | G | P | 1640 |   |
| 8  |   | John [Egerton], Earl of Bridgewater |  |   |   | P | 1649 | DNB |
| 9  | * | William [Compton], Earl of Northampton |  | O | L |   | 1630 |   |
| 10 |   | Robert [Rich], Earl of Warwick |  | C | I | P | 1658 | DNB |
| 11 |   | Henry [Rich], Earl of Holland |  | C |   | P | 1649 | DNB |
| 12 |   | Francis [Fane], Earl of Westmorland [custos rotulorum] |  | C | L | P | 1628 | DNB |
| 13 |   | Edward [Montagu], Viscount Mandeville |  |   |   | P | 1671 |   |
| 14 | * | Thomas [Dove], Bishop of Peterborough |  | C |   |   | 1630 | DNB |
| 15 |   | John [Williams], Bishop of Lincoln |  | C |   |   | 1650 | DNB |
| 16 |   | Mildmay [Fane], Lord de le Spencer |  | C |   | P | 1666 | DNB |
| 17 |   | Edward [Vaux], Lord Vaux |  |   |   |   | 1661 |   |
| 18 |   | John [Mordaunt], Lord Mordaunt |  | O |   | P | 1642 | DNB |
| 19 | * | Robert [Spencer], Lord Spencer |  |   |   |   | 1627 | DNB |
| 20 |   | Edward [Montagu], Lord Montagu |  | O | M | P | 1644 | DNB |
| 21 |   | William [Fitzwilliam], Lord Fitzwilliam |  |   |   |   | 1644 |   |
| 22 |   | Thomas Edmondes, knight |  |   |   | P | 1639 | DNB |
| 23 |   | Richard Hutton, knight |  | O | G | P | 1639 | DNB |
| 24 |   | James Whitlocke, knight |  | O | M |   | 1632 |   |
| 25 |   | Francis Harvy, knight | Adstone |   | M | P | 1632 |   |
| 26 | s | Henry Yelverton, knight | Easton Maudit |   | G | P | 1629 | DNB |
| 27 | * | Richard Cecil, knight | Burghley | C | G | P | 1633 |   |
| 28 | s | William Spencer, knight | Althorp | O |   | P | 1636 |   |
| 29 | * | Edmund Carey, knight | Culham, Oxon. |   |   | P | 1637 |   |

| No. | | Name | Place | | | | Date | |
|---|---|---|---|---|---|---|---|---|
| 30 | | Roland St. John, knight | Woodford | C | | P | 1645 | |
| 31 | r | Thomas Brudenell, knight & baronet | Dene | C | | | 1661 | |
| 32 | | Roland Egerton, knight & baronet | Farthinghoe | | L | P | 1646 | |
| 33 | | Erasmus Dryden, baronet | Canons Ashby | O | M | P | 1632 | |
| 34 | s | Lewis Watson, knight & baronet | Rockingham Castle | O | M | P | 1653 | DNB |
| 35 | | John Hewett, knight & baronet | Hemington | | | | | |
| 36 | s | Baldwin Wake, baronet | Clevedon, Soms. | | | | 1627 | |
| 37 | | Capell Bedell, baronet | Cottesbrooke | C | | P | 1643 | |
| 38 | | Thomas Crewe, knight, serjeant-at-law | Steane | | G | P | 1634 | DNB |
| 39 | * | Robert Osborne, knight | Kelmarsh | | | | | |
| 40 | | Miles Fleetwood, knight | Aldwinkle | | G | P | 1641 | K |
| 41 | s | Hatton Farmer, knight | Easton Neston | O | | | 1640 | |
| 42 | * | Richard Chetwood, knight | Chetwode, Bucks. | | | | 1633 | |
| 43 | * | William Samwell, knight | Samwell | | | | 1628 | |
| 44 | * | Edward Onley, knight | Catesby | O | G | | 1638 | |
| 45 | | Robert Bannastre, knight | Passenham | C | | | 1649 | |
| 46 | s | Thomas Brooke, knight | Great Oakley | | | | 1638 | |
| 47 | s | John Isham, knight | Lamport | C | M | P | 1651 | |
| 48 | * | Thomas Tresham, knight | Newton | | | | 1637 | |
| 49 | | Edmund Hampden, knight | Abingdon | | I | | 1627 | |
| 50 | s | Thomas Cave, knight | Stanford | O | | | 1666 | |
| 51 | | Francis Crane, knight | | | | P | 1636 | DNB |
| 52 | s | William Chauncey, knight | Edgcote | O | | | 1644 | |
| 53 | | William Wilmer, knight | Sywell | C | I | | 1646 | |
| 54 | | Lewis Pemberton, knight | Rushden | | | | 1640 | |
| 55 | s | John Pickering, knight | Titchmarsh | | | P | 1628 | |
| 56 | | Henry Robinson, knight | Cransley | | | | 1637 | |
| 57 | | John Lambe, knight | Peterborough | C | | | 1647 | DNB |
| 58 | | Anthony Haselwood, knight | Maidwell | O | G | | 1660 | |
| 59 | | Humphrey Orme, knight | Peterborough | C | | P | 1648 | |
| 60 | | John Danvers, knight | Culworth | O | | P | 1642 | |
| 61 | | William Beecher, knight | Fotheringhay | | | | 1641 | |
| 62 | s | Richard Samwell, knight | Upton | O | M | | 1668 | |
| 63 | | Richard Wiseman, knight | Lincoln's Inn | C | L | | 1654 | |
| 64 | | Samuel Clarke, doctor of divinity | Northampton | O | | | 1641 | |
| 65 | | Hugh Lloyd, doctor of divinity | Barton Seagrave | C | | | 1629 | |
| 66 | | William Dolben, doctor of divinity | Stanwick | O | | | 1631 | DNB |
| 67 | | Robert Sibthorpe, doctor of divinity | Brackley | C | | | 1662 | DNB |
| 68 | r | Richard Knightley | Fawsley | | G | P | 1639 | DNB |
| 69 | s | Thomas Elmes | Lilford | | M | | 1632 | |
| 70 | | William Lane | Horton | | | | 1637 | |
| 71 | | Francis Nicolls | Hardwick | O | M | P | 1641 | |
| 72 | | Richard Cartwright | Aynho | | I | | 1637 | |
| 73 | | Robert Rainsford | Staverton | | | | 1629 | |
| 74 | | Arthur Gooday | Higham Ferrers | C | G | | 1639 | |
| 75 | | John Bourne | Ufford | | | | 1628 | |
| 76 | | William Conyers | Wakerley | C | M | P | 1648 | |
| 77 | | John Wyrley | Dodford | O | | | 1655 | |
| 78 | | Cuthbert Ogle | Potterspury | | | | 1633 | |
| 79 | | John Thornton | Newnham | O | L | | 1637 | |
| 80 | r | Thomas Andrews | Cherwelton | | M | | 1627 | |
| 81 | | [Edward] Shuckburgh | Naseby? | | L | | 1630 | |
| 82 | | John Hanbury | Kelmarsh | | | P? | 1639 | |
| 83 | s | John Isham | Braunston | | M | | 1627 | |
| 84 | | [Edmund] Mountstephens | Paston | C | | | 1636 | |
| 85 | s | Thomas Dove | | C | | | 1629 | |
| 86 | | Edward Dudley | Clapton | C | I | | 1632 | |
| 87 | | Thomas Jenison | Irchester | | | | 1647 | |
| 88 | r | Francis Quarles | Ufford | C | G | | 1651 | |

| | | | | | | |
|---|---|---|---|---|---|---|
| 89 | s | William Elmes | Lilford | | I | 1641 |
| 90 | | John Norton | Cotterstock | | G | |
| 91 | | Nathaniel Humfrey | Barton Seagrave | | | |
| 92 | | Anthony Palmer | Stoke Doyle | C | M | 1633 |
| 93 | r | George Lynne | Southwick | | | 1672 |
| 94 | | Walter Kirkham | Fineshade | | | |
| | | | Abbey | C | | 1637 |
| 95 | | John Cutts | | | | |
| 96 | | Edmund Sawyer | Kettering? | | | 1630 |
| 97 | | [William] Hacke | Peterborough | | | |
| 98 | | John Breton | Teeton | | | |
| 99 | r | James Pickering | Titchmarsh? | | | 1630 |
| 100 | r | Ambrose Saunders | Sibbertoft? | | | |
| 101 | | William Pargiter | Greatworth | O | I | 1662 |
| 102 | | Moses Tryon | Harringworth | | | |
| 103 | | George Mole | | O | I | 1629 |
| 104 | s | Edward Farmer | Easton Neston | | | |
| 105 | s | Robert Breton | Teeton | O | M | 1641 |
| 106 | | Charles Edmondes | | | | 1652 |
| 107 | | George Catesby | Whiston | | | |
| 108 | | William Saunders | Welford | | | |
| 109 | | John Blincoe | Marston | O | I | 1643 |
| 110 | | Maximilian Lindley | | | | |
| 111 | r | Thomas Kirton | Thorpe | | | |
| | | | Mandeville | O | L | |
| 112 | | Francis Saunders | Syresham | | M | |
| 113 | | Richard Kenwricke | Kings Sutton | | G | 1674 |

| Dignitaries 24 | Court 6 | Gentry 36 | Law 7 | Church 5 | Commerce 0 |
|---|---|---|---|---|---|
| 24 | 6 | 70 | 7 | 5 | 1 |

The Northamptonshire commission of the peace of 1626 presents an enigma. The county had a modest 60 justices in 1621 when Kent reached a peak of 135, and the King promised to redress the complaint of the House of Commons that there were too many J.P.s. In 1625 there were 62 and in 1627 54. Yet in 1626 there were 113, the largest group to be found for any of the six counties here considered at any of the moments analysed in detail. The temporary increase was composed of five knights and forty-five esquires whose names appear in no other *liber pacis*.

Other features of this commission were the sizeable group of men associated with the Court and the increased number of trained lawyers which brought the county up to the level of other shires. More numerous than those of 1584, the courtiers included, however, no man who had the stature of their Elizabethan predecessors, unless the late Queen's cousin, the veteran Sir Edmund Carey, be so considered. Protégé of the Cecils, ambassador to France, Treasurer of the House-hold, Sir Thomas Edmondes was truly a Court figure, an explanation of his membership in the Kent commission—though not in that for Norfolk—but in this year he married Sara, daughter of Sir James Harington of Exton and widow of Lord Zouche. Already a J.P in 1621, he belonged clearly to the circle of county magnates. Sir Miles

Fleetwood also had both county and Court status. Receiver-General  40
of the Court of Wards and Liveries, he was heir to an estate at Ald-
winkle. Sir Francis Crane was a well-known adventurer who operated  51
the tapestry works at Mortlake and became chancellor of the Order
of the Garter. It is not apparent what properties he controlled in 1626
or why he was then a J.P. in Northamptonshire rather than in Norfolk,
with which he was also connected but in 1628 Grafton and other
manors in Northamptonshire were conveyed to him as security for a
large loan to the Crown. Sir Lewis Pemberton, Francis Nicolls, and  54, 71
Cuthbert Ogle were less closely connected with the Court. Pemberton  78
was the son of a gentleman usher to Queen Elizabeth. Nicolls, the
grandson and heir of two eminent lawyers and son of a man who had
been Governor of Tilbury Fort, became secretary to the Elector
Palatine in 1640. Ogle, who must have been in some degree a cousin
of the Barons Ogle, was a royal agent and Lieutenant of Whittlewood
Forest.

The seven lawyers included two judges who were residents of the
county but not assigned to the Midlands circuit: Sir Francis Harvy and  25
Sir Henry Yelverton. Sir Thomas Crewe, Speaker of the Commons in  26, 38
1623-4 and 1625, married a Northamptonshire heiress and bought
out his wife's relatives. He might be classified as a courtier. Sir Richard
Wiseman was another successful lawyer whose wife belonged to the  63
gentry of the county. Richard Cartwright, who established his family  72
at Aynho, William Conyers, who became a serjeant-at-law, and Arthur  76
Gooday, steward of Higham Ferrers, were men who found in the law  74
the basis of unusual careers.

The ecclesiastical members of the Northamptonshire commission
were headed by a lawyer, Sir John Lambe, chancellor of the diocese of  57
Peterborough, who was a supporter of Laud and became Dean of the
Arches. Two prominent members of the clergy were Hugh Lloyd  65
who became archdeacon of Worcester late in 1625 but had not yet
been taken out of the commission in Northamptonshire, and William
Dolben, a relative by marriage of the influential and controversial  66
Bishop of Lincoln (John Williams). Dr. Samuel Clarke, rector of  64
St. Peter's in Northampton, and Dr. Robert Sibthorpe, rector of  67
Brackley, vicar of St. Sepulchre's in Northampton, and chaplain to
the King, joined with Lambe in the administration of ecclesiastical
affairs in the county. It was Sibthorpe's sermon about the royal prerogative which in 1627 led to the suspension of Archbishop Abbot
and a protest in the House of Commons.

Four other members of this commission require comment. Sir
Thomas Brudenell, destined to be raised to the peerage in 1628, was  31
the nephew and heir of a justice of 1584, but like other members
of his family he was a Catholic. Only for a few months was he a J.P.

33 Sir Erasmus Dryden, grandfather of the poet and head of a family which now possessed former monastic property at Canons Ashby, was of Puritan inclination and had been kept out of the commission in 49 1608. Sir Edmund Hampden, the uncle of the more famous John Hampden, was one of the knights who were imprisoned for their opposition to the forced loan of 1626–7. Although never dubbed a 68 knight, Richard Knightley served as knight of the shire in all but one of the parliaments between 1621 and 1629. Presumably he would have represented his county in 1626 also, had he not been one of the men who were pricked for sheriff in order to keep them out of the House. He was the heir to the political and religious opinions as well as to the estates of his cousins; he refused to pay the forced loan and was deprived of his Deputy Lieutenancy. Yet he was a leading J.P. from the time of his succession at the age of 25 until his death in 1639.

Here this analysis would stop if it were based upon the *liber pacis* of 1625. To this point in substance it is not unlike the roster of that year. Four justices had gone: the Earl of Bristol, who was in disgrace, Sir Edward Bromley, who was no longer assigned to the Midland circuit, and Sir Arthur Throckmorton and Sir Euseby Isham, who had both died. Eighteen had been added: four peers, eleven knights, and three simple esquires.[7] They would have constituted an unusual increase in so brief a period, had they been the only additions to the commission, but they were much like their colleagues. The thirty-five remaining esquires were different. If a few had surnames which have already been encountered,[8] they were none the less relatively obscure gentry, and like the others have left so few traces of their lives that little about them can be uncovered. Except for Thomas Jenison, Anthony Palmer, and Charles Edmondes, all thirty-five had been eliminated from the commission before 1630. Only a few need receive comment.

81 Edward Shuckburgh was a member of a distinguished Warwickshire family which had Northamptonshire branches. He was sheriff 102 of the latter county in 1624. Moses Tryon, who had been sheriff in the previous year, was of Dutch extraction. He was one of several Dutch financiers who had been tried in the Star Chamber in 1618 for exporting gold and had been assessed a fine which he was able to discharge by a payment of £5,000. In 1626 he was assigned £1,500 as his share of the forced loan. The owner of an estate at Harringworth, he fulfilled his shrievalty in 1623 without leaving any record that appears in the *Acts of the Privy Council* or in the *Calendar of State Papers*. Charles 106 Edmondes was the son of Sir Clement, who had been a clerk of the Privy Council.

The inferior stature of the last thirty-five justices in the Northamptonshire roster for 1626 is further emphasized by the fact that, while almost all of them were soon removed from the commission, the other members had much of the permanency of tenure which was usual practice. Of the J.P.s between the judges and Cuthbert Ogle, all surviving men were still on the bench in 1636 except seven: Sir William Chauncey and Sir Richard Samwell, both of whom came from families which had earlier given men to the commission, Sir Lewis Pemberton and Sir Anthony Haselwood, both relatively obscure knights, Sir William Beecher, who sold his estate in 1629, and the lawyers Sir Richard Wiseman and William Conyers, neither of whom was firmly established in the county.

The bifurcated nature of the commission is also shown by its record with regard to membership in the House of Commons. With the possible exception of John Hanbury—Gloucester returned a man of that name in 1628—none of the final thirty-five J.P.s was ever elected to the House of Commons. In the other part of the working commission there were nineteen men who did at some time secure a seat in the Commons, while thirty-five did not. Four were elected in 1626: Sir William Spencer and Sir John Pickering for Northamptonshire, Sir Capell Bedell for Hertford, and Sir John Danvers for Oxford University.

The heterogeneous quality of this commission can also be seen from a study of its members with regard to their enrolment in the universities and the inns of court. Among the fifty-four top working members only sixteen, a few more than a quarter, had had no such experience. Among the remaining thirty-five the figure was fifteen or three-sevenths. In none of the other counties was so considerable a proportion denied the training of both university and inn of court.

In short the Northamptonshire commission of 1626 is of unusual interest. Headed by the Lord Lieutenant, the Earl of Exeter, who was a Catholic, and including the Earl of Bridgewater, the Bishop of Lincoln, Richard Knightley, Sir Edmund Hampden, and Moses Tryon, as well as an unprecedented number of relative mediocrities, it was an administrative amalgam. Doubtless its members were never all assembled, but it may have been no accident that its dissensions required the intervention of the Privy Council.

Since the dissension, with its underlying rivalries, seems to be the explanation of the extraordinary size of the commission of 1626, it merits a brief survey. Elements in it were the national eminence of the county's magnates in Elizabeth's time, the sharp distinction between the west, with its Puritan sympathies, and the east, with its Catholics, a tension which seems to have been building up since the early years of the century, and the arrival in the county of Sir Francis Fane to reside at Apethorpe, which his wife had inherited from her Mildmay ancestors; late in December 1624 he secured a peerage as Earl of Westmorland.

After many years in which there seems to have been no serious contest for the county seats in the Commons—they were in effect pre-empted by men named Mildmay, Cecil, Hatton, Spencer, and Knightley, with one going to each side of the county,[9]—there were heated contests in 1624 and 1625 in which the several differences played their parts. With Lords Spencer and Montagu exerting their partly rival authority, Sir Lewis Watson, Sir John Pickering, and Sir John Isham were possible candidates among others.[10] At one moment Lord Spencer wrote to Lord Montagu: 'the papists will work hard this Parliament, . . . and may we have peace and amity, for I assure your good lordship the opposition will be great, for we on this part will not sit down unless you can enforce us to lie down'.[11] The outcome was that in both years Sir William Spencer and Richard Knightley were elected. Both favoured the western side of the county. Lord Burghersh, heir to the Westmorland title, was squeezed out, but was able to be elected a knight of the shire in Kent.[12]

Another dispute erupted in November 1624 over the meeting-place of the quarter sessions and the authority of the *Custos Rotulorum* in that regard. The Privy Council summoned the disputants before them and decreed that if the *Custos* should so wish the January sessions might sit at Kettering, the other three remaining at Northampton. A year later the Earl of Westmorland, recently appointed *Custos*, chose to hold the winter sessions at Kettering for the second time. Justices from the western side appealed against the decision on the grounds that the facilities were inadequate: lodgings, meeting-hall, gaol. The Council reversed their previous ruling, only to have that decision overruled by the King on the appeal of the eastern faction. The signal service of these J.P.s was cited as part reason, and Lord Montagu wrote to Lord Mandeville: 'I am afraid we shall have some scuffling shortly amongst the Justices; the Earl of Westmorland carried such a high hand over his fellow *Justices* by virtue of his Cust Rotulorumship that it cannot be borne.'[13]

Northamptonshire was one of the counties in which the selection of sheriff for 1626 was based upon political expediency. Like Sir Edward Coke and Sir Thomas Wentworth, Richard Knightley was rendered ineligible for election to the Commons. Some change in the Northamptonshire representation was inevitable. Lords Spencer and Montagu combined to secure the return of Pickering as colleague of Spencer's son, 'thus hoping that all bones shall be set to strengthen us that are by birth Northamptonshire men again'.[14] After 1626 Knightley was once more both a J.P. and an M.P.

In this complex schism in the Northamptonshire aristocracy and gentry, membership in the commission of the peace must eagerly have been sought. In spite of the wish of the Commons in 1621 and general royal policy, the pressures were sufficient for a time to enlarge the commission by some fifty men: a few dignitaries, several baronets from neighbouring counties, a small number of courtiers and lawyers, and many simple esquires. Much the largest number were gentry who under ordinary circumstances would not have become justices of the peace. It was in this year that Sir Thomas Brudenell, who had long been suspect and been protected by his friends on the bench, was almost simultaneously convicted of recusancy and put into the commsssion of the peace. He was promptly taken out and was not restored even after he was elevated to the Lords. Even more significant is the fact that most of the additions to the commission were such small gentry that there are few surviving records of their lives. Almost alone among the thirteen hundred men who have been considered here, many cannot be identified with confidence.

## 1636[15]

| | | | | | | | | | | |
|---|---|---|---|---|---|---|---|---|---|---|
| 1 | * | q | Thomas [Coventry], Lord Coventry, lord keeper | | O | I | P | 1640 | DNB | |
| 2 | | q | William [Juxon], Bishop of London, lord treasurer | | O | | | 1663 | DNB | |
| 3 | * | q | Henry [Montagu], Earl of Manchester, keeper of the privy seal | | C | M | P | 1642 | DNB | |
| 4 | * | q | William [Cecil], Earl of Salisbury | | C | G | P | 1668 | | |
| 5 | * | q | William [Cecil], Earl of Exeter [lord lieutenant] | | | G | P | 1640 | | |
| 6 | * | q | John [Egerton], Earl of Bridgewater, president of Wales | | | | P | 1649 | DNB | |
| 7 | s | q | Spencer [Compton], Earl of Northampton | | C | | P | 1643 | DNB | |
| 8 | * | q | Robert [Rich], Earl of Warwick | | C | I | P | 1658 | DNB | |
| 9 | | q | John [Digby], Earl of Bristol | | C | | P | 1653 | DNB | |
| 10 | * | q | Mildmay [Fane], Earl of Westmorland | | C | | P | 1666 | DNB | |
| 11 | * | q | John [Mordaunt], Earl of Peterborough | | O | | P | 1642 | DNB | |
| 12 | * | q | John [Williams], Bishop of Lincoln | | C | | | 1650 | DNB | |
| 13 | | q | Francis [Dee], Bishop of Peterborough | | C | | | 1638 | DNB | |
| 14 | * | q | Edward [Montagu], Lord Montagu | | O | M | P | 1644 | DNB | |
| 15 | | q | George [Goring], Lord Goring | | C | | P | 1663 | DNB | |
| 16 | * | q | Thomas Edmondes, knight, treasurer of the King's household | | | | P | 1639 | DNB | |
| 17 | * | q | Richard Hutton, knight, justice of common pleas | | O | G | P | 1639 | DNB | |
| 18 | | q | Thomas Trevor, knight, baron of exchequer | | | I | P | 1656 | DNB | |
| 19 | | q | Barnaby Bryan [O'Brien], knight | Great Billing | C | | | 1657 | DNB | |
| 20 | * | q | Edmund Carey, knight | Culham, Oxon. | | | P | 1637 | | |
| 21 | * | q | Roland St. John, knight | Woodford | C | | P | 1645 | | |
| 22 | s | q | John Dryden, baronet | Canons Ashby | O | M | P | 1658 | | K |
| 23 | * | q | Lewis Watson, knight and baronet | Rockingham | O | M | P | 1653 | DNB | |
| 24 | * | q | John Isham, knight and baronet | Lamport | C | M | P | 1651 | | |
| 25 | r | q | Christopher Hatton, knight [custos rotulorum] | Kirby | C | G | P | 1670 | DNB | K |
| 26 | * | q | Miles Fleetwood, knight, receiver of the court of wards | | | G | P | 1641 | | K |

| | | | | | | | | |
|---|---|---|---|---|---|---|---|---|
| 27 | * | | Hatton Farmer, knight | Easton Neston | O | | 1640 | |
| 28 | * | q | Edward Onley, knight | Catesby | O | G | 1638 | |
| 29 | * | q | Robert Bannastre, knight | Passenham | C | | 1649 | |
| 30 | * | q | Thomas Brooke, knight | Great Oakley | | | 1638 | |
| 31 | * | q | Thomas Cave, knight | Stanford | O | | 1666 | |
| 32 | * | q | William Wilmer, knight | Sywell | C | I | 1646 | |
| 33 | s | q | Christopher Yelverton, knight | Easton Maudit | C | G | P | 1654 | K |
| 34 | s | q | William Fleetwood, knight | Aldwinkle | C | | 1674 | |
| 35 | * | q | Richard Samwell, knight | Upton | O | M | 1668 | |
| 36 | * | q | John Lambe, knight, master in chancery | | C | | 1647 | DNB |
| 37 | * | q | John Danvers, knight | Culworth | O | | 1642 | |
| 38 | s | q | Robert Wingfield, knight | Upton | C | G | 1652 | |
| 39 | s | q | Richard Lane, knight, attorney of the prince | Ribbesford | C | M | 1650 | DNB |
| 40 | * | | Samuel Clarke, S.T.D. | Northampton | O | | 1641 | |
| 41 | * | | Robert Sibthorpe, S.T.D. | Brackley | C | | 1662 | DNB |
| 42 | * | q | Richard Knightley | Fawsley | | G | P | 1639 | DNB |
| 43 | * | | William Elmes | Lilford | | I | 1641 | |
| 44 | s | q | John Crewe | Steane | O | G | P | 1679 | DNB K |
| 45 | * | | William Lane | Horton | | | 1637 | |
| 46 | * | q | Francis Nicolls | Hardwick | O | M | P | 1641 | |
| 47 | * | q | Charles Edmondes | Hartwell | | | 1652 | |
| 48 | * | q | Richard Cartwright | Aynho | | I | 1637 | |
| 49 | * | q | John Wyrley | Dodford | O | | 1655 | |
| 50 | * | q | Arthur Gooday | Higham Ferrers | C | G | 1639 | |
| 51 | | q | Francis Downes | Pytchley | O | G | P | 1640 | |
| 52 | | q | Robert Tanfield | Loddington | C | M | 1639 | |
| 53 | s | q | Edward Palmer | Stoke Doyle | C | M | 1642 | |
| 54 | * | | Thomas Jenison | Irchester | | | 1647 | |
| 55 | | q | William Downall | | C | M | | |
| 56 | s | q | John Sawyer | Kettering | | | 1646 | |
| 57 | | | George Clarke | Watford | | | 1648 | |

Dignitaries 18; Court 4; Gentry 25; Law 7; Church 2; Commerce 1.

Reduced in 1636 to a much smaller size, the Northamptonshire commission was made up almost entirely of men who either had served themselves already or were descendants of earlier justices. One excep-
19 tion was Sir Barnaby Bryan. Brother and heir of the Earl of Thomond in the Irish peerage, he married a daughter of Sir George Farmer and became a county figure, being nominated Marquess of Billing in 1645, though the patent never passed the Great Seal. There were four
39 lawyers and one merchant who invite comment. Sir Richard Lane was a relative of earlier J.P.s. His career, however, was made at the law; in 1636 he was deputy Recorder of Northampton and Attorney-General to the Prince of Wales. Soon he was to serve as attorney for Strafford during the impeachment proceedings. Although a son of an
53 earlier J.P., Edward Palmer had a career at the bar which won him
52 a readership in the Middle Temple. Robert Tanfield and William
55 Downall were other sons of the county who achieved success in the
57 law. George Clarke, likewise descended from Northamptonshire fore-bears and a relative of Dr. Samuel Clarke, was a member of the

Grocers' Company, alderman of London, and sheriff in 1641, who bought an estate at Watford and qualified for an appointment as J.P. In 1636 the complexion of the Northamptonshire commission was much like that of other counties. No longer could the county boast the national leaders who lent its bench a special quality in the time of Elizabeth I. Yet it did possess the splendid mansions—some open to the public today—which inspired comment by Camden and Norden. 'This Northamptonshire is a most pleasant shire. . . . No shire in this Realme can answer the number of noblemen as are seated in those Partes.'[16] As the civil crisis deepened, the county bench came to have nearly as many lawyers as were to be found in Norfolk and Somerset. The educational experience was also comparable. There were only nine justices who had not been enrolled in either university or one of the inns of court. Parliamentary experience was also similar to that in other counties. While many of the men elected to the Commons in 1640 were reformers, they were not followed by their fellows in their opposition to 'Thorough'. Most of the surviving members of the commission of 1636 were forced to make their peace with the committees for advance of money and compounding.

## NOTES TO APPENDIX C

1. *Cal. Pat. Rolls, Eliz.*, ii (1560–3), 440; Lansdowne MSS. 1218, ff. 21ᵛ, 22.

*1562 roster:*

5. Gladys Scott Thomson, *Two Centuries of Family History* (L. 1930), pp. 167 ff.; *L. & P.* xvi, g1056(60).
14. Ibid. xivв, g249(10); ibid. xvii, g285(6); Barron, *Northamptonshire Families*, pp. 171 ff.
15. Mary E. Finch, *The Wealth of Five Northamptonshire Families* (Oxford, 1956), Ch. III; J. H. Round, *Studies in Peerage and Family History* (L. 1901), p. 281; *DNB*: 'Robert Spencer' and 'John Kytson'; John Bridges, *History and Antiquities of the County of Northampton* (2 vols., L., 1791), i. 479.
16. Finch, *Wealth*, Ch. V.
17. A. L. Rowse, *Ralegh and the Throckmortons* (L., 1962), Ch. II.
18. Bridges, *Hist. of Northampton*, i. 367; *DNB*: 'Ralph Lane'.
19. George Baker, *History and Antiquities of the County of Northampton* (2 vols. L., 1822–41), i. 167, 295–6; Bridges, *Hist. of Northampton*, i. 38.
20. Ibid., p. 290.
21. Baker, *Hist. of Northampton*, i. 73, 524–6; Bridges, *Hist. of Northampton*, i. 114; ibid. ii. 305; *L. & P.* xiiiA, g1115(70); ibid. xx, *passim*; Lincoln's Inn *Black Books*, i. 217, 247, 271, 301, 373 *et passim*; *Complete Peerage*, viii. 458–9; PCC 1571, 32 Holney.
22. Baker, *Hist. of Northampton*, ii. 23; Bridges, *Hist. of Northampton*, i. 232; *Cal. Pat. Rolls, Eliz.* i (1558–60), 281.
23. Baker, *Hist. of Northampton*, i. 732–3; Bridges, *Hist. of Northampton*, i. 215.
24. Baker, *Hist. of Northampton*, i. 364; Bridges, *Hist. of Northampton*, i. 60.

25. Ibid., p. 595; *Middle Temple Bench Book*, p. 150.
26. Bridges, *Hist. of Northampton*, ii. 480.
27. Ibid., p. 470.
28. Ibid., p. 258; Anstruther, *Vaux*, pp. 240, 244.
29. Bridges, *Hist. of Northampton*, i. 389; Revd. Henry Isham Longden (ed.), *The Visitation of the County of Northampton in the year 1681* (Harleian Soc. Publ. lxxxvii, L., 1935), p. 43; *DNB*: 'John Catesby'.
31. Finch, *Wealth*, Ch. IV.
32. Baker, *Hist. of Northampton*, i. 356; Bridges, *Hist. of Northampton*, ii. 276–7; *VCH Hertfordshire* (4 vols., L., 1902–14), iii. 229, 266; *VCH Worcestershire* (4 vols., L. 1901–24), iii. 68, 81, 116, 126, 184, 269, 378, 466; H. Avray Tipping, *English Homes of the Early Renaissance* (L., 1912), pp. 72–3.
33. C. Wise, *The Montagues of Boughton* (Kettering, 1888), pp. 22–8; Bernard Falk, *The Way of the Montagues* (L., n.d.), p. 10.
34. Wake, *Brudenells*, Ch. IV; Finch, *Wealth*, Ch. VI.
35. Bridges, *Hist. of Northampton*, i. 101; *L. & P.* xvi, g678(57); PCC 1559, 52 Chaynay.
36. Barron, *Northamptonshire Families*, pp. 313–14, 322.
37. Ibid., pp. 143, 144; Finch, *Wealth*, p. 5; *Middle Temple Records*, i. 83, 89, 107.
38. Bridges, *Hist. of Northampton*, ii. 343; *Cal. Pat. Rolls, Philip and Mary*, i (1553–4), 22.
39. Bridges, *Hist. of Northampton*, ii. 508; *L. & P.* xviiiA, g981(85); ibid. xixA, g610(103); Barron, *Northamptonshire Families*, p. 27; Bateson, *Original Letters*, p. 36.
40. Bridges, *Hist. of Northampton*, *passim*; *L. & P.* xvi, 134, f. 41; ibid. xviiiA, g226(38); ibid. xixB, g527(4, 30); *Cal. Pat. Rolls, Edw. VI*, i (1547–8), 87 *et passim*; PCC 1561, 16 Loftes.
41. Bridges, *Hist. of Northampton*, i. 579; ibid. ii. 328; *L. & P.* xv, g282(98); ibid. xiiiA, g1115(70).
42. Baker, *Hist. of Northampton*, i. 494; Bridges, *Hist. of Northampton*, i. 119–21; *L. & P.* xxiA, g504(9).
43. Bridges, *Hist. of Northampton*, ii. 600; *VCH Northamptonshire* (4 vols., L., 1902–37), ii. 535.

2. Lansdowne MSS. 737, ff. 18, 18ᵛ, 19.

*1584 roster:*
10. Neale, *House of Commons*, *passim*; Neale, *Elizabeth I and Her Parliaments, 1559–1581, passim*; ibid. *1584–1603, passim*.
12. *Middle Temple Bench Book*, p. 111.
15. Cf. Northants, 1562 roster, no. 15.
17. Ibid., no. 18.
18. Ibid., no. 30.
20. Ibid., no. 31.
22. Anstruther, *Vaux*, pp. 117, 249; cf. Northants, 1562 roster, no. 21.
23. Finch, *Wealth*, Ch. V.
24. *Alum. cantab.*
25. Cf. Northants, 1562 roster, no. 36.
26. Baker, *Hist. of Northampton*, ii. 143, 146; *Northamptonshire Past & Present*, i, no. 5 (1952), pp. 2–3.
27. Cf. Northants, 1562 roster, no. 26.
28. Ibid., no. 40.
30. Barron, *Northamptonshire Families*, p. 185; cf. *supra*, p. 171.

31. Bridges, *Hist. of Northampton*, i. 364, 365; Ingpen, *Middle Temple Bench Books*, p. 172; *DNB*: 'Francis Tate'.
32. Baker, *Hist. of Northampton*, ii. 13; Bridges, *Hist. of Northampton*, i. 122; *L. & P.* xiiA, g539(38); ibid. xiiB, g967(47); ibid. xv, g831(85); ibid. xvi, 381; ibid. xxv, g910(52); *Alum. cantab.*, 'Edward Cope'.
33. Barron, *Northamptonshire Families*, pp. 323–5; cf. *Northamptonshire Past & Present*, i. no. 5, p. 2.
34. Bridges, *Hist. of Northampton*, ii. 258.
35. Cf. Northants, 1562 roster, no. 27.
36. Baker, *Hist. of Northampton*, i. 296.
37. H. Sydney Grazebrook (ed.), *The Visitation of Staffordshire . . . 1583* (vol. iii of William Salt Archaeological Society, *Collections*) (L., 1882); *VCH Buckinghamshire* (4 vols. L., 1905–27), iv. 182; PCC 1597, 31 Cobham.
38. *Pension Book of Gray's Inn*, i. 19, 43, 52, 60; *I.P.M.* 27 Eliz.
39. Finch, *Wealth*, Ch. I.
40. C. Wise, *Rockingham Castle and the Watsons* (Kettering, 1891), Ch. II.
41. Baker, *Hist. of Northampton*, i. 719; Bridges, *Hist. of Northampton*, i. 207; *L. & P.* xivA, g1354(63).
42. Bridges, *Hist. of Northampton*, i. 7, 590; ibid. ii. 97.
43. Baker, *Hist. of Northampton*, i. 10; Bridges, *Hist. of Northampton*, i. 478; *Middle Temple Records*, i. 81, 239, 241, 244, 246.

3. Bateson, 'Original Letters', pp. 35–6; Egerton MS. 2345, f. 22.

4. P.R.O., S.P. 14/33, ff. 44ᵛ, 45, 45ᵛ.

*1608 roster:*
15. Edward Foss, *Judges of England* (9 vols., L., 1848–64), vi. 157.
17. Barron, *Northamptonshire Families*, p. 33.
18. Fairfax Harrison, *The Devon Carys* (2 vols., N.Y., 1920), i. 368–72; Robert Clutterbuck, *History and Antiquities of the County of Hertford* (3 vols., L., 1815–27), iii. 181; PCC 1638, 17 Lee.
20. Cf. Northants, 1584 roster, no. 22.
21. Ibid., no. 26.
23. Rowse, *Ralegh and the Throckmortons, passim*.
24. Bridges, *Hist. of Northampton*, i. 367.
25. Ibid. ii. 39–40.
26. Cf. Northants, 1584 roster, no. 23.
27. *DNB*: 'Lewis Watson'.
28. Bridges, *Hist. of Northampton*, ii. 508.
29. *Middle Temple Bench Book*, p. 134.
30. Finch, *Wealth*, p. 5 n.
31. Baker, *Hist. of Northampton*, i. 296.
32. Ibid. i. 740; Bridges, *Hist. of Northampton*, i. 216.
33. Baker, *Hist. of Northampton*, i. 407; Bridges, *Hist. of Northampton*, i. 76.
34. Baker, *Hist. of Northampton*, i. 494.
35. Ibid. i. 224–5; Bridges, *Hist. of Northampton*, i. 539.
36. Baker, *Hist. of Northampton*, i. 287; Richardson, *Augmentations*, p. 42 *et passim*; *L. & P.* xiiA, g795(10).
37. Bridges, *Hist. of Northampton*, i. 408.
38. Ibid., p. 365; *DNB*: 'Francis Tate'; Keeler, *Long Parliament*, p. 357.
39. *Alum. cantab.*
40. *Alum. oxon.*
41. Cf. Northants, 1584 roster, no. 33.

42. Ibid., no. 34.
43. *Middle Temple Bench Book*, pp. 41, 167; Bridges, *Hist. of Northampton*, i. 521.
44. *VCH Rutland* (2 vols., L., 1908–35), ii. 78, 79; *Students admitted to the Inner Temple*, p. 19.
45. Bridges, *Hist. of Northampton*, i. 586.
46. Ibid., p. 383; Anstruther, *Vaux*, p. 392.
47. Bridges, *Hist. of Northampton*, i. 406–8; PCC 1615, 25 Rudd; *Parliamentary Papers*, 1831, cmd. 231, pp. 189–93.
48. Bridges, *Hist. of Northampton*, ii. 325–7; J. A. Gotch, *The Old Halls and Manor-Houses of Northamptonshire* (L., 1936), pp. 34–5.
49. Finch, *Wealth*, Ch. IV; Bridges, *Hist. of Northampton*, ii. 322.
50. Ibid. i. 595.
51. *VCH Rutland*, ii. 260.
52. Bridges, *Hist. of Northampton*, i. 570.
53. PCC 1558, 29 Welles; *Lincoln's Inn, Admissions*, i. 90.

5. See *supra*, p. 73.

6. P.R.O., C 193/12.
*1626 roster:*
17. *A.P.C., Mar. 1625–May 1626*, pp. 229, 231, 234, 237–8, 248.
24. *Middle Temple Bench Book*, p. 180.
25. Ibid., p. 173; Foss, *Judges*, vi. 319.
26. C. A. Markham and J. C. Cox (eds.), *The Records of the Borough of Northampton* (2 vols., Northampton, 1898), ii. 105.
27. Cf. Northants, 1608 roster, no. 17.
28. *Complete Peerage*: 'Spencer'; *VCH Northamptonshire*, iii. 256; Shaw, *Knights of England*, i. 160.
29. Cf. Northants, 1608 roster, no. 18.
30. *Complete Peerage*: 'St. John'; cf. Northants, 1608 roster, no. 28.
31. Wake, *Brudenells*, pp. 112–14.
32. Baker, *Hist. of Northampton*, i. 621.
33. Barron, *Northamptonshire Families*, p. 45.
35. Baker, *Hist. of Northampton*, i. 434; Joan Wake (ed.), *Quarter Sessions Records of the County of Northampton* (vol. i of Northamptonshire Record Society Publications) (Hereford, 1924), p. 248.
36. Barron, *Northamptonshire Families*, p. 327.
37. Bridges, *Hist. of Northampton*, i. 554.
39. Cf. Northants, 1608 roster, no. 25.
41. Baker, *Hist. of Northampton*, ii. 143; Bridges, *Hist. of Northampton*, i. 290.
42. Cf. Northants, 1608 roster, no. 32.
43. Ibid., no. 35.
44. Ibid., no. 36.
45. Bridges, *Hist. of Northampton*, i. 308.
46. Ibid. ii. 326.
47. Finch, *Wealth*, Ch. II.
48. Cf. Northants, 1608 roster, no. 49.
49. Baker, *Hist. of Northampton*, i. 12, 15; *VCH Northamptonshire*, iv. 67.
50. Bridges, *Hist. of Northampton*, i. 579–80.
51. Thomson, *History of Tapestry*, p. 286.
52. Baker, *Hist. of Northampton*, i. 494; Bridges, *Hist. of Northampton*, i. 120, 121.
53. Ibid. ii. 97, 148.
54. *Alum. cantab.*

55. Bridges, *Hist. of Northampton*, ii. 383; cf. Keeler, *Long Parliament*, 'Gilbert Pickering'.

56. *VCH Northamptonshire*, iv. 164.

58. Bridges, *Hist. of Northampton*, ii. 47–8.

59. *Alum. cantab.*: 'Humphrey Orme', his son.

60. Baker, *Hist. of Northampton*, i. 606; Wake, *Quarter Sessions Records*, p. 247.

61. *VCH Northamptonshire*, iii. 574.

62. Bridges, *Hist. of Northampton*, i. 539; Baker, *Hist. of Northampton*, i. 225. Sir Richard Samwell was son of Sir William, no. 43 *supra*.

63. Bridges, *Hist. of Northampton*, ii. 581.

64. *Visit. Northants, 1681*, p. 54; Markham and Cox, *Records of Northampton*, ii. 238; *Cal. S. P. Dom., Chas. I, 1637 and 1637–8, passim*; PCC 1641, 61 Evelyn.

67. Gardiner, *History of England*, vi. 206, 207, 237; Davies, *Early Stuarts*, pp. 37–8.

68. Barron, *Northamptonshire Families*, p. 185; *Cal. S. P. Dom., Chas. I, 1625–6*, pp. 142, 156; *A.P.C. 1625–6*, p. 238; ibid. *1627*, pp. 25, 395, 430; ibid. *1627–8*, p. 217.

69. Bridges, *Hist. of Northampton*, ii. 242; *VCH Northamptonshire*, iii. 114, 118; PCC 1632, 80 Audley.

70. Bridges, *Hist. of Northampton*, i. 368.

71. *DNB*: 'Augustine Nicholls'.

72. Barron, *Northamptonshire Families*, pp. 11, 12.

73. Emily A. Buckland, *The Rainsford Family* (Worcester, n.d.), p. 195.

74. Bridges, *Hist. of Northampton*, ii. 176; *Pension Book of Gray's Inn*, i. 157, 228; *Northamptonshire Past & Present*, ii (1958), 245; PCC 1639, 38 Harvey.

75. Bridges, *Hist. of Northampton*, ii. 604; PCC 1629, 12 Ridley.

76. *Alum. oxon.*: 'William Conyers', 'Tristram Conyers'; H. W. Woolrich, *Lives of Eminent Serjeants-at-law* (L., 1869), pp. 394–5; *Middle Temple Bench Book*, p. 187.

77. Baker, *Hist. of Northampton*, i. 356; Barron, *Northamptonshire Families*, p. 333; Bridges, *Hist. of Northampton*, i. 52.

78. Ibid., p. 318; PCC 1633, 80 Russell.

81. Barron, *Northamptonshire Families*, p. 370.

86. *Alum. cantab.*; Bridges, *Hist. of Northampton*, iii. 370; *Middle Temple Records*, ii. 645, 680, 691, 713, 823.

87. Bridges, *Hist. of Northampton*, ii. 181; Charles Best Norcliffe (ed.), *The Visitation of Yorkshire in the Years 1563 and 1564* (Harleian Soc. Publ. xvi, L., 1881), p. 174.

96. *VCH Northamptonshire*, iii. 221; *Cal. S. P. Dom., Chas. I, 1635–6*, pp. 112, 118.

102. *Cal. S. P. Dom., Jas. I, 1619–23*, p. 165; *A.P.C., June–Dec. 1626*, p. 111; Walter Metcalfe (ed.), *The Visitations of Essex* (Harleian Soc. Publ. xiii–xiv, L., 1878–9), i. 363.

106. Bridges, *Hist. of Northampton*, i. 381.

7. The new justices were: the Earl of Holland, Viscount Mandeville, Lord Vaux, Lord Fitzwilliam, Sir Richard Hutton, Sir James Whitlocke, Sir Thomas Brudenell, Sir Roland Egerton, Sir John Hewett, Sir William Chauncey, Sir Lewis Pemberton, Sir Henry Robinson, Sir Humphrey Orme, Sir William Beecher, Sir Richard Samwell, Thomas Elmes, William Lane, and John Wyrley.

8. Thomas Andrews, John Isham, Thomas Dove (son of the Bishop of Peterborough), Francis Quarles, William Elmes, George Lynne, Edward Farmer, George Catesby, Thomas Kirton, and three members of the Saunders family: Ambrose, William, and Francis.

9. Neale, *House of Commons*, pp. 33–4, 69, 70; *Members of Parliament*, i, *passim*.

10. *H.M.C., Beaulieu MSS.*, i, 105–10; *H.M.C. Buccleuch MSS.*, i. 258–65.

11. *Beaulieu MSS.*, i. 106.

12. Ibid., p. 110.

13. *A.P.C., 1623–5*, 365–6; ibid., *1625–6*, pp. 256–7, 293; *Buccleuch MSS.*, i. 262.

14. *Beaulieu MSS*, i. 109.

15. P.R.O., S.P. 16/405, ff. 45ᵛ–47ᵛ.

*1636 roster:*
  15. *DNB; VCH Bedfordshire* (3 vols., L., 1904–14), iii. 45.
  20. Cf. Northants, 1608 roster, no. 18.
  21. Cf. Northants, 1626 roster, no. 30.
  24. Ibid., no. 47.
  27. Ibid., no. 41.
  28. Cf. Northants, 1608 roster, no. 36.
  29. Cf. Northants, 1626 roster, no. 45.
  30. Ibid., no. 46.
  31. Ibid., no. 50.
  32. Ibid., no. 53.
  34. *DNB*: 'Charles Fleetwood'.
  35. Cf. Northants, 1626 roster, no. 62.
  37. Ibid., no. 60.
  38. *Alum. cantab.*
  40. Cf. Northants, 1626 roster, no. 64.
  43. Bridges, *Hist. of Northampton*, ii. 242.
  45. Cf. Northants, 1626 roster, no. 70.
  46. Ibid., no. 71.
  47. Ibid., no. 106.
  48. Ibid., no. 72.
  49. Ibid., no. 77.
  50. Ibid., no. 74.
  51. *Cal. S. P. Dom., Chas. I, 1634–5*, pp. 206, 211; PCC 1640, 111 Coventry.
  52. *Middle Temple Bench Book*, p. 183.
  53. Ibid., p. 192.
  54. Cf. Northants, 1626 roster, no. 87.
  55. *Middle Temple Records*, ii. 499, 542, 613.
  56. Cf. Northants, 1626 roster, no. 96.
  57. *Visit. Northants 1681*, p. 52; Frederick George Lee, *The History . . . of Thame* (L., 1883), p. 315; Beaven, *Aldermen of London*, i. 58; ibid. ii. 65.

16. Gotch, *Old Halls and Manor-Houses*, p. vii., quoting Norden.

# SOMERSET

**1562**[1]

| No. | q | Name | Place | | | P | Year | DNB |
|---|---|---|---|---|---|---|---|---|
| 1 | q | Nicholas Bacon, knight [lord keeper] | | C | G | P | 1579 | DNB |
| 2 | q | William [Paulet], Marquess of Winchester [lord treasurer] | | | | P | 1572 | DNB |
| 3 | q | Henry [Fitzalan], Earl of Arundel [lord steward] | | | | | 1580 | DNB |
| 4 | q | Francis [Russell], Earl of Bedford | | C | G | P | 1585 | DNB |
| 5 | q | William [Herbert], Earl of Pembroke | | | | P | 1570 | DNB |
| 6 | q | Gilbert [Berkeley], Bishop of Bath and Wells | | O | | | 1581 | DNB |
| 7 | q | Edward Rogers, knight, comptroller of the household | | | | P | 1567 | DNB |
| 8 | q | Richard Weston, a justice of the common pleas | | | M | P | 1572 | DNB |
| 9 | q | Richard Harper, serjeant-at-law | | | I | | 1577 | |
| 10 | q | Hugh Paulet, knight [*custos rotulorum*] | Hinton St. George | | | P | 1572 | DNB |
| 11 | | Edward Seymour, knight | Berry Pomeroy, Devon | | | | 1593 | |
| 12 | q | William St. Loe, knight | Sutton Court | | | P | 1565 | |
| 13 | q | Maurice Berkeley, knight | Bruton | | L | P | 1581 | |
| 14 | q | Thomas Dyer, knight | Weston | | | P | 1563 | |
| 15 | | George Speke, knight | White Lackington | | | P | 1584 | |
| 16 | | Edward Gorges, knight | Wraxall | | | | 1568 | |
| 17 | | George Norton, knight | Abbots Leigh | | | | 1584 | |
| 18 | q | Ralph Hopton, knight | Witham | | | P | 1571 | |
| 19 | | James FitzJames, knight | Redlynch | | | | 1579 | |
| 20 | q | John Welshe, serjeant-at-law | Cathanger | | M | P | 1572 | |
| 21 | q | William Rosewell | Middle Temple | | M | | 1566 | |
| 22 | q | John Wadham | Merrifield, Devon | O | I | P | 1577 | |
| 23 | | John Horner | Cloford | | | | 1587 | |
| 24 | q | Humphrey Colles | Pitminster | | | | 1571 | |
| 25 | q | Humphrey Walrond | Ilminster | | L | | 1580 | |
| 26 | q | Richard Cooper | Winscombe | | | P | 1566 | |
| 27 | q | Nicholas Halswell | Goathurst | | M | P | 1564 | |
| 28 | | Henry Portman | Orchard Portman | | M | | 1591 | |
| 29 | q | William Hawley | Buckland | | | | 1567 | |
| 30 | q | John Mawdley | Nunney | | M | P | 1573 | |
| 31 | | Richard Warre | Hestercombe | | | | 1603 | |
| 32 | q | John Hippesley | Cameley | | M | P | 1571 | |
| 33 | | Henry St. Barbe | Ashington | | | | 1567 | |
| 34 | | William Clyfton | Barrington | | G | | 1564 | |
| 35 | | Hugh Brooke | Long Ashton | | | | 1586 | |
| 36 | | James Bisse | Batcombe | | | | 1569 | |
| 37 | | John Keynes | Compton Pauncefoot | | | | 1595 | |
| 38 | | Robert Hill | Taunton | | | | 1581 | |
| 39 | | John Wyndham, knight | St. Decumans | | | | 1575 | |
| 40 | | John Thynne, knight | Longleat, Wilts. | | | P | 1580 | DNB |

Dignitaries 9; Court 7; Gentry 13; Law 5; Church 0; Commerce 4.

The Somerset commission of 1562 was characteristic of its time. It included men of national position and men prominent in the county, men whose status derived from inherited estates and those who had benefited notably from the dissolution of the monasteries.

4, 5    Among the dignitaries the Earls of Bedford and Pembroke both held extensive properties in the West Country although their residences were elsewhere. Each was a major figure at the Court of the Queen.

7    Sir Edward Rogers was a resident of Somerset as well as a courtier. Servant of Henry VIII, he had been granted much of the lands of Buckland Priory in 1538 and had gone into exile in the reign of Mary. Now he was a Privy Councillor and Comptroller of the Household.

There were members of the royal Court in the working commission

10    also. Sir Hugh Paulet, head of the senior line of the family of which Lord Treasurer Winchester was a cadet, had served Henry VIII well as both soldier and lawyer. Rewarded with the grant of monastic lands, he was now Governor of Jersey. His was destined to be the most prominent family in the county during the next eighty years. Sir

11    Edward Seymour, the son of the late Lord Protector, was a connection of the royal family, but he was also a resident of Somerset. Sir Maurice

13    Berkeley, who could boast a most distinguished ancestry, was the first Somerset member of the family to achieve prominence. He had been gentleman usher to Henry VIII, and like others had been granted

18    monastic spoils. Sir Ralph Hopton, whose roots were in Suffolk and whose brother was Lieutenant of the Tower, had fought in France with Henry VIII and been granted the monastery of Witham. Sir

14    Thomas Dyer had been a gentleman sewer to Henry VIII and received the grant of Weston from the lands of Glastonbury Abbey. The son of one of Cromwell's agents in the suppression of the monasteries,

19    Sir James FitzJames also owed his fortune to the rape of the Church; a cousin had been Lord Chief Justice between 1526 and 1538. Henry

28    Portman was the son of an eminent lawyer who had been Justice of the King's Bench in Henry's time and Chief Justice under Mary. Monastic lands came his way also. These men are all best classified as courtiers.

Two less prominent men who derived much benefit from the

23    monasteries were Humphrey Colles and John Horner. Since they do not seem to have been active at Court, they may be considered to be gentry. Horner's father was a Henrician J.P., and the son is thought to be the original of the nursery jingle about Christmas pie. A Somerset doggerel went:

> Wyndham and Horner, Berkeley and Thynne,
> When the monks went out, they came in.

24    Colles was a man of means, well acquainted with members of the commission of the peace, with several of whom he seems to have enjoyed a fiduciary relationship. He may have had legal training and he first became a J.P. under Mary.

There were five lawyers in the working part of this commission.

20    Serjeant John Welshe, who was to be made Justice of the Common

Pleas in 1563, might well have been appointed a J.P. merely for his legal competence—he was Recorder of Bristol—but in fact he came from a Somerset family of some note, possessed a considerable estate in that county and in Devon, and was related to members of the gentry. William Rosewell also came from a West Country family. A Middle 21 Temple barrister, he played an active part in the market in monastic lands, and was Solicitor-General at the end of his life. Humphrey Walrond was one of the six clerks and later a master in chancery. 25 John Mawdley and John Hippesley were both Middle Temple 30, 32 readers of Somerset background. Hippesley's grandson, who was one of Buckingham's henchmen in the time of Charles I, has been noted as a J.P. in Kent.

The fortune of four justices was derived from commerce. Sir George Norton, who acquired the monastic property of Abbots Leigh, came 17 from a family of Bristol merchants. His son, Samuel, best known for writings on alchemy, was a J.P. in 1584. James Bisse was said by 36 Somerset's most notable antiquary to have been of 'a very ancient and respectable family', but in a grant of monastic lands to Lord Russell he was described as a clothmaker. It is clear that he acquired considerable property of that sort. Robert Hill may have been related to 38 members of the gentry, but his father was a merchant who generously supported a recently established school in Taunton. William Clyfton 34 was a younger son in a very distinguished Nottinghamshire family. He became a merchant tailor in London, collector of tonnage and poundage, and an original member of the Muscovy Company. In association with Humphrey Colles he engaged in the purchase of monastic lands. His son married a daughter of Lord Monteagle.

The remaining members of this commission may all be classified as gentry though their claim to that status was of varied force. John Wadham's ancestors can be traced in Devon from a fourteenth-century 22 Justice of the Common Pleas. The family acquired such means that in the next generation Nicholas and Dorothy could establish a well-endowed Oxford college. Richard Cooper, 'a person of consideration 26 in the west of England', is somewhat obscure, though he had the means to pay £1,366 for the grant of the manor of Poulet Gauntes from monastic spoils. His descendants became the Earls of Shaftesbury. Henry St. Barbe secured Sir Francis Walsingham as a son-in-law. 33 Sir William St. Loe had a J.P. father, but he is better known as the 12 third husband of Bess of Hardwick. The Gorges family, of which Sir Edward was the head, had been prominent as early as the reign of 16 Edward III, but its most famous member is his son, Ferdinando, who devoted much energy and money to ventures in New England.

Two of the beneficiaries referred to in the Somerset jingle were Wyndham and Thynne. Neither name is found in the patent-roll

39 commission of 1562. Yet Sir John Wyndham, second son in a family which has been encountered in Norfolk and husband of a Somerset heiress, had been a J.P. from the latter years of Henry VIII. When he was pricked for sheriff for 1562, he was removed from the commission as a matter of routine. Even though he lived until 1575, he
40 may not have been restored. Sir John Thynne was introduced into Court circles by his uncle William, a minor official—and also an editor of Chaucer. Knighted at Pinkie Cleugh in 1547, he married the daughter and heiress of the businessman, banker, and courtier, Lord Mayor Sir Richard Gresham. He became a factotum of the Lord Protector and Comptroller of the Household of Princess Elizabeth. He was the recipient of very large grants of monastic and chantry lands—for one he paid £4,340. He purchased Longleat from Sir John Horsey in 1540 and in Elizabeth's reign he erected there the magnificent mansion which has since been the property of his heirs.

The Somerset justices of 1562 were not unlike those of the other counties which have been considered. Yet there were differences. Although a number came from families long prominent in the region and some seem to have been local men newly risen from obscurity— Robert Hill with his burgher background—there were a striking group who had been connected with the Courts of Henry VIII and Edward VI and had profited notably from monastic spoils. The legal profession was important here as elsewhere. Much the same proportion —twelve among the twenty-nine of the working members—were at some time elected to the House of Commons. Six were present in 1563, all sitting for Somerset constituencies except Sir William St. Loe, who must have benefited from his wife's influence in his election as knight for Derbyshire. Sir Edward Rogers and Sir Maurice Berkeley were the county's knights. Serjeant Welshe sat for Bristol, Nicholas Halswell for Bridgwater, and John Hippesley for Wells. Like those for the other counties, the Somerset J.P.s of the early years of Elizabeth I were an enterprising and interesting group of men.

## 1584[2]

| | | | | | | | |
|---|---|---|---|---|---|---|---|
| 1 | q | Thomas Bromley, knight, lord chancellor of England | O | M | P | 1587 | DNB |
| 2 | q | William [Cecil], Lord Burghley, lord treasurer of England | C | G | P | 1598 | DNB |
| 3 | • q | Francis [Russell], Earl of Bedford | C | G | P | 1585 | DNB |
| 4 | q | William [Bourchier], Earl of Bath | C | | | 1623 | |
| 5 | q | George [Tuchet], Lord Audley | C | | | 1617 | |
| 6 | q | Edward [Parker], Lord Morley | C | | | 1618 | |
| 7 | q | John [Stourton], Lord Stourton | O | | | 1588 | |
| 8 | q | Lord Thomas Paulet | | | | 1586 | |
| 9 | q | Roger Manwood, knight [justice of common pleas] | | I | P | 1592 | DNB |
| 10 | q | William Peryam [justice of common pleas] | O | M | | 1604 | DNB |
| 11 | • q | Edward Seymour, knight    Berry Pomeroy, Devon | | | | 1593 | |

| | | | Name | Place | | | | | |
|---|---|---|---|---|---|---|---|---|---|
| 12 | s | q | Amyas Paulet, knight [*custos rotulorum*] | Curry Mallet | | M | | 1588 | DNB |
| 13 | * | q | George Norton, knight | Abbots Leigh | | | | 1584 | |
| 14 | | q | John Young, knight | Bristol | | | P | 1589 | |
| 15 | | | John Sydenham, knight | Brympton | | M | | 1598 | |
| 16 | * | q | John Horner, knight | Cloford | | | | 1587 | |
| 17 | | | John Horsey, knight | Clifton Maybank, Dorset | | | | 1587 | |
| 18 | * | q | Henry Portman, knight | Orchard Portman | | M | | 1591 | |
| 19 | | q | John Stawell, knight | Cothelstone | | I | | 1603 | |
| 20 | s | q | John Clyfton, knight | Barrington | C | M | | 1593 | |
| 21 | | q | John Popham, attorney-general | Wellington | O | M | P | 1607 | DNB |
| 22 | s | q | Edward Seymour | | | | P | 1613 | |
| 23 | s | q | John Thynne | Longleat, Wilts. | O | | | 1604 | |
| 24 | s | q | Nicholas Wadham | Merrifield, Devon | | I | P | 1609 | DNB |
| 25 | s | q | Henry Berkeley | Bruton | | M | P | 1601 | |
| 26 | * | | Richard Warre | Hestercombe | | | | 1603 | |
| 27 | r | q | Edward Popham | Huntworth | | M? | P | 1586 | |
| 28 | | | Christopher Kenne | Kenn | | | | 1592 | |
| 29 | r | | Arthur Hopton | Witham | | G | P? | 1609 | |
| 30 | r | | Richard FitzJames | Redlynch | | | | 1595 | |
| 31 | | q | William Bowerman | Wells | | G | P | 1590 | |
| 32 | | q | John Lancaster | Milverton | O | G | | 1595 | |
| 33 | | | John Buller | North Curry | | M | P? | 1591 | |
| 34 | s | q | Edward St. Barbe | Ashington | | | | 1598 | |
| 35 | | | John Brett | Whitestaunton | | | | 1589 | |
| 36 | r | q | George Sydenham | Combe Sydenham | | | | 1598 | |
| 37 | s | q | John Colles | Pitminster | | G | | 1608 | |
| 38 | | q | Thomas Phelips | Barrington | | | P? | 1590 | |
| 39 | s | q | Gabriel Hawley | Buckland | C | M | | 1603 | |
| 40 | | | Richard Watkyns | Holwell | | | | 1589 | |
| 41 | r | | James Bisse | Croscombe | | M | P | 1606 | |
| 42 | r | | John Sydenham | | | | | | |
| 43 | | q | Alexander Pym | Brymore | | M | P | 1585 | |
| 44 | | | Matthew Ewens | North Cadbury | | M | P | 1598 | |
| 45 | * | | John Keynes | Compton Pauncefoot | | | | 1595 | |
| 46 | r | | William Hill | Yard | | | | 1594 | |
| 47 | s | q | Humphrey Wyndham | Wiveliscombe | | L | | 1622 | |
| 48 | s | q | Samuel Norton | Abbots Leigh | C | | | 1604 | DNB |
| 49 | | | John Francis | Combe Florey | | | | 1619 | |

Dignitaries 10; Court 3; Gentry 26; Law 7; Church 0; Commerce 3.

The dignitaries in the Somerset commission of 1584 were much the usual sort: noblemen who had lands or other interest in the county. The Earl of Bath was the sole peer at this time whose title derived its name from the county; he was the son-in-law of the Earl of Bedford. Lord Morley and Lord Thomas Paulet married women who must have brought them Somerset property. Lords Audley and Stourton had residences in Wiltshire. Because the see of Bath and Wells was vacant there was no episcopal justice. Sir Amyas Paulet might almost have ranked with the dignitaries. Not only was he head of the leading family, but he was a devoted servant of the Queen: Lieutenant-Governor of Jersey, ambassador to France, keeper of Mary Stuart, Chancellor of the Order of the Garter.

In Somerset, as in Kent and Norfolk, the lawyers were outstanding. Already in 1562 the Middle Temple had been the inn selected by most Somerset men. Now this contingent was headed by Attorney-General John Popham. (A group of which he was the focus was discussed in Chapter VI.) In this commission he had as colleagues his elder brother and five barristers. While the records of the Middle Temple—defective at the relevant time—do not indicate that Edward Popham was a member, the return of Bridgwater for the Parliament of 1572 describes him as Recorder of the town, a position conventionally held by a barrister. Matthew Ewens, likewise a Middle Temple barrister and reader who became a Baron of the Exchequer in 1594, was Somerset's other most notable lawyer. William Bowerman and Alexander Pym were also Middle Temple lawyers, Bowerman surely a barrister. Pym, best known as the father of a famous son, is not recorded as having been called to the bar, although he continued to take an active part in the life of the inn after the moment when a call was usual. John Lancaster was a barrister, reader, and treasurer of Gray's Inn, while Humphrey Wyndham—a close friend of Lambarde—was a barrister and bencher of Lincoln's Inn.

Four other justices merit comment. It is not clear whether Sir John Young should be classed as a squire or a merchant. Descended from notable and wealthy Bristol merchants, he seems not to have engaged in commerce, but he described himself as of the city, and there he lived in the 'Great House' where he was knighted by the Queen—in company with John Sydenham—when he entertained her in 1574. Sydenham was the head of one line of a county family which was very prominent for several centuries both before and after 1584. Sir John Stawell and Thomas Phelips are the first members of their families to be encountered in this study. The descendants of both played a large part in county and national affairs.

Most of the men who composed the Somerset commission in 1584 belonged to a tightly knit group and were descended from forebears who had lived in the county for generations. There were many family connections; John Colles is an example. By blood and by marriage he was tied to J.P.s whose names were: Thynne, Mallett, Pym, Popham, Warre, Horner, Rogers, Wyndham, Portman, and Coventry. They in turn had similar bonds. Except for the new arrivals—either immigrant or local parvenu—the Somerset gentry were a compact society.

The tenure of the office of sheriff is also instructive. During the rough quarter-century between 1569 and 1596 eighteen of the thirty-nine working members of this commission served as sheriff. Experience in the Commons, however, was restricted. In a few cases identities are not certain, but it appears that among the working justices no more than thirteen were returned to Parliament at any time. In the election of 1584 there were only six: Thynne, Berkeley, Bisse, and three lawyers—Edward Popham, Pym, and Ewens. Berkeley was knight of the shire with Sir John Horner's son, Thomas, as his colleague. Bisse was returned by Wells, Popham by Bridgwater, Pym by Taunton. Otherwise the county's boroughs selected either their own citizens or strangers. At this time Somerset gentry seem to have had much less interest in Parliament than was the case in other counties.

## 1608[3]

| No. | | | Name | Place | Num | | | P | Year | Ref |
|---|---|---|---|---|---|---|---|---|---|---|
| 1 | | q | Thomas [Egerton], Lord Ellesmere, chancellor of England | | | | L | P | 1617 | DNB |
| 2 | | q | Thomas [Sackville], Earl of Dorset, treasurer of England | | | | I | P | 1608 | DNB |
| 3 | | q | Charles [Howard], Earl of Nottingham, lord great admiral | | | | | P | 1624 | DNB |
| 4 | * | q | William [Bourchier], Earl of Bath | | | C | | | 1623 | |
| 5 | * | q | Edward [Seymour], Earl of Hertford [lord lieutenant] | | | | | | 1613 | |
| 6 | | q | Thomas [Howard], Viscount Howard de Bindon | | | | M | P | 1611 | |
| 7 | | q | John [Still], Bishop of Bath and Wells | | | C | | | 1608 | DNB |
| 8 | * | q | Edward [Parker], Lord Morley | | | C | | | 1618 | |
| 9 | | q | William [Parker], Lord Monteagle | | | | | | 1622 | DNB |
| 10 | | q | Thomas Fleming, knight, chief justice of king's bench } assize | | | | L | P | 1613 | DNB |
| 11 | | q | Lawrence Tanfield, knight, chief baron | | | | I | P | 1625 | DNB |
| 12 | | q | George Snigge, knight, baron of the exchequer | | | O | M | P | 1617 | |
| | | | | | | | | | | |
| 13 | s | q | Edward Phelips, knight, serjeant-at-law [custos rotulorum] | Montacute | 30 | | M | P | 1614 | DNB |
| 14 | * | q | Arthur Hopton, knight | Witham | | | G | P? | 1609 | |
| 15 | s | q | George Speke, knight | White Lackington | 60 | | G | | 1637 | |
| 16 | | | William Courtney, knight | Powderham, Devon | 60 | | M | P | 1630 | |
| 17 | s | q | Francis Popham, knight | Wellington | 30 | O | M | P | 1644 | DNB  K |
| 18 | s | q | Maurice Berkeley, knight | Bruton | 20 | O | M | P | 1617 | |
| 19 | | | John Harington, knight | Kelston | 20 | C | L | P | 1612 | DNB |
| 20 | | q | Hugh Smyth, knight | Long Ashton | 40 | | | | 1627 | |
| 21 | | q | John Rodney, knight | Rodney Stoke | 20 | O | M | P | 1612 | |
| 22 | | | John Jennins, knight | Curry Rivel | 30 | | M | | 1611 | |
| 23 | | | John Carew, knight | Crowcombe | | | | P? | 1637 | |
| 24 | | q | Edward Hext, knight | Low Ham | 24 | | M | P | 1624 | |
| 25 | s | q | John Portman, knight | Orchard Portman | 50 | | M | | 1612 | |
| 26 | s | | Nicholas Halswell, knight | Goathurst | 20 | O | | P | 1633 | |
| 27 | s | q | Edward Gorges, knight | Wraxall | 20 | O | | | 1624 | |
| 28 | | | John Mallett, knight | Enmore | 20 | O | M | | 1616 | |
| 29 | r | | John Cooper, knight | Rockbourne, Hants | 25 | | | | 1611 | |
| 30 | s | | Thomas Phelips, knight | Barrington | 20 | O | G | P? | 1618 | |
| 31 | | q | Francis James, LL.D., master in chancery | Barrow | 15 | O | G | P | 1616 | |
| 32 | | q | Charles Brooke | Temple Combe | 20 | | | | 1610 | |
| 33 | s | q | Thomas Horner | Mells | 40 | | | P | 1612 | |
| 34 | s | q | Henry Walrond | Isle Brewers | 25 | I | | | 1617 | |
| 35 | * | q | John Colles | Pitminster | | | G | | 1608 | |
| 36 | s | q | Samuel Norton | Abbots Leigh | 20 | C | | | 1621 | |
| 37 | | q | John Pyne | Curry Mallet | 20 | | L | | 1609 | |
| 38 | s | q | Edward Rogers | Cannington | 30 | | | | 1627 | |

| | | | | | | | | | |
|---|---|---|---|---|---|---|---|---|---|
| 39 | q | Maurice Gilbert | Witcombe | | | M | | 1610 | |
| 40 | * | Humphrey Wyndham | Wiveliscombe | 15 | | L | | 1622 | |
| 41 | s | John Wyndham | Orchard Wyndham | 20 | | L | | 1645 | |
| 42 | r | Humphrey Sydenham | Dulverton | 22 | | M | | 1625 | |
| 43 | q | Thomas Hughes | Wells | 10 | C | G | P | 1626 | DNB |
| 44 | q | John May | Hinton Charterhouse | 20 | | | | 1637 | |
| 45 | q | John Trevillian | Nettlecombe | 20 | | | | 1623 | |
| 46 | * q | John Francis | Combe Florey | 26 | | | | 1619 | |
| 47 | r q | Alexander Ewens | North Cadbury | 20 | | | | 1620 | |
| 48 | | John Farwell | Wincanton | 20 | | I | | 1616 | |
| 49 | | George Luttrell | Dunster Castle | 60 | C | G | | 1629 | |
| 50 | | Francis Baber | Chew Magna | 20 | O | | | 1643 | |
| 51 | r | George Farwell | Bishop's Hull | 20 | | I | | 1609 | |
| 52 | | John Symes | Poundisford | 20 | O | L | P | 1661 | |
| 53 | | James Clarke | Norton | 20 | | M | | 1612 | |
| 54 | | John Stocker | Chilcompton | 20 | | | | 1610 | |
| 55 | | John Adams | Lincoln's Inn | 12 | O | L | | 1613 | |
| 56 | | Robert Cuffe | Creech St. Michael | 20 | | L | | 1639 | |
| 57 | | Christopher Preston | Cricket St. Thomas | 20 | C | I | | 1623 | |

Dignitaries 12; Court 1; Gentry 32; Law 8; Church 1; Commerce 3.

In 1608 in the Somerset commission the dignitaries included the usual collection of nobility, officers of state, and ecclesiastics. Lords 6, 9 Howard de Bindon and Monteagle were not primarily local figures, but they must have controlled property in the county. Lord Audley, whose residence was now in Ireland, was no longer a J.P. in Somerset, but the current Bishop of Bath and Wells had a place on the bench. 12 Sir George Snigge, now Baron of the Exchequer, had been born in Bristol and became its Recorder. Another eminent Somerset lawyer 13 was Sir Edward Phelips, Speaker of the Commons and soon to be Master of the Rolls; he was *Custos Rotulorum*. His magnificent new mansion at Montacute, which rivalled that of his brother at Barrington, is evidence that he remained a county figure.

Eight other men who had made the law a career gave this commission 31 its particular quality. Francis James, master in chancery and chancellor of the diocese of Bath and Wells, is, however, best classified as a churchman. Sir Edward Hext of a Devon family and the owner of 24 lands there as well as in Somerset, who left London after his call to the bar in the Middle Temple to live the life of an extremely diligent justice of the peace, was in this regard a contrast to the veteran 40, 43 Humphrey Wyndham. Thomas Hughes, who likewise had local connections, was a reader in Gray's Inn but he is best known now as the author of a pre-Shakespearean play performed before the Queen 53, 56 in 1588. James Clarke and his son-in-law Robert Cuffe, also a barrister, 37 were considered in Chapters III and VI. John Pyne was the lawyer father of the barrister opponent of the free gift in 1626 who was discussed in Chapter V. John Adams completes the tale of the legal 55 members of this commission.

A noteworthy justice was Sir John Harington, godson of Elizabeth 19 and a courtier as well as a resident of Somerset. Charles Brooke was the 32 head of the cadet line of the Cobham family who in consequence of the plot inherited some of the assets as well as the obligations of his Kentish cousins. Sir William Courtney, who in 1831 was posthumously recog- 16 nized as *de jure* Earl of Devonshire, merits a line if only because he married Elizabeth Sydenham, widow of Sir Francis Drake. Sir John Rodney was a prominent West Country squire whose family also won 21 historical recognition because of the naval exploits of his descendant. George Luttrell was the head of the wealthy and distinguished family 49 which held Dunster Castle from the fourteenth to the twentieth century. These men were all leading gentry.

Three members of the commission had commercial backgrounds. Sir John Jennins—an ancester of the first Duchess of Marlborough— 22 seems to have come from London and to have owned extensive pro- perties in Hertfordshire and Middlesex as well as in Somerset. John Symes was the son of a merchant of Chard who married a daughter of 52 Robert Hill, the burgher J.P. of 1562. A leading opponent of extra- parliamentary taxation, he was discussed in Chapter V. John Stocker's 54 ancestors were mayors in Winchester and Poole, though he was also descended from the Phelips family in Somerset and the Hales, who were Kentish lawyers. He is only one of many J.P. squires who had both mercantile and legal ancestry.

Except for Lord Audley and Nicholas Wadham (who died in 1609), all the surviving members of the commission of 1584 were still J.P.s in 1608. Yet the troubles of the Stuart period had already been reflected in Somerset. Sir Francis Hastings, who had been a Somerset justice and was Sir Edward Phelips's colleague as knight of the shire, had been put out of the commission because he joined with Northamptonshire Puritans in presenting a petition in behalf of Calvinistic clergy.[4] Seven other Somerset J.P.s were elected to the Commons in 1604. Sir Francis Popham was knight for Wiltshire, while Sir George Snigge, Sir Maurice Berkeley, Sir John Rodney, and Sir John Harington were returned by Bristol, Minehead, Great Bedwin, and Coventry respect- ively. Sir Nicholas Halswell sat for Bridgwater and Francis James for Wareham. The proportion of J.P.s who were at some time members of the Commons was still less than half—probably fifteen out of forty- five non-dignitaries—but the eight M.P.s in 1608 were nearly twenty per cent of the whole working commission. If membership in the Commons be regarded as an index of political interest, Somerset now ranked with Norfolk and Kent.

## 1626⁵

| No. | | Name | | | | Year | | |
|---|---|---|---|---|---|---|---|---|
| 1 | | Sir Thomas Coventry, knight, lord keeper | O | I | P | 1640 | DNB | |
| 2 | | James [Ley], Earl of Marlborough, lord treasurer | O | L | P | 1629 | DNB | |
| 3 | | Henry [Montagu], Earl of Manchester [lord president] | C | M | P | 1642 | DNB | |
| 4 | | Edward [Somerset], Earl of Worcester [lord privy seal] | | | | 1628 | DNB | |
| 5 | | George [Villiers], Duke of Buckingham | | | | 1628 | DNB | |
| 6 | | William [Herbert], Earl of Pembroke | O | | | 1630 | DNB | |
| 7 | | Philip [Herbert], Earl of Montgomery | O | | P | 1650 | DNB | |
| 8 | s | Edward [Bourchier], Earl of Bath | C | | | 1637 | | |
| 9 | | William [Seymour], Earl of Hertford | O | M | P | 1660 | DNB | |
| 10 | | James [Hay], Earl of Carlisle | | | | 1636 | DNB | |
| 11 | | Thomas [Howard], Earl of Berk[shire] | | | P | 1669 | | |
| 12 | | Robert [Wright], Bishop of Bristol | O | | | 1643 | DNB | |
| 13 | s | Henry [Ley], Lord Ley | O | L | P | 1638 | | |
| 14 | | Sir Richard Weston, knight | | M | P | 1635 | DNB | |
| 15 | | Sir John Walter, knight | O | I | P | 1630 | DNB | |
| 16 | | Sir John Denham, knight | | L | | 1639 | DNB | |

| No. | | Name | Place | | | | Year | | |
|---|---|---|---|---|---|---|---|---|---|
| 17 | | Sir Baldwin Wake, baronet | Clevedon | | | | 1627 | | |
| 18 | * | Sir George Speke, knight | White Lackington | | G | | 1637 | | |
| 19 | s | Sir John Stawell, knight | Cothelstone | O | | P | 1662 | DNB | K |
| 20 | * | Sir Francis Popham, knight | Wellington | O | M | P | 1644 | DNB | K |
| 21 | * | Sir Hugh Smyth, knight | Long Ashton | | | | 1627 | | |
| 22 | * | Sir John Wyndham, knight | Orchard Wyndham | | L | | 1645 | | |
| 23 | s | Sir John Horner, knight | Mells | | M | P | 1659 | | |
| 24 | s | Sir Henry Berkeley, knight | Yarlington | O | G | P | 1667 | | K |
| 25 | | Sir John Gill, knight | Buckland | C | | P | 1650 | | |
| 26 | s | Sir Edward Rodney, knight | Rodney Stoke | | M | P | 1657 | | K |
| 27 | s | Sir Robert Gorges, knight | Wraxall | O | | P | 1638 | | |
| 28 | s | Sir Charles Berkeley, knight | Bruton | O | | P | 1668 | | |
| 29 | | Ralph Barlow, dean of Wells | | O | | | 1631 | | |
| 30 | | Gerard Wood, doctor of divinity | Wells | C | | | 1654 | | |
| 31 | | Paul Godwyn, doctor of divinity | Kingweston | O | | | 1645 | | |
| 32 | | John Baber, doctor of divinity | Chew Magna | O | | | 1628 | | |
| 33 | r | John Paulet | Hinton St. George | O | M | P | 1649 | DNB | |
| 34 | s | Robert Hopton | Witham | | | P | 1638 | | |
| 35 | * | Edward Rogers | Cannington | | | | 1627 | | |
| 36 | * | George Luttrell | Dunster Castle | C | G | | 1629 | | |
| 37 | r | John Sydenham | Brympton | | | | 1627 | | |
| 38 | s | John Colles | Pitminster | O | | | 1627 | | |
| 39 | * | John May | Hinton Charterhouse | | | | 1637 | | |
| 40 | * | Francis Baber | Chew Magna | O | | | 1643 | | |
| 41 | s | William Francis | Combe Florey | O | L | | 1636 | | |
| 42 | s | Robert Cuffe | Creech St. Michael | | L | | 1639 | | |
| 43 | s | Matthew Ewens | North Cadbury | | M | | 1628 | | |
| 44 | s | Thomas Wyndham | St. Decumans | | L | | 1635 | | |
| 45 | | William Every | Kittisford | O | | P | 1652 | | |
| 46 | | Thomas Brereton | Taunton | | G | | 1632 | | |
| 47 | | William Walrond | Isle Brewers | | | | 1662 | | |
| 48 | | William Capell | Wrington | | | | | | |
| 49 | s | Anthony Stocker | Chilcompton | O | M | | | | |
| 50 | | Edward Tynte | Chelvey | | M | | 1629 | | |
| 51 | r | John Farwell | Bishop's Hull | | M | | 1648 | | |
| 52 | | Rice Davies | Tickenham | | I | | 1649 | | |

| 53 |   | John Harbyn | Newton Sur- |   |   |   |   |
|----|---|-------------|-------------|---|---|---|---|
|    |   |             | maville     |   | M |   | 1639 |
| 54 | r | Gawen Mallett | Milverton | O | M |   |   |
| 55 |   | James Rosse | Shepton     | O | L |   |   |
| 56 | s | John Harington | Kelston  | O | L | P | 1654 |

Dignitaries 16; Court 2; Gentry 25; Law 7; Church 4; Commerce 2.

Like other counties Somerset had a commission in 1626 in which more than half the members had some recorded dignity, order, or degree, although there was only one baronet. Nearly all the expanded group of nobility can be shown either to have been great officers of state or to have had some local interest. Probably the reigning favourite (Buckingham) and the Scots Earl of Carlisle (who were justices in Kent 5, 10 also) held property in Somerset. Sir Baldwin Wake, unlike other 17 members of his family, made his chief residence at the Somerset estate which they held in addition to their lands in Northamptonshire. In a sense he was a proxy for his brother-in-law, the Earl of Bristol, who was now in disgrace at Court and out of the commission in both counties. Sir John Gill and William Capell both came from Hertford- shire. The younger son of a squire, Gill married a Somerset heiress. 25 When he was knighted in 1613, Somerset was given as his county, and in 1626 he was returned to the Commons by Minehead. A royalist in the civil wars, in his will he gave his residence as London. Though his primary residence was in Hertfordshire, William Capell inherited lands 48 in Wrington which had once belonged to Glastonbury Abbey. Gill and Capell are both best classified as courtiers.

Again like other counties, Somerset felt the temper of Stuart policy. Four leading clergy were J.P.s. Dr. Gerard Wood, as canon and arch- 30 deacon of Wells, was an associate of Dean Barlow. Dr. Paul Godwyn 29, 31 and Dr. John Baber, respectively rector of Kingweston and vicar of 32 Chew Magna, had relatives who belonged to the county's gentry. Chew Magna was the seat of Francis Baber, a prominent squire.                    40

William Every and John Harbyn had mercantile backgrounds. 45 Every came from a family which had prospered greatly in the cloth trade in London as well as in Dorset and Somerset. Harbyn was the 53 eldest son of a mercer of Blandford in Dorset who must have been a man of considerable wealth as he invested heavily in property in both counties. John was sheriff of Dorset in 1623, but he made his chief residence in Somerset. A younger brother was a merchant and alderman of London.

Although the son of a prominent courtier and son-in-law of the Earl of Marlborough, John Harington was an active lawyer who 56 became a bencher in Lincoln's Inn. He was a chairman of sessions and for many years a particularly diligent J.P. in Somerset. Edward Tynte and Rice Davies were both successful barristers. Added to the 50, 52

veteran Cuffe and the relatives of earlier justices—Farwell, Thomas
Wyndham, Francis, and Harington—they raise to seven the number
of barristers in this commission. Tynte came from a family of Somerset
yeomen, but he was able to marry a daughter of Sir Robert Gorges.
Davies was Welsh by birth, and his connection with Somerset seems
to have derived from his two marriages.

The general character of this commission was much like that of
1608; most of the men were Somerset gentry. Sir John Gill, William
Capell, and Rice Davies came from outside. William Every and John
Harbyn had mercantile backgrounds. The county was playing a larger
part in national politics. There was serious opposition to the financial
measures of the government. Sir Robert Phelips was excluded from the
Commons; seven of his associates were members: Sir Francis Popham,
Sir Henry Berkeley, Sir John Gill, Sir John Horner, Sir Edward
Rodney, Sir Robert Gorges, and Sir Charles Berkeley. Five others
were elected on other occasions.

## 1636⁶

| | | | | | | | | | | |
|---|---|---|---|---|---|---|---|---|---|---|
| 1 | * | q | Thomas [Coventry], Lord Coventry, lord keeper | | O | I | P | 1640 | DNB | |
| 2 | | q | William [Juxon], Bishop of London, lord treasurer | | O | | | 1663 | DNB | |
| 3 | * | q | Henry [Montagu], Earl of Manchester, keeper of privy seal | | C | M | P | 1642 | DNB | |
| 4 | * | q | Edward [Bourchier], Earl of Bath | | C | | | 1637 | | |
| 5 | * | q | William [Seymour], Earl of Hertford [lord lieutenant] | | O | M | P | 1660 | DNB | |
| 6 | | q | John [Digby], Earl of Bristol | | C | | P | 1653 | DNB | |
| 7 | * | q | Henry [Ley], Earl of Marlborough | | O | L | P | 1638 | | |
| 8 | | q | William [Piers], Bishop of Bath and Wells | | O | | | 1670 | DNB | |
| 9 | * | q | John [Paulet], Lord Paulet | | O | M | P | 1649 | DNB | |
| 10 | | q | Francis [Cottington], Lord Cottington, chancellor of exchequer | | | | P | 1652 | DNB | |
| 11 | | q | John Finch, knight, chief justice of common pleas | | | G | P | 1660 | DNB | |
| 12 | * | q | John Denham, knight, baron of exchequer | | | L | P | 1639 | DNB | |
| 13 | s | q | John Coventry, esq. [custos rotulorum] | Pitminster | C | I | P | 1658 | | K |
| 14 | s | q | William Portman, baronet | Orchard Portman | O | M | P | 1648 | | K |
| 15 | | q | Edward Powell, knight & baronet, master of requests | Pengethley, Herefs. | O | M | | 1653 | | |
| 16 | * | q | George Speke, knight | White Lackington | | G | | 1637 | | |
| 17 | s | q | Ralph Hopton, knight | Witham | O | M | P | 1652 | DNB | K |
| 18 | * | q | John Stawell, knight | Cothelstone | O | | P | 1662 | DNB | K |
| 19 | s | q | Ferdinando Gorges, knight | Ashton Philips | | | P | 1647 | DNB | |
| 20 | * | q | Francis Popham, knight | Wellington | O | M | P | 1644 | DNB | K |
| 21 | s | q | Robert Phelips, knight | Montacute | | M | P | 1638 | DNB | |
| 22 | * | q | John Wyndham, knight | Orchard Wyndham | | L | | 1645 | | |
| 23 | * | | John Horner, knight | Mells | | M | P | 1659 | | |
| 24 | * | q | Henry Berkeley, knight | Yarlington | O | G | P | 1667 | | K |
| 25 | * | q | John Carew, knight | Crowcombe | | | | 1637 | | |
| 26 | * | q | John Gill, knight | Buckland | C | | P | 1650 | | |
| 27 | * | q | Edward Rodney, knight | Rodney Stoke | | M | P | 1657 | | K |
| 28 | | q | Thomas Wroth, knight | North Petherton | O | I | P | 1672 | DNB | |

| No. | | | Name | Place | | | | | |
|---|---|---|---|---|---|---|---|---|---|
| 29 | * | q | Robert Gorges, of Wraxall, knight | | O | | P | 1638 | |
| 30 | r | q | Robert Gorges, knight | Redlynch | | | P | | |
| 31 | | q | Francis Dodington [knight] | Dodington | O | L | | | |
| 32 | r | q | Thomas Mallett, serjeant-at-law | Poyntington | | M | P | 1665 | DNB |
| 33 | | q | George Warburton, S.T.D., dean of Wells | | O | | | 1641 | |
| 34 | * | q | Gerard Wood, S.T.D. [archdeacon of Wells] | | C | | | 1654 | |
| 35 | * | q | Paul Godwyn, S.T.D. | Kingweston | O | | | 1645 | |
| 36 | | | Edward Kellett, S.T.D. | Bagborough | C | | | 1641 | DNB |
| 37 | * | q | Robert Hopton | Witham | | | P | 1638 | |
| 38 | s | q | George Speke | White Lackington | O | M | | 1637 | |
| 39 | | q | Robert Henley, chief clerk in king's bench | | | M | | 1656 | |
| 40 | s | q | Thomas Luttrell | Dunster Castle | O | L | P | 1644 | |
| 41 | r | q | Thomas Smyth | Long Ashton | O | | P | 1642 | K |
| 42 | * | q | Francis Baber | Chew Magna | O | | | 1643 | |
| 43 | * | q | John Symes | Poundisford | O | L | P | 1661 | |
| 44 | * | q | William Francis | Combe Florey | O | L | | 1636 | |
| 45 | * | | Robert Cuffe | Creech St. Michael | | L | | 1639 | |
| 46 | * | q | William Every | Kittisford | O | | | 1652 | |
| 47 | * | q | John Harington | Kelston | O | L | P | 1654 | |
| 48 | r | q | Arthur Pyne | Cathanger | | L | P | 1639 | |
| 49 | * | q | William Walrond | Isle Brewers | | | | 1662 | |
| 50 | * | q | William Capell | Wrington | | | | | |
| 51 | | q | Thomas Lyte | Lytes Cary | O | M | | 1638 | |
| 52 | s | | James Farwell | Wincanton | | | | 1636 | |
| 53 | | q | William Bassett | Claverton | | L | P | 1656 | K |
| 54 | * | | Anthony Stocker | Chilcompton | O | M | | | |
| 55 | * | q | John Farwell | Bishop's Hull | | M | | 1648 | |
| 56 | * | q | Rice Davies | Tickenham | | I | | 1649 | |
| 57 | * | | John Harbyn | Newton Surmaville | | M | | 1639 | |
| 58 | * | q | Gawen Mallett | Milverton | O | M | | | |
| 59 | * | | James Rosse | Shepton | O | L | | | |
| 60 | s | q | George Paulet | Goathurst | O | M | | 1647 | |
| 61 | | | Rice Cole | Nailsea | | M | | 1650 | |
| 62 | | q | Abraham Burrell | | | | P? | | |
| 63 | | | William Bull | Shapwick | | M | | 1676 | |

Dignitaries 12; Court 2; Gentry 33; Law 9; Church 4; Commerce 3.

Although only thirty-three of the Somerset J.P.s of 1626 were still in the commission ten years later—a considerably smaller proportion than in many counties—its composition was not much changed. Most of the new men were members of the gentry. All except five of the survivors—the Earls of Montgomery and Berkshire, the Bishop of Bristol, Sir Charles Berkeley, and John May—were still included. The peers were not resident in the county. Bristol had been translated to Coventry and Litchfield. May was an old man. Just why Berkeley was so briefly a J.P. that he eluded Barnes in his book on Somerset is not apparent. The usual stability is further shown by the presence of men who had the requisite status. The Earl of Bristol, no longer in 6

19 disfavour, reappeared. Sir Ferdinando Gorges belonged to the county gentry, but his earlier life had been so full of other concerns—particularly maritime and colonial—that only when, some 70 years old, he married again and settled down in the county did he assume the life for
17 which his birth seemed to mark him out. Conversely Sir Ralph Hopton, soon to be a notable royalist soldier, stood far above his father in the
48 roster because he had been knighted. Arthur Pyne, a Lincoln's Inn barrister like his father and grandfather, was made a J.P. shortly after the death of the father whose feud with the Crown was discussed in Chapter V.

There were two justices who are best classified as courtiers. John
13 Coventry, who was the second son of the Lord Keeper and married the co-heiress of John Colles (1626) and made his home at Barton in Pitminster, was *Custos Rotulorum* even though he was not a knight.
15 Sir Edward Powell, a barrister and Master of Requests, was a Herefordshire man whose most obvious connection with Somerset derived from his wife's inheritance of the rectory of North Petherton; only three times did he attend quarter sessions.

In addition to five veteran lawyers—William Francis, Robert Cuffe, John Harington, John Farwell, and Rice Davies—three more
32 barristers were in the commission. Thomas Mallett, a serjeant-at-law and destined to become Justice of the King's Bench, held property in the county although he came from the Cornish branch of the family.
39 Robert Henley, son of a London merchant with a Somerset background who after retirement to Taunton became its first mayor, was a chief clerk of the King's Bench and later a London alderman. He purchased an estate at Melplash, regularly attended quarter sessions, and must
63 have divided his time between Somerset and London. William Bull was a Middle Temple barrister who owned an estate in the county.

The two veterans of mercantile background—William Every and
61 John Harbyn—were joined by Rice Cole, who was the heir of a family of Bristol merchants which intermarried with Somerset gentry. Thomas
51 Lyte was the head of a family which was rising to considerable prominence and was destined to remain among the leading gentry into the
28 twentieth century. Sir Thomas Wroth was a newcomer to Somerset. His family was prominent in Middlesex and contributed several justices to the bench in Kent. He resided at the estate at North Petherton which he purchased from a cousin, and until his death in 1672 he played an important part in the affairs of the county. There were also four clergy in the working part of this commission. All its other members were gentry.

In experience in the House of Commons the Somerset justices did not quite match their fellows in the other counties which have been considered here. Twenty-three were returned to Parliament on some occasion. If only five Somerset J.P.s were present in the Short Parliament, nine were elected in the autumn of 1640. For the Long Parliament John Coventry found a seat at Evesham near his family's chief residence. The others represented Somerset constituencies; half the men returned from the county were members of its commission of the peace. Several were enthusiastic supporters of the King: Sir John Stawell, Sir Henry Berkeley, Sir Ralph Hopton, and Sir Edward Rodney. Sir Francis Popham, however, was a firm parliamentarian who was still a member of the Commons at the time of his death in 1644. In by-elections in 1645 John Harington was elected as knight of the shire, Sir Thomas Wroth, who as sheriff was ineligible in 1640, took the place of his deceased brother at Bridgwater, while Abraham Burrell was chosen for Huntingdon. So far as continued membership in the commission of the peace is evidence, only a few of these J.P.s consistently supported the anti-royalist cause. In 1650 four of the 1636 bench were still justices: Sir Thomas Wroth, Sir John Horner, John Harington, and Rice Cole. A considerable number of the others did not incur the penalty of fine by the committees for the advance of money and for compounding. Yet there can be no question that on the whole the Somerset magistrates supported the King.[7]

## NOTES TO APPENDIX D

1. Lansdowne MS. 1218, ff. 29, 30; *Cal. Pat. Rolls, Eliz.* ii (1560–3), 442, 443; *Cal. Pat. Rolls, Edw. VI*, i (1547–8), 89.

*1562 roster:*

9. *Masters of the Bench of the Inner Temple*, p. 9.
11. *Complete Peerage*: 'Somerset'.
12. Neale, *House of Commons*, p. 24; *Somersetshire Wills*, vi. 24; C. R. Sanders, *The Strachey Family, 1588–1932* (Duke Univ. Press, 1953), pp. 38, 39.
13. *Somersetshire Wills*, vi. 101; *L. & P.* xvi, g678(45), g779(15), *et passim.*
14. *DNB*: 'Edward Dyer'; *L. & P.* xv, g282(87); ibid. xxiA, g91(2); *Somersetshire Wills*, vi. 58, 59.
15. Brown MSS. in archives of Somerset Archaeological Society, Taunton; John Collinson, *History and Antiquities of the County of Somerset* (3 vols., Bath, 1791), i. 68; *Somerset Archaeological Society, Proceedings*, lxxiii (1927), iii.
16. Collinson, *Somerset*, iii. 155–7; *L. & P.* xivA, g1354(26); *DNB*: 'Ferdinando Gorges'.
17. Collinson, *Somerset*, iii. 153; *Som. Arch. Soc. Proc.* lxx (1924), xxiii; *DNB*: 'Samuel Norton'.
18. Brown MSS., ix; *Somersetshire Wills*, vi. 51; *L. & P.* xixA, g1035(74); ibid. XXIB, g476(33).
19. Brown MSS. ix; *L. & P.* xivB, no. 531; *DNB*: 'John FitzJames'.
20. *Middle Temple Bench Book*, p. 147; *Somersetshire Wills*, iv. 7.
21. *Middle Temple Bench Book*, p. 150; *Somersetshire Wills*, vi. 63; Collinson, *Somerset*, i. 229; ibid. ii. 439; *L. & P.* xviiiA, g226(68); ibid. xxA, g282(33).
22. *DNB*: 'Nicholas Wadham'; Collinson, *Somerset*, i. 48; *Somersetshire Wills*, i. 49; *Som. Arch. Soc. Proc.* lxxx (1934), 1.

23. PCC 1588, 33 Rutland; Collinson, *Somerset*, ii. 463; *L. & P.* xviiiA, g981(40), *et passim.*
24. *Somersetshire Wills*, i. 33; *L. & P.* xxA, g624(15), g496(40), g910(82); ibid. xxiA, g1537(35); ibid. xvi, g947(82); ibid. xviiiA, g100(40), g346(37); ibid. xixA, g80(56), g610(116), g812(43); ibid. xixB, g166(82), *et passim; Cal. Pat. Rolls, Edw. VI,* i (1547–8), 32; ibid. iv (1550–3), 142; ibid. v (1547–53), 120, 359; *Cal. Pat. Rolls, Philip and Mary,* i (1553–4), 23.
25. Collinson, *Somerset*, i. 3, 9; *Cal. Pat. Rolls, Eliz.* i (1558–60), 215; *Somersetshire Wills*, i. 60, 61; *Lincoln's Inn Black Books,* i. 381; *Som. Arch. Soc. Proc.* xxviii (1882), 1–24.
26. W. D. Christie, *A Life of Anthony Ashley Cooper* (2 vols., L., 1871), i. 2; *L. & P.* xv, g831(21); PCC 1566, 27 Crymes; Collinson, *Somerset*, ii. 201.
27. Ibid., p. 302; Brown MSS.; *Somersetshire Wills*, vi. 93–4.
28. *DNB*: 'William Portman'; *Som. Arch. Soc. Proc.* lxxxix (1943), 48–9; Collinson, *Somerset*, iii. 275; *L. & P.* xviiiB, g107(20); ibid. xixB, no. 586, g527(10).
29. F. Hancock, *Wifela's Combe—A History of the Parish of Wiveliscombe* (Taunton, 1911); *Somersetshire Wills*, vi. 69; *L. & P.* xxA, 125; ibid. xviiiA, g226(68); ibid. xxA, g282(33).
30. *Middle Temple Bench Book*, p. 137; Collinson, *Somerset*, ii. 219; *Somersetshire Wills*, i. 9.
31. Collinson, *Somerset*, iii. 26, 259–61; *L. & P.* xvi, g878(10), g1154(46), g1311(19).
32. *Middle Temple Bench Book*, p. 152; Collinson, *Somerset*, ii. 124, 136.
33. Ibid. i. 197, 236; ibid. iii. 213; *Somersetshire Wills*, i. 40; ibid. iv. 49; Conyers Read, *Mr. Secretary Walsingham* (3 vols., Camb., 1925), i. 28, 29.
34. *The Visitation of Nottinghamshire . . . 1569* (Harl. Soc. Publ. iv, L., 1871), pp. 16–18; *L. & P.* xiiB, no. 561, no. 682; ibid. xvi, no. 1500 f. 44, g947(40); ibid. xxvA, g496(68); ibid. xxviB, g332(91); *Cal. Pat. Rolls, Edw. VI,* i (1547–8), 19; ibid. ii (1548–9), 227; ibid. iv (1550–3), 416; *Cal. Pat. Rolls, Philip and Mary,* ii (1554–5), 56–7, 234; ibid. iii (1555–7), 93, 334–5; *Cal. Pat. Rolls, Eliz.* i (1558–60), 236, 358; *Somersetshire Wills*, i. 14.
35. Collinson, *Somerset*, ii. 297, 300.
36. Ibid. i. 171; ibid. iii. 467; *L. & P.* xviiiA, g241(15); ibid. xixA, g812(20, 87), g1035(115).
37. Collinson, *Somerset*, iii. 119–20; ibid. ii. 132–3.
38. Ibid. i. 224; ibid. ii. 457; ibid. iii. 287; F. T. Colby (ed.), *The Visitation of the County of Somerset in the Year 1623* (Harl. Soc. Publ. xi, L., 1876), pp. 50–1; *Somersetshire Wills*, i. 67; W. K. Jordan, *The Forming of the Charitable Institutions of the West of England . . . 1480–1660 (Transactions of the American Philosophical Society,* N.S., vol. 50, pt. 8, Oct. 1960), p. 62.
39. Wyndham, *Family History*, pp. 97–111; Collinson, *Somerset*, iii. 289; *Som. Arch. Soc. Proc.* xcii (1946), 82; *Somersetshire Wills*, vi. 104.
40. Neale, *House of Commons*, pp. 97–8; *Som. Arch. Soc. Proc.* lxxviii (1932), 10, 11; *Cal. Pat. Rolls, Edw. VI,* i (1547–8), 89.

2. Lansdowne MS. 737, ff. 157–8.

*1584 roster:*
8. Collinson, *Somerset*, ii. 77; ibid. iii. 436; *Somersetshire Wills*, ii. 92.
10. *Middle Temple Bench Book*, p. 158; *Somersetshire Wills*, v. 27.
11. Cf. Somerset, 1562 roster, no. 11.
13. Ibid., no. 17.
14. *Somersetshire Wills*, i. 25; cf. monumental inscription in Bristol Cathedral.
15. G. F. Sydenham, *The History of the Sydenham Family* (privately printed, 1928), pp. 124–40.

16. Cf. Somerset, 1562 roster, no. 23.
17. J. P. Rylands (ed.), *The Visitation of the County of Dorset* . . . *1623* (Harl. Soc. Publ. xx. 1885), addenda, pp. 2–5; Collinson, *Somerset*, iii. 85.
18. Cf. Somerset, 1562 roster, no. 28.
19. George D. Stawell, *A Quantock Family* (Taunton, 1910), pp. 65–79.
20. Joseph Foster (ed.), *The Visitation of Yorkshire made in the Years 1584/5* . . . [*and*] *1612* (L. 1875), p. 247; *Somersetshire Wills*, iv. 14.
22. *Complete Peerage:* 'Hertford'.
23. *DNB*: 'John Thynne', his father.
25. *Somersetshire Wills*, vi. 102.
26. Cf. Somerset, 1562 roster, no. 31.
27. *Somersetshire Wills*, v. 107; Collinson, *Somerset*, iii. 71–2.
28. Ibid. i, xxxviii; ibid. ii. 123, 284, 295; ibid. iii. 170, 592.
29. *Visitation of Somerset*, p. 57; Brown MSS. ix.
30. Idem; *Cal. S. P. Dom.*, *1581–90*, pp. 240, 242.
31. *Middle Temple Records*, i, 90, 162, 195, 213; *Somersetshire Wills*, i. 68.
32. *Pension Book of Gray's Inn*, i. 76, 79, 83; *Somersetshire Wills*, iii. 48.
33. Ibid. i. 6; Collinson, *Somerset*, iii. 117.
34. *Somersetshire Wills*, i. 22; Collinson, *Somerset*, iii. 213.
35. Ibid., p. 127; *Som. Arch. Soc. Proc.* xxviii (1882), ii, 79; *Somersetshire Wills*, i. 66.
36. Sydenham, *Sydenham Family*, pp. 124–5.
37. *Somersetshire Wills*, iii. 71; Collinson, *Somerset*, iii. 285; *Som. Arch. Soc. Proc.* liv (1908), 16, 17.
38. Collinson, *Somerset*, iii. 113–14, 314; *L. & P.* xiiiA, g1519(16, 32, 33); *Somersetshire Wills*, i. 77.
39. Hancock, *Wifela's Combe*, p. 221; *Somersetshire Wills*, vi. 70.
40. Collinson, *Somerset*, ii. 369; *Visitation of Dorset 1623*, addenda, p. 17.
41. Collinson, *Somerset*, iii. 470; *Somersetshire Wills*, i. 94.
42. Sydenham, *Sydenham Family*, p. 133.
43. S. Reed Brett, *John Pym* (L., 1940), pp. xviii–xx; *Middle Temple Records*, i. 149, 177, 179, 193, 224, 273.
44. *Middle Temple Bench Book*, p. 165; *Somersetshire Wills*, v. 35.
45. Cf. Somerset, 1562 roster, no. 37.
46. Collinson, *Somerset*, iii. 287; *Somersetshire Wills*, i. 35.
47. Wyndham, *Family History*, pp. 108–10, 160–7; *Lincoln's Inn Black Books*, i. 366; ibid. ii. 222, 405; *Somersetshire Wills*, ii. 41.
49. *Som. Arch. Soc. Proc.* lxxxi (1935), 59–60; ibid. lxxxiii (1937), 119–20; Collinson, *Somerset*, iii. 248; *Somersetshire Wills*, vi. 21.

3. P.R.O., S.P. 14/33, ff. 52–4.

*1608 roster:*

12. *Middle Temple Bench Book*, p. 164.
14. Cf. Somerset, 1584 roster, no. 29.
15. Collinson, *Somerset*, i. 68.
16. *Complete Peerage:* 'Devonshire'; *Som. Arch. Soc. Proc.* liv (1908), 88.
19. Ibid. lxxxii (1936), 134; *Somersetshire Wills*, vi. 102.
20. Collinson, *Somerset*, ii. 292–3; Ashton Court MSS. in Bristol County Archives, *passim*.
21. Collinson, *Somerset*, iii. 605.
22. W. C. Metcalfe (ed.), *The Visitations of Hertfordshire* . . . *1572, and* . . . *1634* (Harl. Soc. Publ. xxii., 1886), 148; *Som. Arch. Soc. Proc.* lxxv (1929), 48; ibid. lxxxiv (1938), 123–6; Keeler, *Long Parliament*, p. 233.

23. Collinson, *Somerset*, iii. 516; *Somersetshire Wills*, iii. 25.
24. *Middle Temple Bench Book*, p. 403, n. 4; Collinson, *Somerset*, iii. 445; *Somersetshire Wills*, ii. 57, 58.
25. *Som. Arch. Soc. Proc.* lxxxix (1943), 149; Cokayne, *Baronetage*, i. 90 (cr. 1611).
26. Collinson, *Somerset*, i. 80; ibid. ii. 302.
27. Ibid. iii. 105–7; Raymond Gorges, *The Story of a Family* (Boston, 1944), pp. 165–7.
28. Collinson, *Somerset*, i. 90–92.
29. Ibid. ii. 201; *Somersetshire Wills*, iv. 19.
30. Collinson, *Somerset*, iii. 314; *Som. Arch. Soc. Proc.* lxxv (1929), 47; *Somersetshire Wills*, i. 77.
31. *Alum. oxon.*
32. Cf. Kent, 1608 roster, no. 78.
33. Collinson, *Somerset*, ii. 463; *Somersetshire Wills*, vi. 4.
34. Collinson, *Somerset*, i. 54; *Somersetshire Wills*, i. 91.
35. Cf. Somerset, 1584 roster, no. 37.
36. Collinson, *Somerset*, i. 42; *Lincoln's Inn Black Books*, i. 424; *Somersetshire Wills*, i. 3; P.R.O., St. Ch. 8/272/28.
38. Collinson, *Somerset*, i. 233; *Somersetshire Wills*, ii. 91; *Som. Arch. Soc. Proc.* xxiii (1877), i. 59–60.
39. Collinson, *Somerset*, ii. 361; *Middle Temple Records*, i. 271; I.P.M. 8 Jas. I.
40. Cf. Somerset, 1584 roster, no. 47.
41. Wyndham, *Family History*, pp. 108–11, 141, 157–71, 211.
42. Collinson, *Somerset*, iii. 523; Sydenham, *Sydenham Family*, p. 84.
44. Collinson, *Somerset*, ii. 235; *Som. Arch. Soc. Proc.* lxxxiv (1938), 111; Barnes, *Somerset*, pp. 25, 44, 46.
45. Collinson, *Somerset*, iii, 539; H. Avray Tipping (ed.), *English Houses of the Early Renaissance* (L., n.d.), pp. 139–42.
46. Cf. Somerset, 1584 roster, no. 49.
47. *Som. Arch. Soc. Proc.* xxxvi (1890), ii, 153–5.
48. Collinson, *Somerset*, iii. 255; *Som. Arch. Soc. Proc.* lviii (1912), i. 77; ibid. xxxvii (1891), ii, 41; *Somersetshire Wills*, vi. 65–7.
49. Collinson, *Somerset*, ii. 12; *Som. Arch. Soc. Proc.* lii (1906), i. 62; ibid. xcii (1946), 33; *Somersetshire Wills*, vi. 17; Tipping, *English Houses*, pp. 313–17.
50. Collinson, *Somerset*, ii. 95; *Som. Arch. Soc. Proc.* xiv (1867), ii. 99; Brown MSS.
51. Cf. no. 48, *supra*.
52. *Som. Arch. Soc. Proc.* lxxxii (1936), ii. 141–2; cf. *supra*, p. 75.
53. Cf. *supra*, p. 36.
54. Collinson, *Somerset*, ii. 129–30; *Notes and Queries*, cxlvii (1924), 3; *Notes and Queries for Somerset and Dorset*, xviii (1924–6), 25.
55. *Alum. oxon.*; *Lincoln's Inn Black Books*, ii. 3.
56. Collinson, *Somerset*, i. 76; *Lincoln's Inn Black Books*, ii. 3; cf. *supra*, p. 106.
57. Collinson, *Somerset*, iii. 116–17; *Somersetshire Wills*, i. 31 (John Preston).

4. Cf. *supra*, p. 73.

5. P.R.O., C193/12. There is considerable material on all these men in Barnes, *Somerset*.

*1626 roster:*
17. Barron, *Northamptonshire Families*, p. 327; cf. Northamptonshire, *supra*, passim.

18. Cf. Somerset, 1608 roster, no. 15.
21. Ibid., no. 20.
22. Ibid., no. 41.
23. *Som. Arch. Soc. Proc.* lxxxiii (1937), 145.
25. Clutterbuck, *Hertfordshire*, iii. 471–5; *Somersetshire Wills*, i. 43; C. E. H. Chadwyck Healey, *The History . . . of West Somerset* (L., 1901), pp. 208–14.
27. Gorges, *Story of a Family*, p. 112.
28. *Som. Arch. Soc. Proc.* lxxxii (1936), 139; *Complete Peerage*, ii. 234.
29. *Alum. oxon.*; *Somersetshire Wills*, i. 56.
30. *Alum. cantab.*; *Som. Arch. Soc. Proc.* xliii (1897), 212–17.
31. *Alum. oxon.*; *Som. Arch. Soc. Proc.* iv (1853), ii. 66.
32. Frederick A. Wood, *Collections for a Parochial History of Chew Magna* (Bristol, 1903), p. 202.
34. *Som. Arch. Soc. Proc.* lxxxii (1936), 138.
35. Cf. Somerset, 1608 roster, no. 38.
36. Ibid., no. 49.
37. Sydenham, *Sydenham Family*, p. 143.
38. Collinson, *Somerset*, iii. 286–7; Hancock, *Wifela's Combe*, pp. 240, 241; *Somersetshire Wills*, i. 33.
39. Cf. Somerset, 1608 roster, no. 44.
40. Collinson, *Somerset*, ii. 95; *Notes and Queries for Somerset and Dorset*, v (1896–7), 168; Wood, *Chew Magna*, pp. 140–54.
41. *Lincoln's Inn Black Books*, ii. 35; cf. Somerset, 1584 roster, no. 49.
42. Cf. Somerset, 1608 roster, no. 56.
43. *Som. Arch. Soc. Proc.* xxxvi (1890), ii, 154–5; *Somersetshire Wills*, vi. 65.
44. *Som. Arch. Soc. Proc.* lxxxiii (1937), 144–6; Collinson, *Somerset*, iii. 494; Wyndham, *Family History*, pp. 190 ff.; Keeler, *Long Parliament*, p. 395; *Lincoln's Inn Black Books*, ii. 131, 175.
45. Collinson, *Somerset*, iii. 24; *Notes and Queries for Somerset and Dorset*, xiv (1914–15), 63–4; Brown MSS. xiii; *Somersetshire Wills*, i. 20; *Som. Arch. Soc. Proc.* xlviii (1902), i, 65–6; Jordan, *Charitable Institutions of the West of England*, pp. 54, 59.
46. *Notes and Queries for Somerset and Dorset*, xii (1910–11), 348–50; *Somersetshire Wills*, i. 15.
47. Brown MSS. xxv; *Somersetshire Wills*, iii. 19.
48. Collinson, *Somerset*, i. 207; *Complete Peerage*: '2nd earl of Marlborough'.
49. *Visitation of Somerset*, p. 95; *Som. Arch. Soc. Proc.* lxxxviii (1942), 93.
50. George S. Master, *Collections for a Parochial History of Wraxall* (Bristol, 1900), p. 69; *Middle Temple Records, passim*; *Somersetshire Wills*, vi. 88–9; Collinson, *Somerset*, ii. 317–18.
51. *Masters of the Bench of the Inner Temple*, p. 26.
52. *Som. Arch. Soc. Proc.* lxxxiv (1938), 107–9; *Somersetshire Wills*, ii. 30; *Students admitted to the Inner Temple*, p. 110; St. Ch. 5/D6/19, 5/R29/39.
53. *Som. Arch. Soc. Proc.* lvi (1910), i. 30; *Somersetshire Wills*, ii. 38; Collinson, *Somerset*, iii. 209; *Visitation of Somerset*, p. 46.
54. Ibid., p. 72; Collinson, *Somerset*, i. 92–3.
55. *Visitation of Somerset*, p. 95; *Som. Arch. Soc. Proc.* lxxxviii (1942), 93; Barnes, *Somerset*, p. 29.
56. Ibid., pp. 22, 32, 34–5, *et passim*.

6. P.R.O., S.P. 16/405, ff. 55ᵛ–57ᵛ.

*1636 roster:*
13. Hancock, *Wifela's Combe*, pp. 240–1; *Somersetshire Wills*, i. 33; Keeler, *Long Parliament*, pp. 143–4.

15. Cokayne, *Baronetage*, i. 188 (cr. 1622); *Middle Temple Records*, i. 417; *Cal. S. P. Dom.*, *Chas. I, 1638/9*, pp. 154, 158; Barnes, *Somerset*, p. 24.
16. Cf. Somerset, 1608 roster, no. 15.
19. Gorges, *Story of a Family*, Ch. XI *et passim*.
22. Cf. Somerset, 1608 roster, no. 41.
23. Cf. Somerset, 1626 roster, no. 23.
25. Cf. Somerset, 1608 roster, no. 23.
26. Cf. Somerset, 1626 roster, no. 25.
28. Collinson, *Somerset*, ii. 68–9; *Somersetshire Wills*, ii. 84; Barnes, *Somerset, passim*.
29. Gorges, *Story of a Family*, p. 167 *et passim*.
30. Ibid., pp. 112–14 *et passim*.
31. Collinson, *Somerset*, iii. 519; Shaw, *Knights of England*, ii. 189.
32. *Alum. oxon.*
34. Cf. Somerset, 1626 roster, no. 30.
35. Ibid., no. 31.
37. Ibid., no. 34.
38. *Som. Arch. Soc. Proc.* lxxv (1929), 56.
39. *Middle Temple Bench Book*, p. 188; Collinson, *Somerset*, ii. 393; *Som. Arch. Soc. Proc.* lxxxv (1939), 49; Jordan, *Charitable Institutions of the West of England*, p. 57; Barnes, *Somerset*, p. 24.
40. Collinson, *Somerset*, ii. 12; *Somersetshire Wills*, vi. 17.
42. Cf. Somerset, 1626 roster, no. 40.
43. Cf. Somerset, 1608 roster, no. 52.
44. Cf. Somerset, 1626 roster, no. 41.
45. Cf. Somerset, 1608 roster, no. 56.
46. Cf. Somerset, 1626 roster, no. 45.
47. Ibid., no. 56.
48. *Lincoln's Inn Black Books*, i. 424; ibid. ii. 238; Collinson, *Somerset*, i. 42; *Notes and Queries for Somerset and Dorset*, xix (1927–9), 31–3; *Somersetshire Wills*, i. 3; ibid. ii. 71–2; Keeler, *Long Parliament*, p. 319.
49. Cf. Somerset, 1626 roster, no. 47.
50. Ibid., no. 48.
51. H. C. Maxwell-Lyte, 'The Lytes of Lytescary', *Som. Arch. Soc. Proc.* xxxviii (1892), 1–110; ibid. lxxvii (1931), 125.
52. *Visitation of Somerset*, p. 36.
54. Cf. Somerset, 1626 roster, no. 49.
55. Ibid., no. 51.
56. Ibid., no. 52.
57. Ibid., no. 53.
58. Ibid., no. 54.
59. Ibid., no. 55.
60. Collinson, *Somerset*, ii. 167.
61. *Som. Arch. Soc. Proc.* lxviii (1922), xlvi; *Somersetshire Wills*, v. 109; ibid. vi. 55.
62. Barnes, *Somerset*, p. 313; *Som. Arch. Soc. Proc.* xxii (1876), ii, 89; *Quarter Sessions Records of Somerset*, i, *passim*; ibid. ii, *passim*.
63. Middle Temple Records, ii. 521, 629, 647, 699; Collinson, *Somerset*, i. 151; ibid. iii. 428.

7. Keeler, *Long Parliament*, pp. 61–2; Barnes, *Somerset*, p. 309.

# APPENDIX E

# WORCESTERSHIRE

| | | | | | | | | |
|---|---|---|---|---|---|---|---|---|
| 1 | | q | Nicholas Bacon, knight [lord keeper] | | C | G | P | 1579 | DNB |
| 2 | | q | William [Paulet], Marquess of Winchester [lord treasurer] | | | | P | 1572 | DNB |
| 3 | | q | Henry [FitzAlan], Earl of Arundel [lord steward] | | | | | 1580 | DNB |
| 4 | W | q | Henry Sidney, knight [president of the council of Wales] | | | | P | 1586 | DNB |
| 5 | | q | Edwin [Sandys], Bishop of Worcester | | C | | | 1588 | DNB |
| 6 | | q | Edward [Dudley], Lord Dudley | | | | | 1586 | DNB |
| 7 | | q | Lord Robert Dudley, master of the horse | | | | | 1588 | DNB |
| 8 | | q | Edward Saunders, knight, chief baron of exchequer | | C | M | | 1576 | DNB |
| 9 | | q | Thomas Carus, the queen's serjeant-at-law | | | M | | 1571 | DNB |

| | | | | | | | | |
|---|---|---|---|---|---|---|---|---|
| 10 | | q | Thomas Russell, knight | Strensham | | G | P | 1574 | |
| 11 | | q | Thomas Packington, knight | Hampton Lovett | | | | 1571 | |
| 12 | | q | Thomas Baskerville, knight | Brinsop, Herefs. | | | P | 1572 | |
| 13 | W | q | John Throckmorton, justice of Chester | Feckenham | | M | P | 1580 | |
| 14 | | q | William Sheldon [*custos rotulorum*] | Beoley | | I | P | 1570 | |
| 15 | | | Thomas Hoby | Bisham, Berks. | C | | | 1566 | DNB |
| 16 | | | Thomas Blount of Shillington | Sodington | | | | 1563 | |
| 17 | | q | John Knottesford | Holdfast | | | | 1589 | |
| 18 | | | William Lygon | Madresfield | | | | 1567 | |
| 19 | | | John Littleton | Frankley | | | P | 1590 | |
| 20 | | | John Foliot | Pirton | | | | 1580 | |
| 21 | | | Thomas Smyth | Chipping Campden | | | | | |
| 22 | W | | Thomas Blount of Kidderminster | | | | P | 1568 | |
| 23 | W | | Richard Smyth | Upton-on-Severn | | M | | 1570 | |
| 24 | | | Henry Dingley | Charlton | | | | 1589 | |
| 25 | | | Robert Hunckes | Blockley, Glos. | | | | | |
| 26 | | q | William Jeffreys | Ham Castle | | | | 1565 | |
| 27 | | q | William Cokesey | Wolverton | | M | | 1582 | |
| 28 | | | Richard Ingram | Earls Court | | | | 1562 | |

The following names are found in the *liber pacis* of 1559:

| | | | | | | | | |
|---|---|---|---|---|---|---|---|---|
| 29 | | q | John Bourne, knight | Holt | | | | 1575 | |
| 30 | | q | John Whiddon, knight | Chagford, Devon | | I | P | 1576 | DNB |
| 31 | | | George Blount, knight | Kinlet, Salop. | | | P | 1581 | |
| 32 | | q | John Vaughan, knight | Bewdley | O | | P | 1576 | |
| 33 | | q | Adam Mytton, knight | Shrewsbury | | | P | 1561 | |
| 34 | W | q | Charles Fox | Bromfield, Salop. | | I | P | 1590 | |
| 35 | W | q | John Scudamore | Holme Lacy, Herefs. | | | | 1571 | |
| 36 | | | John Walshe | Shelsley Walsh | | | | | |
| 37 | | q | Reginald Corbett | Moreton Corbet | | M | P | 1566 | DNB |
| 38 | | q | William Symonds | Coventry | | | | 1560 | |
| 39 | W | q | William Gerard | Chester | | G | P | 1581 | DNB |
| 40 | | q | Richard Seybourne | Sutton St. Nicholas | | | | 1566 | |
| 41 | | | Geoffrey Mark[ham] | Feckenham | | | | 1568 | |
| 42 | | q | Walter Blount | Sodington | | | P | 1590 | |
| 43 | | q | Richard Sheldon | Spetchley | | | | 1562 | |

| 44 | q | George Wall, junior | London | I | 1559 |
|----|---|---------------------|--------|---|------|
| 45 | q | Edward Haselwood | Wick | M | 1558 |
| 46 | | William Gower | Wood Hall | | 1566 |
| 47 | | Anthony Daston | Elmley | | 1572 |

Dignitaries 9; Court 4; Gentry 12; Law 2; Church 0; Commerce 1.

The group of professional members of the Council in the Marches of Wales was the outstanding feature of the Worcestershire commission of the peace. Since that council had an ill-defined overriding authority and responsibility, the considerable duplication of personnel between the Council and the commissions of the peace of the counties in its area—indicated in the rosters by W—facilitated effective administration.

In 1562 Worcestershire, with twenty-eight members, had after Norfolk the smallest bench in this study. Save for the element of the Council of Wales its general character was not unusual. Among the
4 dignitaries Sir Henry Sidney, President of the Council and a J.P. in all the counties within its jurisdiction, was a major figure in Elizabethan
5 society. The Bishop of Worcester happened to belong to a family of local prominence, but he owed his membership to his ecclesiastical office. Since the Earl of Worcester, whose principal estate at Raglan was in Monmouthshire, where he was a justice, was not now in the
6 Worcestershire commission, Lord Dudley was the only county nobleman on the bench in the early years of Elizabeth; the Barons Windsor lived at Tardebigge, but their minority or their foreign travel explains their absence from the commission at this and at later moments. Lord
7 Robert Dudley was a principal figure at Court, but only in this county, in Herefordshire, and in Warwickshire was he a J.P. at this time.

In the working part of the commission four men may be regarded as
13 courtiers. Sir John Throckmorton, justice of Chester, might be classified as a lawyer except that his successors were placed among the dignitaries
17 in the roster. John Knottesford, who had been a yeoman of the guard in Henrician days, received a grant of the keepership of Hanley Park and
15 lived well into the reign of Elizabeth. Thomas Hoby, the owner of extensive monastic lands in addition to other property in Berkshire and in Worcestershire, was an important Elizabethan diplomat. The brother-in-law of Bacon and Cecil, he left sons who were justices in
14 Kent and the North Riding. William Sheldon was discussed in Chapter III. Suspected of papistical sentiments, he was, none the less, the holder of very large grants of monastic lands and the effective leader of the county bench at this time.
23 Two lawyers were Richard Smyth and William Cokesey. Smyth, who was solicitor for the Council, was a brother of his colleague,
21 Thomas, later likewise a member of that body. Their background obscure, the brothers failed to leave progeny who succeeded them on
27 the county bench. William Cokesey, a former student in the Middle

Temple, was under-steward of Evesham Abbey before the dissolution of the monasteries and a J.P. as early as 1537; he seems not to have been granted any of the Abbey's lands.

Sir Thomas Packington, the son of a London mercer, possessed an 11 estate in Buckinghamshire. It was the land he inherited from a lawyer uncle, John, Recorder of Worcester and judge in Wales, which explains his standing in this county. The dozen other members of the commission were all gentry of varying eminence. The Russells had 10 been established at Strensham since the time of Edward III. Sir Thomas Baskerville was a Herefordshire gentleman of very ancient 12 lineage who owned property in neighbouring counties as well. The Blounts were a major family. John Foliot and William Lygon were 16,22,20,18 heirs to a less splendid tradition. John Littleton was the descendant of a 19 Justice of the Common Pleas; his marriage with a daughter of the late Sir John Packington enhanced his status and he became *Custos Rotulorum* after the decease of Sheldon.

The small size of this commission—and perhaps its relative lack of lustre—may be attributed in part to the fact that an unusually large number of men who were J.P.s at the moment of Elizabeth's accession had been eliminated. There may have been a deliberate pruning. In addition to three bishops who refused to take the Oath of Supremacy and were deprived of their office, nineteen men were no longer justices when the commission on the patent roll was compiled in February 1562. Three or four had died. Reginald Corbett, William Symonds, William Gerard, and George Wall were all professional lawyers not primarily connected with the county. Anthony Daston, William Gower, and Sir George Blount were declared by the assize judges fit to be put out of the commission. Sir George Blount, Walter Blount, Charles Fox, and Sir John Vaughan, however, were restored not later than 1574. Fox was secretary and principal administrator of the Coun- 34 cil of Wales. Vaughan was an advocate in Doctors Commons. Richard 32 Seybourne and John Scudamore were Herefordshire squires who re- 40, 35 mained in the commission of that county. Only Sir John Bourne, 29 principal Secretary under Mary, was clearly out of sympathy with the new régime; even he took the oath under the Act of Supremacy in 1569. If the bishops, Bourne, and perhaps others were put out of the commission because of their faith, William Sheldon remained and Sir George Blount was restored. More than religion lay behind the considerable adjustment of the Worcestershire commission of the peace in the early months of Elizabeth's reign.

It is not possible to identify the Smyths with confidence, but it is probable that only six members of the working commission in 1562 were ever elected to the House of Commons. Except for John Throckmorton, who sat for a number of constituencies, all were knights of the shire for their county. Droitwich and Worcester city also returned men to Westminster, but not yet were these seats filled by men who were J.P.s. All the county's knights of the shire in the early parliaments of the reign were also members of its commission of the peace. More than other counties Worcestershire had a bench composed of local gentry. Several men had important connections with the royal Court, either past or present. The legal element was comprised solely of members of the Council of Wales and the judiciary. Except for Sir Thomas Packington there was no one with a mercantile background. William Sheldon held extensive monastic lands, and other justices must have had lesser holdings, but in this regard, too, Worcestershire was behind other counties.

## 1584[2]

| | | | | | | | | | |
|---|---|---|---|---|---|---|---|---|---|
| 1 | | q | Thomas Bromley, knight, lord chancellor of England | | O | M | P | 1587 | DNB |
| 2 | | q | William [Cecil], Lord Burghley, lord treasurer of England | | C | G | P | 1598 | DNB |
| 3 | * | W q | Henry Sidney, knight, lord president [of the council of Wales] | | | | P | 1586 | DNB |
| 4 | * | q | Robert [Dudley], Earl of Leicester | | | | P | 1588 | DNB |
| 5 | | W q | Henry [Herbert], Earl of Pembroke | | C | | | 1601 | DNB |
| 6 | | W q | John [Scory], Bishop of Hereford | | C | | | 1585 | DNB |
| 7 | | W q | Nicholas [Robinson], Bishop of Bangor | | C | | | 1585 | DNB |
| 8 | | W q | William [Hughes], Bishop of St. Asaph's | | C | | | 1600 | DNB |
| 9 | * | q | Edward [Dudley], Lord Dudley | | | | | 1586 | DNB |
| 10 | | W q | James Croft, knight, comptroller [of the household] | | | | P | 1590 | DNB |
| 11 | | q | William Ayloffe, justice [of queen's bench] | | | L | | 1585 | DNB |
| 12 | | q | Francis Wyndham, justice [of common pleas] | | C | L | P | 1592 | DNB |
| 13 | | W q | George Bromley, knight, justice [of North Wales] | | | I | P | 1584 | |
| | | | | | | | | | |
| 14 | | W q | John Perrot, knight | | | | P | 1592 | DNB |
| 15 | | W q | Hugh Cholmeley, knight [vice-president of the council of Wales] | | | | | 1597 | DNB |
| 16 | * | W q | John Littleton, knight [custos rotulorum] | Frankley | | | P | 1590 | |
| 17 | | q | Thomas Lucy, knight | Charlecote, Warws. | | | P | 1600 | DNB |
| 18 | s | q | Edward Hoby, knight | Berks. and Kent | O | | P | 1617 | DNB |
| 19 | | W q | John Puckering, serjeant-at-law | | | L | P | 1596 | DNB |
| 20 | | W q | William Aubrey | | O | | P | 1595 | DNB |
| 21 | | W q | Charles Fox | Bromfield, Salop. | | I | P | 1590 | |
| 22 | | W q | Ellis Price, doctor of laws | | C | | P | 1596 | DNB |
| 23 | | W q | Edward Leighton | Wattlesborough, Salop. | | I | P | 1593 | |
| 24 | | W q | William Leighton | Plaish, Salop. | | G | | 1607 | |
| 25 | | W q | Henry Townshend | Cound, Salop. | | L | P | 1621 | |
| 26 | | W q | Richard Pates | Gloucester | | L | P | 1588 | |
| 27 | | W q | Jerome Corbett | Beslow, Salop. | | M | P | 1598 | |
| 28 | | W q | Ralph Barton | | | G | P | 1592 | |
| 29 | | W q | Fabian Phillips | Orleton, Herefs. | | M | P | 1597 | |
| 30 | | W q | William Glasior | Chester | | I | P | 1588 | |
| 31 | s | q | John Russell | Strensham | | | P | 1593 | |

| | | | | | | | | |
|---|---|---|---|---|---|---|---|---|
| 32 | s | q | Richard Lygon | Madresfield | | | | 1584 | |
| 33 | s | q | John Packington | Hampton Lovett | O | L | | 1625 | DNB |
| 34 | | q | Henry Berkeley | Bruton, Soms. | | M | P | 1601 | |
| 35 | s | q | Gilbert Littleton | Frankley | | | P? | 1599 | |
| 36 | s | q | Ralph Sheldon | Beoley | | M | P | 1613 | |
| 37 | W | q | Miles Sandys | Fladbury | C | M | P | 1601 | |
| 38 | s | q | Francis Walshe | Shelsley Walsh | | | | 1596 | |
| 39 | * | q | Walter Blount | Sodington | | | P | 1590 | |
| 40 | | q | Edmund Harwell | Besford | | | | | |
| 41 | * | q | John Knottesford | Holdfast | | | | 1589 | |
| 42 | | | Edmund Colles | Leigh | | I | P | 1606 | |
| 43 | | | Francis Clare | Caldwall | | | | 1608 | |
| 44 | s | | Thomas Foliot | Pirton | | | | 1617 | |
| 45 | s | q | William Sheldon | Beoley | | | | 1587 | |
| 46 | | q | John Washburne | Wichenford | | I | | 1634 | |
| 47 | | | Francis Bracey | Doverdale | | | | 1612 | |
| 48 | | | John Rous | Rous Lench | | | G | 1603 | |
| 49 | | | George Wynter | Huddington | C | | | 1594 | |
| 50 | | q | Robert Wythe | Droitwich | | I | | 1586 | |
| 51 | | q | William Childe | Blockley, Glos. | | | | 1601 | |
| 52 | | | Edward Pytts | Kyre Magna | | I | | 1618 | |

Dignitaries 13; Court 4; Gentry 22; Law 13; Church 0; Commerce 0.

More clearly than in 1562 the Worcestershire commission of the
peace in 1584 reflected the conditions of the marches. A majority of
the dignitaries were members of the Council of Wales; together with a
dozen lawyer colleagues they dominated the roster. The Comptroller
of the Royal Household—Sir James Croft—and the Lord Deputy of 10
Ireland—Sir John Perrot—were important members of the royal 14
Court and can have played little direct part in the affairs of the region,
but inherited lands there easily explain a formal membership in the
county bench. Sir Hugh Cholmeley, Vice-President of the Council of 15
Wales, and John Puckering, now justice of the Carmarthen circuit, 19
Speaker of the Commons, and already a distinguished lawyer, were
other men closely associated with the Court who may have been not
merely nominal justices in Worcestershire. Their active colleagues in
the Council of Wales, if not necessarily in the administration of this
county, included the eleven men who followed Puckering in the roster.
Except for Edward Leighton, whose legal studies did not secure for
him a call to the bar, they all had had significant legal training in either
the common or the civil law. They were professional members of the
Council. None had a primary residence in the county. Edward Leighton was *Custos Rotulorum* in Shropshire, his own county. The dozen
were members of the commissions in the other marcher counties and
in Wales. There is more than a suggestion of the bureaucratic ex-
pedients of a later day. The interlocking between the Worcestershire
bench and the Council is further shown by the inclusion in the Council
of men who were leading gentry of the county; the veteran Sir John
Littleton and Miles Sandys, barrister and later treasurer of the Middle 16, 37

Temple, younger brother of Bishop Edwin (now translated to York), were already members. Sir Thomas Lucy and Edmund Colles were admitted in 1590 and 1601 respectively. Altogether nearly half this commission were at some time members of the Council.

There were no justices of ecclesiastical or mercantile background, but two other lawyers sat on the bench. Robert Wythe was the second son of a relatively undistinguished family who after some years in London became the heir of his elder brother. Edward Pytts, originally of Hertfordshire, was a bencher in the Inner Temple who purchased an estate in the county, was knighted in 1603, and became sheriff in 1612.

The remaining members of the commission were gentry of varying antiquity and prominence. Edmund Colles, whose father had been bailiff for the abbot of Pershore and had purchased the inheritance of the manor, was said to be 'a grave and learned justice' but, 'being loaded with debts (which like a snowball from the Malvern Hills gathered increase)', was forced to sell his estate. John Washburne 'was the best continual housekeeper and best beloved gentleman in the county' but his chiefest distinction was his sixty years' service as a J.P. While John Rous was the heir of a line which has been tracked back to the Conquest, it was his grandfather who won for the family marked local prestige. George Wynter is known chiefly as the father of two sons who were principal participants in the Gunpowder Plot. Two outsiders whose status in the county derived from their wives were Henry Berkeley of Somerset (a J.P. there also) and Sir Thomas Lucy, who became sheriff of Worcestershire in 1586, although he is known best as the owner of the magnificent mansion at Charlecote which has figured in so much Shakespearean lore.

It was the professional members of the Council of Wales who gave this bench most of its connection with the universities, the inns of court, and the House of Commons. They contributed seven of the twelve barristers in the working part of the commission and two of the six university men. All except William Leighton served in Parliament on some occasion, while only nine of the other members were ever elected. Usually the councillors were returned by constituencies outside the county. In the Commons in 1584 were Croft, Lucy (as knight of the shire for Warwickshire), Puckering, Corbett, Russell, and Berkeley (as knight for Somerset). Croft, Russell, and Berkeley were back again in 1586, when Hoby, Pates, and Sandys were their colleagues. In both years the Worcestershire knights were John Russell and John Littleton (son of Gilbert). In participation in Parliament, in concern for the experience which was available at the universities and the inns of court, as in industry and in wealth, the gentry of the marcher countries lagged behind those of other parts of England.

## 1608[3]

| | | | | | | | | |
|---|---|---|---|---|---|---|---|---|
| 1 | W | q | Thomas [Egerton], Lord Ellesmere, chancellor of England | | L | P | 1617 | DNB |
| 2 | | q | Thomas [Sackville], Earl of Dorset, treasurer of England | | I | P | 1608 | DNB |
| 3 | W | q | Ralph [Eure], Lord Eure, president in Wales [lord lieutenant] | C | G | | 1617 | |
| 4 | W | q | Edward [Somerset], Earl of Worcester, master of the horse | | | | 1628 | DNB |
| 5 | | q | Gervase [Babington], Bishop of Worcester | C | | | 1610 | DNB |
| 6 | | q | Anthony [Rudd], Bishop of St. David's | C | | | 1615 | DNB |
| 7 | s | q | Edward [Dudley], Lord Dudley | O | | | 1643 | |
| 8 | W | q | John [Harington], Lord Harington | | | P | 1613 | DNB |
| 9 | | q | Christopher Yelverton, knight, justice of king's bench | | G | P | 1612 | DNB |
| 10 | | q | David Williams, knight, justice of king's bench, assize | | M | P | 1613 | DNB |
| 11 | W | q | Richard Lewknor, knight, justice of Chester assize | | M | P | 1616 | |

| | | | | | | | | | | |
|---|---|---|---|---|---|---|---|---|---|---|
| 12 | s | | q | Edmund Harwell, knight | Besford | 20 | O | | | |
| 13 | r | W | q | Thomas Leighton, knight | Feckenham | 20 | | I | P | 1611 |
| 14 | | W | q | William Herbert, knight | Swansea | | | | P | 1609 |
| 15 | | W | q | Henry Poole, knight | Sapperton, Glos. | | | I | P | 1616 |
| 16 | * | | q | John Packington, knight [custos rotulorum] | Hampton Lovett | 40 | O | L | | 1625 DNB |
| 17 | s | | q | Thomas Russell, knight | Strensham | 20 | O | | P | 1632 |
| 18 | s | | q | William Lygon, knight | Madresfield | 20 | | M | P | 1609 |
| 19 | r | | q | William Walshe, knight | Abberley | 20 | | | P | 1622 |
| 20 | s | | q | William Sandys, knight | Fladbury | 20 | | | | 1640 |
| 21 | s | | q | Samuel Sandys, knight | Ombersley | 20 | | | P | 1623 |
| 22 | | | q | Thomas Biggs, knight | Lenchwick | 20 | O M | | P | 1613 |
| 23 | | | | Francis Egiocke, knight | Feckenham | 10 | O M | | | 1622 |
| 24 | r | | | Arnold Lygon, knight | Beauchamp Court | 20 | | | | 1612 |
| 25 | * | | q | Edward Pytts, knight | Kyre Magna | 20 | | I | | 1618 |
| 26 | | | q | Richard Grevis, knight | Moseley | 20 | | | | 1632 |
| 27 | | | q | William Whorewood, knight | West Bromwich | 20 | | | L | 1614 |
| 28 | * | W | | Henry Townshend, knight | Cound, Salop. | 10 | | L | P | 1621 |
| 29 | * | | q | Francis Clare, knight | Caldwall | | | | | 1608 |
| 30 | | | | Francis Kettleby, knight | Cotheridge | 7 | | | | 1616 |
| 31 | | | q | John Amy, master in chancery | | 40 | C | | | 1621 |
| 32 | | W | q | Richard Atkins | Gloucester | 40 | O | L | | 1610 |
| 33 | | W | q | Thomas Cornewall | Burford, Salop. | 20 | | M | | 1617 |
| 34 | * | | q | John Washburne | Wichenford | 13 | | I | | 1634 |
| 35 | | | q | William Savage | Elmeley Castle | 20 | | M | | 1616 |
| 36 | * | | | Thomas Foliot | Pirton | 13 | | | | 1617 |
| 37 | | | q | William Combe | Stratford-on-Avon | 28 | | M | P | 1611 |
| 38 | s | | q | Francis Dingley | Charlton | 20 | | | | 1624 |
| 39 | | | q | Arthur Salway | Stanford | 20 | | | | 1616 |
| 40 | | W | | George Wilde | Droitwich | 10 | | I | P | 1616 |
| 41 | | | q | Walter Jones | Chastleton, Oxon. | 10 | | L | P | 1632 |
| 42 | | | q | John Fleete | Hallow | 10 | | I | | 1619 |
| 43 | | | q | Walter Savage | Broadway | 20 | | | | 1622 |
| 44 | | | q | William Horton | Staunton | 10 | | M | | 1612 |
| 45 | s | | q | William Ingram | Earls Court | 10 | | I | | 1635 |

Dignitaries 11; Court 1; Gentry 25; Law 7; Church 0; Commerce 1.

In Worcestershire between 1584 and 1608, unlike most counties, there was a reduction in the size of the commission of the peace. The elimination of all but two of the dozen professional—barrister—members of the Council of Wales is a full explanation. Much as only a few justices held over from 1562 until 1584, so there were few members of the bench in the latter year still in the commission two decades later. On both occasions nearly all the surviving justices remained in office. During the former interval only two elderly men—Henry Dingley and Robert Hunckes—were put off the bench; in the latter four men were eliminated in Worcestershire, though two were still justices in other counties—Sir Edward Hoby, *Custos Rotulorum* in Kent, and Sir Henry Berkeley, a leading figure in Somerset. Ralph Sheldon was a recusant who had promised to conform but did not; the problem is rather why he was a J.P. in 1584 than why he was later removed from the bench.[4] In the case of Francis Bracey there seems to be no ready explanation of the interruption in the usual continuity of office.

The only noteworthy name in the list of dignitaries is the Earl of Worcester. Since he was able so to combine steadfast Catholic faith with unwavering loyalty to his sovereign that he could be a favourite both with Elizabeth and with James, his membership in the Council of Wales and the commission of the peace is not surprising. In the working group also the single courtier invites mention; Arthur Salway was a minor official in the Exchequer, a wealthy man who held property in the county. Commerce too had a sole representative: Walter Jones, the barrister considered in Chapter III, was the heir of very successful woollen merchants of Witney.

Although they were fewer than in 1584, there were seven lawyer members in the commission. Sir Edward Pytts and Sir Henry Townshend were veterans, Townshend being the sole survivor of the phalanx of legal councillors. A Lincoln's Inn reader who became Recorder or Steward of several boroughs in the region of the Marches, he was now second justice of Chester. Richard Atkins lived in Gloucester, and William Combe in Warwickshire. John Fleete, who purchased an estate in the county, became Crown attorney in the principality and Marches of Wales. John Amy resided in Cambridgeshire. A master in chancery, he seems to have been put in this commission in pursuance of a plan to include in each English commission at least one man who was familiar with the procedures of the civil law. Finally George Wilde was the sole indigenous lawyer. From him alone among the legal members do quarter-sessions papers survive, and he may possibly be the only man in his category who really acted as a J.P. in the county.

Four of the gentry justices were veterans of the commission of 1584, and seven were relatives in the male line of earlier J.P.s. Sir Thomas Leighton, whose wife was a daughter of Sir Francis Knollys and thus a cousin of Queen Elizabeth, had been Governor of Jersey. Sir Francis

*(marginal numbers: 4, 39, 41, 25,28, 32, 37,42, 31, 40, 13)*

Kettleby and Sir William Whorewood resided in neighbouring counties. The remaining men were Worcestershire gentlemen of no great distinction. The county still lagged in educational and parliamentary experience. In the working commission seven had attended a university and nineteen one of the inns of court. Twelve were returned to the Commons at some time. In 1604 Sir Henry Bromley and Sir William Lygon were elected as knights of the shire, and Sir Samuel Sandys was returned in a by-election after Lygon's death. Droitwich sent the lawyers William Combe and George Wilde. Walter Jones, who had been a burgess for Worcester between 1584 and 1593, was again chosen for that city. Sir Henry Poole sat for Cricklade in Wiltshire. Worcestershire was remote from the capital. Its gentry did not have the political ambitions of their counterparts in other counties. It did not produce enough able and ambitious lawyers to fill even the seats of its two boroughs, and less than elsewhere did the citizens of its towns enter the ranks of the gentry.

*(margin note: 30, 27)*

## 1626[5]

| No. | mark | W | Name | Place | | | | Year | |
|---|---|---|---|---|---|---|---|---|---|
| 1 | | W | Sir Thomas Coventry, knight, lord keeper | | O | I | P | 1640 | DNB |
| 2 | | W | James [Ley], Earl of Marborough, lord treasurer | | O | L | P | 1629 | DNB |
| 3 | | W | Henry [Montagu], Earl of Manchester [lord president] | | C | M | P | 1642 | DNB |
| 4 | * | W | Edward [Somerset], Earl of Worcester [lord privy seal] | | | | | 1628 | DNB |
| 5 | | W | William [Compton], Earl of Northampton [president of the council of Wales, lord lieutenant] | | O | L | | 1630 | |
| 6 | | W | Francis [Godwin], Bishop of Hereford | | O | | | 1633 | DNB |
| 7 | | W | John [Thornborough], Bishop of Worcester | | O | | | 1641 | DNB |
| 8 | * | W | Edward [Dudley], Lord Dudley | | O | | | 1643 | |
| 9 | | | Thomas [Windsor], Lord Windsor | | | M | | 1641 | |
| 10 | | W | Sir John Doddridge, justice | | O | M | P | 1628 | DNB |
| 11 | | W | Sir William Jones, justice | | O | L | P | 1640 | DNB |
| 12 | | W | Sir John Bridgman, knight, justice of Chester | | O | I | | 1638 | |
| 13 | r | | Sir Thomas Littleton, knight & baronet | Frankley | O | I | P | 1650 | |
| 14 | s | W | Sir Ralph Clare, knight | Caldwall | O | M | P | 1670 | DNB |
| 15 | * | | Sir Thomas Russell, knight | Strensham | O | | P | 1632 | |
| 16 | * | W | Sir William Sandys, knight | Fladbury | | | | 1640 | |
| 17 | s | | Sir James Pytts, knight | Kyre Magna | | I | | 1640 | |
| 18 | * | | Sir Richard Grevis, knight | Moseley | | | | 1632 | |
| 19 | | | Sir John Bucke, knight | Kempsey | O | I | P | 1648 | |
| 20 | r | | Sir John Rous, knight | Rous Lench | | M | P | 1645 | |
| 21 | | | Sir Henry Spiller, knight | Eldersfield | | L | P | | |
| 22 | | | Joseph Hall, dean of Worcester | | C | | | 1656 | DNB |
| 23 | | | Hugh Lloyd, doctor of divinity | Worcester | C | | | 1629 | |
| 24 | | | John Charlett, doctor of divinity | Cropthorne | O | | | 1640 | |
| 25 | | | Christopher Helme, doctor of laws | Worcester | O | | | 1628 | |
| 26 | * | | John Washburne | Wichenford | | | | 1634 | |

| | | | | | | | | | | |
|---|---|---|---|---|---|---|---|---|---|---|
| 27 | s | | Giles Savage | Elmley Castle | | M | | 1632 | | |
| 28 | r | | Leonard Jeffreys | Earls Croome | | | | 1629 | | |
| 29 | | | Edward Seabright | Besford | O | | | 1658 | | |
| 30 | | | John Read | Bredon | | I | | 1626 | | |
| 31 | * | | Walter Jones | Chastleton, Oxon. | | L | P | 1632 | | |
| 32 | * | | William Ingram | Earls Court | | I | | 1635 | | |
| 33 | | | John Colepeper | Feckenham | O | M | P | 1660 | | |
| 34 | | | Robert Barnefield | Severn Stoke | | | | | | |
| 35 | | W | Robert Berkeley | Spetchley | | M | P | 1656 | DNB | |
| 36 | s | | Humphrey Salway | Stanford | O | I | P | 1652 | DNB | K |
| 37 | s | W | John Wilde | Droitwich | O | I | P | 1669 | DNB | K |
| 38 | r | | William Jeffreys | Ham Castle | O | | | 1631 | | |
| 39 | | | William Childe | Northwick, Glos. | O | I | | 1633 | | |
| 40 | | | Edward Cookes | Norgrove | | M | | 1637 | | |
| 41 | | | Richard Skinner | Cofton Hackett | O | G | | 1633 | | |

Dignitaries 12; Court 0; Gentry 18; Law 3; Church 4; Commerce 4.

In 1626 the Worcestershire commission of the peace was still smaller, but its general character was not much changed. All the surviving justices of 1608 were on the bench. Except for membership in the Council of Wales, the Stuart inflation of titles and dignities was less evident than in other counties. If all but one of the dignitaries were members, that Council included only four of the working group: two knights who were leading members of the gentry and two lawyers. A list of the Council compiled in 1633 shows that a considerable group were J.P.s in Worcestershire, but in contrast to 1584 it was the magnates and not the active members who enjoyed dual status.[6] Men were given honour when it was cheap.

1
29 In this instance the Lord Keeper requires mention. He was a son of the county, and his wife was a sister of Edward Seabright. The latter became a baronet in December of 1626 and from a City background was well on his way into the ranks of the gentry. He was the heir of an uncle who had been a town clerk of London and must have been a man of wealth. Seabright's second wife was a daughter of Lord

21 President Manchester. Sir Henry Spiller was another intruder from London. Although he purchased an estate in Worcestershire in 1613, he was described as of London when he was chosen knight of the shire

31 for Middlesex in 1628. The veteran Walter Jones and Richard
41 Skinner, who was a son of a rich clothier of Ledbury, Herefordshire, were the third and fourth mercantile members of the commission.

35 There were three practitioners of the common law. Robert Berkeley had a commercial background, but he was a very successful barrister

37 who was raised to the King's Bench. John Wilde, lawyer son of a lawyer, became a Baron of the Exchequer during the Commonwealth.
40 Edward Cookes, another barrister, was less eminent. The civil law was

represented by Christopher Helme, while the Dean of Worcester and 25 two doctors of divinity gave the bench the ecclesiastical element which was usual in the time of Charles I.

Among the gentry who were neither veterans nor relatives of earlier justices John Colepeper stands out. A younger son of a very prominent family in Sussex and in Kent, where he was a J.P. in 1636, he inherited property in this county from an uncle and here he lived for a number of years, appropriately a member of the commission. Like ten of his working colleagues on this bench he was returned to the Commons at one time. Five were returned in 1626: Sir Henry Spiller for Midhurst, Sir Ralph Clare for Bewdley, John Wilde for Droitwich, and Sir Thomas Littleton and Sir John Rous as knights of their own shire.

## 1636[7]

| | | | | | | | | | | |
|---|---|---|---|---|---|---|---|---|---|---|
| 1 | * | W | q | Thomas [Coventry], Lord Coventry, lord keeper | | O | I | P | 1640 | DNB |
| 2 | | | q | William [Juxon], Bishop of London, lord treasurer | | O | | | 1663 | DNB |
| 3 | * | W | q | Henry [Montagu], Earl of Manchester, keeper of privy seal | | C | M | P | 1642 | DNB |
| 4 | | W | q | John [Egerton], Earl of Bridgewater, president of council of Wales [lord lieutenant] | | | | P | 1649 | DNB |
| 5 | | W | q | Mountjoy [Blount], Earl of Newport | | | | | 1666 | DNB |
| 6 | * | W | q | John [Thornborough], Bishop of Worcester | | O | | | 1641 | DNB |
| 7 | | W | q | George [Coke], Bishop of Hereford | | O | | | 1646 | DNB |
| 8 | * | W | q | Edward [Dudley], Lord Dudley | | O | | | 1643 | |
| 9 | | W | q | William [Craven], Lord Craven | | | | | 1697 | DNB |
| 10 | | W | q | Humphrey Davenport, knight, chief baron of exchequer | | O | G | P | 1645 | DNB |
| 11 | * | W | q | William Jones, knight, justice of king's bench | | O | L | P | 1640 | DNB |
| 12 | * | W | q | Robert Berkeley, knight, justice of king's bench | | | M | P | 1656 | DNB |
| 13 | * | W | q | John Bridgman, knight, justice of Chester | | O | I | | 1638 | |
| 14 | s | W | q | Thomas Coventry, esquire [custos rotulorum] | Croome D'Abitot | | | P | | |
| 15 | | W | q | Walter Devereux, knight & baronet | Lye | | | P | 1659 | |
| 16 | * | | q | Edward Seabright, knight & baronet | Besford | O | | | 1658 | |
| 17 | s | | q | William Russell, baronet | Strensham | O | M | P | 1669 | |
| 18 | * | W | q | Ralph Clare, knight | Caldwall | O | M | P | 1670 | DNB |
| 19 | | W | q | Henry Herbert, knight, master of the revels | Ribbesford | | | P | 1673 | DNB K |
| 20 | * | W | q | William Sandys, knight | Fladbury | | | | 1640 | |
| 21 | * | | q | James Pytts, knight | Kyre Magna | | I | | 1640 | |
| 22 | * | | | John Bucke, knight | Kempsey | O | I | P | 1648 | |
| 23 | * | | q | John Rous, knight | Rous Lench | | M | P | 1645 | |
| 24 | * | | q | Henry Spiller, knight | Eldersfield | | L | P | | |
| 25 | | | q | Arthur Smythes, knight | Dodderhill | | | | | |
| 26 | * | | q | John Wilde, serjeant-at-law | Droitwich | O | I | P | 1669 | DNB K |
| 27 | | | | Richard Cresheld, serjeant-at-law | Evesham | | L | P | 1652 | K |
| 28 | | | | William Smythe, S.T.D. | Alvechurch | O | | | 1658 | |
| 29 | * | | q | John Charlett, S.T.D. | Cropthorne | O | | | 1640 | |

| 30 |   | q | James Littleton, chancellor of | | | | | | |
|----|---|---|-------------------------------|-----------|---|---|---|------|---|
|    |   |   | Worcester                     |           | O |   |   | 1645 |   |
| 31 | r |   | Edward Dingley                | Charlton  | O |   |   | 1647 |   |
| 32 | * | q | Humphrey Salway               | Stanford  | O | I | P | 1652 | DNB | K |
| 33 | s |   | William Childe                | Northwick, Glos. | | | | | |
| 34 |   |   | Thomas Good                   | Redmarley D'Abitot | | | | | |
| 35 |   |   | William Warmistry             | Worcester | O |   |   | 1640 |   |

Dignitaries 13; Court 2; Gentry 11; Law 2; Church 4; Commerce 3.

The Worcestershire commission in 1636 was the smallest in any of the six counties since the early years of Elizabeth. Half its members were veterans from 1626 and half were members of the Council of Wales. Only six were simple esquires. Several new men deserve comment.

14    The Court element was strong. The Lord Keeper's eldest son, though not a knight, was *Custos Rotulorum* (like his brother in Somer-
9    set). Another relative was Lord Craven, son of a very wealthy deceased Lord Mayor of London, whose sister Coventry had married. Craven, whose other obvious connection with the county was his appointment to the Council of Wales, was already well embarked on his spectacular career of service to the Stuart family. Probably he held some property in the region, but he cannot have been more than a nominal member
19    of this commission. Sir Henry Herbert, who clearly owned a significant estate in the county, was another member of this bench who was more
5    a national than a county figure. The Earl of Newport likewise was a favourite of the King and a member of the Council but hardly a county magnate. Although he succeeded a cousin as third Earl of
15    Essex in 1646, Sir Walter Devereux had purchased an estate in Worcestershire and seems to fit properly in the category of gentry.

Three clergy, one lawyer, and one merchant were new members of
28    the bench. Dr. William Smythe was the second Warden of Wadham College, who had become rector of Alvechurch and canon of Wor-
30    cester. James Littleton, later a master in chancery, had family con-nections in the county but must have owed his nomination as J.P. to
35    his ecclesiastical position. William Warmistry, registrar of the diocese of Worcester, an office which had earlier been filled by both his father and his grandfather, seems to fit best in the ecclesiastical category.
27    Richard Cresheld was a Lincoln's Inn barrister who married the daughter of the man whom he succeeded as a Recorder of Evesham.
25    Sir Arthur Smythes was the son and heir of a London alderman who had purchased extensive property in the county.

Eleven members of the working commission were elected to the House of Commons at some time. In the Long Parliament were four Worcestershire justices: the favourite Sir Henry Herbert, the knights

of the shire—serjeant Wilde and Humphrey Salway—and serjeant
Cresheld for Evesham. Wilde and Salway were reformers, but theirs
was a point of view which was not common in this county. Most of the
J.P.s who survived until 1645 were subject to a fine for their political
activities. Although the commission for Worcestershire in 1650 contained half a dozen surnames which had been found earlier, the only
veterans from 1636 were the two knights of the shire, Humphrey
Wilde—now Chief Baron—and Humphrey Salway. The sentiment of
the Worcestershire commission of the peace was predominantly
royalist.[8]

## NOTES TO APPENDIX E

1. Lansdowne MS. 1218, ff. 32–2$^v$, 82$^v$; *Cal. Pat. Rolls, Eliz.* ii (1560–3), 44.

*1562 roster:*

10. T. R. Nash, *Collections for the History of Worcestershire* (2 vols. and suppl.,
    L. 1781–99), ii. 395; *VCH Worcs.* iv. 204; W. R. Williams, *The Parlia-
    mentary History of the County of Worcester* (Hereford, 1897), p. 31.

11. W. P. W. Phillimore (ed.), *The Visitation of the County of Worcester . . . 1569*
    (Harl. Soc. Publ. xxvii, L. 1888), pp. 102–3; *VCH Worcs.* iii. 155; Nash,
    *Collections*, i. 352; *L. & P.* xvii, g1012(28); ibid. xix, index.

12. William Henry Cooke, *Collections towards the History and Antiquities of the
    County of Hereford* (L. 1886), p. 157; *VCH Worcs.* iv. 73; Williams, *Parlia-
    mentary History*, p. 33.

13. *DNB*: 'Francis Throckmorton'.

14. See *supra*, p. 34.

16. Nash, *Collections*, ii. 162a, 163; *Visitation of Worcester*, pp. 16–22.

17. *VCH Worcs.* iv. 126, 130, 473; *L. & P.* viii, g632(22); A. T. Butler (ed.),
    *The Visitation of Worcestershire 1634* (Harl. Soc. Publ. xc, L., 1938), p. 57.

18. *VCH Worcs.* iv. 120; Nash, *Collections*, ii. 118.

19. Ibid. i. 492a; I. H. Jeayes, *Descriptive Catalogue of the Charters and Muni-
    ments of the Lyttleton Family* (L., 1893), pp. iv, xv; *Visitation of Worcester
    1569*, pp. 92–4.

20. *VCH Worcs.*, iv. 182, 211; Nash, *Collections*, ii. 258.

21. Penry Williams, *The Council in the Marches of Wales* (Cardiff, 1958), p. 356.

22. Williams, *Parliamentary History*, p. 33; *VCH Worcs.* iii. 169.

23. Williams, *Council of Wales*, pp. 334, 356; *Middle Temple Records*, i. 105, 111.

24. Nash, *Collections*, i. 272, 272b.

25. *Visitation of Worcester 1569*, p. 81; *VCH Worcs.* iii. 270.

26. Nash, *Collections*, i. 244–5; ii suppl. 69; *VCH Worcs.* iv. 249; Bateson,
    *Original Letters*, p. 5; *Visitation of Worcester 1634*, p. 54.

27. *Middle Temple Records*, i. 68, 74; *Visitation of Worcester 1569*, p. 44; Nash,
    *Collections*, i. 194; Bateson, 'Original Letters', p. 4.

28. *VCH Worcs.* iii. 507; *Visitation of Worcester 1569*, pp. 82–3.

29. Oddly, Sir John Bourne was omitted from the *DNB*. The identity is clear
    from many sources. The oath is recorded in P.R.O., S.P. 12/21, f. 59. His
    will is PCC 1575, 29 Pyckering.

31. PCC 1581, 28 Darcy.

32. *Alum. oxon.*; BM Egerton MS. 2345, f. 27$^v$.

33. PCC 1561, 30 Loftes.

34. Williams, *Council of Wales*, p. 348.
35. J. Duncumb, *et al.*, *Collections towards the History and Antiquities of the County of Hereford* (6 vols., Hereford, 1804–1916), iii. 37.
36. *Visitation of Worcester 1569*, p. 140.
38. PCC 1560, 36 Mellershe.
40. *Cal. Pat. Rolls, Ed. VI*, i. 84; ibid. iii. 230; ibid. iv. 272.
41. *VCH Worcs.* iii. 118–19; Lansdowne MS. 1218, f. 90ᵛ.
42. Egerton MS. 2345, f. 36ᵛ.
43. PCC 1562, 9 Chayre.
44. PCC 1559, 19 Mellershe.
45. *VCH Worcs.* iv. 170.
46. Cf. no. 41, *supra*; *VCH Worcs.* iii. 454; Lansdowne MS. 1218, f. 90ᵛ.
47. PCC 1572, 31 Daper; *VCH Worcs.* iii. 346; Lansdowne MS. 1218, f. 90ᵛ.

2. Lansdowne MS. 737, ff. 160–1.

*1584 roster:*
13. Williams, *Council of Wales*, p. 344.
16. Cf. Worcestershire, 1562 roster, no. 19.
21. Ibid., no. 34.
23. George Grazebrook and J. P. Rylands (eds.), *The Visitation of Shropshire . . . 1623* (2 vols., Harl. Soc. Publ. xxviii, xxix, 1889), ii. 324.
24. Williams, *Council of Wales*, p. 350.
25. Ibid., p. 358.
26. Ibid., p. 354.
27. Ibid., p. 346.
28. Ibid., p. 344.
29. Ibid., p. 354.
30. Ibid., p. 348.
31. *VCH Worcs.* iv. 204; Nash, *Collections*, ii. 395.
32. *VCH Worcs.* iv. 120.
34. Cf. Somerset, 1584 roster, no. 25.
35. Cf. Worcestershire, 1562 roster, no. 19.
36. Cf. pp. *supra*, pp. 34–5.
37. *Middle Temple Bench Book*, p. 153; Williams, *Council of Wales*, p. 356.
38. *VCH Worcs.* iv. 335.
39. Nash, *Collections*, ii. 162a, 163.
40. *VCH Worcs.* iv. 21; Nash, *Collections*, i. 27.
41. Cf. Worcestershire, 1562 roster, no. 17.
42. *VCH Worcs.* iv. 103, 108; Nash, *Collections*, i. 472; ibid. ii. 75, 397, 400.
43. Ibid. i. 264; ibid. ii. 44; *VCH Worcs.* iii. 170; *DNB*: 'Ralph Clare'.
44. *VCH Worcs.* iv. 182.
45. *Visitation of Worcester 1569*, p. 128.
46. *VCH Worcs.* iii. 563; Nash, *Collections*, ii. 365–6, 460; *Visitation of Worcester 1634*, p. 100.
47. *Visitation of Worcester 1569*, p. 24; Nash, *Collections*, i. 335; Bateson, 'Original Letters', p. 6.
48. *VCH Worcs.* iii. 498–9; *Worcestershire Archaeological Society Transactions*, N.S. ix (1932), 31, 33; Nash, *Collections*, ii. 85.
49. *VCH Worcs.* iii. 410, 459; ibid. iv. 10; John Morris (ed.), *The Condition of Catholics under James I*, by John Gerard (L., 1871), p. 70.
50. *VCH Worcs.* iii. 86; *Visitation of Worcester 1569*, pp. 149–50.
51. Nash, *Collections*, i. 99; *Visitation of Worcester 1569*, pp. 36–7.
52. *VCH Worcs.* iv. 282–3.

3. P.R.O., S.P. 14/33, ff. 64ᵛ-6.

*1608 roster:*

11. *Middle Temple Bench Book*, p. 160.
12. *VCH Worcs.* iv. 21.
13. *Visitation of Shropshire*, ii. 324; *VCH Worcs.* iii. 114, 374; *DNB*: 'Francis Knollys'; Neale, *House of Commons*, p. 295.
14. Sir Samuel Rush Meyrick (ed.), *Heraldic Visitations of Wales and Part of the Marches* (2 vols., Llandovery, 1846), ii. 55 n.; Thomas Nichols, *The History and Antiquities of Glamorganshire and its Families* (L. 1874), p. 136; Williams, *Council of Wales*, pp. 350–1.
15. Sir John Maclean and W. C. Heane (eds.), *The Visitation of the County of Gloucester taken in the Year 1623* (Harl. Soc. Publ. xxi, L., 1885), p. 126; Williams, *Council of Wales*, pp. 346–7.
16. *VCH Worcs.* iv. 204.
18. Nash, *Collections*, I, xix, 162; ibid. ii. 118; *VCH Worcs.*, iv. 30; PCC 1619, 39 Parker.
19. *VCH Worcs.*, iv. 87, 335–6; *Visitation of Worcester 1569*, p. 140.
20. *Worcestershire Archaeological Society Transactions*, N.S. xvi (1939), 45–50.
21. Ibid.
22. Nash, *Collections*, ii. 198; *Visitation of Worcester 1569*, p. 16; PCC 1614, 61 Lawe.
23. *VCH Worcs.* iii. 429; *Visitation of Worcester 1569*, p. 52; PCC 1623, 5 Swann.
24. Cf. *supra*, no. 18.
25. Cf. Worcestershire, 1584 roster, no. 52.
26. *VCH Worcs.* iii. 189; *Visitation of Worcester 1634*, p. 42; PCC 1632, 111 Audley.
27. Thomas Harwood (ed.), *Survey of Staffordshire* (L. 1844), p. 394 n.; *VCH Worcs.* iii. 185–7; PCC 1616, 11 Cope; William Salt Archaeological Society, *Collections for a History of Staffordshire* (Birmingham, 1880– ), V, pt. ii. 311.
28. Cf. Worcestershire, 1584 roster, no. 25.
29. Ibid., no. 43.
30. *Visitation of Shropshire*, ii. 288; PCC 1616, 49 Cope.
31. *Alum. cantab.*
32. *Lincoln's Inn Black Books*, i. 356, 393.
33. *Visitation of Shropshire*, i. 148; Williams, *Council of Wales*, pp. 346–7.
34. Cf. Worcestershire, 1584 roster, no. 46.
35. *Visitation of Worcester 1569*, pp. 124–5; Nash, *Collections*, i. 384; *VCH Worcs.* iii. 342; ibid. iv. 39.
36. Cf. Worcestershire, 1584 roster, no. 44.
37. *Middle Temple Records*, i. 181, 224; ibid. ii. 584.
38. Nash, *Collections*, ii, 272–2b.
39. *Visitation of Worcester 1569*, pp. 121–2; Keeler, *Long Parliament*, p. 332; PCC 1616, 26 Cope.
40. *VCH Worcs.* iii. 62.
41. Cf. *supra*, p. 35.
42. *VCH Worcs.* iii. 484; ibid. iv. 475; *Cal. S. P. Dom., Eliz. 1598–1601*, p. 209.
43. Cf. *supra*, no. 35.
44. Nash, *Collections*, ii. 372; PCC 1613, 22 Capel.
45. *VCH Worcs.* iii. 507.

4. *A.P.C., 1580–1*, pp. 166, 254, 301; ibid., *1587–8*, p. 137; *Cal. S. P. Dom., Eliz. 1581–90*, p. 142; ibid., *1591–4*, pp. 91–4, 531, 546, 554; *Cal. S. P. Dom., Jas. I, 1603–10*, pp. 26–8, 591.

5. P.R.O., C 193/12.

*1626 roster:*

12. *Alum. oxon.*
13. Cf. Worcestershire, 1562 roster, no. 19; *Alum. oxon.*
15. Cf. Worcestershire, 1608 roster, no. 17.
16. Ibid., no. 20.
17. *VCH Worcs.* iv. 282–3.
18. Cf. Worcestershire, 1608 roster, no. 26.
19. *Visitation of Worcester 1569*, p. 27; Nash, *Collections*, ii. 19–20.
20. *VCH Worcs.* iii. 498–9.
21. Nash, *Collections*, i. 373; *VCH Worcs.* iv. 78.
23. *Alum. oxon.*
24. Ibid.
25. Ibid.
26. Cf. Worcestershire, 1608 roster, no. 34.
27. *VCH Worcs.* iii. 342–4.
28. Nash, *Collections*, i. 267; *Visitation of Worcester 1569*, p. 83; *Visitation of Worcester 1634*, p. 53.
29. Nash, *Collections*, i. 79; *Visitation of Worcester 1569*, pp. 125–6.
30. Nash, *Collections*, i. 131–2; *VCH Worcs.* iii. 287–9.
33. Nash, *Collections*, i. 442; *VCH Worcs.* iii. 119; *Sussex Archaeological Collections*, xlvii (1904), 65, 72; cf. *supra*, p. 138.
31. Cf. Worcestershire, 1608 roster, no. 41.
32. Ibid., no. 45.
34. Nash, *Collections*, ii. 343; *Visitation of Shropshire*, i. 34.
38. *VCH Worcs.* iv. 249; Nash, *Collections*, i. 245, 267.
39. Ibid., p. 99; *Visitation of Worcester 1634*, pp. 20, 21.
40. Nash, *Collections*, i. 440*a*; *VCH Worcs.* iii. 116, 198.
41. Nash, *Collections*, i. 251; *VCH Worcs.* iii. 55–6.

6. *Archaeologia Cambrensis*, 6th Series, xvii (1927), 194–6.

7. P.R.O., S.P.16/405, ff. 67ᵛ–68ᵛ.

*1636 roster:*

7. *Alum. oxon.*
13. Cf. Worcestershire, 1626 roster, no. 12.
14. Cf. *DNB*, sub his father, the Lord Keeper.
15. Cokayne, *Baronetage*, i. 89 (cr. 1611); *VCH Worcs.* iv. 103.
16. Cf. Worcestershire, 1626 roster, no. 29.
17. Cokayne, *Baronetage*, ii. 9 (cr. 1627).
20. Cf. Worcestershire, 1626 roster, no. 16.
21. Ibid., no. 17.
22. Ibid., no. 19.
23. Ibid., no. 20.
24. Ibid., no. 21.
25. *VCH Worcs.* iii. 64.
28. *Alum. oxon.*
29. Cf. Worcestershire, 1626 roster, no. 24.
30. *Alum. oxon.*
31. Nash, *Collections*, ii. 272–2*b*.
32. Cf. Worcestershire, 1626 roster, no. 36.
33. Ibid., no. 39.

34. *Visitation of Worcester 1634*, p. 39; *VCH Worcs.* iii. 557; Nash, *Collections*, ii. 305.

35. *Visitation of Worcester 1634*, p. 99.

8. Thomas Walkley, *The Names of the Justices of the Peace in . . . 1650* (L., 1650), pp. 59–60.

# THE NORTH RIDING

## 1562[1]

| | | | | | | | | | |
|---|---|---|---|---|---|---|---|---|---|
| 1 | | | Nicholas Bacon, knight [lord keeper] | | C | G | P | 1579 | DNB |
| 2 | N | q | Thomas [Young], Archbishop of York | | O | | | 1568 | DNB |
| 3 | | q | William [Paulet], Marquess of Winchester [lord treasurer] | | | | P | 1572 | DNB |
| 4 | N | q | Henry [Fitzalan], Earl of Arundel [lord steward] | | | | | 1580 | DNB |
| 5 | N | q | Henry [Manners], Earl of Rutland [lord president of the council of the North] | | | | | 1563 | DNB |
| 6 | N | q | Thomas [Percy], Earl of Northumberland | | | | | 1572 | DNB |
| 7 | N | q | Henry [Neville], Earl of Westmorland | | | | | 1563 | DNB |
| 8 | N | q | George [Talbot], Earl of Shrewsbury | | | | | 1590 | DNB |
| 9 | N | q | Henry [Clifford], Earl of Cumberland | | | | | 1570 | DNB |
| 10 | | | William [Dacre], Lord Dacre of Gilsland | | | | | 1563 | |
| 11 | | | Henry [Scrope], Lord Scrope | | | | | 1592 | DNB |
| 12 | N | | John [Lumley], Lord Lumley | | C | | | 1609 | DNB |
| 13 | | | Robert [Ogle], Lord Ogle | | | | | 1562 | |
| 14 | N | | William [Eure], Lord Evers [Eure] | | | | | 1594 | |
| 15 | N | | Thomas [Wharton], Lord Wharton | | | | P | 1568 | |
| 16 | N | | John [Darcy], Lord Darcy | | | | | 1602 | |
| 17 | | q | Nicholas Powtrell [serjeant-at-law] | | | G | P | 1580 | |
| 18 | | q | John Welshe [serjeant-at-law] | | | M | P | 1572 | |

| | | | | | | | | | |
|---|---|---|---|---|---|---|---|---|---|
| 19 | N | q | Thomas Gargrave, knight | Wragby | | | P | 1579 | DNB |
| 20 | N | q | Henry Gate, knight [custos rotulorum] | Seamer | | | P | 1589 | |
| 21 | | q | Christopher Danby, knight | Thorpe Perrow | | G | P | 1581 | |
| 22 | N | q | George Bowes, knight | Streatlam, Durham | | | P | 1580 | DNB |
| 23 | | | William Bellasis, knight | Newburgh | | | | 1604 | |
| 24 | | | William Fairfax, knight | Gilling | | G | P | 1599 | |
| 25 | N | q | Robert Mennell, serjeant-at-law | | | L | | 1563 | |
| 26 | N | q | Ralph Skynner, dean [of Durham] | | O | | | 1563 | |
| 27 | N | q | Henry Sayvell [Savile] | Lupset | O | | P | 1569 | |
| 28 | | | Leonard Dacre | Naworth, Cumbs. | | | P | 1573 | DNB |
| 29 | | | Thomas Rokeby | Mortham | | | | 1568 | |
| 30 | | | Roger Radcliffe | Mulgrave Castle | | | | 1589 | |
| 31 | | q | John Sayer | Worsall | | | P? | 1585 | |
| 32 | | q | John Herbert | Overton | | | P? | 1569 | |
| 33 | | q | Nicholas Wanfourth [Michael Wandesforde] | Kirklington | | | | 1575 | |
| 34 | | | Roger Dalton | Kirkby Misperton | | G | | 1587 | |
| 35 | | | Anthony Caterick | Stanwick St. John | | L | | 1585 | |

The following men were listed in the *liber pacis* of 1559 and in some cases in that of 1561 also.

| | | | | | | | | |
|---|---|---|---|---|---|---|---|---|
| 36 | N | q | Nicholas [Heath], Archbishop of York | | C | | 1578 | DNB |
| 37 | | q | Cuthbert [Tunstall], Bishop of Durham | | O | | 1559 | DNB |
| 38 | N | q | Francis [Talbot], Earl of Shrewsbury | | | | 1560 | DNB |
| 39 | | | John [Latimer], Lord Latimer | | | | 1577 | |
| 40 | N | q | William Dalison, knight, justice of queen's bench | | C | G | 1559 | DNB |

| 41 | N | q | William Rastell, justice of queen's bench | | O | L | P | 1565 | DNB |
|---|---|---|---|---|---|---|---|---|---|
| 42 | N | q | George Conyers, knight | Sockburn | | | | 1567 | |
| 43 | N | | Nicholas Fairfax, knight | Gilling | | M | P | 1571 | |
| 44 | | | Edward Gower, knight | Stittenham | | | | 1579 | |
| 45 | | | Anthony Hunter | Thornton | | | | 1561 | |
| 46 | | | Richard Bowes | Streatlam, Durham | | | | 1559 | |
| 47 | N | | Thomas Eynns | Heslington | | | P | 1578 | |
| 48 | N | | Richard Norton | Norton Conyers | | | | 1588 | DNB |
| 49 | | q | Richard Whalley | Screveton, Notts. | | G | P | 1583 | DNB |
| 50 | | | George Dakins | East Cowton | | | | 1578 | |
| 51 | | | Christopher Lepton | Kepwick | | | | 1586 | |
| 52 | | q | Robert Trystram | Guisborough | | | | 1574 | |
| 53 | | | James Fox | Kirby Knowle | | | | 1562 | |
| 54 | | q | James Grene | Landmoth | | | | 1579 | |

The following man was listed in the *liber pacis* of 1561:

| 55 | | | Richard Cholmeley, knight | Whitby | | | P | 1583 | |
|---|---|---|---|---|---|---|---|---|---|

Dignitaries 18; Court 6; Gentry 10; Law 0; Church 1; Commerce 0.

The peculiar conditions of the north country were reflected in the commission of the peace for the North Riding of Yorkshire in 1562. Just over half its members were dignitaries, and of the other seventeen only nine were merely esquire. Here, too, there was a regional council —its members designated by N in the accompanying rosters—which had overriding administrative authority.

The dignitaries included three elements: holders of important office; heirs to ancient titles, such as the Earls of Northumberland and Shrewsbury; and Tudor parvenus, such as Lords Ogle and Eure. Like the ancient nobility some of the knights in the working part of the commission enjoyed a quasi-feudal status: Sir William Bellasis, Sir Christopher Danby, Sir William Fairfax.

Thus the distinction between the dignitaries and the working group is less satisfactory than elsewhere. The heirs of the feudal aristocracy had fully as much effective power as did the men who are best described as courtiers. Both were members of the Council of the North. Sir Thomas Gargrave, who had once been the servant of the late Lord [19] President—the fifth Earl of Shrewsbury—had been Speaker of the House of Commons in 1559 and was now *Custos Rotulorum* in the West Riding. Sir Henry Gate, born in Middlesex and at one time [20] Receiver-General of the Court of Augmentations, was deputy steward and constable of Pickering and Pickering Lythe and *Custos* in the North Riding. A native of Yorkshire and Marshall of Berwick, Sir George Bowes was a soldier by profession whose robust courage in [22] 1569 did much to contain the rebellion headed by the northern earls, his fellows on the Yorkshire bench. Serjeant Robert Mennell was [25] seneschal and comptroller of the palatine bishopric of Durham, where the Dean, Ralph Skynner, was an administrator rather than a priest. [26]

27 Henry Savile, knight of the shire in 1559 as colleague of Gargrave,
32 was surveyor of crown lands north of the Trent. With John Herbert, who had served as agent for the Crown with regard to the properties of suppressed monasteries near York, these men make up the category of courtiers.

Three other members of the commission merit comment. Thomas
29 Rokeby was the head of a family which included two learned lawyers; his brother John was doctor of civil law and chancellor of York, while his son Ralph—a close friend of William Lambarde—was a serjeant and Master of Requests; both were at a later time members of the
31 Council of the North and J.P.s in the North Riding. John Sayer of Worsall on the Tees in the extreme north of the county was a J.P. for at least the thirty years between 1554 and 1584. Of undistinguished ancestry, he owed his position to his marriage with Dorothy Bulmer, heiress to their estate. 'Nicholas Wanfourth' must represent a
33 clerk's error for Michael Wandesforde, a cadet member of the Kirklington family which consistently contributed members to the bench, whose name appears in the *libri pacis* of both 1559 and 1561, in the quarter sessions records, and in 1564 in Archbishop Young's report about the faith of the J.P.s.

Brief comment should be made about some of the twenty men listed in those *libri pacis* who were not in the patent-roll commission. The bishops were deprived; the Earl of Shrewsbury and others had died;
41 William Rastell, a firm Catholic, resigned his office as Justice of the
43 Queen's Bench. Sir Nicholas Fairfax was sheriff in 1562 when his son
55 was already a justice. Sir Richard Cholmeley, a man of great wealth and
50 position, and George Dakins, of lesser stature, both returned to the
42, 47 commission later. Sir George Conyers and Thomas Eynns, a professional lawyer, remained members of the Council until their deaths,
48 although no longer J.P.s in the North Riding. Richard Norton—'Old Norton'— a member of an ancient Yorkshire family, and Richard
49 Whalley, a Tudor politician, were both to be seriously involved in the rebellion of 1569; perhaps their dissatisfaction may have been suspected as early as 1562. This is a diverse group, larger than its equivalent in other counties. The accession of Elizabeth was followed by more change in the North Riding than in most counties, but there is no clear pattern, even if, as was shown in Chapter IV, Cecil gave careful consideration to the personnel of this commission. Norton and Whalley, who were Catholics, did not remain as J.P.s. Sir Christopher Danby, Leonard Dacre—also a leader in the rebellion—Thomas Rokeby, John Sayer, Michael Wandesforde, and Anthony Caterick were continued in office although their views were such as to secure for them in 1564 Archbishop Young's epithet: 'no favorers of religion'.[2]

The educational and parliamentary experiences of the North Riding J.P.'s of the early years of Elizabeth's reign reflected the persistence there of the conditions of an earlier time. Relatively few men were ever members of a university, an inn, or the Commons. Among the nineteen J.P.s of 1562 who were not members of the House of Lords, probably nine, including the assize justices, were at some time returned to Parliament. It is not likely that the John Sayer who served for Southwark in 1553 and 1554 and the John Herbert who was elected by Much Wenlock in 1553 were the men who were later North Riding J.P.s. In the Parliament of 1563 there were present: John Welshe, Sir Thomas Gargrave, Sir Henry Gate, and Leonard Dacre, none of them a characteristic squire.

In Yorkshire as elsewhere former monastic properties were in the possession of men who were J.P.s in the early years of Elizabeth. In addition to the Earls of Shrewsbury and Rutland, who were national rather than north-country figures, the Earls of Cumberland and Westmorland had received important grants in the time of Henry VIII. Sir Thomas Wharton and Sir William Eure, both subsequently ennobled, were awarded more extensive lands. Of the North Riding justices who did not hold titles, however, the names of Bellasis and Cholmeley are the only ones to appear prominently among the recipients of the royal grants which are now calendared in the *Letters and Papers of Henry VIII*. In spite of the wide estates controlled by the Yorkshire houses, the spoils held by North Riding J.P.s in the first decade of Elizabeth I seem to have been relatively small.[3]

## 1584[4]

| # | | | | Name | | | | | |
|---|---|---|---|---|---|---|---|---|---|
| 1 | | | q | Thomas Bromley, knight, lord chancellor of England | O | M | P | 1587 | DNB |
| 2 | | N | q | Edwin [Sandys], Archbishop of York | C | | | 1588 | DNB |
| 3 | | | q | William [Cecil], Lord Burghley, lord treasurer of England | C | G | P | 1598 | DNB |
| 4 | | N | q | Henry [Hastings], Earl of Huntingdon | | | | 1595 | DNB |
| 5 | * | N | q | George [Talbot], Earl of Shrewsbury | | | | 1590 | DNB |
| 6 | s | N | q | Edward [Manners], Earl of Rutland | | | | 1587 | DNB |
| 7 | s | N | q | George [Clifford], Earl of Cumberland | C | | | 1605 | DNB |
| 8 | | N | q | Richard [Barnes], Bishop of Durham | O | | | 1587 | DNB |
| 9 | | N | q | John [May], Bishop of Carlisle | C | | | 1598 | DNB |
| 10 | s | | q | Gilbert [Talbot], Lord Talbot | | | P | 1616 | DNB |
| 11 | | N | q | Henry [Carey], Lord Hunsdon | | | P | 1596 | DNB |
| 12 | | | q | Edward [Parker], Lord Morley | C | | | 1618 | |
| 13 | * | N | q | Henry [Scrope], Lord Scrope | | | | 1592 | DNB |
| 14 | r | N | | Cuthbert [Ogle], Lord Ogle | | | | 1597 | |
| 15 | * | N | q | John [Darcy], Lord Darcy | | | | 1602 | |
| 16 | * | N | q | William [Eure], Lord Eure | | | | 1594 | |
| 17 | s | | | Philip [Wharton], Lord Wharton | C | G | | 1625 | |
| 18 | | | q | Christopher Wray, knight [chief justice of queen's bench] | C | L | P | 1592 | DNB |
| 19 | | | q | John Clench, serjeant-at-law | | L | | 1607 | DNB |

| No. | | | | Name | Place | | | | Year | |
|---|---|---|---|---|---|---|---|---|---|---|
| 20 | | N | q | Francis Rodes, serjeant-at-law | Staveley | C | G | | 1589 | DNB |
| 21 | r | | q | John Manners, knight | | C | G | P | 1588 | |
| 22 | s | | | Ralph Eure, knight | Malton | C | G | | 1617 | |
| 23 | | N | q | Matthew Hutton, dean | York | C | | | 1606 | DNB |
| 24 | | N | q | John Foster, knight | Bamborough Castle | | | | 1602 | |
| 25 | * | N | q | Henry Gate, knight [*custos rotulorum*] | Seamer | | | P | 1589 | |
| 26 | * | N | q | William Fairfax, knight | Gilling | | G | P | 1599 | |
| 27 | | N | q | William Mallory, knight | Studley | | | | 1602 | |
| 28 | | N | q | Christopher Hilliarde, knight | Winestead | | | P | 1602 | |
| 29 | r | N | q | Thomas Fairfax, knight | Steeton | | | P | 1599 | |
| 30 | s | | q | Thomas Danby, knight | Thorpe Perrow | | | | 1590 | |
| 31 | * | | q | William Bellasis, knight | Newburgh | | | | 1604 | |
| 32 | | | q | John Dawney, knight | Sessay | | | P | 1598 | |
| 33 | | | q | Ralph Bourchier, knight | Beningborough | | | P | 1598 | |
| 34 | r | N | q | Robert Bowes, knight | Aske | C | L | P | 1597 | DNB |
| 35 | | N | q | Lawrence Meres | York | | G | P | 1592 | |
| 36 | s | N | q | Ralph Rokeby | Lincoln's Inn | C | L | | 1596 | DNB |
| 37 | | N | q | Ralph Hurleston | Gray's Inn | | G | P | 1587 | |
| 38 | | N | q | Humphrey Purefey | Barwell, Leics. | C | G | | 1598 | |
| 39 | | N | q | Lawrence Blundeston | Gray's Inn | C | G | | 1588 | |
| 40 | | N | q | John Gibson, D.C.L. | Welburn | C | | | 1613 | |
| 41 | | N | q | Henry Cheke | Yearsley | C | | P | 1586 | DNB |
| 42 | | | q | Martin Berkheade [Birkett] | York | | G | P | 1590 | |
| 43 | | | q | Henry Constable | Constable Burton | | L | P | 1607 | |
| 44 | r | N | q | Christopher Wandesforde | Kirklington | C | L | | 1590 | |
| 45 | r | | q | William Hilliarde | Winestead | C | I | P | 1608 | |
| 46 | s | N | q | William Bowes | Streatlam, Durham | C | G | P | 1611 | |
| 47 | | | | Thomas Grimston | Grimston Garth | | | | 1586 | |
| 48 | * | | | Roger Radcliffe | Mulgrave Castle | | | | 1589 | |
| 49 | * | | q | Roger Dalton | Kirkby Misperton | | G | | 1587 | |
| 50 | | | | Marmaduke Wyvell | Constable Burton | C | L | P | 1617 | |
| 51 | | | q | Thomas Calverley | Littleburn, Durham | | L | | 1614 | |
| 52 | | | q | Thomas Layton | Sexhow | | | P | 1584 | |
| 53 | s | | q | Francis Cholmeley | Whitby | | | | 1586 | |
| 54 | | | | Thomas Savile | Welburn | | | | 1588 | |
| 55 | r | | | Christopher Wandesforde | Walburn | | | | 1601 | |
| 56 | r | | q | John Constable | Dromonby | | | | 1620 | |
| 57 | | | q | Anthony Talboys | Skirmingham, Durham | C | L | P | 1584 | |
| 58 | s | | | Edward Gate | Seamer | C | L | P | 1622 | |
| 59 | | | q | Robert Briggs | Old Malton | | M | P | 1615 | |
| 60 | | | q | William Watenhall | Henning | | | | | |
| 61 | r | | q | Robert Rokeby | Marske | | L | | 1608 | |
| 62 | | | | William Maliverer | Arncliffe | C | | | 1618 | |
| 63 | | | q | Cuthbert Pepper | East Cowton | | G | P | 1609 | |

Dignitaries 19; Court 5; Gentry 25; Law 13; Church 1; Commerce 0.

Between 1562 and 1584 the number of justices in the North Riding almost doubled. There were nine veterans and ten sons of earlier J.P.s. Conspicuously absent were participants in the rebellion of 1569: the brother and heir of the Earl of Northumberland, now in the Tower; the Earl of Westmorland; Leonard Dacre; Richard Norton. Lord Lumley, a recusant, Anthony Caterick, a probable one, and John Sayer, who must have been very elderly, had also been eliminated. Present, however, was the Catholic Lord Morley, who in the right of his wife, a daughter of the late Lord Monteagle—a J.P. in 1580—represented the Stanley interest in the region.

The members of the Council of the North were also more numerous—thirty—more than twice the total in 1562. All the Councillors were J.P.s in the North Riding; they comprised a large part of the men in the categories of Court, law, and Church. The Court group were: the veteran Sir Henry Gate; Sir John Manners, who was brother and 21 heir of the Earl of Rutland; Henry Cheke, a nephew of Burghley's 41 first wife, who was secretary and Keeper of the Signet of the Council; and the two Bowes, William, who was a son of the late justice Sir 46 George, and Sir Robert, treasurer and ambassador to Scotland, who 34 was a brother. The sole churchman in the working group was the Dean of York.                                                        23

Much more conspicuous in the roster were the professional lawyers who formed the legal staff of the Council of the North. Like their counterparts in the Council of Wales, their names formed a phalanx in the middle of the list: from Lawrence Meres down to John Gibson. With them belongs Francis Rodes, who because he was a serjeant 20 appeared immediately after the assize judges. Only Rokeby was a 36 Yorkshireman by birth. All except Gibson, who was judge of the 40 Prerogative Court of York and later master in chancery, were readers and benchers of their inns of court. This must be a reflection of policy.

Six other professional lawyers were members of the commission but not of the Council. Martin Berkheade (or Birkett) was Queen's 42 Attorney at York. William Hilliarde, a brother of Sir Christopher, 45 was Recorder of York. Thomas Calverley was administrator of the 51 temporalities of the diocese of Durham, Cuthbert Pepper, who had 63 just become a J.P., was later Surveyor of the Court of Wards and a member of the Council. Anthony Talboys and Robert Briggs were 57, 59 barristers with north-country backgrounds. Calverley had been a reader in Lincoln's Inn, and Pepper was later to win that distinction in Gray's Inn. Conditions in the North Riding were changing.

None the less much the largest group of J.P.s were gentry of diverse background and standing. Sir John Foster, warden of the middle 24 march, keeper of Tynedale and Redesdale, was not primarily a York-shire figure, though he was a north-country leader. Sir William Mallory 27 was steward of Ripon and later of York; his mother had been a Norton. Less eminent but still prominent members of the gentry were Sir Thomas Fairfax—of a different branch of his family than the earlier 29 J.P.s—and Sir Christopher Hilliarde. Sir Ralph Bourchier was the 28, 33 son of a soldier of perhaps noble and illegitimate birth, but he was selected as knight of the shire in 1588, when his colleague was Henry Constable, whose family had long been known in the county. Among 43 the less prominent gentry there were J.P.s for whom the traditions of an earlier age must have been strong even after the failure of the rebellion of 1569. The formal education of North Riding justices reflected their social position. Among the dignitaries there had not been much increase in the number of those who had attended either a university or an inn. In the working group the figure for the inns had risen strikingly and that of the universities somewhat less. The lawyers are the explanation. Among forty-four men, twenty-one were elected to the Commons at some time. At least three sat in 1584: Sir Ralph Bourchier for Newport in the Isle of Wight, Henry Cheke for Boroughbridge, and Henry Constable for Hedon. The knights of the shire are unknown. In 1586 Sir Henry Gate and Sir Thomas Fairfax were the members for Yorkshire. Sir John Dawney, Sir Ralph Bourchier, Henry Constable, William Hilliarde, and Robert Briggs were returned for other seats in the county. Although this record is similar to that of Worcestershire, the J.P.s of the North Riding were well behind those of the other counties here studied in their membership in either a university, an inn, or the House of Commons.

## 1608[5]

| No. | | N | q | Name | Place | Age | Univ. | Inn | P | Death | DNB |
|---|---|---|---|---|---|---|---|---|---|---|---|
| 1 | | | q | Thomas [Egerton], Lord Ellesmere, chancellor of England | | | | L | P | 1617 | DNB |
| 2 | | | q | Tobias [Matthew], Archbishop of York | | | O | | | 1628 | DNB |
| 3 | | | q | Thomas [Sackville], Earl of Dorset, treasurer of England | | | | I | P | 1608 | DNB |
| 4 | | N | q | Edmund [Sheffield], Lord Sheffield, president of the council [of the north, lord lieutenant] | | | O | | | 1646 | DNB |
| 5 | * | N | q | Gilbert [Talbot], Earl of Shrewsbury | | | | | P | 1616 | DNB |
| 6 | s | | q | Roger [Manners], Earl of Rutland | | | C | I | | 1612 | DNB |
| 7 | | | q | George [Lloyd], Bishop of Chester | | | C | | | 1615 | DNB |
| 8 | | | q | John [Thornborough], Bishop of Bristol | | | O | | | 1641 | DNB |
| 9 | s | N | q | Thomas [Scrope], Lord Scrope | | | | G | P | 1609 | |
| 10 | * | N | q | Ralph [Eure], Lord Eure | | | C | G | | 1617 | |
| 11 | | | q | John [Stanhope], Lord Stanhope, vice-chamberlain of household [custos rotulorum] | | | C | G | P | 1621 | DNB |
| 12 | | | q | Edward [Bruce], Lord Bruce, master of the rolls | | | | | | 1611 | DNB |
| 13 | | | q | James Altham, knight, baron of exchequer, assize | | | C | G | P | 1617 | DNB |
| 14 | | | q | Edward Phelips, knight, serjeant-at-law, assize | | | | M | P | 1614 | DNB |
| 15 | s | | q | William Eure, knight | Ayton | | O | G | P | 1646 | |
| 16 | s | | q | John Sheffield, esquire | | | | | P | 1614 | |
| 17 | * | N | q | Cuthbert Pepper, knight, attorney of court of wards | East Cowton | | | L | P | 1609 | |
| 18 | | | q | Edward Yorke, knight | Ripon | | C | | | 1621 | |
| 19 | | N | q | Thomas Posthumous Hoby, knight | Hackness | 25 | O | G | P | 1641 | |
| 20 | | N | q | Thomas Lascells, knight | Sowerby | 24 | | | | 1619 | |
| 21 | s | N | q | Henry Bellasis, knight | Newburgh | 30 | C | | P | 1624 | |
| 22 | | | q | Richard Musgrave, knight | Norton Conyers | 15 | C | G | P | 1618 | |
| 23 | | N | q | Francis Boynton, knight | Burton Agnes | 30 | | | | 1617 | |

| | | | | | | | | | | |
|---|---|---|---|---|---|---|---|---|---|---|
| 24 | s | q | Thomas Dawney, knight | Sessay | 30 | | G | | 1644 | |
| 25 | r | q | Conyers Darcy, knight | Hornby Castle | 16 | C | I | | 1654 | |
| 26 | | q | Thomas Metcalfe, knight | Nappa | 10 | | | | 1655 | |
| 27 | | q | William Bamburgh, knight [N, 1611] | Howsham | 25 | C | G | | 1623 | |
| 28 | | | Richard Theakston, knight | Theakston | 20 | | G | P | 1609 | |
| 29 | * N | q | John Gibson, knight [D.C.L.] | Welburn | 20 | C | | P | 1613 | |
| 30 | | q | Richard Vaughan, knight | Thorpe | 20 | | | | 1624 | |
| 31 | | q | Richard Etherington, knight | Ebberston | 20 | | L | | | |
| 32 | | q | Henry Jenkins, knight | Busby | 20 | C | L | P | 1646 | |
| 33 | | q | Timothy Whittingham, knight | Holmside, Durham | 7 | C | M | | 1630 | W |
| 34 | | q | Stephen Proctor, knight | Fountains Abbey | 20 | | | | 1620 | |
| 35 | N | q | Charles Hales, knight | Newland, Warws. | 12 | O | G | | 1618 | |
| 36 | N | q | John Bennet, knight, doctor of laws | York | 20 | O | G | P | 1627 | DNB |
| 37 | N | q | Richard Williamson, knight | York | 20 | | G | P | 1609 | |
| 38 | N | q | John Ferne, knight | Temple Belwood | 4 | C | I | P | 1609 | DNB |
| 39 | * | | Marmaduke Wyvell, knight | Constable Burton | 25 | C | L | P | 1617 | |
| 40 | r | | Richard Cholmeley, knight | Whitby | 20 | C | | P | 1631 | |
| 41 | | q | Arthur Dakins, knight | Long Cowton | 20 | C | G | | 1623 | |
| 42 | s | | Timothy Hutton, knight | Marske | 20 | C | G | | 1629 | |
| 43 | s | | John Gibson, minor, knight [N. 1616] | Welburn | 20 | | G | | 1638 | |
| 44 | N | q | Richard Hutton, serjeant-at-law | Goldsborough | 20 | O | G | P | 1639 | DNB |
| 45 | | q | Thomas Mallory, archdeacon of Richmond | | | C | | | 1644 | |
| 46 | * | q | William Maliverer | Arncliffe | | C | | | 1618 | |
| 47 | * | q | William Hilliarde | Winestead | | C | I | P | 1608 | |
| 48 | * | q | Robert Briggs | Old Malton | 10 | | M | P | 1615 | |
| 49 | | q | Walter Bethell | Alne | 8 | C | L | | 1623 | |
| 50 | * | | John Constable | Dromonby | 10 | | | | 1620 | |
| 51 | | q | Christopher Aske | York | 10 | | | | 1610 | |
| 52 | | | Thomas Davile | Newstead | 6 | C | | | 1624 | |
| 53 | s | | Charles Layton | Sexhow | 20 | | | | 1614 | |
| 54 | | | Richard Aldborough | Ellenthorpe | 10 | C | | | 1613 | |
| 55 | | | Hugh Frankland | Thirkleby | | | | | 1607 | |
| 56 | | | Thomas Scudamore | Overton | 20 | | I | | 1621 | |
| 57 | | | Thomas Norcliffe | Nunnington | 20 | | | | 1616 | |
| 58 | | q | Henry Tankard | Arden | 6 | C | L | | 1626 | |
| 59 | | | Richard Darley | Buttercrambe | 15 | C | G | P | 1654 | |
| 60 | | q | Robert Hungate | Sand Hutton | 20 | C | L | | 1620 | |
| 61 | | | John Theaker | York | | | | | 1608 | |
| 62 | | | Adam Midlam | | 4 | | G | | 1621 | |

Dignitaries 14; Court 4; Gentry 25; Law 14; Church 1; Commerce 4.

The North Riding commission of 1608 was substantially the same in size as that of 1584, but there were twice as many knights and half as many members of the Council of the North. There were fewer esquires and fewer Yorkshire peers, many more members of the royal Court. There were the usual proportions of veterans and sons of former justices. There were six instances in which a surviving J.P. was no longer a member of the bench, but the explanations seem to be individual. Lord Morley, for example, whose son had now inherited the

Monteagle title of his mother, no longer enjoyed the same standing in the county, but both father and son were justices in Somerset. Evidence is lacking with regard to several families to explain why a son had not followed his father in the North Riding commission. Yet the pattern of 1608 was much like that of 1584.

11          Among the dignitaries were two royal favourites, Lord Stanhope,
12  Vice-Chamberlain and Master of the Posts, and Scottish Lord Bruce,
8  both of whom held extensive lands in Yorkshire. The Bishop of Bristol had been Dean of York and did not relinquish the preferment until he was translated to Worcester in 1617. Richmondshire in the North
7  Riding lay within the diocese of the Bishop of Chester. There was a reason for the membership of these men in the commission.

34          In the working group were a quartet of courtiers. Stephen Proctor, probably of Yorkshire descent, acquired in London and Westminster the means with which he bought the holdings of the Gresham family at Fountains. His several patents of monopoly won him great popular disfavour and a bitter attack by the Commons in 1610. He seems to have been equally unpopular with the neighbours among whom he built the splendid house which is still a tourist attraction. Thomas
56  Scudamore was the son of a Monmouthshire man who had been the Queen's Receiver-General. Since he was not a lawyer, this seems also
43  the best category for the younger John Gibson, though he might be
16  regarded as a member of the gentry. Similarly John Sheffield, son of the new Lord President of the Council of the North, owed his status to his father. Here, too, might be put Thomas Sheffield—the name crossed out appears near the end of the roster between Thomas Scudamore and Thomas Norcliffe—if he were in fact a North Riding J.P. Lord Sheffield's son Thomas was born after 1608; there are a number of clerical errors in the *liber*; three Thomases in sequence seems suspect. 'Thomas Sheffield', however, appears in a *liber pacis* of 1604. Since the J.P., if such he really was, is now no more than a name, he has not been accepted for purposes of this study.

Although in Yorkshire, as in Worcestershire, the phalanx of lawyers associated with the regional council no longer distinguished the middle of the roster, there were still several legal members of the Council and as many other men skilled in the law. In addition to two veterans— the elder John Gibson and Cuthbert Pepper—there were five lawyer Councillors, none a Yorkshireman by birth. Born in Cumberland,
44  serjeant Richard Hutton was Recorder of York and later Justice of the
38  Common Pleas. Sir John Ferne was Recorder of Doncaster. Sir John
36  Bennet was a civilian, chancellor of the diocese of York; later he became judge of the Prerogative Court of Canterbury and was ulti-
35  mately disgraced for his dishonesty. Sir Charles Hales of a Kent family
37  and Sir Richard Williamson of Lincolnshire were other prominent

lawyers. Little need be said of the seven lawyers who were not members of the Council: Sir Richard Etherington, Sir Henry Jenkins, Robert Briggs, Walter Bethell, Henry Tankard, Robert Hungate, and John Theaker. Their backgrounds were various, largely in the county; all barristers except Theaker—a notary—they played active parts in 61 the work of quarter sessions.

Thomas Mallory, archdeacon of Richmond, was clearly a church- 45 man, though he was a son of the notable gentry family of Studley. There were four justices who, while rather difficult to classify, seem to be best put in the category of commerce though the Court and the gentry are not impossible. Sir Edward Yorke, although of a Yorkshire 18 family, was the son of a man who had been sheriff of London, a member of the Muscovy Company, and Master of the Mint. Before serving in the commission of the peace, the son attended Cambridge, became Vice-Admiral, and was knighted. Surely of Welsh extraction, Sir Richard Vaughan was described as resident in Herefordshire when he 30 was knighted in 1603. Just what were the means with which he acquired the land requisite for his knighthood and for his appointment as J.P. is not apparent. Hugh Frankland was the nephew and heir of a 55 wealthy member of the Clothworkers' Company. Thomas Norcliffe, 57 a Yorkshireman from the West Riding, acquired from his operations in the market in land enough wealth to purchase an estate in the North Riding and to achieve the status of esquire.

Christopher Aske, Thomas Davile, and Adam Midlam are also elusive. Since they seem to have been related to earlier men who were members of the commission in Yorkshire, they are best described as gentry. Sir Arthur Dakins, clearly related to gentry, may also be so 41 classified, although without being called to the bar he was for some twenty years associated with Gray's Inn.

Finally among the men who were certainly gentry a few invite comment. Sir Thomas Hoby and Sir Richard Cholmeley, who were 19, 40 considered in Chapter III, were both members of this commission to their mutual discomfort. Sir Timothy Whittingham was a son of a 33 prominent Dean of Durham, Sir Francis Boynton of the East Riding, 23 who held land in the North Riding also, was descended from a proud line already prominent in the thirteenth century.

Some study at one of the universities was now common for North Riding J.P.s: almost as great a proportion as in Norfolk, and more than in the other counties, had had this experience. In the working group eighteen—not quite forty per cent—were at some time M.P.s. Five men were elected to the Parliament of 1604: John Sheffield and Sir Richard Musgrave as knights of the shire for Lincolnshire and Westmorland respectively, Sir Thomas Hoby, Sir Henry Jenkins, and Sir John Ferne for Yorkshire constituencies.

## 1626[6]

| # | | N | Name | | | | | Year | DNB | |
|---|---|---|------|---|---|---|---|------|-----|---|
| 1 | | | Sir Thomas Coventry, knight, lord keeper | | O | I | P | 1640 | DNB | |
| 2 | * | N | Toby [Matthew], Archbishop of York | | O | | | 1628 | DNB | |
| 3 | | | James [Ley], Earl of Marlborough, lord treasurer | | O | L | P | 1629 | DNB | |
| 4 | | | Henry [Montagu], Earl of Manchester, lord president | | C | M | P | 1642 | DNB | |
| 5 | | | Edward [Somerset], Earl of Worcester, lord privy seal | | | | | 1628 | DNB | |
| 6 | s | N | Emanuel [Scrope], Lord Scrope [lord president of the council of the north, lord lieutenant] | | O | | | 1630 | | |
| 7 | r | | Francis [Manners], Earl of Rutland | | | | P | 1632 | DNB | |
| 8 | r | | Francis [Clifford], Earl of Cumberland | | | | P | 1641 | | |
| 9 | s | | William [Cecil], Earl of Exeter | | | G | | 1640 | | |
| 10 | * | N | Edmund [Sheffield], Earl of Mulgrave | | O | | | 1646 | DNB | |
| 11 | s | | Henry [Constable], Viscount Dunbarre | | | | | 1645 | DNB | |
| 12 | r | | Algernon [Percy], Lord Percy | | C | | P | 1668 | DNB | |
| 13 | s | N | Henry [Clifford], Lord Clifford | | O | | P | 1643 | DNB | |
| 14 | * | | William [Eure], Lord Eure | | O | G | | 1646 | | |
| 15 | | N | Sir John Savile, knight | | C | | P | 1630 | DNB | |
| 16 | | | Sir Francis Harvy, knight ⎫ | | | M | P | 1632 | | |
| 17 | | | Sir Henry Yelverton, knight ⎬ justices | | | G | P | 1629 | DNB | |
| 18 | * | | Sir Richard Hutton, knight ⎭ | | O | G | P | 1639 | DNB | |
| 19 | | N | Sir Thomas Wentworth, knight & baronet | Wentworth | C | I | P | 1641 | DNB | |
| 20 | s | | Sir Thomas Bellasis, knight & baronet | Newburgh | C | | P | 1653 | | |
| 21 | r | N | Sir Marmaduke Wyvell, baronet | Constable Burton | C | L | P | 1648 | | |
| 22 | | N | Sir David Foulis, knight & baronet | Ingleby | | | | 1642 | DNB | |
| 23 | | | Sir Thomas Gower, knight & baronet | Stittenham | | | | 1654 | | |
| 24 | s | N | Sir Thomas Fairfax of Gilling, knight | | C | | P | 1636 | | |
| 25 | * | | Sir Thomas Dawney, knight | Sessay | | G | | 1644 | | |
| 26 | * | N | Sir Richard Cholmeley, knight | Whitby | C | | P | 1631 | | |
| 27 | * | | Sir Conyers Darcy, knight | Hornby Castle | C | I | | 1654 | | |
| 28 | * | | Sir Timothy Whittingham | Holmside, Durham | C | M | | 1630 | | |
| 29 | * | | Sir Timothy Hutton, knight | Marske | C | G | | 1629 | | |
| 30 | * | N | Sir John Gibson, knight | Welburn | | G | | 1638 | | |
| 31 | * | N | Sir Henry Tankard, knight | Arden | C | L | | 1626 | | |
| 32 | | N | Sir Arthur Ingram, knight | Sheriff Hutton | C | L | P | 1642 | DNB | K |
| 33 | | N | Sir Thomas Tildesley, knight | York | C | G | | 1635 | | |
| 34 | s | | Sir Thomas Norcliffe, knight | Nunnington | C | M | P | 1628 | | |
| 35 | s | | Sir William Sheffield, knight | | | L | P | | | |
| 36 | | N | Sir William Ellis, knight | Lincoln | | G | | 1636 | | |
| 37 | | N | Sir Thomas Ellis, knight | Grantham | C | G | P | 1627 | | |
| 38 | s | | Sir Thomas Layton, knight | Sexhow | | | | 1651 | | |
| 39 | * | | Sir Richard Darley, knight | Buttercrambe | C | G | P | 1654 | | |
| 40 | | N | Sir John Lowther, knight | Lowther, Westmorland | | I | P | 1637 | | |
| 41 | | N | John Wilson, dean of Ripon | Bedale | O | G | | 1635 | | |
| 42 | | | Henry Bankes, D.D. | Seamer | C | | | 1640 | | |
| 43 | | | William Pennyman | Marske | | I | | 1628 | | |
| 44 | r | | William Mallory | Studley | C | | P | 1646 | | K |
| 45 | | | Henry Griffith [Griffin] | Burton Agnes | C | | | 1643 | | |
| 46 | s | | William Aldborough | Aldborough | C | | | 1628 | | |
| 47 | | | Roger Gregory | Thirsk | | G | | | | |
| 48 | | | Matthew Jobson | Middleham | | G | | 1637 | | |

| 49 |   | Nicholas Conyers | Boulby |   |   |   | 1636 |   |
|----|---|------------------|--------|---|---|---|------|---|
| 50 |   | Thomas Heblethwayte | Malton | C | M | P | 1647 | K |
| 51 | r | Roger Wyvell | Osgodby |   | L |   | 1657 |   |
| 52 |   | Thomas Gilby | Stainton, Lincs. |   | G |   |   |   |

Dignitaries 18; Court 4; Gentry 21; Law 7; Church 2; Commerce o.

Superficially the North Riding commission of 1626 was much like those of other counties—except Northamptonshire, where rivalries had induced a remarkable growth. In Yorkshire, also, there was intense rivalry. Sir Thomas Hoby had shown such disrespect for the Lord President of the Council that he had been removed from that body in 1622 and put out of the commission. And this was not the only occasion where a J.P. was removed. In 1625 the competition of Sir Thomas Wentworth and Sir John Savile for election as knight 19 of the shire meant a disputed return which was disallowed by the House. Wentworth was pricked for sheriff to prevent his re-election in 1626; then he was put out of the commission of the peace and deprived of his office as *Custos Rotulorum* in a fashion designed to be humiliating. Since Wentworth is included, this *liber pacis* must have been compiled earlier in the year, but as deputy President of the Council Savile appeared in the roster ahead of the assize justices. 15 Temporarily he was triumphant. Another former J.P. had also been deprived of office. In 1617 Sir Thomas Metcalfe led an armed attack against a house in what was probably the last episode of private war south of the Tweed. Such disorderly conduct was unsuitable for a justice of the peace.

Beside these happenings an analysis of the commission seems tame. Except for Savile the dignitaries were all routine appointments: the incumbents of various offices and the nobility of the area, all relatives of earlier justices. The Court group in the working commission included the veteran Sir John Gibson and three new men. Sir David Foulis was a Scotsman who came to England with James I and made 22 a career which gained him wealth, lands in Yorkshire, and membership in the Council of the North before he pitted himself against Wentworth, was deprived of all offices, and incarcerated in the Fleet. Born in Yorkshire, Sir Arthur Ingram gained a fortune in London, 32 secured lucrative appointments, became a leading figure at Court and very important in the administration of the north. Sir William Sheffield 35 was a son of the former President of the Council of the North.

Professional members of that council included four of the seven lawyers in the commission. Sir Henry Tankard was a veteran member. Sir Thomas Tildesley was attorney-general in the palatine administra- 33 tion of Lancashire. The cousins Sir William and Sir Thomas Ellis, 37 and Sir John Lowther were all barristers; Sir William Ellis had been 40, 36 a reader in Gray's Inn. Not members of the Council but men who had

43 major interests in the county were William Pennyman, who was one
50 of the six clerks of chancery, and Thomas Heblethwayte.
41, 42  John Wilson and Henry Bankes provided the clerical element that
was usual at this time. Except for Ingram there were no men who
were mercantile in their provenance. The rest of the roster were
gentry who do not require comment.

By 1626 the J.P.s of the North Riding had come to be men who had
enjoyed much the same experience in the inns of court and the
universities as their counterparts in other counties. None of the other
five counties had fewer J.P.s who had never been enrolled in either an
inn or a university. While not identical with Kent or Norfolk,
Yorkshire was no longer different in this respect.

Election to the House of Commons was secured by thirteen of the
working justices at least once in their lives, always for a Yorkshire
constituency except for the return of Sir Thomas Ellis by Grimsby in
1597. There were two North Riding J.P.s who were members of the
Commons in 1626: Sir Thomas Fairfax for Hedon and Sir Arthur
Ingram for York. The Yorkshire knights of the shire were Sir John
Savile and Sir William Constable. Doubtless Wentworth would also
have been in the House had he not been pricked for sheriff deliberately
to disqualify him.

## 1636[7]

| | | | | | | | | | | | |
|---|---|---|---|---|---|---|---|---|---|---|---|
| 1 | | | q | William [Laud], Bishop [sic] of Canterbury, primate of all England | | O | | | 1644 | DNB | |
| 2 | * | | q | Thomas [Coventry], Lord Coventry, lord keeper | | O | I | P | 1640 | DNB | |
| 3 | | N | q | Richard [Neile], Archbishop of York, primate of England | | C | | | 1640 | DNB | |
| 4 | | | q | William [Juxon], Bishop of London, lord treasurer | | O | | | 1663 | DNB | |
| 5 | | | q | Henry [Montagu], Earl of Manchester, keeper of privy seal | | C | M | P | 1642 | DNB | |
| 6 | | N | q | Thomas [Howard], Earl of Arundel and Surrey, earl marshal | | C | | | 1646 | DNB | |
| 7 | * | N | q | Thomas [Wentworth], Viscount Wentworth, president of York [lord lieutenant] | | C | I | P | 1641 | DNB | |
| 8 | * | N | q | Algernon [Percy], Earl of Northumberland | | C | | P | 1668 | DNB | |
| 9 | * | | q | Francis [Clifford], Earl of Cumberland | | | | P | 1641 | | |
| 10 | * | | q | William [Cecil], Earl of Exeter | | | G | P | 1640 | | |
| 11 | * | N | q | Edmund [Sheffield], Earl of Mulgrave | | O | | | 1646 | DNB | |
| 12 | s | | q | Thomas [Fairfax], Viscount Fairfax of Elmeley | | | | P | 1641 | | |
| 13 | | | q | George Vernon, knight, justice of common pleas | | | I | P | 1639 | DNB | |
| 14 | | | q | Robert Berkeley, knight, justice of king's bench | | | M | P | 1656 | DNB | |
| 15 | * | | q | Richard Hutton, knight, justice of common pleas | | O | G | P | 1639 | DNB | |
| 16 | s | | q | Henry Bellasis, esquire | Newburgh | C | L | P | 1647 | | K |
| 17 | * | | q | Thomas Gower, knight & baronet | Stittenham | | | | 1654 | | |
| 18 | | N | q | Edward Osborne, baronet | Kiveton | C | I | P | 1647 | | |
| 19 | | N | q | John Hotham, knight & baronet | Scorborough | | M | P | 1645 | DNB | K |

| # | | N | q | Name | Place | | | P | Year | DNB | K |
|---|---|---|---|------|-------|---|---|---|------|-----|---|
| 20 | s | | q | William Pennyman, baronet | Marske | O | I | P | 1643 | DNB | K |
| 21 | * | N | q | William Ellis, knight, council of north | Lincoln | | G | | 1636 | | |
| 22 | * | N | q | John Lowther, knight, council of north | Lowther | | I | P | 1637 | | |
| 23 | | N | q | Richard Dyott, knight, council of north | Durham | O | I | P | 1659 | | |
| 24 | | N | q | John Melton, knight, secretary and keeper of signet in north | York | C | | P | 1640 | DNB | K |
| 25 | | N | q | George Radcliffe, knight, attorney of the king in the north | Thornhill | O | G | P | 1657 | DNB | |
| 26 | * | N | q | Thomas Posthumous Hoby, knight | Hackness | O | G | P | 1641 | | |
| 27 | * | | q | Thomas Dawney, knight | Sessay | | G | | 1644 | | |
| 28 | * | N | q | John Gibson, knight | Welburn | | G | | 1638 | | |
| 29 | * | N | q | Arthur Ingram, knight | Sheriff Hutton | C | L | P | 1642 | DNB | K |
| 30 | * | | q | William Sheffield, knight | | | L | P | | | |
| 31 | * | | q | Thomas Layton, knight | Sexhow | | | | 1651 | | |
| 32 | * | | q | Richard Darley, knight | Buttercrambe | C | G | P | 1654 | | |
| 33 | | | q | Robert Napier, knight | Seamer | | G | P | 1661 | | K |
| 34 | s | | q | Hugh Cholmeley, knight | Whitby | C | G | P | 1657 | DNB | K |
| 35 | s | | q | Hugh Bethell, knight | Ellerton | C | | P | 1663 | | |
| 36 | | | | William Strickland, knight | Boynton | | G | P | 1673 | DNB | K |
| 37 | r | | q | Thomas Danby, knight | Thorpe Perrow | C | | P | 1660 | | K |
| 38 | | | q | James Morley | Normanby | | | | | | |
| 39 | * | | q | William Mallory | Studley | C | | P | 1646 | | K |
| 40 | s | | q | Matthew Hutton | Marske | C | | P | | | |
| 41 | r | | q | William Frankland | Thirkleby | | G | P | 1640 | | |
| 42 | | | q | Richard Egerton | Allerston | | L | | | | |
| 43 | r | N | q | Christopher Wandesforde | Kirklington | C | G | P | 1640 | DNB | |
| 44 | | | q | Thomas Harrison | Cayton | | G | | 1642 | | |
| 45 | * | | q | Thomas Heblethwayte | Malton | C | M | P | 1647 | | K |
| 46 | r | | | James Pennyman | Ormsby | O | I | | 1655 | | |
| 47 | * | | q | Roger Wyvell | Osgodby | | L | | 1657 | | |
| 48 | | | q | Thomas Best | Middleton Quernow | | | P | | | |
| 49 | | | | John Dodsworth | Thornton Watlass | | | | 1644 | | |
| 50 | | | q | John Wastell | Scorton | C | G | P | 1659 | | K |
| 51 | | | q | Robert Barwicke | York | | G | | | | |
| 52 | | | | George Metcalfe | Northallerton | C | G | | 1642 | | |
| 53 | | | q | William Caley | Thormanby | | G | | 1681 | | |
| 54 | | | | Richard Wynne | Guisborough | | L | | 1653 | | |

Dignitaries 15; Court 4; Gentry 23; Law 7; Church 0; Commerce 5.

The apparent character of the commission of the peace for the North Riding in 1636 was similar to that of other commissions of the same date, in size and composition. Eight survivors of the bench of 1626 were no longer included, but several of them were members of other commissions, and there seems to be no reflection of the disturbed political situation. Sir David Foulis may have been a victim of Wentworth's power; Lord Eure had been forced to sell most of his lands to meet his debts and had forcibly resisted the sheriff's efforts to levy a tax. Sir Thomas Hoby had not only been restored to the commission and to the Council of the North, but had become *Custos Rotulorum* and probably still held that honour—no *Custos* is shown in this *liber pacis*. Archbishop Laud had been added to the roster of all three Yorkshire Ridings, although the only other counties in which he was a J.P. were Kent, Surrey, and Middlesex; Laud's close friendship with new Lord President and Lord Deputy of Ireland is a plausible explanation. The cross-currents of the time surely affected the North Riding commission, but the situation was not simple; membership was not confined to Wentworth's faction.

In the working part of the commission the three surviving justices in the Court group—Gibson, Ingram, Sheffield—had been joined by
24 Sir John Melton, secretary and Keeper of the Signet of the Council of the North. A politician, the author of books on politics and astro-
18 logy, he had been a successful entrepreneur. Sir Edward Osborne, however, is better classified in the commercial group. Although he was Vice-President of the Council of the North, he qualified for a marriage with a daughter of Lord Fauconberg by the wealth inherited from two Lord Mayors of London and a Master of the Mint. He is better known as the father of the Restoration statesman who became the Earl of Danby. Another justice whose status came from mercantile
33 success was Sir Robert Napier, a distant cousin of the inventor of logarithms, who also married a nobleman's daughter. Since his principal residence was at Luton, his membership in the North Riding commission must have been in consequence of his Yorkshire property.
44 Thomas Harrison belonged to a family which included several mayors
48 and aldermen of York. Thomas Best is a nebulous figure, probably the son of a Fleet Street scrivener with a Yorkshire background who
54 participated actively in the market in land. Finally Richard Wynne, as the possibly fabricated pedigree of the visitation of 1612 declares, may well have come from Wales. He must have owned land in the county, but he has left only minimal traces of his life.

Again there were seven lawyers in this commission, Ellis, Lowther, and Heblethwayte being veterans from the bench in 1626. Sir George
25 Radcliffe, perhaps a distant cousin of Roger Radcliffe (J.P. in 1559 and 1584), was a Gray's Inn barrister who became a close friend and political associate of Wentworth. He was King's Attorney in the
23 north and a major figure in the life of the region. Sir Richard Dyott, also a barrister, was chancellor of the county palatine of Durham and a
50 member of the Council of the North. John Wastell, a son of a York-shire gentleman, found a call to the bar to be the basis of a very success-
51 ful career. Robert Barwicke lived in York, where he practised law probably with less success than Wastell.

Since in contrast to the other counties there were no non-episcopal clergy in this commission, there remain only a few gentry to consider.
19 Sir John Hotham, the controversial and tragic governor of Hull in the

civil wars, was a descendant of a Yorkshire family of considerable prominence since the early fifteenth century. Sir William Strickland 36 was a grandson of Peter Wentworth, the Elizabethan Puritan, with whom his other grandfather had been associated in Parliament; his Boys cousins were Kentish J.P.s. His brother-in-law, Sir Hugh Cholmeley, who married a daughter of Sir William Twysden, also had 34 Kent connections.

There was no appreciable change with regard to enrolment in the universities and the inns of court, but the political unrest of the county and the nation must be reflected by the number of senior J.P.s who obtained election to Parliament. Twenty-four of the thirty-nine members of the working commission sat at Westminster at some time, and eight North Riding J.P.s were members of the Short Parliament, while the Long Parliament contained ten. Except for Sir John Lowther (Westmorland on several occasions), Sir Robert Napier (Corfe Castle, Weymouth, Peterborough), Sir Richard Dyott (Litchfield, Stafford), all these North Riding J.P.s were returned by Yorkshire seats at least once. In the Short Parliament Sir Edward Osborne was one of the knights of the shire, while Sir Arthur Ingram, who had represented York city several times, was returned in 1640 by Windsor and by Callington. In the Long Parliament both of the Yorkshire knights of the shire—Henry Bellasis and Sir Ferdinando Fairfax— were opponents of Strafford, while the other constituencies were divided between reformers and supporters of the King. Nearly all the justices who lived into the war years became opponents of the men who controlled Parliament, but Sir William Strickland and John Wastell remained firm in their support of the 'popular' cause. In 1650 they, Sir Richard Darley, and (Sir) Robert Barwicke were still in the commission of the peace for the North Riding.[8]

## NOTES TO APPENDIX F

1. *Cal. Pat. Rolls, Eliz.* ii (1560–3), 436–7; Lansdowne MS. 1218, ff. 13, 13ᵛ, 65ᵛ.

*1562 roster:*

17. *Register of Admissions to Gray's Inn*, p. 8.
18. Cf. Somerset, 1562 roster, no. 20.
19. Neale, *Elizabeth and Her Parliaments, 1559–1581*, p. 43; R. R. Reid, *The King's Council of the North* (L., 1921), pp. 167 n., 492.
20. A. Gooder, *The Parliamentary Representation of the County of York* (Yorkshire Archaeological Society Record Series, ii, 1938), pp. 20–3; Joseph Foster (ed.), *The Visitation of Yorkshire . . . 1584/5 . . . [and] 1612, etc.* (L., 1875), pp. 262–3; Richardson, *Augmentations*, pp. 258, 282–3; *VCH North Riding*, ii. 485 *et passim*; Reid, *King's Council*, p. 493.
21. C. B. Norcliffe (ed.), *The Visitation of Yorkshire in the Years 1563 and 1564*

(Harl. Soc. Publ. xvi, L. 1881), p. 88; Gooder, *Parliamentary Representation*, pp. 14–15; *VCH North Riding*, i. 351.

23. Joseph Foster, *Pedigrees of the County Families of Yorkshire*, vol. ii: *North Riding* (L. 1874); *Visitation of Yorkshire, 1584/5 and 1612*, pp. 231–2.

24. Reid, *King's Council*, p. 492; Lansdowne MS. 1218, f. 91ᵛ.

25. *Lincoln's Inn Black Books*, i. 230, 281.

26. *Alum. oxon.*

27. Gooder, *Parliamentary Representation*, pp. 19–20; *Yorkshire Archaeological Society Journal*, xxv (1918–20), 16–21.

29. *Visitation of Yorkshire, 1584/5 and 1612*, p. 128; J. J. Cartright, *Chapters in the History of Yorkshire* (Wakefield, 1872), p. 67; *DNB*: 'John Rokeby'; *Alum. cantab.*: 'John Rokeby'; Reid, *King's Council*, p. 252.

30. *Visitation of Yorkshire, 1584/5 and 1612*, p. 206; Cartright, *Yorkshire*, p. 67; *VCH North Riding*, ii. 395.

31. Ibid. i. 98; *Cal. S. P. Dom. 1547–80*, p. 26.

32. *L. & P.* xiiiB, no. 1172; ibid. xv. 563; ibid. xviiiA, 546; ibid. xxA, g623(7); ibid. xxiA, 770, 775, 784; *Cal. Pat. Rolls, Edw. VI*, ii (1548–9), 136; *Cal. Pat. Rolls, Eliz.* ii (1560–3), 181; William Page (ed.), *The Certificates of the Commissioners Appointed to Survey the Chantries* (Part II, Surtees Soc. Publ. xcii. 1893), 371; *Index of Wills in the York Registry* (Yorks. Arch. Soc. Record Ser. xix, 1895), 69.

33. H. B. M'Call, *The Story of the Family of Wandesforde* (L., 1904), *passim*; Bateson, 'Original Letters', p. 71.

34. *VCH North Riding*, ii. 445; *Visitation of Yorkshire, 1563–4*, pp. 85–7.

35. *VCH North Riding*, i. 129; *Visitation of Yorkshire, 1584/5 and 1612*, p. 255; *Yorks. Arch. Soc. Journal*, xix (1906–7), 73–7.

42. *VCH North Riding*, i. 451.

43. Gooder, *Parliamentary Representation*, pp. 5–8.

44. *Visitation of Yorkshire, 1563–4*, p. 144.

45. *Wills in York Registry* (Yorks. Arch. Soc. Record Ser. xiv, 1893), 86.

46. *Visitation of Yorkshire, 1584/5 and 1612*, pp. 596, 597; I.P.M., 1 Eliz., York 122/43.

47. Reid, *King's Council*, pp. 170–1.

50. *VCH North Riding*, i. 161; Egerton MS. 2345, f. 15.

51. *VCH North Riding*, ii. 53.

52. Ibid., p. 355.

53. Ibid., p. 97.

54. Ibid. i. 414.

55. Gooder, *Parliamentary Representation*, pp. 17–19; S.P. 12/145, f. 14ᵛ.


2. Bateson, 'Original Letters', p. 71.


3. *L. & P.* xiiiA, g1519(29), g1309(22); ibid. xivA, g904(22); ibid. xvii, g283(11); ibid. xixB, g800(5); ibid. xxA, g282(46), g504(41); ibid. xxB, g266(2), g648(7), g910(7); ibid. xxiA, g504(2); ibid. xxiB, g476(6).


4. Lansdowne MS. 737, ff. 47ᵛ–48ᵛ.

*1584 roster:*

22. Gooder, *Parliamentary Representation*, pp. 26–30.

24. Reid, *King's Council*, pp. 6 n. 229, 494; James Raine, *History and Antiquities of North Durham* (L., 1852), p. 306.

25. Cf. North Riding, 1562 roster, no. 20.

26. Ibid., no. 23.

27. Shaw, *Knights of England*, ii. 71; *Visitation of Yorkshire, 1584/5 and 1612*, pp. 156–7; Keeler, *Long Parliament*, p. 265; Gooder, *Parliamentary Representation*, pp. 30–3.
28. *Visitation of Yorkshire, 1584/5 and 1612*, p. 51; Neale, *House of Commons*, pp. 191–2.
29. Gooder, *Parliamentary Representation*, pp. 31–3.
30. *Visitation of Yorkshire, 1584/5 and 1612*, p. 264; cf. North Riding, 1562 roster, no. 21.
31. Ibid., no. 23.
32. *Visitation of Yorkshire, 1584/5 and 1612*, pp. 80–1; Legard, *Legards of Anlaby*, pp. 196–7.
33. Gooder, *Parliamentary Representation*, pp. 34–5.
35. *Pension Book of Gray's Inn*, i. 8 n. 1.
37. Ibid., p. 17.
38. Ibid., p. 32; Reid, *King's Council*, p. 251.
39. *Pension Book of Gray's Inn*, pp. 42, 54.
40. *Alum. cantab.*
42. F. A. Inderwick (ed.), *The Inner Temple* (L., 1896), p. 471; *Wills in York Registry* (Yorks. Arch. Soc. Record Ser. xxii, 1897), 13; Reid, *King's Council*, p. 251 n.; *Cal. S. P. Dom. 1547–80*, p. 538, no. 27.
43. *Visitation of Yorkshire, 1584/5 and 1612*, pp. 56–8; Gooder, *Parliamentary Representation*, pp. 33–4; Reid, *King's Council*, p. 196; Neale, *House of Commons*, pp. 190–1.
44. C. Jackson (ed.), *The Autobiography of Mrs. Alice Thornton* (Surtees Soc. Publ. lxii, 1873), 344.
45. *Students admitted to the Inner Temple*, p. 37; *Masters of the Bench of the Inner Temple*, p. 15.
46. *Alum. cantab.*; cf. *DNB*: 'George Bowes'; *Visitation of Yorkshire, 1584/5 and 1612*, pp. 596–7.
47. Ibid., p. 154.
48. Ibid., p. 206.
49. *VCH North Riding*, ii. 445.
50. *Visitation of Yorkshire, 1584/5 and 1612*, p. 380; Cokayne, *Baronetage*, i. 103 (cr. 1611).
51. *Visitation of Yorkshire, 1563–4*, p. 4 n.; *Lincoln's Inn Black Books*, i. 369.
52. *Visitation of Yorkshire, 1584/5 and 1612*, p. 540.
53. Ibid., p. 220.
54. Ibid., p. 184 *et passim*; *Yorks. Arch. Soc. Journal*, xxv (1918–20), 1 ff.
55. M'Call, *Wandesford*, p. 239; *Autobiography of Alice Thornton* (Surtees Soc. Publ. lxii. 1873), 344.
56. *Visitation of Yorkshire, 1584/5 and 1612*, p. 196.
57. *Lincoln's Inn Black Books*, i. 339, 364–5; Robert Surtees, *The History and Antiquities of the County Palatine of Durham* (4 vols., L., 1816–40), iii. 254.
58. *Visitation of Yorkshire, 1584/5 and 1612*, p. 60.
59. *Middle Temple Records*, i. 162, 206; *Yorks. Arch. Soc. Journal*, xxvii (1923–4), 357.
60. *Visitation of Yorkshire, 1584/5 and 1612*, p. 257; *Quarter Sessions Records*, iii. *passim*.
61. *Visitation of Yorkshire, 1584/5 and 1612*, p. 199; *Wills in York Registry* (Yorks. Arch. Soc. Record Ser. xxvi, 1899), 197.
62. *Visitation of Yorkshire, 1584/5 and 1612*, pp. 200–1; *Yorks. Arch. Soc. Journal*, xvi (1900–1), 173–4.
63. *Pension Book of Gray's Inn*, i. 109, 500; *Visitation of Yorkshire, 1584/5 and 1612*, p. 560.

5. P.R.O., S.P. 14/33, ff. 22–3ᵛ.

*1608 roster:*

11. *VCH North Riding*, i. 60, 249; Neale, *House of Commons*, pp. 34, 83, 86–92, 223, 225.
12. *VCH North Riding*, i. 107, 267, 346, 432; ibid. ii. 313.
15. *Yorks. Arch. Soc. Journal*, xxiii (1914–15), 359; *Complete Peerage*: 'Eure'.
16. Ibid. '2nd Earl of Mulgrave'.
17. Cf. North Riding, 1584 roster, no. 63.
18. *DNB*: 'John York'.
19. Cf. *supra*, pp. 37 ff.
20. *Visitation of Yorkshire, 1584/5 and 1612*, p. 61; *VCH North Riding*, i. 177–8; ibid. ii. 66.
21. *Visitation of Yorkshire, 1584/5 and 1612*, pp. 232–3; *Yorks. Arch. Soc. Journal*, xxvii (1923–4), 358.
22. *Visitation of Yorkshire, 1584/5 and 1612*, pp. 142–3; *VCH North Riding*, i. 393; *Cal. S. P. Dom., Jas. I, 1611–18*, p. 434.
23. *Visitation of Yorkshire, 1584/5 and 1612*, p. 8; *VCH North Riding*, ii. 368–9; Cokayne, *Baronetage*, i. 114 (cr. 1618): 'Walter Boynton', his son.
24. *Visitation of Yorkshire, 1584/5 and 1612*, p. 81.
25. *Yorks. Arch. Soc. Journal*, xxiii (1914–15), 358.
26. *Visitation of Yorkshire, 1584/5 and 1612*, p. 409; *VCH North Riding*, i. 202, 204–5; F. R. Raines (ed.), *The Journal of Nicholas Assheton* (Chetham Soc. xiv. 1848), pp. 9–11.
27. *Visitation of Yorkshire, 1584/5 and 1612*, p. 85; *North Country Wills* (2 vols., Surtees Soc. cxvi and cxxi, 1908 and 1912), ii. 152; PCC 1572, 4 Peter [William Bamburgh, gent.]; C. W. Foster (ed.), *Calendars of Lincoln Wills* (2 vols., L., 1902, 1910), i. 45; *VCH North Riding*, ii. 114–15.
28. Ibid. i. 358–62.
29. Cf. North Riding, 1584 roster, no. 40.
30. *Visitation of Yorkshire, 1584/5 and 1612*, p. 584; *VCH North Riding*, i. 462, 551; ibid. ii. 464; Shaw, *Knights of England*, ii. 121.
31. *Lincoln's Inn, Admissions*, i. 97; *Visitation of Yorkshire, 1584/5 and 1612*, p. 516; Shaw, *Knights of England*, ii. 118; *VCH North Riding*, ii. 451; *Quarter Sessions Records*, i. *passim*.
32. *Lincoln's Inn Black Books*, ii. 51; *Visitation of Yorkshire, 1584/5 and 1612*, p. 371; *VCH North Riding*, ii. 304.
33. *Alum. cantab.*; *DNB*: 'William Whittingham'.
34. *VCH North Riding*, ii. 57; William Dugdale (ed.), *The Visitation of Yorkshire 1665* (Surtees Soc. xxxvi, Durham, 1860), p. 78; *North Country Wills*, ii. 68–9; John R. Wilbran, *Memorials of the Abbey of St. Mary of Fountains*, ii (Surtees Soc. Publ. lxvii, 1876), 345–53; M. W. Beresford, 'The Common Informer, the Penal Statutes, and Economic Regulation', *Economic History Review*, 2nd Series, x (1957–8), 221–37; St. Ch. 5/P14/21; St. Ch. 8/184/33.
35. *Alum. oxon.*; Reid, *King's Council*, p. 228.
37. *Register of Admissions to Gray's Inn*, p. 60; *Pension Book of Gray's Inn*, i. 153, 209; Shaw, *Knights of England*, ii. 132.
39. Cf. North Riding, 1584 roster, no. 50.
40. *Visitation of Yorkshire, 1584/5 and 1612*, pp. 220, 221; Reid, *King's Council*, pp. 231, 234; cf. *supra*, p. 39.
41. *Pension Book of Gray's Inn*, i. 137; *Alum. cantab.*; *Visitation of Yorkshire, 1584/5 and 1612*, pp. 169, 511; Lansdowne MS. 1218, f. 13ᵛ; Egerton MS. 2345, f. 15.
42. *DNB*: 'Matthew Hutton'; *Alum. cantab.*

43. *Visitation of Yorkshire, 1584/5 and 1612*, p. 520.
45. *Alum. cantab.*
46. Cf. North Riding, 1584 roster, no. 62.
47. Ibid., no. 45.
48. Ibid., no. 59.
49. *Lincoln's Inn Black Books*, ii. 52; *Visitation of Yorkshire, 1584/5 and 1612*, p. 241; *VCH North Riding*, ii. 87.
50. Cf. North Riding, 1584 roster, no. 56.
51. *Visitation of Yorkshire, 1584/5 and 1612*, pp. 118–19; *Wills in York Registry* (Yorks. Arch. Soc. Record Ser. xxvi, 1899), 133.
52. *Alum. cantab.*: 'William Davile'; *Visitation of Yorkshire, 1584/5 and 1612*, p. 215; *VCH North Riding*, ii. 19.
53. J. W. Walker (ed.), *Yorkshire Pedigrees* (3 vols., Harl. Soc. Publ. xciv, xcv, xcvi, 1942–4), ii. 270–2.
54. *Visitation of Yorkshire, 1584/5 and 1612*, p. 279; *VCH North Riding*, i. 369.
55. Ibid. ii. 57; *Visitation of Yorkshire 1665*, p. 78; *North Country Wills*, ii. 68–9.
56. *Students admitted to the Inner Temple*, p. 90; *Visitation of Yorkshire, 1584/5 and 1612*, p. 573.
57. *Visitation of Yorkshire 1665*, p. 341; *Quarter Sessions Records*, i–iii, *passim*; F. Collins (ed.), *Yorkshire Fines* (4 vols., Yorks. Arch. Soc. Record Ser. ii (1886), v (1888), vii (1889), viii (1889)), ii. 3, 21, 53, 189; ibid. iii. 3, 197; ibid. iv. 112, 116; *VCH North Riding*, ii. 114; *Middle Temple Records*, ii. 452; *Yorks. Arch. Soc. Journal*, iii (1873–4), 66; ibid. xv (1898–9) 142; *VCH North Riding*, ii. 114.
58. *Visitation of Yorkshire, 1584/5 and 1612*, p. 216; *VCH North Riding*, ii. 33, 34, 36; *Lincoln's Inn Black Books*, ii. 12; *Alum. cantab.*; Reid, *King's Council*, pp. 184 n., 196, 210.
59. *Visitation of Yorkshire, 1584/5 and 1612*, p. 87; *VCH North Riding*, ii. 93 ff.; Keeler, *Long Parliament*, p. 133; Gooder, *Parliamentary Representation*, p. 74.
60. *Visitation of Yorkshire, 1584/5 and 1612*, pp. 141–2; *Alum. cantab.*; *Yorks. Arch. Soc. Journal*, xviii (1901–5), 46–7; Jordan, *Charities of Rural England*, pp. 334, 377.
61. Will: York Registry, 19 March 1607/8.
62. *Register of Admissions to Gray's Inn*, p. 53; *Quarter Sessions Records*, iii, *passim*.

6. P.R.O., C 193/12.

*1626 roster:*
16. *Middle Temple Bench Book*, p. 173.
20. *Yorks. Arch. Soc. Journal*, xxiii (1914–15), 352; *Complete Peerage*: 'Fauconberg'.
21. Cokayne, *Baronetage*, i. 103 (cr. 1611); cf. North Riding, 1584 roster, no. 50.
22. *VCH North Riding*, ii. 245, *et passim*.
23. *Visitation of Yorkshire, 1584/5 and 1612*, p. 226; *Yorks. Arch. Soc. Journal*, xxiii (1914–15), 381.
24. *Complete Peerage*: 'Viscount Fairfax'.
25. Cf. North Riding, 1608 roster, no. 24.
26. Ibid., no. 40.
27. Ibid., no. 25.
28. Ibid., no. 33.
29. Ibid., no. 42.
30. Ibid., no. 43.
31. Ibid., no. 58.

32. Anthony F. Upton, *Sir Arthur Ingram* (L., 1961).
33. *Alum. cantab.*; *Pension Book of Gray's Inn*, i. 64, 175.
34. Cf. North Riding, 1608 roster, no. 57. He is discussed along with his father.
35. *Alum. cantab.*
36. Reid, *King's Council*, p. 497; *Pension Book of Gray's Inn*, i. 83, 137, 223.
37. Ibid., pp. 231, 252; A. R. Maddison (ed.), *Lincolnshire Pedigrees* (4 vols., Harl. Soc. Publ., l, li, lii, lv, 1902–4), i. 324–5.
38. J. R. Walker (ed.), *Yorkshire Pedigrees* (3 vols., Harl. Soc. Publ. xciv–xcvi, 1942–4), ii. 270–2.
39. Cf. North Riding, 1608 roster, no. 59.
40. *Students admitted to the Inner Temple*, p. 155.
41. *Alum. oxon.*; J. Le Neve, *Fasti Ecclesiae Anglicanae* (3 vols., Oxford, 1854), iii. 180.
42. *Alum. cantab.*, where he is confused with another man; *Quarter Sessions Records*, ii, iii, *passim*.
43. *DNB*: 'William Pennyman', 1607–43; Keeler, *Long Parliament*, p. 312; *Students admitted to the Inner Temple*, p. 115; *VCH North Riding*, ii. 282.
45. *Visitation of Yorkshire, 1584/5 and 1612*, p. 524; Cokayne, *Baronetage*, ii. 26 (cr. 1627).
46. Cf. North Riding, 1608 roster, no. 54: Richard Aldborough.
47. *Visitation of Yorkshire, 1584/5 and 1612*, p. 525.
48. Ibid., p. 622; *North Country Wills*, ii. 171–3; *VCH North Riding*, i. 248; will: York Registry, admon., 26 April 1637.
49. *Visitation of Yorkshire 1665*, p. 340; *VCH North Riding*, ii. 342.
51. *Yorks. Arch. Soc. Journal*, xxiii (1914–15), 381; *VCH North Riding*, ii. 433; *Visitation of Yorkshire, 1584/5 and 1612*, p. 189.
52. *Lincolnshire Pedigrees*, ii. 402.


7. P.R.O., S.P. 16/405, ff. 21ᵛ–23ᵛ.

*1636 roster:*
17. Cf. North Riding, 1626 roster, no. 23.
18. Cokayne, *Baronetage*, i. 153 (cr. 1620).
21. Cf. North Riding, 1626 roster, no. 36.
22. Ibid., no. 40.
23. *Alum. oxon.*; *Students admitted to the Inner Temple*, p. 181.
26. Cf. North Riding, 1608 roster, no. 19; *Cal. S. P. Dom., Ch. I, 1629–31*, p. 301; P.R.O., S.P. 16/212, f. 21ᵛ.
27. Cf. North Riding, 1608 roster, no. 24.
28. Ibid., no. 43.
30. Cf. North Riding, 1626 roster, no. 25.
31. Ibid., no. 38.
32. Cf. North Riding, 1608 roster, no. 59.
35. *Alum. cantab.*
38. *Visitation of Yorkshire, 1584/5 and 1612*, p. 194; *VCH North Riding*, ii. 33, 281, 292.
40. *Visitation of Yorkshire 1665*, p. 173.
41. *VCH North Riding*, ii. 57.
42. Ibid., p. 422; *Visitation of Yorkshire 1665*, p. 71.
44. *Visitation of Yorkshire, 1584/5 and 1612*, p. 527; *Visitation of Yorkshire 1665*, pp. 216–17; *VCH North Riding*, i. 322, 380, 382.
46. *Visitation of Yorkshire 1665*, p. 198.
47. Cf. North Riding, 1626 roster, no. 51.
48. Foster, *Yorkshire Pedigrees*; *VCH North Riding*, i. 392.

49. *Visitation of Yorkshire, 1584/5 and 1612,* p. 266; *VCH North Riding,* i. 345.
51. *Register of Admissions to Gray's Inn,* p. 231; *Pension Book of Gray's Inn,* i. 227, 310.
52. *Visitation of Yorkshire, 1584/5 and 1612,* pp. 409, 554; *Visitation of Yorkshire 1665,* p. 325; *VCH North Riding,* ii. 420, 425.
53. *Pension Book of Gray's Inn,* ii. 125; *VCH North Riding,* ii. 210, 427; Cokayne, *Baronetage,* iii. 186 (cr. 1661).
54. *Visitation of Yorkshire, 1584/5 and 1612,* p. 593.

8. Keeler, *Long Parliament,* pp. 73–6; Walkley, *Justices of the Peace in 1650,* p. 18.

# ASSESSMENTS OF J.P.S IN 1609

I N the Ellesmere papers in the Huntington Library is a memorandum in Latin listing the working portions of the commissions of the peace in 1609 which shows what must be assessments for the subsidy.[1] Its date happens to fall only ten years from the mid-point of our period, at the time when working portions of the commissions were in general larger than at either earlier or later moments. It was also a time when the commissions combined many of their Elizabethan characteristics with the new tendencies which appeared in the Stuart era. Thus the document is particularly interesting, though it is not so readily available as the *libri pacis*. Just as the commissions for other counties in 1562 show how representative the six counties actually were then, so does this document for its time. It contributes to the whole study, and it should also prove useful in work on cognate questions.

Since most of the data for the six counties are given in the rosters of 1608, for those shires only the changes have been given here. Their small number shows how very stable the commissions were.

The names have been translated and are reproduced with the standardized spelling which has been the practice in other lists. The figures have been converted into arabic numerals and the abbreviation for pounds—*li.*—omitted. In the original the notation of most small assessments—chiefly £5—is expressed in shillings.

### BEDFORDSHIRE

| | |
|---|---|
| Edward Radcliffe, knight, in lands | 20 |
| John Crofts, knight, in lands | 20 |
| John Rotherham, knight | 20 |
| Francis Anderson, knight | 26 |
| Robert Newdigate, knight | 20 |
| Thomas Tyrringham, knight | Bucks. |
| William Fleetwood, knight | |
| Richard Conquest, knight | 20 |
| John Butler, knight | 10 |
| John Osborne, esq. | 25 |
| Nicholas Luke | 20 |
| William Gostwicke | 20 |
| Edmund Mordaunt | 20 |
| Thomas Cheyney | 20 |
| Nicholas Potts | 10 |
| George Francklin | 20 |
| Launcelot Lowther | 20 |
| John Lea | 20 |
| William Plomer | 10 |
| William Fishe | 5 |
| Thomas Anstell | 20 |
| Oliver Harvy | 6 |

### BERKSHIRE

| | |
|---|---|
| Thomas Challenor, knight | Bucks. |
| Henry Neville, knight, in lands | 30 |
| William Forster, knight | 20 |
| George Hyde, knight | 20 |

[1] Huntington Library MSS., EL 2513.

| | | | |
|---|---|---|---|
| Edward Hoby, knight | Kent | William Burlas, knight | 25 |
| Francis Knollys, knight | 20 | Henry Longvill, knight | 40 |
| Michael Mollins, knight | 20 | Thomas Denton, knight | 20 |
| Richard Lovelace, knight | | Anthony Tyrringham, knight | 40 |
| Richard Fettiplace, knight, in lands | 10 | Christopher Hoddesdon, knight | 20 |
| Edmund Fettiplace, knight | 24 | Jerome Horsey, knight | 20 |
| John Norris, knight | 23 | Edmund Ashfield, knight | 20 |
| Valentine Knightley, knight | 20 | Fleetwood Dormer, knight | 10 |
| William Fleetwood, knight | Bucks. | Richard Ingolsby, knight | 20 |
| Richard Coningsby, knight, house- | | William Andrews, knight | 25 |
| hold | 20 | Anthony Greeneway, knight | 20 |
| Francis Castillion, knight | 20 | Henry Savile, knight | |
| Vice-chancellor of Oxford University | | William Garrett, knight | dead |
| for the time being | | Thomas Lee, knight | 20 |
| Robert Wright, S.T.D. | | Paul Darrell, in goods | 3 |
| Basil Fettiplace | 10 | William Tothill | 20 |
| Edmund Dunch, in lands | 40 | Christopher Hampden | 10 |
| Thomas Read | 26 | John Phelips, in lands | 6 |
| Henry Sadler | 20 | Edward Salter, in lands | 10 |
| Samuel Bakehouse | 23 | Thomas Ducke | 20 |
| Thomas Doleman | 20 | Anthony Chester | 20 |
| Francis Moore | 10 | Richard Moore | 8 |
| William Stubbs | 10 | Paul Risley | 13 |
| Anthony Blagrave | 22 | Edward Woodward | 14 |
| Edward Clarke | 10 | Richard Cotton | |
| William Stonehouse | 10 | | |
| Walter Darell | 4 | | |
| Henry Martin, LL.D., Oxford City | 2 | | |

## CAMBRIDGESHIRE

| | | | |
|---|---|---|---|
| | | Oliver Cromwell, knight | Hunts. |
| | | Thomas Jermy, knight | 30 |
| BUCKINGHAMSHIRE | | John Cutts, knight | 30 |
| | | John Cotton, knight | 50 |
| John Egerton, knight | | John Peyton, knight | 50 |
| Henry Lee, knight, in lands | 70 | Miles Sandes, knight | 20 |
| Thomas Challenor, knight | 30 | John Woode, knight | 20 |
| Edmund Carey, knight, London | 50 | Vice-chancellor of Cambridge for the | |
| Francis Fortescue, knight | 30 | time being | |
| Edward Hoby, knight | Kent | Thomas Neville, dean of Canterbury | |
| John Packington, knight | 60 | Humphrey Tyndall, dean of Ely | |
| Robert Dormer, knight | 60 | John Palmer, dean of Peterborough | |
| William Clarke, knight | 30 | Roger Good, S.T.D. | |
| Francis Goodwyn, knight | 40 | Edward Hynde, in lands | 6 |
| Richard Mompesson, knight | 20 | Thomas Wendie | 30 |
| George Fleetwood, knight | 20 | John Cage | 30 |
| William Fleetwood, knight | 20 | John Pigott | 10 |
| William Bowyer, knight | 20 | Robert Millisent | 20 |
| Alex Hampden, knight | 28 | Henry Vernon | 20 |
| Marmaduke Darrell, knight, in lands | | Francis Brakyn | 10 |
| and in fee, household | 30 | Richard St. George | |
| John Croke, sr., knight | 30 | John Batisford | 20 |
| Francis Cheyney, knight | 20 | John Goldwell | 20 |
| Henry Drury, knight | 20 | Robert Castell | 12 |
| William Willoughby, knight | 25 | Michael Dalton | 20 |
| George Throckmorton, knight | 20 | Roger Thornton | 20 |

## CORNWALL

| | | |
|---|---|---|
| Reginald Mohun, knight, in lands | 50 | |
| John Parker, knight | | |
| William Killigrew, knight | Middx. | |
| Anthony Rous, knight | 30 | |
| William Wraye, knight | 30 | |
| Nicholas Halls, knight | 20 | |
| Nicholas Prideaux, knight | 30 | |
| Christopher Harris, knight | Devon | |
| William Hutchinson, S.T.D. | | |
| Richard Carew of Antony | 20 | |
| John Arundell of Trerise | | |
| Hannibal Vivian | 25 | |
| Thomas St. Aubyn | 20 | |
| Tristram Arscott | Devon | |
| John Hender | 20 | |
| Arthur Harris | Devon | |
| John Harris of Llandrest | 20 | |
| Derory Chamond | 20 | |
| Edward Cosworth | 20 | |
| Walter Kendall | 20 | |
| Richard Warre | | |
| Otwell Hill | 20 | |
| Richard Trefuses | 10 | |
| William Parker, S.T.B. | | |
| Philip Bevill | 20 | |
| Richard Penwaring | 20 | |
| Alex Arundell | 20 | |
| John Rashleigh | 20 | |
| Gilbert Michell | 8 | |
| William Roscaricke | 23 | |
| Richard Trevanion | 10 | |
| Thomas Kendall | 20 | |

## DERBYSHIRE

| | | |
|---|---|---|
| John Manners, knight, in lands | 50 | |
| Anthony Ashley, knight, household | 25 | |
| William Browne, knight | 40 | |
| Francis Luke, knight | 60 | |
| German Poole, knight | 13/6/8 | |
| John Stanhope, knight | 30 | |
| John Ferrers, knight | Warws. | |
| Thomas Greisley, knight | 30 | |
| Peter Fretchvill, knight | 30 | |
| John Harper, knight | 40 | |
| John Bentley, knight | 10 | |
| Philip Stanhope, knight | 13/6/8 | |
| Henry Leigh, knight | 12 | |
| Henry Sacheverell | 26 | |
| William Kniveton | 20 | |
| Francis Fitzherbert | 10 | |
| Richard Harper | 10 | |

| | |
|---|---|
| William Jessopp | 13/6/8 |
| Robert Bainebrigge | 10 |
| Francis Rodes | |
| John Parker | 10 |

## DEVON

| | | |
|---|---|---|
| Robert Chichester, knight, in lands | 40 | |
| Thomas Wise, knight | 23 | |
| Thomas Dennys, knight | 30 | |
| Ferdinand Gorges, knight | | |
| William Strode, knight | 30 | |
| George Carew of Cockington, knight | 40 | |
| Richard Champernowne, knight | 35 | |
| Thomas Ridgeway, knight | 40 | |
| William Killigrew, knight | Middx. | |
| Warwick Heale, knight | 20 | |
| Thomas Harris, knight, serjeant-at-law | | |
| Amias Bamfield, knight | 40 | |
| Thomas Browne, knight | 20 | |
| Richard Hawkins, knight | 20 | |
| Thomas Reynell, knight | 20 | |
| Thomas Drew, knight | 20 | |
| George Southcott, knight | 25 | |
| Henry Roll, sen., knight | 60 | |
| John Ackland, knight | 20 | |
| George Smyth, knight | 30 | |
| John Specott, knight | 28 | |
| William Poole, knight | 20 | |
| John Doddridge, knight, serjeant-at-law | Westminster | |
| Christopher Harris, knight | 20 | |
| Edward Seymour | 40 | |
| Charles Brooke | Somerset | |
| John Stukeley of Aston | 30 | |
| Richard Carew of Antony | Cornwall | |
| William Abbott | 27 | |
| Edmund Parker | 45 | |
| John Drake | 20 | |
| Hugh Ackland | 20 | |
| Anthony Monck | 22 | |
| Thomas Heale | 21 | |
| William Walrond | 20 | |
| William Crymes | 30 | |
| Arthur Harris | 36 | |
| Francis Glanville | 20 | |
| John Copleston | 40 | |
| Edmund Prideaux | 20 | |
| Robert Haydon | 20 | |
| William Carie | 20 | |
| John Norcotte | 20 | |

| | |
|---|---|
| Anthony Copleston | 20 |
| Richard Prideaux, junior | 20 |
| Thomas Huison | 20 |
| William Bastard | 20 |
| Nicholas Gilbert | 20 |
| Richard Waltham | 10 |
| Richard Reynell | 20 |
| Arthur Tremayne | 20 |
| Richard Warre | |
| Ambrose Bellott | 20 |
| John Arscott | 20 |
| George Sprint | 20 |
| Marcus Cottell | 20 |
| Nicholas Frye | 20 |
| Tristram Arscott | 20 |

### DORSET

| | |
|---|---|
| George Trenchard, knight, in lands | 40 |
| Ralph Horsey, knight | 60 |
| Robert Naper, knight | 25 |
| Anthony Ashley, knight, household | 50 |
| Arthur Gorges, knight | |
| Carew Raleigh, knight | |
| George Moreton, knight | 40 |
| John Rogers, knight | 40 |
| John Browne, knight | 40 |
| Thomas Freake, knight | 60 |
| Robert Miller, knight | 30 |
| John Jeffreys, knight | 15 |
| John Williams, knight | 30 |
| George Somers, knight | 12 |
| John Rivers, knight | 20 |
| John Strangways, knight | 30 |
| Francis James, master in chancery | |
| | Somerset |
| Charles Brooke | Somerset |
| James Hussey, LL.D. | |
| Edmund Uvedall | 15 |
| John Fitzjames | 20 |
| John Clavell | 20 |
| William Gibbs | 8 |
| Christopher Anketill | 10 |
| Thomas Jesopp, M.D. | 10 |
| Richard Symons | 12 |
| Richard Swayne | 10 |
| John Strode | 10 |
| Richard Collier | |
| John Luttrell | 20 |
| Thomas Uvedall | 12 |
| George Hull | 20 |
| Francis Ashley | 10 |
| Richard Warre | |

| | |
|---|---|
| Robert Coker | 15 |
| John Williams of Tinam | 20 |
| Robert Tiderkey | 10 |

### YORKSHIRE, EAST RIDING

| | |
|---|---|
| Edward Phelips, knight, king's serjeant-at-law [crossed out] | |
| William Eure, knight | |
| Thomas Posthumous Hoby, knight | N.R. |
| Thomas Metham, knight, in fee, household | 20 |
| Launcelot Alford, knight, in lands | 20 |
| William Alford of Muse, knight | |
| John Bennet, knight | 20 |
| Stephen Proctor, knight | W.R. |
| Charles Hales, knight, in lands and in fee, Coventry | 20 |
| Richard Williamson, knight | Lindsey |
| John Ferne, knight | 4 |
| Philip Constable, knight, in lands | 35 |
| Henry Griffith, knight | 25 |
| Hugh Bethell, knight | 20 |
| Francis Boynton, knight | 30 |
| William Bamburgh, knight | 25 |
| Christopher Hilliarde, knight | 30 |
| Arthur Dakins, knight | 20 |
| William Gee, knight | 20 |
| Richard Hutton, serjeant-at-law | W.R. |
| John Hotham | 20 |
| William Hilliarde | 20 |
| William Watkinson | 20 |
| Jonas Waterhouse, in goods | 6 |
| Henry Alured, in lands | 5 |
| Richard Hodgeson | 10 |
| Thomas Southaby | 20 |
| Roger Thorpe | 20 |
| John Payler, in goods | 4 |
| John Legard, in lands | 20 |
| Philip Moncton | 8 |
| William Hilliarde, knight [sic] | 6/13/4 |
| Roger Southaby | 10 |

### YORKSHIRE, WEST RIDING

| | |
|---|---|
| Edward Phelips, knight, king's serjeant-at-law [crossed out] | |
| Edward Talbott, esquire | |
| John Savile, knight, in lands | 45 |
| Thomas Fairfax of Denton, knight | 20 |
| Edward Yorke, knight | |
| John Savile of Howley, knight | 30 |

Francis Palmer, knight                26/13/4
Henry Slingsby, knight                      22
John Mallory, knight                        20
Robert Swift, knight                        25
Richard Gargrave, knight                    26
Mauger Vavasor, knight                      20
Henry Goodricke, knight                     20
Edward Stanhope, knight                     21
Richard Tempest, knight                     21
George Savile, junior, knight
William Slingsby, knight
Henry Savile, knight                        20
Robert Mounson, knight                      21
Stephen Tempest, knight                     21
John Bennet, knight                     Middx.
Stephen Proctor, knight                     20
Charles Hales, knight                    Warw.
John Ferne, knight                       E.R.
John Jackson, knight                        20
Thomas Blande, knight                       21
Richard Hutton, serjeant-at-law             20
William Wentworth                           35
Thomas Wentworth of Elmsall                 20
Robert Key of Woodsome                      20
William Rokeby                              20
Henry Farrer                                20
George Twisleton                            22
William Ramesden                            20
Mathew Wentworth                            20
Thomas Heaber                               20
John Talbott                                20
George Chaworth                             20
William Phelips
John Maliverer                              20
George Shellito                             20
John Estofte                                20
Lionel Rolleston                            20
Thomas Mountney                              7
John Payler                              E.R.
Charles Rickard                             20
Peter Watson, in goods                       7

### YORKSHIRE,
### NORTH RIDING

Identical with pp. 231–2 except:

Omitted:

Cuthbert Pepper, knight
Edward Yorke, knight
John Constable
Christopher Aske
Hugh Frankland
John Theaker

New J.P.s:

Henry Frankland, knight                     15
John Payler                              E.R.
Roger Thorpe                                20
Ralph Salvin                                10

### ISLE OF ELY

John Cutts, knight                      Cambs.
John Peyton, knight, governor of
    Guernsey, in lands                      15
John Peyton of Islam, knight                50
John Peyton of Dodington, junior,
    knight, in lands                        15
Miles Sandes, knight                        20
Simeon Steward, knight                      15
Richard Cope, knight                        10
John Claypoole, knight                      20
Thomas Steward, knight                      20
Thomas Hewar, knight                        20
John Jolles, knight                     London
Thomas Neville, dean of Canterbury
Humphrey Tyndall, dean of Ely
Robert Tinley, archdeacon of Ely
James Taylor, S.T.D.
John Day, LL. D.                            10
John Reppes                                 15
Francis Tyndall                             10
Francis Brakyn                          Cambs.
Henry Vernon
James Weston                                10
Daniel Goodricke                            10
Richard Arkenstall                        dead
William Stermyn                             12

### ESSEX

John Grey, knight, in lands                 20
Daniel Dunne, master of the court of
    requests                                20
Christopher Hatton, knight                  25
John Cutts, knight                      Cambs.
Thomas Lucas, knight                        40
John Sames, knight                          30
Henry Maynard, knight                       40
Thomas Edmondes, knight, house-
    hold                                    10
Henry Fanshawe, knight                   Herts.
Gamaliel Capell, knight                     20
William Smith, knight                       20
Ralph Wiseman, knight                     dead
William Ayloffe, knight                     20
John Deane, knight                          20

| | | | | |
|---|---|---|---|---|
| Robert Leigh, knight | 20 | | John Tanfield | 20 |
| Robert Wroth, knight | 20 | | Francis Ramme | 20 |
| Francis Bacon, knight, solicitor- | | | Thomas Perient | 7 |
| general | Middx. | | Anthony Ward | 20 |
| John Tyndall, knight, master in | | | | |
| chancery | 20 | | GLOUCESTER | |
| Richard Weston, knight | 20 | | | |
| Edward Seyliard, knight | 20 | | Edmund Carey, knight, in lands, | |
| Thomas Mildmay of Barnes, knight | 30 | | London | 50 |
| Edward Coke, knight | 20 | | Henry Bridges, esquire, in lands | 10 |
| Henry Maxey, knight | 20 | | Henry Poole, knight | 50 |
| Barnard Whitestones, knight | Sussex | | John Poyntz, knight | 20 |
| Thomas Gardiner, knight | 20 | | John Tracy, knight | 30 |
| Thomas Meade, knight | 25 | | Henry Winston, knight | 30 |
| Thomas Harris, knight | 20 | | John Hungerford, knight | 40 |
| Nicholas Coote, knight | 20 | | Edward Winter, knight | 40 |
| Richard Saltonstall, knight | 20 | | Edward Greville, knight | Warws. |
| Thomas Joslin, knight | 25 | | William Cooke, knight | 20 |
| Edward Butler, knight | 25 | | George Huntley, knight | 20 |
| James Bourchier, knight | 20 | | Henry Blomer, knight | 10 |
| Michael Hickes, knight | 20 | | Thomas Seymour, knight | 20 |
| Stephen Powle, knight | 20 | | John Chamblame, knight | 30 |
| Reginald Argall, knight | 20 | | Robert Woodroffe, knight | 20 |
| George Sayer, knight | 10 | | Henry Townshend, knight | Salop. |
| William Cutts, knight | 10 | | Giles Fettiplace, knight | 20 |
| Edward Grimston, master in chan- | | | Richard Atkins | 15 |
| cery, in lands | 20 | | Thomas Edwards, LL.D., master in | |
| Robert Barker, serjeant-at-law | 10 | | chancery | |
| William Tabor, S.T.D. | 20 | | Thomas Baynham | 40 |
| Edmund Pirton | 10 | | Richard Berkeley | 20 |
| Humphrey Mildmay | 20 | | Nicholas Boteler | 20 |
| John Boteler | 20 | | Paul Tracy | 30 |
| Geoffrey Nightingale | 12 | | Thomas Stephens, attorney of the | |
| William Tomse | 20 | | prince, London | 20 |
| William Higham | 20 | | William Dutton | 40 |
| Richard Francke | 20 | | Giles Reade | 30 |
| William Wiseman | 20 | | John Throckmorton | 20 |
| William Ayloffe of Little Chissell | 20 | | Joseph Baynham | 20 |
| Thomas Waldgrave | 14 | | William Norwood | 20 |
| Thomas Fanshawe | 20 | | Richard Codrington | 20 |
| Edward Waldgrave | 20 | | Richard Daston, in goods | 10 |
| Henry Gent | 20 | | William Guies, in lands | 17 |
| Thomas Wiseman | 20 | | Arnold Oldisforth, keeper of the | |
| Thomas Warren | 20 | | hanaper in chancery, in goods | 10 |
| Thomas Kighley | 15 | | Anthony Smyth, in lands | 20 |
| John Killingworth | 20 | | William Barnes | 20 |
| Charles Cliborne | 20 | | George Thorpe, household | 30 |
| Robert Rich | 12 | | Nicholas Overbury | 10 |
| John Darcy | 20 | | Richard Delabere | 6 |
| John Argall | 20 | | Henry Fleetwood | 12 |
| Edward Elrington | 20 | | George Huntley | 20 |
| John Hurleston | 20 | | Thomas Escourt | 20 |
| Francis Barnard | 20 | | Jasper Selwin | 8 |
| William Ayloffe, junior | 10 | | Giles Forster | 20 |

| | |
|---|---|
| William Kingston | 20 |
| William Bourcher | 20 |
| John Pleydall | |
| Thomas Hunckes | |
| Robert Bathurst | 20 |
| Richard George | 6 |

## HEREFORD

| | |
|---|---|
| Robert Harley, knight | |
| Thomas Coningsby, knight, in lands | 23 |
| John Scudamore, knight | |
| William Herbert, knight, in lands, London | 40 |
| Henry Poole, knight ⎱ | Glos. |
| John Poyntz, knight ⎰ | |
| James Scudamore, knight | 20 |
| Thomas Cornewall, knight | |
| Richard Hopton, knight | 10 |
| Henry Townshend, knight | Salop. |
| Eustace Whitney, knight | 20 |
| Richard Atkins, Glos. | 15 |
| Thomas Cornewall | Salop. |
| Richard Davies | 7 |
| James Bayly, LL.D., in goods | 8 |
| George Chute, household | 26 |
| William Rudhall, in lands | 20 |
| John Vaughan | 10 |
| Thomas Harley | 20 |
| Elias Walwin | 10 |
| William Saxey, in goods | 12 |
| James Baskerville, in lands | 10 |
| Humphrey Cornewall | 5 |
| John Curle | 10 |
| John Scudamore | 10 |
| Henry Vaughan | 10 |
| Richard Hyett | 6 |
| Roland Vaughan | 10 |
| James Tomkins | 20 |
| Paul Delahey | 10 |
| Thomas Jones | 6 |
| Thomas Coningsby | 6 |
| John Berrington | 10 |
| John Hoskins | |
| John Blunte | 8 |
| Nicholas Garnons | dead |
| William Dauncey | 20 |
| Robert Curle | 6 |
| Thomas Welford | 10 |
| Owen Hopton | 5 |

## HERTFORDSHIRE

| | |
|---|---|
| John Egerton, knight | |
| Edward Carey, knight, household | 66 |

| | |
|---|---|
| Thomas Challenor, knight | Bucks. |
| John Cutts, knight | Cambs. |
| Henry Cocke, knight, cofferor of the household, in lands, household | 50 |
| Arthur Capell, knight | 50 |
| Henry Carey, knight | |
| John Brockett, knight | 20 |
| Ralph Coningsby, knight | 40 |
| Roland Litton, knight | 25 |
| John Brograve, knight | 30 |
| Henry Butler, knight | 20 |
| Henry Maynard, knight | Essex |
| Richard Spencer, knight | 28 |
| John Leventhorpe, knight | 25 |
| Thomas Pope Blunte, knight | 20 |
| Henry Fanshawe, knight | 30 |
| John Ferrers, knight | 10 |
| John Luke, knight | 20 |
| William Fleetwood, knight | Bucks. |
| Thomas Harris, knight, serjeant-at-law | |
| Francis Bacon, knight, solicitor-general | Middx. |
| Leonard Hyde, knight | 20 |
| Robert Chester, knight | 20 |
| Thomas Dacres, knight | 25 |
| Robert Boteler, knight | 27 |
| Ralph Sadler | 50 |
| William Purvaye | 20 |
| Walter Tooke, auditor of court of wards | 20 |
| Andreas Grey | 15 |
| Thomas Dockwra | 20 |
| Edward Poulter | 20 |
| Thomas Hanchett | 20 |
| Ralph Ratcliffe | 20 |
| William Curle, auditor of court of wards | 20 |
| John Hare, clerk of foregoing court | 20 |
| Lucas Norton | 20 |
| John Shotbolt | 20 |
| Ralph Wilbraham | 10 |
| William Cocke | 20 |
| John Brockett | 8 |
| Nicholas Trott, in lands | 20 |
| Henry Frowicke, in goods | 6 |
| William Cade, in lands | 10 |
| Edward Cason | 20 |
| William Newte | 20 |
| Robert Bath | 10 |

## HUNTINGDONSHIRE

| | |
|---|---|
| Oliver Cromwell, knight | 50 |
| Robert Bevell, knight | 30 |

Robert Cotton, knight 30
John Bedell, knight 20
Anthony Forest, knight 20
Robert Payne, knight
Othonell Hill, LL.D., in goods 10
Robert Cromwell, in goods 4
Henry Cromwell, in lands 10
Francis Brakyn Cambs.
Paul Thompson, S.T.B.
Francis Browne, in lands 20
Edward Mary Wingfield 20
Christopher Hodson 20
Robert Castle 10
Thomas Hetley 10
Robert Andeley 10

### KENT

Identical with pp. 126–8 except:

Omitted:
John Smyth, knight

New J.P.s:
Samuel Lennard, knight 20
Thomas Twysden 10
William Mann

### LEICESTERSHIRE

Walter Hastings, esquire, in lands 20
John Grey, knight Essex
Thomas Compton, knight 20
Henry Harington, knight
William Skipwith, knight 20
Henry Hastings, knight 20
Thomas Cave, knight 20
William Turpyn, knight 20
Basil Brooke, knight 10
Thomas Beaumont, knight 20
Thomas Humphrey, knight 20
Thomas Beaumont, junior, knight 10
William Smyth, knight 20
Wolstan Dixey, knight 20
Thomas Heselrigge, knight 20
Samuel Flemming, S.T.D.
John Chippendale, LL.D. 10
William Cave 10
Henry Cave 10
Mathew Saunders 10
Edward Turvill 14
William Nowell 20
Henry Smyth 10

Thomas Grey 10
Bartholomew Laxton 4

### LINCOLN, KESTEVEN

Edward Fynes, esquire
George St. Poole, knight ⎫
William Wraye, knight ⎬ Lindsey
Thomas Mounson, knight, house-
hold 30
Thomas Grantham, knight Lindsey
William Armyn, knight, in lands 25
Edward Bushey, knight 22
Edward Carre, knight 25
Peter Eure, knight 20
John Meres, knight 20
Charles Dymocke, knight 20
John Hatcher, knight 20
Charles Hussey, knight 22
Thomas Lambart, knight Holland
William Rigden, knight 20
Laurence Staunton, dean of Lincoln 10
Alex Thorold 15
Edward King 15
Henry Hall 20
Thomas Harington
Daniel Harley 15
Anthony Thorold 15
Thomas Butler, in goods 4

### LINCOLN, LINDSEY

Edward Fynes, esquire
Richard Amcotts, knight, in lands 15
George St. Poole, knight 50
William Mounson, knight London
William Wraye, knight, in lands 50
Thomas Mounson, knight, household
John Savile, knight W.R.
William Petham, knight 20
Philip Tyrwhitt, knight 30
Roger Dalison, knight, household 32
Thomas Grantham, knight 30
Edward Ayscough, knight 20
Edward Tyrwhitt, knight 20
Nicholas Saunderson, knight 30
John Thorold, knight 20
William Hickman, knight 20
Gervase Helwis, knight 20
Vincent Skinner, knight Middx.
Peter Eure, knight 20
John Langton, knight 20
John Read, knight Holland
Thomas Darnell, knight 20

Adrian Scroope, knight
Roger Halton, knight                20
Thomas Dalison, knight              10
Thomas Darrell, knight              20
Richard Skipwith, knight            20
Francis South, knight               20
John Aylmer, knight                 20
Richard Williamson, knight          20
John Ferne, knight                E.R.
Charles Dymocke, knight      Kesteven
Miles Sandes, knight           Cambs.
John Guevara, knight             dead
George Fitzwilliam, knight, in lands 20
John Bowyer, knight                  8
Laurence Staunton, dean of Lincoln
                               Kesteven
Andreas Gedney                      20
Thomas Hatcliffe                    10
William Heneage                     35
Nicholas Girlington                 15
William Ayscough                    10
Robert Tyrwhitt                     20
Thomas Massingbord                  20
John Jon[es ?]                      20
Edward Skipwith                     15
John Newcomen                       20
Richard Totheby                      5
Henry Skinner                       10
Thomas Bard                         20
Robert Bryan                        20
George Ashton                       10


LINCOLN, HOLLAND

William Welby, knight, in lands     28
Edward Heron, knight                20
George St. Poole, knight       Lindsey
William Mounson, knight
Thomas Mounson, knight, house-
  hold
William Carre, knight               35
Richard Ogle, knight                25
John Langton, knight           Lindsey
John Meres, knight        ⎱
Charles Dymocke, knight   ⎰  Kesteven
Thomas Lambart, knight              22
John Read, knight                   20
William Rigden, knight              20
Mathew Gamlin, knight               25
Anthony Jebie                        8
Thomas Ogle                         10
Leonard Bawtree                      8
Henry Skinner                  Lindsey

## MIDDLESEX

Roger Aston, knight, master of
  wardrobe, household
Edward Carey, knight, master of the
  jewels, household
Thomas Challenor, knight      Bucks.
Edmund Carey, knight, London     50
Thomas Vavasor, knight, marshall of
  household, in lands             40
Jerome Bowes, knight, in goods   15
William Waade, knight, *locum tenens*,
  Tower of London, in fee, house-
  hold                            25
Edward Phelips, knight, serjeant-at-
  law                        Somerset
Drew Drury, knight, in fee, house-
  hold                            30
Edmund Tilney, master of revels, in
  fee, household                  20
Edward Hoby, knight               Kent
William Cornwallis, knight, in lands 30
Francis Darcy, knight             20
Anthony Ashley, knight, household
George Carey, knight, in lands    40
Robert Brett, knight              24
Ludovic Lewkener, knight, London  30
Walter Cope, knight               20
Richard Wigmore, knight           20
Ralph Coningsby, knight        Herts.
William Killigrew, knight         20
Vincent Skinner, knight           20
William Bowyer, knight            20
William Fleetwood, knight         20
Richard Baker, knight             25
Robert Leigh, knight            Essex
Thomas Fowler, knight             20
Thomas Smyth, knight, clerk of
  parliament                      20
Thomas Lake, knight, in goods     20
Henry Hobart, knight, attorney-
  general                      London
William Fleetwood, knight      Bucks.
Robert Wroth, knight            Essex
Henry Baker, knight, in lands     20
John Leake, knight                20
Francis Bacon, knight, solicitor-
  general                         20
Henry Montagu, knight, recorder
  of London                        5
George Carew, knight, master in
  chancery
Thomas Crompton, knight, judge of
  admiralty, in lands             20

George Coppin, knight, clerk of
  the crown, in goods 20
John Bennet, knight, in lands 20
Robert Ashley, knight 20
Gideon Ansham, knight 20
John Brett, knight 20
Robert Bannastre, knight, household 20
John Doddridge, knight, serjeant-at-
  law, in goods 10
Owen Wood, dean of Armagh
Henry Thoresby, master in chancery,
  in lands 20
Richard Brownelowe, chief proto-
  notary of the bench, in lands 20
John Hare, clerk of the court of
  wards and liveries Herts.
John Keys, in lands 20
John Barnes 20
William Gerard 20
Nicholas Collin 10
Tobias Wood 20
James Walrond 20
Valentine Saunders 20
Chidiac Wardour, in goods 20
John Machell
Edward Vaughan, in lands 20
Richard Sutton 20
Richard Blunte 20
Francis Roberts 20
William Harrison, in goods 6
Edward Forcett, in lands 20
Henry Spiller, in lands 20
Francis Mingane
Nicholas Kemp, in lands 20
Ralph Hatry 20
Christopher Merrick 20
Henry Farmer

Henry Morgan, in lands 10
William Morgan of Newport 10
William Rawlins 10
Edward Kemys 10
Valentine Pritchard 10
Roland Williams 10
William Jones 4
Maurice Griffin 10
William Price, in lands 10
Roger Bathern, in lands 5
Andreas Powell 10
Charles Jones 10
Hugh Jones 10

## NORTHAMPTONSHIRE

Identical with pp. 170–1 except:

  Omitted:

Euseby Andrews, knight
Tobias Chauncey, knight
Thomas Mulsho

  New J.P.s:

William Chauncey, knight 20
Augustine Nicolls, knight, serjeant-
  at-law 6
Erasmus Dryden 20
Gilbert Pickering 12

## NORFOLK

Identical with pp. 150–2 except:

  New J.P.s:

John Heveningham, knight 10
Richard Stubbe 15
William Gibbons 14

## MONMOUTH

Thomas Somerset, knight
Edmund Morgan, knight, in lands 10
Walter Montagu, knight Northants.
Henry Billingsley, knight, in lands,
                                    Glos. 20
Roland Morgan, knight
Henry Townshend, knight Salop.
William Powell, knight, in lands 40
Charles Somerset 10
William Herbert 10
Robert Hopton 10
John Gamsford 10
Richard Kemys 10

## NOTTINGHAMSHIRE

Charles Candishe [Cavendish ?],
  knight, in lands 40
John Hollis, knight 40
Francis Leake, knight Derbys.
Henry Pierpoint, knight 45
John Biron, knight 40
John Stanhope, knight Derbys.
Roger Ayscough, knight 20
William Sutton, knight 20
Brian Lascells, knight 20
John Thornehaugh, jun. knight 20
John Thorold, knight 10
George Lascells, knight 5

George Gillie, knight 20
George Chaworth, knight 20
William Willoughby, knight 25
Philip Stanhope, knight, Derbys. 20/4
John Thornhaugh, in lands 20
William Cooper, in lands 20
Edward North 20
Robert Pierpoint 20
Fulke Cartwright 10
Humphrey Pipe 20
John Harker 20
Thomas Simcocks 20
Hardulph Wastnes, in lands 20
Gervase Markham, in lands 20
Lancelot Rowlston

### OXFORDSHIRE

Henry Lee, knight Bucks.
Francis Eure, knight, in lands 8
Francis Fortescue, knight Bucks.
Michael Blunte, knight 25
William Spencer, knight 30
Anthony Cope, knight 30
Michael Mollins, knight Berks.
James Harington, knight Rutland
Richard Mompesson, knight Bucks.
William Greene, knight, in lands 20
Michael Dormer, knight 20
William Paddy, knight, in fee,
London 20
Edmund Fettiplace, knight Berks.
George Tipping, knight, in lands 25
Roland Lacy, knight, in lands 25
Vice-chancellor of Oxford University for the time being
George Abbot, S.T.D.
Anthony Blincoe, LL.D.
John Doyley, in lands 15
George Brome 20
Walter Colepeper, in lands 15
John Throckmorton 20
John Wellisborne 20
William Frere 20
Thomas Chamblame 10
Henry Samborne Wilts.
Edmund Taverner 8
Richard Light, in lands 20
George Rives, S.T.D.

### RUTLAND

James Harington, knight, in lands 25
William Bulstrode, knight 10

Guy Palmes, knight 10
William Boddenden, knight 10
Basil Fielding, Warws. 10
John Wingfield 10
Thomas Mackworth 16
Anthony Dyatt 5
Tobias Houghton 6
Richard Cony, in lands 10

### SHROPSHIRE

John Egerton, knight, junior 40
William Herbert, knight, in lands
London
Henry Poole, knight Glos.
Henry Bromley, knight Worcs.
Robert Needham, knight, in lands 20
George Manwaring, knight 20
Robert Vernon, knight 8
Francis Layton, knight
Henry Wallopp, knight Southants.
Francis Newport, knight, in lands 20
Edward Fox, knight 20
Roger Owen, knight 15
Walter Chetwind, knight Staffs.
Henry Townshend, knight, in lands 10
Richard Hussey, knight 8
Robert Parslowe, knight 8
Vincent Corbett, knight 10
Thomas Harris, serjeant-at-law 5
Richard Atkins Glos.
Thomas Cornewall 20
Richard Barker 4
Andreas Charleton 10
Humphrey Lee 10
John Marker 6
Francis Wolrich 8
Thomas Oteley 3
Richard Mitton, in lands 4
Edward Bromley 5
Francis Newton 6
Thomas Corbett 6
Peter Corbett 5
Edward Lutwich 4
Thomas Powell, in goods 5
Thomas Edwards, in lands 4
Hugh Lloyd 1/10
James Skeffington, in goods, Coventry 14
Humphrey Briggs, in lands 10
Charles Fox, knight [sic] 8
Roger Kynaston, in lands 6
Bonham Norton 4

| | | | |
|---|---|---|---|
| Thomas Horde | 5 | John Harmer, S.T.D., in goods | 3 |
| Edward Littleton | 2 | Nicholas Steward, LL.D., in lands | 20 |
| Edward Lloyd, in lands | 5 | Thomas Ridley, LL.D. | 15 |
| Stephen Smalman | | William St. John, in lands | 20 |
| | | Edward Savage | 10 |
| | | Edward Richards | 16 |

## SOMERSET

Identical with pp. 193–4 except:

Omitted:

Arthur Hopton, knight
John Carew, knight
John Colles

New J.P.:

| | |
|---|---|
| Barnaby Sambourne | 20 |

## SOUTHAMPTON

| | |
|---|---|
| Francis Vere, knight, in lands | 50 |
| Thomas Gorges, knight, household | |
| Thomas West, knight, in lands | 20 |
| Thomas Dennys, knight | Devon |
| Walter Sandes, knight | 25 |
| John Seymour, knight | 30 |
| Walter Longe, knight | Wilts. |
| Michael Mollins, knight | Berks. |
| Oliver Lambart, knight | |
| Thomas Smyth, knight, in fee, household | 20 |
| Henry Wallopp, knight | 50 |
| Giles Wroughton, knight | Wilts. |
| Edward Moore, knight, in lands | 40 |
| Robert Oxenbridge, knight | 25 |
| William Kingsmill, knight | 10 |
| Francis Palmes, knight | 25 |
| Benjamin Titchborne, knight | 25 |
| Hampden Paulet, knight | |
| Richard Norton, knight | 25 |
| William Uvedall, knight | 25 |
| Richard Mills, knight | 25 |
| Richard White, knight | 30 |
| William Killigrew, knight | Middx. |
| William Sandes, knight | |
| Richard Titchborne, knight | 20 |
| Mathew Carew, knight | 20 |
| Thomas Clarke, knight | 20 |
| William Abarrowe, knight | 20 |
| William Dodington, knight | 40 |
| John Leigh, knight | 16 |
| Henry Whitehead, knight | 20 |
| Thomas Cornwallis, knight | |
| William Oglander, knight | 20 |
| Ambrose Button, knight | 10 |

| | |
|---|---|
| William Wallopp | 20 |
| Francis Cotton, in lands | 10 |
| Adrian Stoughton | Sussex |
| John Moore | 10 |
| William Brock | 10 |
| Thomas Creeke | |
| Richard Warre | |
| John Warner | 20 |
| Arthur Wilmot | 20 |
| Thomas Kirkby, in lands | 20 |
| Thomas Brooke | 20 |
| Andreas Read | 8 |

## STAFFORDSHIRE

| | |
|---|---|
| Walter Aston, knight, in lands | 30 |
| John Bowes, knight | 20 |
| Edward Littleton, knight | 20 |
| John Egerton, knight | 26/13/4 |
| Thomas Crompton, knight, Middx. | 20 |
| Simon Weston, knight | 5 |
| John Leigh, knight, in fee, household | |
| | 33 |
| Henry Griffith, knight | E. R. |
| Edward Littleton, knight | 20 |
| Edward Leigh, knight | 20 |
| Gilbert Wakering, knight | 20 |
| Walter Chetwind, knight | 20 |
| William Chetwind, knight | 20 |
| William Whorewood, knight | 20 |
| Henry Townshend, knight, justice of Chester | Salop. |
| William Tooker, dean of Litchfield | |
| Ralph Sneade | 20 |
| George Greisley | 3 |
| Robert Meverall | 20 |
| Francis Trentham | 20 |
| Walter Bagot | 20 |
| William Skeffington | 20 |
| Walter Wrottesley | 20 |
| Anthony Kinnersley | 10 |
| Roger Fowke | 3 |
| Robert Aston | 3 |
| Humphrey Wirley | 10 |
| Thomas Rudyard | 10 |
| Thomas Crompton | 10 |
| Arthur Radcliffe | |

## SUFFOLK

| | |
|---|---|
| Robert Carey, knight, in fee, household | 32 |
| Henry Gawdy, knight | Norfolk |
| Anthony Felton, knight, in lands | 30 |
| William Walgrave, knight | 50 |
| Arthur Heveningham, knight | Norfolk |
| Robert Jermyn, knight | 60 |
| Thomas Barnardston, knight | 30 |
| Nicholas Bacon, knight | 100 |
| John Higham, knight | 20 |
| Robert Drury, knight | 20 |
| Henry Glenham, knight | 50 |
| Robert Gardiner, knight | 25 |
| John Cotton, knight | Cambs. |
| Edward Withipoole, knight | 30 |
| William Pooly, knight | 20 |
| Michael Stanhope, knight | 50 |
| Francis Baildon, knight | 10 |
| Henry Warner, knight | 20 |
| Calthrop Parker, knight | 20 |
| Thomas Eden, knight | 25 |
| John Gilbert, knight | 20 |
| George Waldegrave, knight | 20 |
| Harbottle Grimston, knight, in goods | 5 |
| Robert Hitcham, knight, in lands | 20 |
| James Bacon, knight, Middx. | 20 |
| Thomas Wingfield, knight | 30 |
| Robert Crane, knight | 20 |
| Thomas Plaiters, knight | 20 |
| Martin Stuteville, knight | 20 |
| Robert Barker, serjeant-at-law | 10 |
| Robert Ashfield | 20 |
| Francis Jermy | 35 |
| John Gurden | 25 |
| Mathew Cratcherwood | 7 |
| Nicholas Garnish | 20 |
| Lionel Tollemache | 40 |
| Edward Bacon | 28 |
| John Rivett, in lands | 15 |
| John Laney, in goods | 8 |
| Thomas Crofts, in lands | 20 |
| Edmund Pooly | 20 |
| Thomas Jermyn | 12 |
| John Blennerhassett | 20 |
| Edward Honing | 20 |
| Edward Buckenham | 20 |
| Samuel Blennerhassett | 20 |
| Thomas Kemp | 15 |
| William Clapton | 10 |
| Thomas Tilney | 15 |
| Robert Gosnold | 20 |

| | |
|---|---|
| Robert Rolfe | 12 |
| James Smyth | 8 |
| Anthony Pening | 20 |
| William Barroughe | 20 |
| Humphrey Wingfield | 15 |
| George Lehunt | 20 |
| Thomas Wolrich | 20 |
| Thomas Walton | 6 |

## SURREY

| | |
|---|---|
| Charles Howard, knight | Sussex |
| Thomas Challenor, knight | Bucks. |
| Thomas Gorges, knight, household | |
| Francis Leigh, knight | 20 |
| Thomas Vavasor, knight | Middx. |
| George Moore, knight, in lands | 50 |
| Edward Tilney, master of the revels, household | |
| Francis Carew, knight | 50 |
| John Egerton, knight, Staffs. | 20 |
| Oliver St. John | |
| Oliver Leigh, knight | 20 |
| Thomas Vincent, knight | 20 |
| Edward Howard, knight | 30 |
| Francis Wolley, knight | 30 |
| William Fleetwood, knight | Bucks. & Middx. |
| Edmund Bowyer, knight | 20 |
| Nicholas Saunders | 20 |
| William Gardiner, knight | 20 |
| John Trevor, knight, in goods | 10 |
| Nicholas Throckmorton, knight, in lands | 20 |
| Robert Moore, knight | 20 |
| Francis Vincent, knight | 20 |
| Thomas Gardiner, knight | 20 |
| Thomas Crymes, knight | 20 |
| Francis Stidolfe, knight | 20 |
| Christopher Parkins, knight | |
| Henry Montagu, knight, recorder at London, | Northants. |
| Richard Cooper, knight | 20 |
| John Hill, knight, household | 26 |
| Nicholas Lusher, knight | 20 |
| Thomas Hunt, knight | 20 |
| William Mynn, knight, household | 40 |
| William Gresham, knight | 20 |
| Thomas Gresham, knight | 20 |
| John Parker, knight | |
| Thomas Muschampe, knight | 20 |
| Robert Wright, knight | 20 |
| Thomas Hoskins, knight | 20 |

| | | | | |
|---|---|---|---|---|
| George Rivers, knight | Kent | John Shirley, serjeant-at-law | 15 |
| George Paule, knight | 20 | William Thorne, dean of Chichester | |
| Thomas Blague, dean of Rochester | | Francis Cox, S.T.D. | |
| Thomas Ridley, LL.D. | | Thomas Pelham | 50 |
| John Hamond, M.D. | 20 | John Drury, LL.D. | |
| Richard Goddard | | John Colepeper | 12 |
| Laurence Stoughton | 20 | Henry Shelley | 20 |
| John Evelyn | 20 | Herbert Morley | 20 |
| Francis Angier | 20 | Anthony Shirley | 12 |
| John Denham | 20 | John Sackville | 6 |
| Francis Drake, household | 26 | Adrian Stoughton | 20 |
| Francis Clarke | | John Clarke | 6 |
| John Hawarde | 20 | George Blincoe | 20 |
| Nicholas Kemp | Middx. | Thomas Churcher | 10 |
| John Warner, in lands | 5 | Alexander Shepherd | 8 |
| John Harris | 10 | Nicholas Jordan | 10 |
| Richard Elliott | 20 | Richard Amherst | 4 |
| Anthony Benn | 10 | John Middleton | 8 |
| William Haynes | 20 | Robert Casey | |
| Laurence Elliott | 20 | Anthony Apsley | 7 |
| Bostock Fuller | 20 | Bradshaw Drew | 10 |
| William Wignell | 13 | | |

## SUSSEX

## WARWICKSHIRE

| | | | |
|---|---|---|---|
| Charles Howard, knight, in lands | 20 | Edward Devereux, esquire, in lands | 20 |
| Francis Neville, esquire | 20 | Thomas Leigh, knight | 40 |
| Thomas Leeds, knight | 25 | Edward Littleton, knight | Staffs. |
| Richard Lewknor, knight, justice of Chester | | Edward Greville, knight | 66/13/4* |
| Walter Covert, knight | 40 | Robert Digby, knight | 20 |
| Nicholas Parker, knight | 30 | William Goodyer, knight | 20 |
| Thomas Waller, knight | | Henry Goodyer, knight | |
| George Moore, knight | Surrey | Thomas Holt, knight | 20 |
| Thomas Bishop, knight | 30 | John Ferrers, knight | 20 |
| Edward Carrell, knight | 30 | William Fielding, knight | 30 |
| Henry Goring, knight | 40 | Richard Verney, knight | 26/13/4 |
| Thomas Carrell, knight | 20 | Thomas Lucy, knight | 20 |
| John Shirley, knight | 20 | Thomas Beaufoe, knight | 26/13/4 |
| Thomas Eversfield, knight | 25 | William Somerville | 20 |
| Edward Burton, knight | 6 | John Newdigate, knight | 20 |
| Edward Bellingham, knight | 10 | Clemens Throckmorton, knight | 20 |
| Thomas Palmer, knight | 10 | Clemens Fisher, knight | 20 |
| Barnard Whitestones, knight | 16 | Henry Dymocke, knight | 20 |
| Edward Colepeper, knight | 30 | Thomas Spencer | 26/13/4 |
| John Morley, knight | 25 | Basil Fielding | 30 |
| John Ashburnham, knight | | William Combe | 26/13/4 |
| William Browne, knight | Surrey | Bartholomew Hales | 20 |
| George Gunter, knight | 25 | Robert Burgin | 20 |
| George Rivers, knight | Kent | Edward Boughton | 20 |
| William Oglander, knight | 20 | John Hickford | 20 |
| | | Thomas Wright | 20 |

\* In the manuscript this assessment is stated as C marks.

### WORCESTERSHIRE

Identical with p. 213 except:

New J.P.:

| | |
|---|---|
| Henry Bromley, knight | 40 |

### WILTSHIRE

| | |
|---|---|
| Edmund Carey, knight, London | 50 |
| Anthony Mildmay, knight, Northants. | |
| James Marvin, knight, in lands | 45 |
| Thomas Gorges, knight, household | |
| Walter Long, knight | 40 |
| William Eure, knight | 30 |
| John Hungerford, knight, Glos. | 40 |
| Anthony Ashley, knight, household | |
| Francis Popham, knight | 30 |
| Giles Wroughton, knight | 30 |
| Henry Bainton, knight | 35 |
| Carew Raleigh, knight | |
| Walter Vaughan, knight | 50 |
| Richard Coningsby, knight, household | 20 |
| Edward Penruddock, knight | 25 |
| John Dauncey, knight | 25 |
| John Earnely, knight | 20 |
| Jasper Moore, knight | 30 |
| Thomas Snell, knight | 20 |
| James Ley, knight | |
| Alexander Tutt, knight | 20 |
| George Ivie, knight | 20 |
| Edward Escourt, knight | 25 |
| Anthony Hungerford, knight | 20 |
| Owen Wood | |
| William Tooker | |
| William Wilkinson, in goods | 5 |
| Henry Sadler, in lands | 20 |
| John Warneford | 20 |
| John Hungerford | 20 |
| John Ayloff | 20 |
| Henry Martin | 20 |
| Edmund Long | 20 |
| Edmund Lambart | 20 |
| William Bailiffe | 20 |
| Laurence Hyde | 8 |
| Edward Read, in goods | 4 |
| Giles Tooker | 8 |
| William Blacker, in lands | 10 |
| John Hall, in lands | 20 |
| William Chaffin | 10 |

The meaning of this document, originally in the files of the man who had responsibility for appointments to the commissions of the peace, is not immediately apparent. Since the compilation required significant labour, there must have been some serious purpose, one which becomes clearer in the light of comparable evidence. The notes in Cecil's hand beside the Yorkshire rosters in the *liber pacis* of 1559 seem to be his estimates of actual incomes. They varied between £400 and 40 marks. Even the latter, moreover, was well above the statutory minimum of £20 for a J.P., which as Lambarde indicated had been rendered obsolete by the inflation of money.[1] Cecil, however, must have been concerned with the financial means of those justices, and a number of the least affluent disappeared from the commission by 1562. Likewise men who were forced to sell their estates or were outlawed for debt ceased to be justices, although they might remain Deputy Lieutenants.[2] Justices were expected to be men of significant means.

In 1596 a list was compiled of J.P.s whose assessments for the subsidy were below £20. Its purpose seems to have been fiscal since at its

[1] Cf. *supra*, p. 48.

[2] e.g., William, fifth Lord Eure (*supra*, p. 237), Edmund Colles of Pershore, Worcestershire (*supra*, p. 212), Sir Nicholas Halswell of Somerset (*supra*, p. 108), Thomas Wattes of Northamptonshire (*supra*, p. 169).

end was the number—188—of justices whose assessments were below standard and the sum of their deficiencies. The identity of some of the men and the levels of assessment add meaning to the document. Among eleven in Kent were Sir Thomas Wilford (£17), Anthony St. Leger (£10), the very prosperous lawyer, John (later Sir John) Boys (£15), and William Redman, archdeacon of Canterbury (£6). The North Riding had fourteen, including Sir William Bowes (£15), John Constable (£8), Robert Rokeby (£8), and Cuthbert Pepper (£5), who later became an attorney for the Court of Wards and a member of the Council of the North. In Worcestershire there were an even dozen, among them Francis Walshe, Thomas Foliot, and John Washburne, all assigned the sum of £12. 6s. 8d. Northamptonshire had nine, Norfolk six, and Somerset only five. They included from Northamptonshire John Wake (£10), from Norfolk Christopher Yelverton (£5), and from Somerset the eminent lawyers George Snigge and Edward Phelips, both set down at £15. These men were major figures in county or legal circles. Their deficiency can have been only technical. None the less here is a tangible sign of the official concern with the financial affairs of justices of the peace.[1]

Yet many of the men whose assessments were below £20 in 1596 remained in the commissions, although some were assessed at a higher figure in 1609, sometimes still below £20. In 1621, moreover, a Privy Council letter which dealt with the subsidy of that year contained a threat: '. . . as wee presume that there is no man admitted to the office of justices of the peace . . . but such as shalbe found to have in land XX *li.* per annum, as by statute is provided, soe it is expected that none of them be assessed under that rate at the least uppon danger of the disgrace to be put out of the commission . . .'.[2] This language hardly suggests ruthless discipline, and it is unlikely that after 1621 there were no J.P.s assessed at less than £20.

The variation between the counties seems to indicate not only important differences in wealth and the accident of the holdings of the men who happened to be members of the commissions, but also the process by which assessments were made. The average assessments of J.P.s ranged, county by county, from several which were less than £16—Herefordshire £14. 3s., Lindsey £15. 9s., Shropshire £9. 2s.— to Buckinghamshire at £27. 4s. The figures for the counties herein considered were: Somerset £23. 5s., Northamptonshire £20. 6s., Kent £19. 9s., Norfolk £17. 4s., North Riding £16. 8s., Worcestershire £15. 5s.[3] There was great variation in the assessments from the £100 of

[1] Harleian MS. 6822, ff. 291–5.
[2] *A.P.C.*, Jas. 1, *1621–3*, p. 24.
[3] These are my own calculations from the data in EL (lesmere MS.) 2513.

Sir Nicholas Bacon to the £3 of a few J.P.s. There must none the less have been some not wholly capricious relationship between the worth of the property and the income which it produced. In addition to other interests the Ellesmere memorandum is one clue to the vexed problem of the wealth of the gentry.

# A NOTE ON THE WEALTH OF
# THE GENTRY

WILLS are the readiest source of knowledge about the estates of most J.P.s. If they are almost universally concerned with the disposition of property, those of the Tudor and Stuart periods hardly ever provide unambiguous evidence about the values of either the land holdings or the total wealth of the decedent. None the less, their wills provide eloquent testimony that J.P.s were men of much wealth.

One element in many wills—one usually stated in pounds and shillings, which had great enough weight so that it affords real evidence of the value of the total estate—was the legacies, marriage portions, or dowries left to unmarried daughters. If custom, the competition of the market place, or other social pressures may often have played an important part in the decisions which fathers made in behalf of their daughters, they could not make such bequests beyond the total of their assets, nor did this generosity—other clauses in many wills are manifest reflections of genuine affection—usually impoverish the eldest son, whatever the lot of younger brothers.[1] Thus many wills indicate the fortunes of the gentry in monetary terms.

During the completion of this study more than 400 wills have been examined. Although use has been made of texts printed in biographical and other studies and in collections such as Brown's *Somersetshire Wills*, most have been found in the registers in Somerset House. Many other wills are available, but it became apparent that the added information did not repay the hours spent in the search. Care was taken, however, to ensure that each period of twenty years and each of the five selected counties in the province of Canterbury is well represented. Occasionally particular wills were sought out; in some cases the successive heads of families were chosen; in other instances a will was searched in the hope of solving such a problem as the identity of a J.P.; the wills of all the men named in Lambarde's *Ephemeris* were examined. Otherwise the selection was random.

Ninety-seven wills included major bequests to daughters in terms of money. In a few cases there were annuities which have been capitalized at the twenty years' purchase rate which was a common basis for the sale of land. There follow the number and the average totals of such legacies arranged by periods and counties.

[1] Cf. Stone, *Crisis of the Aristocracy*, pp. 637–45; Finch, *Wealth, passim.*

| | 1558–79 | | 1580–99 | | 1600–19 | | 1620–40 | | |
|---|---|---|---|---|---|---|---|---|---|
| Kent | 4 | £1,214 | 7 | £1,538 | 3 | £1,733 | 5 | £3,380 | |
| Norfolk | 8 | 854·2 | 3 | 2,400 | 6 | 2,223 | 4 | 2,250 | |
| Northants. | 5 | 743·2 | 8 | 2,213·5 | 2 | 2,000 | 8 | 2,127·5 | |
| Somerset | 4 | 372·5 | 5 | 1,027·6 | 5 | 1,940 | 6 | 2,238·7 | |
| Worcs. | 5 | 508 | 3 | 1,100 | 3 | 3,100 | 3 | 2,766·7 | |
| Total | 26 | | 26 | | 19 | | 26 | | 97 | (total) |
| Average | | £748 | | £1,696 | | £1,777 | | £2,486·6 | | £1,668·6 (aver.) |

The most striking feature of these statistics is the continuing rise in the total amounts of money bequeathed to daughters. This judgement emerges even through data as thin as the two Northamptonshire wills of the period 1600 to 1619. The rise from £748 to £2,486. 6s. is suggestive both of the progress of inflation and of the wealth of the gentry.

# GENERAL INDEX

Admiralty, Court of, 98.
Ale-houses, 9–13.
American Revolution, 122.
*Archainomia*, 2.
Arches, Dean of the, 24, 175.
Armada, 14, 100.
Assizes, 11, 23, 59, 103.
  Justices of, 15, 22, 40, 47, 60, 61, 84.
  Northamptonshire, in 1627, 76–7.
Attorney-General, 84, 137, 149.
Augmentations, Court of, 18, 34, 45, 166, 225.
Aylesford, Lathe of, 9, 12, 21, 26.

Baronets, 53, 55 ff., 79.
Barristers, *see* lawyers.
Bedfordshire, J.P.s in, 102.
Benevolence, 74.
Birling, 17.
Bishops, 15, 53 f., 64.
  reports by, on J.P.s, 71–2, 81, 226.
Bridgwater, 103, 108.
Bristol, 6, 192.

Cambridge, 58, Chapter VI *passim*.
  Clare College, 171.
  Corpus Christi College, 25.
Canon Law, 130.
Canterbury, 6, 24, 33, 44, 103 ff.
Catholics, *see* recusants.
Chancery, Court of, 24, 100, 129.
  Clerk of, 129, 189, 236.
  Master in, 2, 19, 31, 134, 147, 171, 189, 194, 214, 218, 229.
  Registrar of, 24, 161.
Chastleton, 35, 43.
Chatham, 6, 24.
Chester, Chief Justice of, 84, 94, 208.
Cinque Ports, 6.
  Chancery Court of the, 33.
Civil Law, 17, 18, 51, 130, 216, 226, 232.
Civil Wars, 121 f.
Clergy, 31, 46.
  in the Commission of the Peace, 49, 51, 57.
  non-conforming, 73.
Cobham (Kent), 17, 18.

Cobham Plot, 119, 129.
Commerce, *see* Merchants.
Commissions, special, 34, 41, 61, 77, 79, 96, 100 ff., 149.
  on chantries, 34.
  for musters, 9.
  for sewers, 9, 14.
Common Pleas, Judges of the, 98, 137, 149, 152, 166, 188, 232.
  Protonotary of the, 130.
Constables, 11, 79.
Courtiers, 19, 28, 31, 49, 51, 147.
Courts, central, 96.
Crime, 9–13, 66.
  bastardy, 12, 13.
  murder, 12.
  robbery, 9.
Criminal jurisdiction, 1, 103.
*Custos Rotulorum*, 3, 24, 34, 37–9, 41, 43, 75, 107, 178, 209, 211, 214, 225, 235, 237.
  deputy *Custos*, 37, 43.

Deptford, 6, 24.
Deputy Lieutenant, 19, 32, 73, 81, 130, 176.
Devon, 62, 74.
Dignitaries, 15, 31, 46, 48 f.
Diplomacy (diplomats), 17, 24, 38, 84, 134, 152, 191, 208, 229.
Doctors Commons, 209.
Durham, Palatine County of, 51, 64.

East India Company, 130.
Education, Chapter VI *passim*.
*Eirenarcha*, 1, 2, 8, 21, 102, 103.
Ely, Isle of, 6.
*Ephemeris*, Chapter II *passim*, 28 n., 31, 100, 105, 113, 117, 263.
Esquires, 15, 42, 57.
Essex Rebellion, 32, 41, 130.
Exchequer, Barons of the, 9, 24, 32, 130, 150, 166, 192, 194, 216.

Fawsley, 73.
'Five Knights', 76.
Forced Loan, 75–80, 102, 176.
'Free Gift', 75–6.

Garter, Chancellor of the Order of the, 175, 191.
Gentry, 25, 28, 31, 45, 46, 49, 52, 57, 61, 66–7, 76, 79, 83, 85, 121, 139, 183.
  controversy over the, 3–4, 20, 116, Appendix H.
Gray's Inn, 26, 28 n., 83, 86–7, 91–3.
Great Yarmouth, 120.
Green Cloth, Clerk of the, 125, 129.
Greenwich, 8, 100.
Gunpowder Plot, 35, 56, 119, 212.

*Habeas Corpus*, 76–7.
Hackness, 38–9.
Halling, 8, 15, 17, 21–2.
Helmsley, 110.
Henley, 78.
*Hidalgos*, 116.
Household, Comptroller of the, 188, 190, 211.
  Marshall of the, 129.
  Treasurer of the, 174.
  Vice-chamberlain of the, 171.
Hull, 102.
Humanism, 89.
Huntingdonshire, 102.

Ightham, 8, 9, 14, 15, 21–2.
Ilchester, 80, 103, 105, 107.
Inner Temple, 28 n., 86–7, 91–3.
Inns of Court, 21, 28 n., 58, Chapter VI *passim*, 121; *see also each* Inn.
*Intendants*, 79, 116.
Ireland, Lord Deputy of, 23, 165, 211, 238.

Jewel House, Master of the, 24.
J.P.s, categories of, Chapter III *passim*, 49.
  level of activity of, 112–15.
  numbers of, 6–7, 49 ff., 128.

Kent, 4, 6, 7, Chapter II *passim*, 31, 49, 61, 87–8, 90 ff., Appendix A.
  Quarter Sessions in, 104 ff.
Kettering, 104, 178.
King's Bench, chief clerk of the, 200.
  Chief Justice of the, 37, 59, 152, 166, 171.
  Justice of the, 171, 188, 200, 216.
King's Lynn, 120, 146–7.
Knights, 15, 42, 57, 79.
  of the Bath, 34.

Knights of the Shire, 23, 24, 27, 32, 34, 69, 125, 149–50, 152–3, 169, 172, 176, 178, 190, 193, 195, 201, 210, 212, 215–18, 226, 230, 233, 235–6, 239.
Knole, 11, 23.

Lancaster, County of, 6.
  Duchy of, 6; Chancellor of the, 53, 134.
Lawyers, 8, 18, 19, 26, 28, 31, 45–6, 49–51, 57, 64, 117, 122, 125, 129, 134, 137–9, 147, 149, 152, 155, 157, 166, 169, 171, 175, 180, 188, 192, 200, 208, 211, 214, 226, 229, 232, 235, 238.
  barristers, 24, 26, 81, 93–5, 125, 129, 134, 149, 152, 155, 157, 171, 192, 198, 200, 212, 216, 229, 233, 235.
  serjeants-at-law, 84, 98, 125, 137, 149, 152, 155, 175, 219, 226.
*Libri Pacis*, 5–7, 17, 22, 60–2, 69, 70, 72, 73, 128, 260.
  *marginalia* on, 61–2, 69–71, 260.
Lincoln's Inn, 2, 14, 18, 21, 26, 28 n., 36, 86–7, 91–3, 129.
Litigation, 37, 39–40, 43, 45, 65, 100, 120.
Liveried Companies (of London), 8, 18, 24, 41, 130, 166, 181, 189, 209, 235.
London, 6, 18, 24, 26, 28, 44, 120.
  Lord Mayor of, 19, 25, 32, 79, 125, 130, 149, 165, 190, 238.
  Lord Chancellor (Lord Keeper), 22, 47, 57–9, 63–5, 83, 96, 216.
  Lord Lieutenant, 4–5, 32, 47, 53–4, 155.
  Lord Treasurer, 22.

Maidstone, 8, 9, 13, 15, 103, 106.
Malling, 32.
Malton, 110.
Marprelate press, 73.
Merchants, 18, 19, 24, 28, 31, 35, 46, 49, 52, 130, 146–7, 158, 165, 169, 189, 192, 195, 197, 200, 216, 235, 238.
Middlesex, J.P.s in, 102.
Middle Temple, 28 n., 33, 36–7, 58, 86–7, 91–3, 129.
  Somerset men enrolled in the, 92–3.
Monastic lands, 18, 34, 124, 126, 146–7, 166–7, 188–90, 208, 227.
Muscovy Company, 189, 233.

Navy, Royal, 24, 32, 129, 134, 152.
Nettlebed, 78.
Norfolk, 6, 42, 49, 51, 58-9, 62, 86-7, 90-1, Appendix B.
North, Council of the, 6, 38-41, 51, 74, 94, 109-12, 117, 225, 229, 231-3, 235, 237-8.
Lord President of the Council of the, 38, 54, 75, 235, 238.
Vice-President of the Council of the, 39.
Northampton, 77, 104, 178.
Northamptonshire, 4, 6, 42, 49, 50, 61-2, 86-7, 91, Appendix C.
Commission of the Peace in (1626), 49, 52, 66, 77, 87, 118, 174 ff.
Forced Loan in (1626), 76-7.
J.P.s in, 102.
Record Society, 6, 167.
Quarter Sessions in (1626), 104, 120.
Ship Money in, 79-81.
Northern Earls, Rebellion of the, 119, 228.
North Riding, 4, 6, 49, 70, 86-7, 91, Appendix F.
Quarter Sessions in the, 104-5, 108-12, 120.
Norwich, 6, 120.

Oxford, 17, 19, 58, Chapter VI *passim*.
Queen's College, 32.
Trinity College, 35, 38.
Wadham College, 189, 218.

Parliament, 1604-10, 73, 131, 195.
1614, 74.
1621, 51, 63-4, 73.
1626, 75, 135, 155, 198, 236.
1628, 78.
Long, 121, 138, 153, 158, 201, 218, 239.
Short, 38, 138, 201, 239.
House of Commons, 2, 26-8, 45, 51, 58, 122.
Puritan M.P.s, 73.
Sheriffs excluded from, 75, 198, 236.
Patent Rolls, 5-7.
Peace, Clerk of the, 40.
Commission of the, 4-5, 8, 9, Chapter IV *passim*; appointment to the, 2, 8, Chapter IV *passim*; distribution of members of the, 53, 60; oath under the Act of Uniformity required of the, 71,

81; operation of the, 9 ff., 22, 39-40, Chapter VII *passim*; organization of the, 22; Puritans in the, 73, 77; readmission to the, 66, 75-6; recusancy and the, 71-2; religion as a factor in the, Chapter V *passim*; removal from the, 63-6, Chapter V *passim*; secular politics as a factor in the, Chapter V *passim*; size of the, 48-52, 63, 66; terms of the, 96 ff.
Peers (peerage) in the Commission of the Peace, 15, 17, 49, 53-4, 85-9.
Penshurst, 10, 23.
*Perambulation of Kent*, 2, 19, 21.
Peterborough, Soke of, 6, 167.
Petition of Right, 78.
Piracy, 33, 97-8.
Plague, relief from the, 102.
Poor House (hospital, House of Correction), 11-12, 34.
Poor Law, 78-9.
Population, 53.
Posts, Master of the, 18, 171, 232.
Prerogative Court of Canterbury, 19, 24, 232.
Privy Council, 9, 14, 38, 64, 71, 74, 77, 81, 96-8, 101, 118, 155, 177-8, 188, 261.
Puritans, 38, 73, 77, 81, 176.

Quarter Sessions, 3-5, 9-11, 13-15, 32, 39-40, 75, 102-12.
attendance at, 105-12.
barristers in, 112-14.
chairman of, 43.
jury at, 13-14, 40.
organization of, 103-12.
recognizances certified at, 106-12.
Quorum (of the Commission of the Peace), 4.

Recognizances, 9, 10, 36, 103, 112-14.
Recorder, 33, 98, 107, 125, 137, 149, 152, 155, 158, 169, 189, 192, 194, 209, 218, 229, 232.
Recusancy and Recusants, 14, 36, 39-40, 53-4, 56, 69-72, 81, 101, 175, 179, 214, 228.
Regicides, 41, 158.
Religion, 13-14, 34, 62, Chapter V *passim*, 169, 226.
Requests, Masters of, 21, 129, 200, 226.

Restoration, 1, 122.
Richmond (Yorks.), 110.
Rochester, 11, 15, 21.
  Diocese of, 19.
Rolls, Master of the, 64, 134, 137, 194.

Saint John of Jerusalem, Hospital of, 69, 125, 166.
Sandwich, 24, 32–3.
  Grammar School, 101.
Secretary of State, 18, 96, 134, 209.
Serjeants-at law, see lawyers.
Sevenoaks, 15.
Sheriff, 25, 33–4, 41, 55, 59, 61, 75–6, 78–81, 147, 150, 153, 155, 176, 178, 190, 192, 197, 201, 212, 226, 235.
Ship Money, 78–80.
Signet, clerk of the, 18.
Solicitor-General, 137, 189.
Somerset, 6, 36–7, 49, 51, 74, 90, 91–3, Appendix D.
  J.P.s in, 1614, 74–6.
  Quarter Sessions in, 103 ff.
  Sheriff of, 79.
  Ship Money in, 78–80.
Speaker of the Commons, 149, 175, 194, 211, 225.
Star Chamber, Court of, 37, 39–41, 43, 45, 60, 63, 65, 73, 100, 115, 120, 176.
Subsidy, assessments for the, 43, 46, 62, 174, Appendix G.
  failure of Parliament to grant a, 117.
Supremacy, Act of, 71, 209.
Sussex, 62.

Tapestries, 35, 44, 119, 175.

Taunton, 100, 103, 108, 189.
Thirsk, 104–5, 109–10.
Tonbridge, 9, 18.
Tower of London, 24, 53, 69, 71, 125, 129, 149–50, 188, 228.
Trent, Council of, 68.

Uniformity, Act of, 71.
Universities, 21, Chapter VI passim, 121.
  doctors of, 15.
Upnor Castle, 32.

Vice-Chamberlain, 232.

Wales, Council of, 6, 51, 94, 108, 117, 208, 211; Lord President of the, 23, 58, 166, 208.
  Marches of, 6, 34, 118.
Wardrobe, Marshall of the, 129.
Wards and Liveries, Court of, 125, 134, 175, 229.
Wells, 103, 105, 107.
Wills, 19, 20, 32–4, 37, 44, 172, 263–4.
Woollen trade, 6, 35, 120, 214.
Worcester, 36.
Worcestershire, 6, 24, 35–6, 49, 50, 86–7, 90 ff., 103, Appendix E.
  Quarter Sessions in, 104, 120.
  recognizances of J.P.s of, 112–14.
Wrotham, 10, 15, 21.
Wyatt's Rebellion, 119, 125, 130.

York, 6.
Yorkshire, 19, 62; see also North Riding.

# INDEX OF NAMES OF PERSONS

Since the data about most J.P.s are shown in the several rosters, those entries are indicated by bold-face type.

Abbot, George, 101, **131**, 175.
Adams, John, **194**, 195.
Aldborough, Richard, **231**.
— William, **234**.
Alforth, Sir William, 101.
Alleyn, Sir Christopher, 15, 16, 18, 20, 21, **123**.
Altham, Sir James, **230**.
Amy, John, 51, **213**, 214.
Anderson, Sir Edmund, **148**, 149.
Andrews, Sir Euseby, **170**.
— Sir Thomas (d. 1564), **164**.
— Thomas (d. 1594), **168**.
— Thomas (d. 1627), **173**.
Annesley, Brian, **16**.
Appleyard, John, **145**.
Argall, Richard, **17**, 23, 24.
Aske, Christopher, **231**, 233.
Astley, Sir Francis, **157**, 158.
— John, **16**, 22, 23, 24, 27.
Aston, Sir Roger, **126**, 129.
Athowe, John, **157**, 158.
—, Thomas, 101, **151**, 152, **154**, 155.
Atkins, Richard, **213**, 214.
Aubrey, William, **210**.
Audley, Baron, *see* Tuchet.
Ayloffe, William, **210**.
Ayscough, John, **17**.

Baber, Francis, **194, 196, 197, 199**.
— John, **196**, 197.
Babington, Gervase, 113, **213**.
Bacon, Ann, 97.
— Sir Edmund, **153, 156**.
— Sir Francis, 38, 63, **119**.
— Sir Nathaniel, 58, 96 f., 101, **114, 148, 151**.
— Sir Nicholas (d. 1579), 38, 42, 58, 62, 83, 84, Chapter VII *passim*, **123, 145,** 146, **164,** 165, **187, 207, 224**.
— Sir Nicholas (d. 1624), 43, **56,** 58, 59, **148,** 150, **151**.
Baker, Sir Henry, 55.
— Sir John, 55.
— Sir Richard, **16, 123**.

Baker, Sir Thomas, **127**.
Balcanquall, Walter, **133, 136**.
Bamburgh, Sir William, 110, **231**.
Bancroft, John, **133, 136**.
— Richard, **126**.
Bankes, Henry, **234,** 236.
— Sir John, **136,** 137.
Bannastre, Sir Robert, **173, 180**.
Bargrave, Isaac, **133, 136**.
Barham, Nicholas, **123,** 125.
Barkham, Sir Edward, 57.
Barkley, Robert, **128**.
Barlow, Ralph, **196, 197**.
— William, **126**.
Barnard, Francis, **168,** 169.
Barnefield, Robert, **216**.
Barnes, Richard, **227**.
— Thomas G., 2, 78, 114.
— Sir William (d. 1619), **127,** 130.
— William, **157**.
Barney, John, **145,** 147.
— Martin, **148**.
— Sir Richard, 56, **153, 156,** 158.
— Robert, **145,** 147.
— Sir Thomas, **151**.
Barnham, Sir Francis, **132,** 135, 139.
— Martin, **17,** 25, 129.
Barrington, Sir Francis, 73.
Barroughe, Thomas, **148**.
Barton, Ralph, **210**.
Barwicke, Robert, 112, **237,** 238, 239.
Baskerville, Sir Thomas, **207,** 209.
Bassett, William, **199**.
Beard, Charles A., 2.
Beaupre, Edmund, **145,** 146, 150.
Bedell, Sir Capell, 56, **173,** 177.
Bedingfield, Sir Henry, 101.
Beecher, Edward, 15, **17,** 18, 20.
— Sir William, **173,** 177.
Belcher, William, **171**.
Bell, Sir Robert (d. 1577, 150).
— Sir Robert (d. 1639), **154,** 156, **157**.
Bellasis, Sir Henry (d. 1624), 109 f., **230**.
— Henry, esq. (d. 1647), 111, **236,** 239.
— Sir Thomas, 110, **234**.
— Sir William, **224,** 225, **228**.

Bendlowes, William, **164**, 169.
Bennet, Sir John, **231**, 232.
Berkeley, Sir Charles, **196**, 198, 199.
— Gilbert, **187**.
— Henry (d. 1601), **191**, 193, **211**, 212, 214.
— Sir Henry (d. 1667), **196**, 198, **198**, 201.
— Sir Maurice (d. 1581), **187**, 188, 190.
— Sir Maurice (d. 1617), 74, **193**, 195.
— Robert, **216**, 216, **217**, **236**.
Berkheade [Birkett], Martin, **228**, 229.
Berresforde, Michael, **128**.
Bess of Hardwick, *see* Talbot, Elizabeth.
Best, Thomas, 110, **237**, **238**.
Beswick, William, **128**, 130, 135.
Bethell, Sir Hugh, **237**.
— Walter, **231**, 233.
Beyer, John, **124**.
Biggs, Sir Thomas, **213**.
Binge, Francis, **124**.
— George, **128**, 131.
— Robert, 15, **17**, 19, 20, 22, **124**, 139.
— Dr. Thomas, 20.
Bisse, James (d. 1569), **187**, 189.
— James (d. 1606), **191**, 193.
Blague, Thomas, **127**, 130.
Blennerhassett, Sir Edward, **151**.
— John, **145**, 146.
— William, **148**.
Bletchenden, Thomas, **137**.
Blincoe, John, 77 n., **174**.
Blount, Sir George, **207**, 209.
— Mountjoy, Earl of Newport, **217**, 218.
— Thomas of Kidderminster (d. 1568), **207**, 209.
— Thomas of Shillington (d. 1563), **207**, 209.
— Walter, **207**, 209, **211**.
Blundeston, Lawrence, **228**.
Blunt, Thomas, **137**, 138.
Boleyn, Sir James, **145**, 147.
Bonner, Edmund, 69, 70.
Borough, Lord, *see* Burgh, Thomas.
Bossevile, Sir Henry, **133**, **136**.
— Ralph (d. 1581), **123**, 125.
— Sir Ralph (d. 1635), **127**, 135.
— Sir Robert, **127**.
Bourchier, Edward, Earl of Bath, **196**, **198**, 199.
— Sir Ralph, **228**, 229, 230.
— William, Earl of Bath, **190**, 191, **193**.

Bourne, Sir John (d. 1575), 34, 69, 71, **207**, 209.
— John (d. 1628), **173**.
Bowerman, William, **191**, 192.
Bowes, Sir George, **224**, 225.
— Sir Martin, **123**, 125.
— Richard, **225**.
— Sir Robert, **228**.
— William, **228**, 229.
Boynton, Sir Francis, 40 ff., 110, **230**, 233.
Boys, Edward (d. 1597), **17**.
— Sir Edward (d. 1635), **127**, **133**.
— Edward (d. 1646), **133**, **136**, 138.
— Sir John, **17**, 24, 33, 106, **127**, 129, 131.
— Samuel, 104, 106, **128**, **133**.
— William, **137**.
Bracey, Francis, **211**, 214.
Brampton, William, **145**, 147.
Bramston, Sir John, **156**, 158.
Brantingham, Elias, **151**, 152, **154**, 155.
Brente, Robert, **124**, 125.
Brereton, Thomas, **196**.
Breton, John, 77 n., **174**.
— Robert, **174**.
Brett, John, **191**.
Bridgman, Sir John, **215**, 217.
Briggs, Robert, **228**, 229, 230, **231**, 233.
Bristol, Earl of, *see* Digby, John.
Bromley, Sir Edward, **176**.
— Sir George, **210**.
— Sir Henry, **215**.
— Thomas, 16, 22, 58, **148**, **167**, **190**, 210, 227.
Brooke, Arthur, **171**.
— Charles, **127**, 129, **193**, 195.
— Henry, 27.
— Hugh, **187**.
— Sir Thomas, **173**, **180**.
— William, Lord Cobham (d. 1597), 15, **16**, 17, 18, 20, 21, 83, **123**.
— Sir William (d. 1643), **136**.
Brown, Anthony (d. 1567), **145**.
Browne, Anthony, Viscount Montagu (d. 1592), 71.
— Sir Anthony, **151**, 155.
Bruce, Edward, Lord, **230**, 232.
Brudenell, Edmund, **164**, 166, 167, **168**.
— Sir Thomas, 54, 56, **173**, 175, 179.
Bryan, Sir Barnaby [O'Brien], 79, **179**, 180.
Buck, Sir Peter, **127**, 129.

Bucke, Sir John, 113, **215**, **217**.
Buckeridge, John, 101, **132**.
Buckhurst, Baron, *see* Sackville, Thomas.
Buckworth, William, **157**, 158.
Bull, William, 106 f., **199**, 200.
Buller, John, **191**.
Bulmer, Dorothy, 226.
Burgavenny, Lord, *see* Neville, Henry.
Burgh, Thomas, Lord, **16**, 23.
— William, Lord Borough, **123**.
Burghley, Lord, *see* Cecil, William.
Burnaby, Thomas, **170**.
Burrell, Abraham, **199**, 201.
Butler, John, **164**.
Butt, Sir William, 98, **145**, 146.
Button, Sir William, 56.
Buxton, John, **157**, 158.
Byng, Andrew, **154**, 156, **157**.

Caesar, Sir Julius, **132**, 134.
Caley, William, 111, **237**.
Calthorpe, Sir James, **151**, 153.
Calverley, Thomas, **228**, 229.
Calvert, Sir George, 64.
Camden, William, 181.
Campion, Edmund, 69.
— William, **128**, 130.
Capell, William, **196**, 197, 198, **199**.
Carew, George, Earl of Totnes, **132**.
— Sir John, **193**, **198**.
Carey, Sir Edmund, **170**, 171, 172, **172**, 174, **179**.
— Sir George, **16**, 23.
— Henry, Lord Hunsdon (d. 1596), **16**, 23, **123**, 227.
— Henry, Viscount Rochford (d. 1666), **132**, 135.
Carleton, Dudley, Lord, 73, **132**.
Carnarvon, Earl of, *see* Dormer, Robert.
Carr, Robert, Earl of Somerset, 54.
Cartwright, Hugh, **124**, 125.
— Richard, **173**, 175, **180**.
Carus, Thomas, **207**.
Cary, Henry, Viscount Falkland, **132**.
Caspari, Fritz, 89.
Caterick, Anthony, 71, **224**, 226, 228.
Catesby, George, **174**.
— Sir Richard, 165.
— Robert, 35.
— Thomas, **164**.
Catlin, Hugh, **124**.
Catlyn, Sir Robert, **145**.

Cave, Richard, **164**.
— Roger, **168**.
— Sir Thomas, **173**, **180**.
Cecil, Richard, **170**, 172, **172**.
— Sir Robert, 18, 38.
— Sir Thomas, 72, **168**, 169, **170**.
— William, Lord Burghley (d. 1598), **16**, 22, 24, 38, 60 ff., Chapter V *passim*, **148**, **164**, 165, **167**, **190**, **210**, 226, **227**, 229.
— William, Earl of Exeter (d. 1640), 4, 54, **172**, 177, **179**, **234**, **236**.
— William, Earl of Salisbury (d. 1668), **132**, **135**, **172**, **179**.
Champneys, Justinian, **17**, 25, 28.
Charles I, 75, 77, 118, 121, 178.
Charlett, John, 113, **215**, **217**.
Chaucer, Geoffrey, 190.
Chauncey, Sir Tobias, **170**.
— William (d. 1585), **164**, 167, **168**.
— Sir William (d. 1644), 77, 77 n., **173**, 177.
Cheke, Henry, **228**, 229, 230.
Chetwood, Sir Richard, **170**, **173**.
Cheyney, E. P., 2.
— Henry, Lord, **16**, 23, **123**.
Childe, William (d. 1601), **211**.
— William (d. 1633), **216**.
— William, **218**.
Cholmeley, Francis, 228.
— Sir Hugh (d. 1597), **210**, 211.
— Sir Hugh (d. 1657), 38, 111, **237**, 239.
— Ranulph, **123**.
— Sir Richard (d. 1583), **225**, 226.
— Sir Richard (d. 1631), 39, 42, **231**, 233, **234**.
Chowne, Sir George, 21, **127**.
Chute, Edward, **133**, **137**.
— Sir Walter, **127**.
Clare, Francis, **211**, **213**.
— Sir Ralph, **215**, 217, **217**.
Clarke, George, **180**, 180.
— Henry, **136**.
— James, 36 ff., 92, 100, **194**, 194.
— Samuel, **173**, 175, **180**. 181,
— William, **168**.
Clench, John, **227**.
Clere, Sir Edward, **148**, 149.
— Sir Henry, **151**.
Clerke, George, **124**.
— Henry, 135.
— Sir Rowland, **124**.
Clifford, Francis, Earl of Cumberland, **234**, **236**.

Clifford, George, Earl of Cumberland
(d. 1605), **227**.
— George, **17**.
— Henry, Earl of Cumberland (d.
1570), **224**, 227.
— Henry, Lord (d. 1643), **234**.
Clyfton, Sir John, **191**.
— William, **187**, 189.
Cobham, Sir Henry, **16**, 21, 24, 27,
100, 128.
— John, **16**, 24, 27, 83, **123**.
— Lord, *see* Brooke, William.
Cockayne, Charles, 79.
Cockett, William, **145**, 147.
Coke, Sir Edward, 59, 64, 94, 119, 149,
**151**, 155, **170**, 171.
— George, **217**.
— Sir John, **132**, 134.
— Robert, **145**, 147.
Cokesey, William, 84, **207**, 208.
Cole, Rice, **199**, 200, 201.
Colepeper, John, **137**, 138, **216**, 217.
Colles, Edmund, 113, **211**, 212.
— Humphrey, **187**, 188, 189.
— John (d. 1608), **191**, **193**.
— John (d. 1627), **196**, 200.
Combe, William, **213**, 214, 215.
Compton, Henry, Lord, **168**, 168 f.
— Spencer, Earl of Northampton, **179**.
— William, Lord, **170**, **172**, **215**.
Constable, Henry, **228**, 229, 230.
— Henry, Viscount Dunbarre, **234**,
236.
— John, **228**, **231**.
— Sir William, **39**, 101, **236**.
Conway, Edward, Lord (d. 1631), **132**,
134.
— Edward, Viscount Conway (d. 1655),
54.
Conyers, Sir George, 70, **225**, 226.
— Nicholas, **235**.
— Reginald, **164**.
— William, **173**, 175, 177.
Cooke, Sir Anthony, 38.
Cookes, Edward, 113 f., **216**, 216.
Cooper, Sir John, **193**.
—Richard, **187**, 189.
Cope, Sir Anthony, 73.
— Edward, **168**, 171.
Corbett, Clemens, **154**, 156, 157.
— Jerome, **210**, 212.
— Sir John, 56, 76, 78, **154**, 156.
— Miles, **157**, 158.
— Reginald, **207**, 209.

Corbett, Thomas, **151**.
Cornewall, Thomas, **213**.
Cornwallis, Sir Charles, **151**, 152, **154**.
Cosin, Richard, **16**, 23, 24, 28.
Cottington, Sir Francis, **132**, 134, **136**,
**198**.
Cotton, Bartholomew, **152**.
— Sir Thomas, **16**, 18, 21, **123**.
Courtney, Sir William, **193**, 195.
Coventry, John, 107, **198**, 200, 201.
— Sir Thomas, 58, 107, **131**, **135**, **153**,
**156**, **172**, **179**, **196**, **198**, **215**, 216,
**217**, **234**, 236.
— Thomas, **217**, 218.
Crane, Sir Francis, 119, **173**, 175.
Cranfield, Lionel, Earl of Middlesex, 54.
Cranmer, Robert, **128**.
Craven, William, Lord, **217**, 218.
Crawley, Sir Francis, **136**.
Cresheld, Richard, **217**, 218, 219.
Crewe, John, **180**.
— Sir Thomas, **173**, 175.
Crispe, Sir Henry, **123**, 125.
— Nicholas, **123**, 125.
Croft, Sir James, **210**, 211, 212.
Croke, Sir John, **126**.
Cromer, William, **16**, **123**.
Cromwell, Henry, Lord, 53, **148**.
— Thomas, 146, 166, 169, 188.
Crooke, George, **156**.
Cuffe, Robert, 100, 106, **194**, 194, **196**,
**199**.
Curtis, Mark H., 89 f.
Cutts, John, **174**.

Dacre, Baron, *see* Lennard, Francis.
— Leonard, 70 f., **224**, 226 f., 228.
— William, Lord, **224**.
Dakins, Sir Arthur, **231**, 233.
— George, **225**, 226.
— Margaret (Lady Margaret Hoby), 38.
Dale, Roger, **170**, 175.
Dalison, Sir Maximilian, **127**, **132**.
— Sir William, 8, **224**.
Dalton, Roger, **224**, **228**.
Damsell, Sir William, **123**, 125.
Danby, Sir Christopher, 70, **224**, 225,
226.
— Sir Thomas (d. 1590), **228**.
— Sir Thomas (d. 1660), **237**.
Daniel, William, **151**.
Danvers, Sir John, 77 n., **173**, 177, **180**.
Darcy, Sir Conyers, 109, **231**, **234**.
— Sir Edward, **127**.

Darcy, John, Lord, **224, 227**.
Darley, Sir Richard, 109 f., **231, 234, 237,** 239.
Darnell, Sir Thomas, 76.
Darrell, Hugh, **124,** 125.
— Sir Robert, **133, 136**.
Daston, Anthony, **208,** 209.
Davenport, Sir Humphrey, **217**.
Davies, Margaret Gay, 2.
— Rice, 107, **197, 198, 199**.
Davile, Thomas, 110, **231,** 233.
Dawney, Sir John, **228,** 230.
— Sir Thomas, **231, 234, 237**.
Deane, Robert, 8.
Dee, Francis, **179**.
de Gray, Sir William, **154,** 155.
Denham, Sir John, **196, 198**.
Denn, Thomas, **137,** 138.
Denny, Sir William, **157,** 158.
Dennys, Sir Maurice, **123,** 125.
Derby, Earl of, *see* Stanley, Edward.
Dereham, Sir Thomas, **154,** 155, **157**.
Dering, Sir Anthony, **127,** 130, **132**.
— Sir Edward, **136,** 138.
Devereux, Robert, Earl of Essex, 38.
— Walter (d. 1576), 53.
— Sir Walter (d. 1659), 56, **217,** 218.
Digby, John, Earl of Bristol, 176, **179,** 197, **198,** 199.
Digges, Sir Dudley, 64, **132,** 134, **136,** 137.
— Thomas, **136**.
Dingley, Edward, **218**.
— Francis, 113, **213**.
— Henry, **207,** 214.
Dixon, Henry, **133,** 134, **137**.
Doddridge, Sir John, **215**.
Dodington, Sir Francis, **199**.
Dodsworth, John, 111, **237**.
Dolben, William, **173,** 175.
Donne, John, 120.
Dormer, Robert, Earl of Carnarvon, 54.
Dove, Thomas (d. 1629), **173**.
— Thomas (d. 1630), **170,** 172.
Downall, William, **180,** 180.
Downes, Francis, **180**.
Downing, Joshua, **133,** 134.
Doyle, Thomas, **124**.
Doyley, Edmund (d. 1612), **151**.
— Edmund (d. 1638), **154**.
— Henry, 72, **148,** 150.
Drake, Sir Francis, 101, 119, 195.
Drury, Sir Anthony, **154, 156**.

Drury, Sir Drew (d. 1617), **148,** 149, 150, **151**.
— Drew (d. 1632), **154**.
Dryden, Sir Erasmus, 56, 73, 77, 77 n., **173,** 176.
— Sir John, **179**.
Dudley, Edward, Lord (d. 1586), **207,** 208, **210**.
— Edward (d. 1632), **173**.
— Edward, Lord (d. 1643), **213, 215, 217**.
— Robert, Earl of Leicester, **168,** 168, 207, 208, **210**.
Duke, Sir Edward, **133, 136**.
Dyer, Sir James, **164**.
— Sir Thomas, **187,** 188.
Dyott, Sir Richard, **237,** 238, 239.

Edmondes, Charles, **174,** 176, **180**.
— Sir Thomas, **132,** 134, **136, 153, 154,** 172, 174, **179**.
Edolphe, Sir Robert, **127**.
Edwards, Reginald, **137**.
Egerton, John, Earl of Bridgewater, 58, **132,** 172, 177, **179, 217**.
— Richard, **237**.
— Sir Roland, 56, **173**.
— Thomas, Lord Ellesmere, 21, 58 ff., **126, 150, 170, 193, 213, 230**.
Egiocke, Sir Francis, **213**.
Eliot, Sir John, 76.
Elizabeth I, 63, 68.
Ellesmere, Baron, *see* Egerton, Thomas.
Ellis, James, **168,** 169.
— Sir Thomas, **234,** 235, 236.
— Sir William, 40 ff., **234,** 235, **237**.
Elmes, Edmund, **164, 168**.
— Thomas, 77, 77 n., 78, **173**.
— William, **174, 180**.
Elton, G. R., 3.
Empson, Richard, **165**.
Engham, Sir Thomas, **127**.
Erle, Sir Walter, 76.
Erskine, Thomas, Earl of Kelly, **132**.
Essex, Earl of, *see* Devereux, Robert.
Etherington, Sir Richard, **231,** 233.
Eure, Ralph, Lord, **213, 218, 230**.
— William, Lord Evers (d. 1594), **224,** 225, 227, **227**.
— William, Lord (d. 1646), 39, 54, 101, **230, 234,** 237.
Every, William, **196,** 197, 198, **199**.
Ewens, Alexander, **194**.
— Matthew (d. 1598), **191,** 192, 193.

Ewens, Matthew (d. 1628), **196**.
Exeter, Earl of, *see* Cecil, William.
Eyer, John, **145**, 147.
Eynns, Thomas, **225**, 226.

Fairfax, Sir Ferdinando, 239.
— Sir Nicholas, **225**, 226.
— Sir Thomas (d. 1599), **228**, **229**, 230.
— Sir Thomas (d. 1636), 111, **234**, 236.
— Thomas, Viscount (d. 1641), **236**.
— Sir William, **224**, 225, **228**.
Fane, Francis, Earl of Westmorland, 77, **126**, 129, 131, **132**, **172**, 177, 178.
— George (d. 1572), **124**.
— Sir George (d. 1640), **126**, 129, 131, **132**, 135, **136**, 138.
— Mildmay, Earl of Westmorland, 18, **132**, **135**, **172**, 178, **179**.
— Sir Thomas (d. 1589), **16**, 18 ff.
— Thomas (d. 1607), **17**, 19, 21, 28.
Farmer, Edward, **174**.
— Sir George, **168**, **170**, 180.
— Sir Hatton, **173**, 180.
— Sir John, **164**, 165.
— Thomas, **148**, 149, 152.
Farwell, George, **194**.
— James, **199**.
— John (d. 1616), **194**.
— John (d. 1648), **196**, **199**.
Ferne, Sir John, **231**, 232, 233.
Filmer, Sir Edward, **127**, 130, **132**.
— Sir Robert, **136**, 138.
Finch, George, **17**.
— Sir Heneage, 25.
— Henry, 25, **106**, **128**, 129.
— Sir John, 25, 135, **136**, 137, **198**.
— M. E., 42.
— Sir Moyle, **16**, 25, 27, 106, **126**.
— Sir Thomas (d. 1563), **123**.
— Thomas, Earl of Winchelsea (d. 1639), 55, **135**.
Fineux, John, **17**.
Fitzalan, Henry, Earl of Arundel, **123**, **145**, 164, 165, **187**, **207**, **224**.
FitzJames, Sir James, **187**, 188.
— Richard, **191**.
Fitzwilliam, Sir William (d. 1599), **164**, 165, **168**.
— Sir William (d. 1618), **168**, 169, **170**.
— William, Lord (d. 1644), **172**.
Fleete, John, **213**, 214.

Fleetwood, Sir Miles, **173**, 175, **180**.
— Sir William, **180**.
Fleming, Sir Thomas, **193**.
Flowerdew, Edward, **148**, 149.
Fludd, Thomas, **17**, 18, 20 f., 106.
Foliot, John, **207**, 209.
— Thomas, **211**, **213**.
Foster, Sir John, **228**, 229.
— Sir Thomas, **170**.
Fotherby, Charles, **127**, 130.
Foulis, Sir David, 111, **234**, 235, 237.
Fox, Charles, **207**, 209, **210**.
— James, 70, **225**.
Francis, John, **191**, **194**.
— William, 100, **196**, **199**.
Frankland, Hugh, **231**, 233.
— William, **237**.
Franklyn, James, **137**, 137.
Freake, Edward, **148**, 149.
Freeman, John, **171**, 171.
Fuller, Bostock, 113.
— Nicholas, 73.
Fulmerston, Sir Richard, **145**, 146, 147.

Gardiner, S. R., 37.
— Thomas, **136**, 137.
Gargrave, Sir Thomas, **224**, 225, 227.
Gate, Edward, **228**.
— Sir Henry, **224**, 225, 227, **228**, 230.
Gawdy, Bassingbourne (d. 1590), **148**.
— Sir Bassingbourne (d. 1606), 59.
— Sir Clypsby, **151**.
— Framlingham, **154**, **157**.
— Francis, 16, 23, **148**, 149.
— Sir Henry, **148**, **151**.
— Philip, 59.
— Sir Robert, **151**, **154**, **157**.
— Sir Thomas the elder (d. 1589), **16**, 22, 145, 146, **148**, 149.
— Thomas, junior, **145**.
— Thomas, **148**.
Gerard, Dutton, Baron, 54.
— Gilbert, **123**, **145**, 147.
— Thomas, Lord, **170**, 171.
— William, **207**, 209.
Gibbons, Thomas, **145**, 146.
Gibson, John (d. 1613), **228**, 229, **231**.
— Sir John (d. 1638), 110, 111, **231**, 232, **234**, 237.
Gilbert, Maurice, **194**.
Gilborne, Sir Edward, **133**, 134, **136**.
— Sir Nicholas, 101, 104, 106, **127**, 130, **132**.
Gilby, Thomas, **235**.

Gill, Sir John, **196**, **197**, **198**, **198**.
Glasior, William, **210**.
Godfrey, Thomas, **137**.
Godwin, Francis, **215**.
Godwyn, Paul, **196**, **197**, **199**.
Goldwell, John, **17**, 25, 27, 28, 139.
Good, Thomas, **218**.
Gooday, Arthur, **173**, **175**, **180**.
Gorges, Sir Edward (d. 1568), **187**, 189.
— Sir Edward (d. 1624), 108, 172, **193**.
— Sir Ferdinando, 119, 189, **198**, 200.
— Sir Robert (d. 1638), **196**, 198, **199**.
— Sir Robert, **199**.
Goring, George, Lord, **179**.
Gower, Sir Edward, 70, **225**.
— Sir Thomas, 111, **234**, **236**.
— William, **208**, 209.
Gregory, Roger, 110, **234**.
Grene, James, **225**.
Gresham, Sir John, 25.
— Sir Richard, 190.
— Sir Thomas (d. 1579), 25.
— Sir Thomas (d. 1630), **132**.
— William, **16**, 19, 25, 148, 149, 152.
Greville, Fulke, Lord Brooke, **132**.
Grevis, Sir Richard, 113, **213**, **215**.
Griffin, Edward (d. 1570), **164**, 166.
— Sir Edward (d. 1625), **168**, **170**.
Griffith, Henry, 101, **234**.
Grimston, Sir Henry, **133**, **136**.
— Thomas, **228**.
Grindal, Edmund, 54.
Grymes, John, **128**, 130, 134.
Gwynn, Richard, **151**, 152, **154**, 155.

Habington, Thomas, 44.
Hacke, [William], **174**.
Hadd, Edward, **137**, 137.
— Matthew, 106, **127**, 129.
Hales, Sir Charles (d. 1618), **231**, 232.
— Sir Charles (d. 1623), **127**.
— Sir Edward, 55, **127**, 131, **132**, 135, **136**, 138.
— Humphrey, **123**.
— Sir James, **16**, 25.
— Thomas, **17**, 25, **124**.
Hall, Henry, **128**, 129.
— Joseph, **215**, 217.
Halswell, Nicholas (d. 1564), **187**, 190.
— Sir Nicholas (d. 1633), 74, 100, 108, **193**, 195.
Hampden, Sir Edmund, 76 ff., 77 n., 80, 119, **173**, 176, 177.
— John, 80, 119, 176.

Hanbury, John, **173**, 177.
Hannam, Thomas, 92, 93.
Harbyn, John, **197**, 197, 198, **199**.
Harcourt, Michael, **168**, 169.
Hardres, Richard, **17**, 127.
Hare, Sir John, **154**, 156, **157**.
— Nicholas, 72, **148**, 149, 150.
— Sir Ralph, 101, **151**.
Harfleete, Sir Thomas, **127**.
Harington, Sir John (d. 1612), **193**, 195.
— John, Lord (d. 1613), **213**.
— John (d. 1654), 106 f., **197**, 197, **199**, 201.
— Sara, 174.
Harlackenden, Thomas, **124**, 125.
Harper, Richard, **187**.
Harrington, Sir James, 174.
Harrison, Thomas, **237**, 238.
Harsnett, Samuel, **153**.
Harte, Sir George, **16**.
— Sir Percival (d. 1580), **123**.
— Sir Percival (d. 1642), **126**, **132**, **136**.
Harvy, Sir Francis, **172**, 175, **234**.
Harwell, Edmund, **211**.
— Sir Edmund, 113, **213**.
Haselwood, Sir Anthony, 77 n., **173**, 177.
— Edward, **208**.
Hasted, Edward, 44.
Hastings, Sir Edward, 53, 69, 71.
— Sir Francis, 66, 73, 195.
— Henry, Earl of Huntingdon, **227**.
Hatton, Sir Christopher (d. 1591), **16**, 23, **168**, 168, 169.
— Sir Christopher (d. 1670), **179**.
Hawarde, John, 63, 65.
Hawkins, John, **16**, 23, 27, 28, 119.
Hawley, Gabriel, **191**.
— Sir Henry, 100.
— William, **187**.
Hay, Sir George, **132**.
— James, Earl of Carlisle, **132**, **196**, **197**.
Heale, Sir Francis, 74.
Hearne, Nicholas, **152**, 152.
— Sir Thomas, **154**, 156, **157**.
Heath, Nicholas, 69, 70, **224**.
— Sir Robert, **132**, 134, **136**, **137**.
Heblethwayte, Thomas, 112, **235**, 236, **237**.
Helme, Christopher, **215**, 217.
Hendon, Edward, **128**, 129, 134, **136**.
— John, **137**.
Heneage, Sir Thomas, 55.

Henley, Robert, **199**, 200.
— Thomas, **17, 124.**
— Sir Walter, 18, 126.
Henrietta Maria, Queen of England, 102.
Herbert, Henry, Earl of Pembroke
(d. 1601), **210.**
— Sir Henry (d. 1673), **217,** 218.
— John, **224,** 226.
— Philip, Earl of Montgomery and
Pembroke, 4, **131, 135, 196,** 199.
— William, Earl of Pembroke (d. 1570),
**123, 187,** 188.
— Sir William (d. 1609), **213.**
— William, Earl of Pembroke (d. 1630),
**131, 196.**
Herdson, John, **128,** 130.
Hereford, Viscount, *see* Devereux,
Walter.
Heveningham, Sir Arthur, **148,** 149,
**151, 154.**
— Sir John, 76, 78, **154.**
— William, **157.**
Hewar, Thomas (d. 1585), **148.**
— Sir Thomas (d. 1630), 101, **151,** 155.
Hewett, Sir John, 56, **173.**
Hext, Sir Edward, 106, **193,** 194.
Heydon, Sir Christopher, 98, **145,** 146.
— Sir John, 146.
— Sir William, **148,** 149.
Heyman, Henry, **128.**
— Sir Peter, 139.
— Ralph, 17.
Hickman, Henry, **170,** 171.
Hill, Robert, **187, 189,** 190.
— William, **191.**
Hilliarde, Sir Christopher, **228.**
— William (d. 1608), **228,** 229, 230, **231.**
— Sir William (d. 1632), **39** ff.
Hippesley, John (d. 1571), **187,** 189,
190.
— Sir John (d. 1655), **133,** 134.
Hobart, Anthony, **154, 157.**
— Sir Henry, 119, **149, 151.**
— Sir John, 56, **153,** 156, **156,** 158.
— Miles, **148.**
— Miles (d. 1639), **154,** 155, **157,** 158.
— Sir Miles (d. 1639), **156,** 158.
Hoby, Sir Edward, **16,** 24, 27, 28, **126,**
129, 131, **210,** 212, 214.
— Lady Margaret (Margaret Dakins),
38.
— Thomas, 84, **207,** 208.
— Sir Thomas Posthumous, **37** ff., 75,
101, 111, **230,** 233, 235, **237,** 237.

Hodges, Henry, 79.
Hogan, Thomas, **148.**
Holdsworth, Sir William, 1, 91, **122.**
Holdyche, Henry, 59, **152.**
— John, **148.**
— Robert, **145,** 147.
Holl, Thomas, **154,** 156.
Holland, Sir John, **156,** 158.
Holman, Philip, 79.
Honiwood, Sir John, **133,** 134, **136.**
— Robert, **17, 127,** 134.
— Thomas, 27, **124,** 125.
— Thomas (d. 1622), **127.**
Hopton, Arthur, **191, 193.**
— Sir Ralph (d. 1571), **187,** 188.
— Sir Ralph (d. 1652), **198,** 200, 201.
— Robert, **196,** 199.
Horner, John (d. 1587), **187,** 188, **191.**
— Sir John (d. 1659), 92, **196,** 198, **198,**
201.
— Thomas, 92 f., **193,** 193.
— Tristram, 92.
Horsey, Sir John, **190, 191.**
Horton, William, **213.**
Hotham, Sir John, 39 ff., 111, **236,**
238.
Houghton, Robert, **151,** 152.
— Tobias, **171.**
Howard, Charles, Earl of Nottingham,
**126, 193.**
— Sir George, **123.**
— Henry, Earl of Northampton (d.
1614), **126,** 170.
— Henry, Lord Maltravers (d. 1652),
**156,** 158.
— Philip, Earl of Arundel, **148.**
— Theophilus, Earl of Suffolk, **135, 153,**
**156**
— Thomas, Duke of Norfolk (d. 1572),
**145, 146,** 147.
— Thomas, Viscount Howard de Bin-
don (d. 1611), **193.**
— Thomas, Earl of Suffolk (d. 1626),
**150.**
— Thomas, Earl of Berkshire (d. 1669),
**196,** 199.
— Thomas, Earl of Arundel and Surrey
(d. 1646), **156, 236.**
Howell, Sir John, **136.**
Hubberd, Henry, **145.**
Hughes, Thomas, 119, **194,** 194.
— William, **210.**
Humfrey, Nathaniel, **174.**
Hunckes, Robert, **207,** 214.

Hungate, Robert, 109, 231, 233.
Hunter, Anthony, 225.
Hurleston, Ralph, 228.
Hurstfield, Joel, 2.
Hutton, Matthew (d. 1606), 228, 229.
— Matthew, 111, 237.
— Sir Richard, 112, 172, 179, 231, 232, 234, 236.
— Sir Timothy, 231, 234.

Ingram, Sir Arthur, 119, 234, 235, 236, 237, 239.
— Richard, 207.
— William, 213, 216.
Isham, Sir Euseby, 170, 176.
— Giles, 164, 166 f.
— John (d. 1596), 166, 168, 169.
— John (d. 1627), 173.
— Sir John (d. 1651), 173, 178, 179.
Isley, William, 123, 125.

Jackson, Thomas, 136, 138.
James I, 63, 72, 74.
James, Francis, 193, 194 f.
— Martin, 17, 23 f.
Jeffreys, Leonard, 216.
— William (d. 1565), 207.
— William (d. 1631), 216.
Jegon, John, 151.
Jenison, Thomas, 173, 176, 180.
Jenkins, Sir Henry, 231, 233.
Jenkinson, Sir Henry, 233.
— Richard, 152.
Jennins, John, 193, 195.
Jermy, Francis, 157, 158.
— John, 154, 155.
Jermyn, Sir Thomas, 154, 155 f.
Jerningham, Sir Henry, 153, 155, 156.
Jobson, Matthew, 110, 234.
Jones, Inigo, 155.
— Walter, 35 ff., 113, 213, 214, 215, 216, 216.
— Sir William, 215, 217.
Jordan, W. K., 34.
Juxon, William, 135, 156, 179, 198, 217, 236.

Keeler, Mary Frear, 42.
Kellett, Edward, 199.
Kemp, John, 152.
— Robert (d. 1595), 148, 149.
— Robert (d. 1612), 151.
— Sir Robert (d. 1647), 157, 158.

Kempe, Nicholas, 128, 129.
— Sir Thomas, 123, 125.
Kenne, Christopher, 191.
Kenricke, Richard, 77 n., 174.
Kettleby, Sir Francis, 213, 215.
Keynes, John, 187, 191.
Kirkham, Walter, 174.
Kirton, Thomas (d. 1606), 168, 169.
— Thomas, 174.
Knatchbull, Sir Norton, 127, 131, 133.
Knightley, Edmund, 166.
— Sir Richard (d. 1615), 73, 168, 169, 170.
— Richard (d. 1639), 77, 77 n., 80, 173, 176, 177, 178, 179, 180.
— Sir Valentine (d. 1566), 164, 166.
— Valentine (d. 1618), 73, 168, 170, 171, 172.
Knollys, Sir Francis, 214.
— William, Earl of Banbury, 132.
Knottesford, John, 207, 208, 211.
Knyvett, Sir Philip, 56, 151, 155.
— Sir Thomas (d. 1569), 145, 147.
— Sir Thomas (d. 1594), 148.
— Sir Thomas (d. 1617), 151.
— Thomas (d. 1658), 157.

Lambarde, William, 1, Chapter II passim, 17, 31 f., 47 f., 83, 93, Chapter VII passim, 117, 192, 226.
Lambe, Sir John, 80, 81, 173, 175, 180.
Lancaster, Edward, 108.
— John, 191, 192.
Lane, Sir Richard, 180, 180.
— Sir Robert, 164, 168.
— Sir William (d. 1616), 73, 170.
— William (d. 1637), 173, 180.
Lascells, Sir Thomas, 110, 230.
Latimer, John, Lord, 53, 224.
Laud, William, 135, 138, 236, 238.
Layton, Charles, 231.
— Thomas (d. 1584), 228.
— Sir Thomas (d. 1651), 234, 237.
Lee, Richard, 137.
Legard, John, 39 ff., 111.
Le Groos, Sir Charles, 154, 155, 156, 157, 158.
Leigh, Sir Francis, 136.
— Oliph, 126.
Leighton, Edward, 210, 211.
— Sir Thomas, 213, 214.
— William, 210.
Lennard, Francis, Baron Dacre, 18.
— John, 16, 18, 20, 123.

Lennard, Richard, Lord Dacre, **132**, 133.
— Sir Samuel, **127**, 129.
Lepton, Christopher, **225**.
Lestrange, Sir Hamond, 101, **151**, **154**, 157, 158.
— Sir Nicholas, *see* Strange, Sir Nicholas.
Leveson, Sir John, 15, **17**, 19, 20, 21, 27, 32, 100, 106, **126**, 130, 131.
Lewin, William, **16**, 19, 20, 21, 27, 28.
Lewis, Michael, **168**, 169.
Lewkener, Sir Robert, **133**, **136**.
Lewknor, Sir Richard, **213**.
Ley, Henry, Lord, **196**, **198**.
— James, Earl of Marlborough, 56, **131**, **153**, **172**, **196**, **215**, **234**.
Lindley, Sir Henry, **126**, 130.
— Maximilian, **174**.
Littleton, Sir Edward, **136**, 137.
— Gilbert, **211**, 212.
— James, **218**, 218.
— John, **207**, 209, **210**, 211.
— Sir Thomas, 56, **215**, 217.
Lloyd, George, **230**, 232.
— Hugh, **173**, 175, **215**.
Longvill, Sir Henry, **170**.
Lovelace, John, Baron, 54.
— Lancelot, **137**, 137.
— Thomas, **123**, 125.
— William (d. 1577), 27, **123**, 125.
— Sir William (d. 1628), **126**, **134**.
Lovell, Charles, **154**, 157.
— Thomas (d. 1604), 72.
— Sir Thomas (d. 1567), **145**, 146.
Lovett, Thomas, **164**, 169.
Lowe, Sir Timothy, **127**, 130.
Lowther, Sir John, **234**, 235, **237**, 239.
Lucy, Sir Thomas, **210**, 212.
Lumley, John, Lord, **224**, 228.
Luttrell, George, 108, **194**, **195**, **196**.
— Thomas, 108, **199**.
Lygon, Sir Arnold, **213**.
— Richard, **211**.
— William (d. 1567), **207**, 209.
— Sir William (d. 1609), 113, **213**, 215.
Lynne, George (d. 1593), **164**, 167, **168**.
— George (d. 1672), **174**.
Lyte, Thomas, **199**, 200.

Malett, George, 92.
— Thomas, 92.
Maliverer, William, **228**, **231**.
Mallett, Gawen, **197**, 199.

Mallett, Sir John, 93, **193**.
— Thomas, **199**, 200.
Mallory, Thomas, **231**, 233.
— Sir William (d. 1602), **228**, 229.
— William (d. 1646), **234**, 237.
Mann, Bartholomew, **128**, 129.
— Sir Christopher, **133**.
Manners, Edward, Earl of Rutland, **227**.
— Francis, Earl of Rutland, **172**, **234**.
— Henry, Earl of Rutland, **224**, 227.
— Sir John, **228**, 229.
— Roger, Earl of Rutland, **230**.
Mansell, Sir Robert, **126**, 129, 131, **132**, **136**, **151**, 152, 153, 155.
Manwood, Sir Peter, 106, **126**, 129, 131.
— Sir Roger, **16**, 24, 27, 101, **123**, **190**.
Mapes, Francis, **154**, 156, 157.
Mark[ham], Geoffrey, **207**.
Matthew, Tobias, **230**, **234**.
Mawdley, John, **187**, 189.
May, Sir Humphrey, **132**, 134, **153**, 154.
— John (d. 1598), **227**.
— John (d. 1637), **194**, **196**, 199.
Meade, Thomas, **168**.
Melton, Sir John, **237**, 238.
Mennell, Robert, 70, 94, **224**, 225.
Meres, Lawrence, **228**.
Mershe, John, **164**, 167.
Metcalfe, George, 111, **237**.
— Sir Thomas, **231**, 235.
Meyney, Sir Anthony, **126**, 131.
— John, **124**, 125.
Michell, Sir Francis, 63, 65.
Middlesex, Earl of, *see* Cranfield, Lionel.
Midlam, Adam, **231**, 233.
Mildmay, Anthony, **168**, 169, **170**.
— Sir Walter, **164**, 165, **168**, 169.
Mole, George, **174**.
Monins, Edward, **17**.
— Sir William, 55, **127**, **135**.
Montagu, Sir Edward (d. 1602), **164**, 166, 167, **168**.
— Edward, Lord (d. 1644), 73, 77, **172**, **172**, **178**, **179**.
— Edward, Viscount Mandeville (d. 1671), **172**, 178.
— Henry, Earl of Manchester, **131**, **135**, **153**, **156**, **172**, **179**, **196**, **198**, **215**, 216, **217**, **234**, **236**.
— Viscount, *see* Browne, Anthony.
— Sir Walter, **170**.

Monteagle, Lord, *see* Stanley, William;
 Parker, William.
Moore, Sir George, 73.
Mooreton, George, **17**, 26.
Mordaunt, Henry, Lord, **170**.
— John, Lord (d. 1562), 71, **164**, 165.
— John, Lord (d. 1642), 77, 80, **172, 179**.
— Sir Lestrange, 56, **151, 153**.
— Louis, Lord, **168**.
More, Sir Thomas, 69, 133.
Morgan, Francis, **170**, 171.
Morley, James, **237**.
Moulton, George, 8, 15, **16**, 19, 20, 22,
 **124**.
Moundford, Sir Edmund (d. 1617), **151**.
— Edmund (d. 1643), **154, 157**.
— Osbert, **145**.
Mountstephens, [Edmund], **173**.
Moyle, Sir Thomas, 139.
Mulsho, Thomas (d. 1562), **164**.
— Thomas (d. 1608), **168, 170**.
Musgrave, Sir Richard, **230**, 233.
Mytton, Sir Adam, **207**.

Napier, Sir Robert, **237**, 238, 239.
Nash, T. R., 44.
Naunton, Sir Robert, **132**, 134.
Neale, Sir John, 68.
Needham, Sir John, **170**, 171.
Neile, Richard, **236**.
Neville, Edward, Lord Burgavenny, **126**.
— Henry, Earl of Westmorland (d.
 1563), **224**, 227, 228.
— Henry, Lord Burgavenny (d. 1587),
 **16**, 17, 18, 20, 21, 24, **123**.
— Sir Henry (d. 1641), **126**, 129, **132**.
— Thomas, **127**, 130.
Newman, George, **127**, 130, **133**, 134.
Newton, Sir Adam, 55, **127**, 130, **132**,
 134.
Nicolls, Francis, 77 n., **173**, 175, **180**.
Norcliffe, Thomas (d. 1616), 109, **231**,
 233.
— Sir Thomas (d. 1628), 110, **234**.
Norden, John, 181.
Norris, Sir John, 100.
Northumberland, Earl of, *see* Percy,
 Thomas.
Norton, Sir George, **187**, 189, **191**.
— John, **174**.
— Richard, 70, **225**, 226, 228.
— Samuel (d. 1604), 119, **191**.
— Samuel (d. 1621), 108, **193**.
Notestein, Wallace, 2.

Ogle, Cuthbert, Lord (d. 1597), **227**.
— Cuthbert (d. 1633), **173**, 175.
— Robert, Lord, **224**, 225.
Onley, Sir Edward, **170**, **173, 180**.
Orme, Sir Humphrey, **173**.
Osborne, Sir Edward, 111, **236**, 238,
 239.
— Sir Robert, **170**, 172, **173**.
— Thomas, Earl of Danby, **238**.
Oxborough, Thomas, 101, **151, 152**.
Oxford, Earl of, *see* Vere, John de.

Packington, Sir John (d. 1560), 209.
— John (d. 1625), 56, **211**, 213.
— Sir Thomas, **207**, 209.
Page, Sir William, **127**.
Paget, William, Baron, 71.
Palgrave, Sir Augustine, **154**, 155,
 **157**.
— John, **148**, 149, **151**.
Palmer, Anthony, **174**, 176.
— Edward, **180**, 180.
— Henry (d. 1611), **126**, 129.
— Sir Henry, **133, 136**.
— James, 135.
— Roger, 135.
— Thomas, **17**, 55, **127**.
Paramore, Henry, **128**.
— Thomas, **133, 137**.
Pargiter, William, 77 n., **174**.
Parker, Edward, Lord Morley, 72, **148**,
 149, 152, **190**, 191, **193**, **227**, 228,
 231.
— Henry, Lord Monteagle, 54.
— John, **16**, 25, 28, 129.
— Matthew, 83, **123**.
— Richard, **133**, 134, **137**, 138.
— William, Lord Monteagle, 72, **189**,
 **193, 194**.
Parkhurst, John, 146.
Parkins, Sir Christopher, **127**, 129.
Parlett, Francis, **154**, 155, **157**.
Parr, Katherine, Queen of England,
 165.
— William, Marquess of Northampton,
 **164**, 165.
Partrige, Edward, 139.
— William, **17**, 27.
Paston, Clemens, 72, **148**.
— William, **145**, 146, **148**, 151.
Pates, Richard, **210**, 212.
Paulet, Sir Amyas, **191**, 191.
— George, **199**.
— Sir Hugh, **187**, 188.

Paulet, John, Lord, 74 ff., **196**, **198**.
— Thomas, Lord, **190**, 191.
— William, Marquess of Winchester, **123**, **145**, **164**, 165, **187**, **207**, **224**.
Pawle, Sir George, **127**, 130, 134.
Payne, Richard, **16**.
Pemberton, Sir Lewis, **173**, 175, 177.
Pembroke, Earl of, *see* Herbert, Philip.
Pennyman, James, **237**.
— William (d. 1628), **234**, 236.
— Sir William (d. 1643), **237**.
Pepper, Sir Cuthbert, 110, **228**, 229, **230**.
Percy, Algernon, Lord, **234**, **236**.
— Thomas, Earl of Northumberland, 69, **224**, 225.
Perrot, Sir John, **210**, 211.
Peryam, William, **190**.
Peyton, Sir John, **148**, 150, **151**, 155.
— Sir Samuel, 55.
— Sir Thomas (d. 1611), **127**.
— Sir Thomas (d. 1684), 55.
Phelips, Sir Edward, **193**, 194, 195, **230**.
— Sir Robert, 75, 80, **198**, 198.
— Thomas (d. 1590), **191**, 192.
— Sir Thomas (d. 1618), **193**.
Philip II, 68.
Phillips, Fabian, **210**.
Pickering, James (d. 1612), **171**.
— James (d. 1630), **174**.
— Sir John, 77 n., **173**, 177, 178.
Piers, William, 107, **198**.
Plowden, Edmund, 69 ff.
Poole, Sir Henry, **213**, 215.
Pooley, Robert, 135.
Pope, Elinor Dorothy, 35.
— Sir Thomas, 35.
Popham, Edward, **191**, 192, 193.
— Sir Francis, 74 f., 93, 108, **193**, 195, **196**, 198, **198**, 201.
— Sir John, 37, 58 f., 92, 119, **191**, 192.
Porter, John, **137**, 138.
Portman, Henry, **187**, 188, **191**.
— Sir John, **193**.
— Sir William, 56, **198**.
Potter, Thomas, **17**, 19, **127**, 139.
Potts, John, **154**, **157**.
Powell, Sir Edward, 56, **198**, 200.
Powtrell, Nicholas, **224**.
Pratt, Gregory, **151**.
Preston, Christopher, **194**.
Price, Ellis, **210**.
Pritherough, William, **170**, 171.

Proctor, Sir Stephen, 119, **231**, 232.
Prothero, G. W., 3.
Puckering, John, **210**, 211, 212.
Puleston, Roger, 59.
Purefey, Humphrey, **228**.
Putnam, Bertha, 2.
Pym, Alexander, 119, **191**, 192, 193.
— John, 64, 119.
Pyne, Arthur, **199**, 200.
— Hugh, 75 f.
— John, **193**, 194.
Pytts, Edward, **211**, 212, **213**, 214.
— Sir James, **215**, **217**.

Quarles, Francis (d. 1570), **164**, 167.
— Francis (d. 1651), **173**.

Radcliffe, Edward, Earl of Sussex, 54.
— Sir George, 78, **237**, 238.
— Henry, Earl of Sussex, **148**.
— Robert, Earl of Sussex, **151**, 153.
— Roger, **224**, **228**.
— Thomas, Earl of Sussex, **145**.
Rainsford, Robert, **173**.
Rand, John, **171**, 171.
Randolph, Thomas, **16**, 17, 20, 27.
Rastell, William, **225**, 226.
Read, Conyers, 3.
— John, **216**.
Redman, Robert, **151**, 152.
Reeve, Edmund, **154**, 155, **157**, 157.
Reppes, Henry, **145**.
— John, **151**.
Rich, Henry, Earl of Holland, **132**, **172**.
— Robert, Earl of Warwick, **153**, 154, **156**, **172**, **179**.
Richardson, Sir Thomas (d. 1635), **152**, 152, **154**, 155.
— Sir Thomas (d. 1643), **156**, 158.
Richers, John, 21, **151**.
— Robert, **15**, 17, 18, 19, 20, 22, **124**.
Rivers, Sir George, **127**, 130, 134.
— Sir John, 55, **132**, 134, **136**, 139.
Roberts, Sir Thomas, 55, **132**.
— Sir Walter, **136**.
Robinson, Sir Henry, **173**.
— Nicholas, **210**.
Robsart, Lucy, 150.
Rodes, Francis, **228**, 229.
Rodney, Sir Edward, **196**, 198, **199**, 201.
— Sir John, **193**, 195.
Rogers, Sir Edward (d. 1567), **187**, 188, 190.

Rogers, Edward (d. 1627), 74, 93, 193, 196.
— Francis, 133, 136.
Rokeby, John, 226.
— Ralph, 21, 226, 228, 229.
— Robert, 228.
— Thomas, 71, 224, 226.
Roper, John, Lord Teynham, 132, 133.
— William, 69, 71.
Rosewell, William, 187, 189.
Rosse, James, 197, 199.
— Peter, 92.
Rous, John (d. 1603), 211, 212.
— Sir John (d. 1645), 215, 217, 217.
Rowse, A. L., 2.
Rudd, Anthony, 213.
Rudston, Robert, 16, 19, 20, 22, 123.
Rugg, William, 72, 148, 149, 151.
Russell, Francis, Earl of Bedford, 164, 165, 168, 187, 188, 190.
— John, 210, 212.
— Sir Thomas (d. 1574), 84, 207, 209.
— Sir Thomas (d. 1632), 213, 215.
— William, Lord (d. 1613), 170.
— Sir William (d. 1669), 56, 217.

Sackville, Edward, Earl of Dorset, 77, 132, 135.
— Sir Richard, 83, 123, 124.
— Robert, Lord Buckhurst, 126, 131.
— Thomas, Lord Buckhurst, Earl of Dorset, 16, 23, 124, 125, 126, 150, 170, 193, 213, 230.
St. Barbe, Edward, 191.
— Henry, 187, 189.
St. John, Oliver, Viscount Grandison, 132.
— Sir Roland, 173, 179.
St. Leger, Sir Anthony, 24, 124, 125.
— Nicholas, 17, 27.
— Sir Warham, 16, 24, 123, 130.
St. Loe, Sir William, 187, 189, 190.
Salway, Arthur, 213, 214.
— Humphrey, 216, 218, 219.
Samwell, Sir Richard, 77 n., 81, 173, 177, 180.
— Sir William, 170, 171, 173, 177.
Sandys, Edwin (d. 1588), 83, 207, 208, 212, 227.
— Sir Edwin (d. 1629), 73, 132.
— Miles, 211, 211, 212.
— Sir Samuel, 213, 215.
— William, Lord (d. 1623), 168, 169, 171.

Sandys, Sir William (d. 1640), 213, 215, 217.
Saunders, Ambrose, 174.
— Sir Edward, 164, 166, 207.
— Francis (d. 1585), 164, 166, 169.
— Francis (d. 1674), 174.
— William (d. 1623), 171.
— William, 174.
Savage, Giles, 216.
— Thomas, Viscount, 153, 155.
— Walter, 213.
— William, 113, 213.
Savile, Sir John, 75, 234, 235, 236.
— Thomas (d. 1588), 228.
— Thomas, Baron (d. c. 1659), 54.
Sawyer, Edmund, 174.
— John, 180.
Sayer, John, 70, 224, 226, 228.
Sayvell, Henry, 224, 226.
Scamler, Adam, 154, 155, 157.
— Edmund, 164, 168, 169.
— James, 151, 155, 172.
Scory, John, 210.
Scott, Sir Edward, 132, 135.
— Sir John, 16, 21, 25, 126, 131.
— Reginald, 25.
— Sir Thomas (d. 1594), 16, 25, 27, 123.
— Thomas (d. 1611), 127.
— Zachary, 106, 128, 129.
Scrope, Emanuel, Lord, 75, 234.
— Henry, Lord, 224, 227.
— Thomas, Lord, 230.
Scudamore, John, 207, 209.
— Thomas, 231, 232.
Seabright, Edward, 56, 216, 216, 217.
Sedley, Sir Isaac, 55, 132.
— Sir John, 132, 136.
— Sir William, 55.
— Sir William (d. 1618), 17, 18, 19, 21, 100, 106, 127, 129.
Selby, Sir William, 132.
Seybourne, Richard, 207, 209.
Seyliard, Thomas, 133, 137.
Seymour, Sir Edward (d. 1593), 187, 188, 191.
— Sir Edward (d. 1613), 191, 193.
— William, Earl of Hertford, 196, 198.
Sheffield, Edmund, Lord, 230, 234, 236.
— John, 230, 232, 233.
— Thomas, 232.
— Sir William, 234, 235, 237.

Sheldon, Ralph, 35, 98, 211, 214.
— Richard, 207.
— William (d. 1570), 34, 84, 119, 207, 208, 209.
— William (d. 1587), 211.
Sheppard, Owen, 154, 156.
Shorte, Samuel, 137.
Shuckburgh, [Edward], 173, 176.
Shute, Robert, 168.
Sibthorpe, Robert, 77, 80 f., 173, 175, 180.
Sidney, Sir Henry (d. 1586), 16, 23, 27, 123, 150, 207, 208, 210.
— Sir Henry (d. 1612), 151.
— Sir Philip, 27, 38.
— Robert, Viscount Lisle, Earl of Leicester (d. 1626), 126, 132.
— Robert, Earl of Leicester (d. 1677), 135.
— Thomas, 148, 150.
Simpson, Alan, 2, 42.
— John, 133.
Skinner, Richard, 216, 216.
Skynner, Ralph, 224, 225.
Smyth, Sir Hugh, 193, 196.
— Sir John (d. 1609), 127, 130, 131, 139.
— John (d. 1638), 154, 157.
— Sir Owen, 157, 158.
— Richard (d. 1570), 84, 94, 207, 208.
— Sir Richard (d. 1628), 127, 130, 132.
— Thomas 207, 208.
— Thomas (d. 1591), 16, 24.
— Sir Thomas (d. 1625), 119, 127, 130.
— Thomas (d. 1642), 199.
Smythe, William, 217, 218.
Smythes, Sir Arthur, 217, 218.
Snelgrave, Henry, 128, 133, 136.
Snigge, Sir George, 193, 194, 195.
Somers, John, 16, 18, 20.
Somerset, Earl of, see Carr, Robert.
— Edward, Earl of Worcester, 131, 153, 172, 196, 213, 214, 215, 234.
— Sir George, 124, 125.
— William, Earl of Worcester, 208.
Sondes, Sir George, 136.
— Sir Michael, 17, 27, 28, 106, 126, 131.
— Sir Richard, 101, 127, 132.
— Sir Thomas, 16, 25.
Southwell, Sir Thomas, 154, 155, 157.
Southworth, Thomas, 106 f.
Speke, Sir George (d. 1584), 187.

Speke, Sir George (d. 1637), 74, 108, 193, 196, 198.
— George (d. 1637), 199.
Spelman, Sir Henry, 101, 120, 151, 153, 154, 157.
— John (d. 1643), 157, 158.
— John (d. 1662), 157.
Spencer, Sir John (d. 1522), 165.
— Sir John (d. 1586), 164, 165, 168.
— Richard, 136.
— Sir Richard (d. 1624), 73.
— Robert, Lord, 170, 172, 178.
— Thomas, 164, 167.
— Sir William, 172, 177.
Spiller, Sir Henry, 215, 216, 217, 217.
Spratling, Sir Adam, 127.
Stafford, Sir Humphrey, 164, 166, 167, 168.
Stanhope, John, Lord, 40 ff., 126, 131, 170, 171, 230, 232.
Stanley, Edward, Earl of Derby, 53.
— Henry, Lord Strange, 53.
— Thomas, 123, 124.
— William, Lord Monteagle, 53, 189.
Stawell, Sir John (d. 1603), 191, 192.
— Sir John (d. 1662), 196, 198, 201.
Steede, Sir William, 127, 134.
Steninge, Thomas, 145, 146.
Steward, John, 148.
Stile, Edmund, 127, 134.
— Sir Humphrey, 133, 134, 136.
— Sir Thomas, 136.
Still, John, 193.
Stocker, Anthony, 196, 199.
— John, 194, 195.
Stone, Lawrence, 3.
Stourton, John, Lord, 190, 191.
Strafford, Earl of, see Wentworth, Sir Thomas.
Strange, Lord, see Stanley, Henry.
— Sir Nicholas, 145, 146.
Strangways, James, 70.
Strickland, Sir William, 237, 239.
Strode, Sir William, 73.
Stroode, George, 137, 138.
Strype, John, 72.
Stuart, Mary, Queen of Scots, 102, 119, 149, 165, 191.
Suckling, Charles, 154, 154, 157.
— Edmund, 154, 154, 156.
— Sir John, 132, 134, 153, 154, 156.
Sussex, Earl of, see Radcliffe, Edward.
Sybell, John, 124.
Sydenham, Elizabeth, 195.

Sydenham, George, **191**.
— Humphrey, 108, **194**.
— Sir John (d. 1598), **191**, 192.
— John, **191**.
— John (d. 1627), **196**.
Symes, John, 75, 76, 108, **194**, 195, **199**.
Symonds, William, **207**, 209.

Talbot, Elizabeth, Countess of Shrewsbury (Bess of Hardwick), 189.
— Francis, Earl of Shrewsbury, **224**.
— George, Earl of Shrewsbury, **224**, 225, 226, 227, **227**.
— Gilbert, Lord, **227**, 230.
Talbott, Thomas, **157**, 158.
Talboys, Anthony, 228, 229.
Tanfield, Sir Lawrence, **193**.
— Robert, 180, 180.
Tankard, Sir Henry, **231**, 233, 234.
Tanner, J. R., 3.
Tate, Bartholomew, 168.
— Sir William, **170**.
Theaker, John, **231**, 233.
Theakston, Sir Richard, **231**.
Theobald, Stephen, **128**, 129.
Thomond, Earl of, 79.
Thornborough, John, **215**, 217, 230, 232.
Thornhill, Sir Timothy, **136**.
Thornton, John, **173**.
Throckmorton, Sir Arthur, **170**, 176.
— John, **207**, 208, 209.
— Sir Nicholas, **164**, 165, 167.
Thursby, Francis, **145**, 147.
Thynne, Sir John (d. 1580), **187**, 189.
— John (d. 1604), **191**, 193.
Tildesley, Sir Thomas, **234**, 235.
Tollemache, Sir Lionel, 56, **153**, 155, **156**, 158.
Tooke, John, **124**, 125.
Townshend, Henry, **210**, 213, 214.
— Sir Roger, 56, **153**, 155, **156**.
— Thomas, **124**.
— Thomas (d. 1590), 72, **148**, 149, 150.
Tresham, Sir Lewis, 56.
— Sir Thomas (d. 1559), 69, 70, **164**, 166.
— Sir Thomas (d. 1637), **171**, 173.
Trevelyan, George Macaulay, 1, 120.
Trever, Sir John, **127**, 129, 131, 134.
Trevillian, John, **194**.

Trevor, Sir Thomas, **153**, 155, **179**.
Tryon, Moses, **174**, 176, 177.
Trystram, Robert, 70, **225**.
Tuchet, George, Lord Audley, **190**, 191, 194, 195.
— James, Baron Audley, 54.
Tufton, Sir Humphrey, **136**, 138.
— John (d. 1567), **124**.
— John, Earl of Thanet (d. 1676), 55, **135**.
— Sir Nicholas, **126**, 132.
Tunstall, Cuthbert, 224.
Twysden, Roger (d. 1604), 17, **19**, 21.
— Sir Roger (d. 1672), **136**, 138.
— Sir William, 55, **132**, 239.
Tyndall, Sir Thomas, **145**, 147.
Tynte, Edward, **196**, 198.

Vane, Sir Henry, **136**, 138.
Vaughan, Sir John, **207**, 209.
— Sir Richard, 109, **231**, 233.
Vaux, Edward, Lord, 54, 72, **172**.
— William, Lord, 53, 69, 71.
Vavasor, Sir Thomas, **126**, 129, 131.
Vere, John de, Earl of Oxford, 146.
Vernon, Sir George, **236**.
Villiers, George, Duke of Buckingham, 50, **131**, 133, **153**, 154, **196**, 197.

Wadham, Dorothy, 189.
— John, **187**, 189.
— Nicholas, 189, **191**, 195.
Wake, Sir Baldwin, 56, **173**, **196**, 197.
— John, **168**, 170.
— Thomas, **164**, 167.
Wall, George, **208**, 209.
Waller, George, **127**, 133.
— Sir Thomas, **126**, 129, 131.
Walmesley, Sir Thomas, **126**.
Walpole, John, **148**, 150.
Walrond, Henry, **193**.
— Humphrey, **187**, 189.
— William, **196**, 199.
Walshe, Francis, **211**.
— John, **207**.
— Sir William, **213**.
Walsingham, Edmund, **124**, 125.
— Sir Francis, 18, 189.
— Thomas (d. 1584), 17, 18, **123**, 125.
— Sir Thomas (d. 1630), **126**, 131, **132**, 135.
— Sir Thomas (d. 1669), **133**, 135, **136**, 138.

Walter, John (d. 1626), 133.
— Sir John (d. 1630), 196.
Wandesforde, Christopher (d. 1590), 228.
— Christopher (d. 1601), 228.
— Christopher (d. 1640), 111, 237.
Wanfourth, Nicholas [Michael Wandesforde], 71, 224, 226.
Warburton, George, 199.
— Sir Peter, 170.
Warmistry, William, 218, 218.
Warner, John, 136.
Warre, Richard, 37, 92, 100, 187, 191.
— Roger, 93.
— Thomas, 92.
Washburne, John, 211, 212, 213, 215.
Wastell, John, 112, 237, 238, 239.
Washington, Lawrence, 106, 127, 129.
Watenhall, William, 228.
Watkyns, Richard, 191.
Watson, Edward (d. 1584), 168, 169.
— Sir Edward (d. 1617), 170.
— Sir Lewis, 56, 173, 178, 179.
Wattes, Thomas, 164, 169.
Watton, Thomas, 123, 125, 126.
Weldon, Anthony, 123, 125.
— Sir Ralph, 127, 129.
Welshe, John, 187, 188, 190, 224, 227.
Wentworth, Sir John, 157, 158.
— Peter, 70, 239.
— Sir Thomas, 54, 66, 75, 76, 78, 111, 234, 235, 236, 236, 237, 238, 239.
Westmorland, Earl of, see Fane, Francis; Fane, Mildmay.
Weston, Richard (d. 1572), 187.
— Sir Richard (d. 1635), 132, 134, 196.
— Sir Richard (d. 1652), 136.
Whalley, Richard, 225, 226.
Wharton, Philip, Lord (d. 1625), 227.
— Philip, Lord (d. 1696), 54.
— Thomas, Lord, 224, 227.
Whiddon, Sir John, 207.
Whitfield, Sir Ralph, 136.
Whitgift, John, 54, 130.
Whitlocke, Sir James, 172.
Whittingham, Sir Timothy, 109, 231, 233, 234.
Whorewood, Sir William, 213, 215.
Wilde, George, 213, 214, 215.
— John, 216, 216, 217, 217, 219.
Wilford, Sir Thomas (d. 1611), 106, 126.

Wilford, Sir Thomas (d. 1646), 133, 136.
Wilkinson, Richard, 127, 129.
Willcox, W. B., 2.
Williams, Sir David, 213.
— John, Lord (d. 1559), 164, 166.
— John (d. 1650), 172, 177, 179.
Williamson, Sir Richard, 231, 232.
Willoughby, Thomas, 16, 19.
Wilmer, Sir William, 77, 77 n., 80, 173, 180.
Wilson, John, 111, 234, 236.
Wilton, Robert, 157.
Windsor, Edward, Baron Windsor of Stanwell, 71, 208.
— Thomas, Lord, 215.
Wingfield, Robert (d. 1576), 164, 167.
— Sir Robert (d. 1609), 73, 170.
— Sir Robert (d. 1652), 180.
Wiseman, Sir Richard, 173, 175, 177.
Withens, Sir William, 127, 130, 132.
Wolrich, Francis, 59.
Wood, Gerard, 196, 197, 199.
Woodhouse, Henry, 42, 97, 98, 148, 151.
— Sir Philip, 151.
— Sir Roger (d. 1560), 145, 147.
— Sir Roger (d. 1588), 148.
— Sir Thomas (d. 1572), 145, 146.
— Sir Thomas (d. 1658), 56, 151, 153, 153, 156.
— Sir William (d. 1564), 145, 146.
— Sir William (d. 1639), 154, 156.
Wotton, Edward, Lord, 21, 24, 27, 126, 132.
— Sir Henry, 24.
— Thomas, 16, 24, 123.
Wray, Sir Christopher, 148, 149, 227.
Wren, Matthew, 156, 158.
Wright, Robert, 54, 196.
Wroth, Sir Thomas, 199, 200, 201.
Wyatt, George, 128, 130.
Wyndham, Sir Edmund, 145, 146.
— Francis, 98, 148, 149, 210.
— Sir Henry, 151, 152, 155.
— Humphrey, 93, 107, 191, 192, 194, 194.
— Sir John (d. 1575), 187, 189.
— John (d. 1645), 108, 194, 196, 198.
— Thomas (d. 1635), 196.
— Thomas (d. 1653), 157, 158.
Wynne, Richard, 237, 238.
Wynter, George, 211, 212.
Wyrley, John, 77 n., 173, 180.
Wythe, Robert, 211, 212.

Wyvell, Marmaduke (d. 1617), **228, 231.**
— Sir Marmaduke (d. 1648), **234.**
— Roger, 110, 111, **235, 237.**

Yelverton, Sir Christopher (d. 1612), **168,** 169, **170,** 171, **213.**
— Sir Christopher (d. 1654), **180.**
— Sir Henry, **172,** 175, **234.**
— William (d. 1587), **145,** 146, **148,** 149.

Yelverton, Sir William (d. 1631), 57, **151, 153.**
Yorke, Sir Edward, **230,** 233.
Young, Sir John (d. 1590), **191,** 192.
— John (d. 1605), **16,** 23.
— Thomas, 71, **224,** 226.

Zouche, Edward, Lord, **168, 170.**
— George, Lord, **164,** 165.

PRINTED IN GREAT BRITAIN
AT THE UNIVERSITY PRESS, OXFORD
BY VIVIAN RIDLER
PRINTER TO THE UNIVERSITY

## DATE DUE

| | | | |
|---|---|---|---|
| | | | |
| | | | |
| | | | |
| | | | |
| | | | |
| | | | |
| | | | |
| | | | |
| | | | |
| | | | |
| | | | |
| | | | |
| | | | |
| | | | |
| | | | |
| | | | |

HIGHSMITH 45230